ONE BOOK

THE WHOLE UNIVERSE

ONE BOOK
THE WHOLE UNIVERSE

Plato's *Timaeus* Today

Edited by

Richard D. Mohr
and Barbara M. Sattler

PARMENIDES
PUBLISHING

Las Vegas | Zurich | Athens

PARMENIDES PUBLISHING
Las Vegas | Zurich | Athens

Published 2010
Printed in the United States of America

ISBN: 978-1-930972-32-2
E-Book ISBN: 978-1-930972-61-2

Library of Congress Cataloging-in-Publication Data

One book, the whole universe : Plato's Timaeus today / edited by Richard D. Mohr
and Barbara M. Sattler
      p. cm.
Proceedings of a conference held Sept. 13–16, 2007 at the University of Illinois (Urbana).
   Includes bibliographical references and index.
   ISBN 978-1-930972-32-2 (pbk.)
   1. Plato. Timaeus. 2. Cosmogony, Ancient. I. Mohr, Richard D. II. Sattler, Barbara
M., 1974–
   B387.O53 2010
   113–dc22
                              2010000651

Typeset in Garamond and OdysseaUBSU (Greek), and Indexed by 1106 Design,
www.1106design.com. | Cover design by *the*BookDesigners.com
Printed and lay-flat bound by Edwards Brothers, Inc., www.edwardsbrothers.com.

1-888-PARMENIDES
www.parmenides.com
www.platostimaeustoday.com

Table of Contents

"Necessity"

What is the curse
That makes the universe
So all bewilderin'?

What is the hoax
That just provokes the folks
They call God's childerin?

What is the jinx
That gives a body
And his brother
And ev'ry one aroun'
The run aroun'?

Necessity, necessity
That most unnecessary thing,
Necessity.
What throws the monkey wrench in
A fellow's good intention,
That nasty old invention,
Necessity!

My feet wanna dance in the sun,
My head wants to rest in the shade,
The Lord says, "Go out and have fun,"
But the landlord says,
"Your rent ain't paid!"

Necessity,
It's plain to see
What a lovely old world
This silly old world
Could be—
But man, it's all in a mess
Account of necessity.

Necessity, necessity
There ought to be a law against necessity.
I'd love to play some tennis,
Or take a trip to Venice,
But sister, here's the menace,
Necessity.

Old Satan's the father of sin
And Cupid's the father of love.
Oh, hell is the father of gin
But no one knows the father of
Necessity, Necessity,

That's the maximum
That a minimum
Thing can be.

There's nothing lower than less,
Unless it's Necessity.

— E. Y. "YIP" HARBURG

"Necessity" is a lyric from the renowned musical play, *Finian's Rainbow* (1947). Music by Burton Lane.

Plato's Cosmic Manual:
Introduction, Reader's Guide, and Acknowledgements

Richard D. Mohr

Introduction

This collection of essays brings together physicists, philosophers, classicists, and architects to assess the meaning and impact of one of the most profound and influential works of Western letters—Plato's *Timaeus,* a work which comes as close as any to giving a comprehensive account of life, the universe, and everything, and does so in a startlingly narrow compass. Its core is but sixty-five pages long.

This core gives an account of the nature of god and creation, a theory of knowledge that explains various grades of cognition, a comprehensive taxonomy of the soul and perception, and an account of the objects that gods and souls might know or encounter, call them collectively, in John Wesley's phrase, the furniture of the universe. The analytical inventory of this furniture includes theories of what is and is not eternal, of the basic constituents of material objects, of how material objects compound into large scale, even cosmic, structures, of time and of space. There are elaborate accounts of both physical processes and life processes, the nature of making, morality, sickness and health. There are even accounts of accounts, of what can and cannot be said. We have then, in a single book the length of a modest novella, a comprehensive theology, metaphysics, physics, epistemology, and psychology, with significant excursions into logic, biology, astronomy, medicine, and ethics.

Hovering over all of this is the notion that the objects and structures in the world around us—both sub-atomic and cosmic—are, at some deep level, perhaps the deepest level, mathematical constructs. Building on a cosmic scale consists of adjusting ratios and measures found in the materials that confront the builder. Structures at the largest scale are numerical progressions, while the sub-atomic components of the primary bodies, earth, air, fire, and water, are not granules or other bits of stuff, but triangles and squares. When, in Douglas Adams' *Hitchhiker's Guide to the Galaxy*, the answer to the ultimate question of life, the universe, and everything turns out to be the number

1

forty-two, we are meant to chuckle at both the incongruity and the banality of the answer, but we have in fact wandered deep into Platonic turf. What is basic is quantitative, not qualitative. The basic constituents of material reality are going to be things like number, proportion, and the regular polyhedrons, not properties like yellow, blue, warm-blooded, feathered, hot, cold, dry, wet. Hardly any historians of thought now believe that Plato personally made any significant contributions to mathematics, but his basic vision that the intelligibility of physical reality is fundamentally mathematical has turned out to be right, at least as things now stand in science. Those who view various elements of Plato's theology and metaphysics as at best bloated, should remember that he held out the correct model for science unheralded for over two thousand years until Kepler used regular polyhedrons, the Platonic solids, to get astronomy and, by analogy, all of science back operating on a mathematical paradigm.

It is not surprising then that physicists remain fascinated by the *Timaeus,* even when they reject what many see as its metaphysical excesses. In this volume, we have two contrasting physicists. Sir Anthony Leggett, 2003 Nobel Laureate for Physics, gives a sympathetic account of the *Timaeus'* general bearings, while astrophysicist Sean Carroll, the *New York Times'* go-to guy for all things cosmological, thinks we can get along just fine without the *Timaeus* as an intellectual antecedent. Two additional contrasting essays explore the extent to which Plato's geometrizing of the universe is a coherent project. Thomas Johansen argues that Plato overreaches in this project, while Alan Code argues that the geometrizing project has been misunderstood.

So we have gods, some eternal objects, material objects, space, time, and numbers. But wait, there's more. In addition to the *Timaeus'* synoptic presentation of life, the universe, and everything, the dialogue and its companion fragment, the *Critias*, present one thing more, myth. They contain one of the West's most enduring myths, the legend of Atlantis. As disappointing as the news may be to some New Age-ers and mystics, it appears that the myth is wholly an invention of Plato's imagination. Near the start of the *Timaeus*, Critias gives a short version of the myth, which *he* holds to be an account of actual history, but which no critics now think Plato believed to be actual history. Critias begins to give the full version of the myth as the dialogue named after him, but this 'dialogue' breaks off in mid-sentence after only a dozen pages of what is mostly geographical description. The body of the *Timaeus*, that is, Timaeus' account of life, the universe, and everything, is wedged in between the short version and the severely truncated, long version of the myth.

The myth recounts events said to have occurred nine thousand years in the past. At that time, the evil island empire of Atlantis has a world-historical battle with a wholly just Athens, an Athens that realizes the principles of the paradigmatically just society laid out in Plato's *Republic* or in the close approximation of it that Socrates has spun out to Timaeus, Critias, and two others just the day before. Critias recounts the myth in answer to a request by Socrates to be shown his ideal state realized in action. Athens wins the battle, but then, just as in a hurricane that sinks pirates and admirals alike, a terraqueous disaster of cosmic proportion befalls the Mediterranean catchment. The island of Atlantis sinks below the ocean and earthquakes and floods level Athens, killing all its soldiers and virtually all of its inhabitants. As in a gangland massacre, somebody has to be left standing to tell the tale.

The Atlantis myth has provided the West with the concept of the lost world, the displaced world, the other world, and the world of the other. From these points of departure, the myth has enchanted the Western mind and launched a thousand variants in utopias, novels, movies, and resorts. But as much as it has enchanted the storyteller, it has puzzled the critic. In particular, the two dialogues leave maddeningly unclear what the relationship is between the cosmology of the *Timaeus* and the content of the myth. With literary explorations of Plato on the rise, this problem has become an important topic and is addressed by a number of the essays in this collection, as is the reception of the myth into the West. See especially the contributions of Barbara Sattler, Kathryn Morgan, and Jon Solomon. In addition, two essays address the nature and status of myths and stories within the epistemological framing of the dialogue—those by Gábor Betegh and Alexander Mourelatos.

Even the metaphysics of the *Timaeus* is spun out in the manner of a story. But virtually all critics now think that Timaeus' story about the universe, unlike Critias' about Atlantis, is one in which Plato advances his own views—to the extent, that is, that Plato's own views can be found in his dialogues. A lot of critics deny this latter position. For them, Plato's writings are 'just' literature or rhetoric or prods to thought, but not a body of thought. Pursuing this debate would take us well beyond the four corners of this book. For the sake of full disclosure, though, let it be known that all of the contributors here who write on the content of Timaeus' speech work on the unstated presumption that the speech represents Plato's views.

But given that the thoughts of Timaeus *are* spun out in narrative form, it comes as no surprise that lively debates rage over what in the speech is to be taken literally, at face value, and what figuratively, 'merely' as an aid for exposition. These debates go as far back as Plato's Academy itself, where there was a debate over whether Timaeus' account of creation was meant to be read literally when it says that the organized universe at some point had a beginning and that before that beginning every sensible thing was in a chaotic flux *or* whether this "In the beginning" trope—it's a fixed formula in Greek—was just a highly effective literary device for Plato to sort out for the reader conflicting strands that have always jointly existed in the universe—order and disorder—and that there actually was no first moment at which God intervened into the world around us.

The last few decades have seen a general, though not universal, shift toward literal readings of the *Timaeus*, especially surrounding the creation story. Perhaps part of this shift is the result of the theory of the Big Bang having made talk of origins in physics respectable again. And perhaps another part of the shift is a consequence of there being less pressure now to see Plato's views as invariant across his career. The non-literal reading of the creation story, going clear back to the Academy, was driven in large part by an effort to make the *Timaeus* consistent with two other dialogues—the earlier *Phaedrus* and Plato's last work, the *Laws*—both of which view each soul as a self-moving motion that has always existed, while the *Timaeus*, when read literally, views at least most souls as creations in time with external sources of motion. Critics worry less about this sort of inconsistency now than they did through most of the twentieth century.

But one thing is certain: not everything in the *Timaeus* can be read literally. At one point, Timaeus reports that a soul that extends through the whole universe (more on this later) was whipped up by God in a *kratêr*, the Greek word from which we get "crater" and which refers to a large footed and handled ceramic bowl in which the Greeks diluted their muddy, sweet wines with water to make them palatable. No one thinks that Plato believes that out there in the universe somewhere there is floating around a giant ceramic vessel at least the size of California. And what sense does it make to speak of mixing up a non-material thing in a material thing to begin with? Literal readings of the *Timaeus* may generally be correct, but they are not universal access badges.

So how *does* the creation story go? In the beginning, . . . or rather even before the beginning, there is a supreme God, who exists outside the world and is chiefly viewed as a craftsman or demiurge—*dêmiourgos*—a Greek notion that can apply to any type and rank of craftsmanship from lowly potting, a job fit for a slave, on up to the marble-carving of Phidias, the sculptor of the Parthenon statuary. Such a supreme craftsman god first appears in Plato's *Republic*, in the seventh book's discussion of astronomy, where, as in the late *Timaeus,* he creates the heavenly bodies and establishes their function as temporal markers—for days, months, years. A craftsman god also appears in each of the rest of the late group of Platonic dialogues—the *Sophist, Statesman, Philebus*, and *Laws*. In the *Timaeus*, the Craftsman or Demiurge is further characterized as being a father and a maker, and as a builder, carpenter, and timber framer, a person who makes things hang together. He is eternal. He is rational in his agency and is himself an object of reason. He has a personality: he isn't jealous, he harbors no grudges, he wants things to be as good as they can be. He is providential: he intervenes in the world. He creates the heaven and the earth. So far at least, this Platonic God is quite similar to the Judeo-Christian God, but surprisingly new when set against earlier Greek literature and philosophy. Indeed we would be shocked by his newness if we were not familiar with the Judeo-Christian God.

But he also differs in a number of significant ways from the Christian God. First, the Christian God draws not just his agency from within himself—his will and motive powers flow from himself—but the content of his mind, his ideas, his plans, have their origin internally to himself as well. This is not so for Plato's God or for Greek craftsmen more generally. They create with an eye to models or paradigms that are external to them and which they aim to realize or instantiate perfectly in the things upon which they work. We might say that while the Demiurge's motives are (largely) internal to him, his intentions, the things and conditions that he wants to realize, are not.

The models, which the Demiurge uses for his creation of the orderly world, are another Platonic first. They are what Plato calls Forms or Ideas, capitalized here to distinguish them from both forms that are the mere shapes of material objects and ideas that are thoughts in the mind. Forms or Ideas are mind-independent, eternal, non-material *objects* of knowledge. They are what guarantee that knowledge is knowledge and not some lesser grade of cognition. They serve as paradigms or standards for our moral and productive activities. They allow us to accurately identify things in this world and, in some sense, are the cause of them as well. They are said to be the things that really are, in contrast to the objects around us that are said sort of to be and sort of not to be. Forms exist in themselves, not in relation to other things. The rule seems to be that there is exactly one Form for each general concept that we have. But as with nearly every feature of Forms, their exact range is contested by critics. Still, the traditional list of Forms include moral and aesthetic notions (Justice Itself, Goodness Itself, Beauty Itself), mathematical concepts (Three, Oddness, Even, Square, Sphere), Relations (Double, Half, Large, Small, Octave, Speed), notions that range widely over other notions (Being, Sameness, Difference, Motion, Rest), and in the *Timaeus* at least, there is a clear commitment to Forms of natural kinds—the species and genera of living things and the primary bodies (Earth, Air, Fire, and Water). These Forms of natural kinds are said in particular to provide the eternal paradigms after which the Demiurge crafts the world.

A plurality of twentieth-century Platonic scholarship was devoted to a war over the nature and status of Platonic Forms. Critics disputed over what Forms are, whether they have any merit, when Plato came to believe in them, and whether Plato changed his mind about them over the course of his fifty-year philosophical and literary career. These debates have tended to wane of late, as critics have found other things of interest in Plato, and too, perhaps, this vein has been somewhat mined out. After five-hundred articles on whether the Form of good is good, there may not be much more to be said on the subject. In any case, the theory of Forms is not the exclusive or even primary focus of any of the contributions to this collection, even though traditionally the *Timaeus* has been a major site in the debates about Forms. By contrast, there is rising critical interest in theological matters in Plato, and five of the essays in the volume take the Demiurge as their central focus or at least point of departure—the essays by Anthony Long, Allan Silverman, Charles Kahn, Matthias Vorwerk, and Thomas Robinson.

So far we have the Craftsman and his model. But on what does he work? Another major way in which the Demiurge differs from the Christian God relates to the materials that he crafts. In Christian theology, God is omnipotent—there is nothing he can't do—and spectacularly, with such power he makes the world from nothing. Neither of these conditions—omnipotence and creation ex nihilo—holds of the Platonic Demiurge. He desires everything to be orderly because he believes that order is everywhere better than disorder, but he is confronted with a blooming buzzing confusion, a chaotic flux, over which he has limited control and of which, at least on a literal reading of the dialogue, he is not the cause. The pre-cosmic world is like a flooding river that turns back upon itself, leaps its banks, and sweeps everything along with it, tossing things to and fro, flipping them about, and doing so again. The Demiurge can do a pretty good job at controlling the flux. He is even able to use some of the same forces that in some contexts are so destructive and disordering (e.g., fire) to enable him to produce good things (like, sunlight and vision). These enabling capacities adapted from the pre-cosmos into the orderly world are called auxiliary or accompanying causes. But even after the Demiurge's best efforts, there remains a certain cussedness in things, a recalcitrance to good. The world's permanent undertow is called Necessity, the thing that trips up the best laid plans and intentions, even God's: "The Lord says, 'Go out and have fun,'/ But the landlord says, 'Your rent ain't paid!' / Necessity, it's plain to see / What a lovely old world this silly old world could be, / But man, it's all in a mess, account of Necessity."

In consequence of his view that God's capacities for good deeds are limited, Plato does not have to, as his Christian counterparts must, work through the tangles and trammels of the problem of evil. Plato does not frame tornados as tests of belief in God, mass slaughter as the product of valuable free-wills. That children come down with incurable cancers is not something about which Plato must wring his hands or expend cleverness of mind. The *Timaeus* does not and need not offer a theodicy—a justification for the presence of evil in a world where Providence is all powerful and all good.

The *Timaeus* says next to nothing, even metaphorically, about the instrumentalities of God, the *means* he uses when he confronts the world as given to him. In Christian iconography, the instruments of God standardly are his fingers and hands: In Exodus, God writes the Ten Commandments with his forefinger, the same one with which on the ceiling of the Sistine Chapel he gives Adam the spark of life, and according to folk song, "He has the whole wide world in his hands." The Demiurge has no such iconography. This aspect of his nature is left vague, passed over in silence. By contrast, in the *Timaeus* we learn a great deal more of the *manners* or *respects* of the Demiurge's creation than Bible or tradition reports of the Christian God's. The Demiurge creates by introducing, or maybe more accurately, adjusting the conditions of, unity, order, harmony, proportion, measure, and number in the world.

Until quite recently, the overwhelming majority of critics have taken these properties of unity, order, and the like, not as manners or respects of creation, but as the very ends or goals of the Demiurge's creation, and so traditionally, though often tacitly, it has been assumed that the chief aims of the Demiurge are aesthetic: the goodness with which he invests the world is primarily to be understood as beauty; his primary aim is to make the world a more beautiful place, as beautiful as it can be. The cosmos is a work of art. But of late, some critics have begun viewing the Demiurge less as a producer of beauty than as a producer of rationality. In this collection, versions of this newer view are reflected in Anthony Long's and Barbara Sattler's contributions. Here, the aim of the Demiurge is not so much to make the world look good as to make it intelligible and have intelligence. Rationality is the supreme good of which this world is capable. Proportionality, number, and the like are vehicles for this end, not the project's end itself. Understood in this way, Timaeus' creation story at least stands some chance of linking up with the ethical and political concerns found in his speech, in the literary frame of the dialogue, and in other late dialogues that combine moral and cosmological concerns—notably the *Statesman* and *Philebus*.

The rationality project has three prongs. First, there will need to be creatures who have the developed capacity to be rational. Those would be creatures like you and me in good circumstances. But too frequently circumstance is not good. Our souls' very encounter with the cussedness of the material world causes us to fall far away from being able to develop our rational capacities. One of the most dramatic passages of the dialogue is the description of the newly incarnate infant soul maddened and deranged by its contact with the flux of the phenomena. As a result of our naturally deranged nature, if we are to have a capacity for rationality, we will need to have a model of it present to mind, so that we can begin to set aright our ability to think by reference to it. So second, there will need to be a fully, properly rational soul available to serve as a paradigm after which we can model our mental *processes*. And finally, even with our rational capacities in order and developed to the point of proper use, we will still need to have *objects* about which to think correctly. For Plato, rationality is not just a matter of method and process; it's a matter of taking in the right sorts of things. For the vast majority of humans, the things that finalize rationality by giving it proper objects will not be Platonic Forms, rather most of us will have to find rational objects in the world present to hand. The Demiurge leaves the creation of potentially rational creatures—humans—to the lesser gods. And takes on for himself the two larger projects that will make potential rationality actual rationality for humans. Along the way, he makes the world as thoroughly rational and as full of intelligence as is possible, a project to which, at our best, we humans contribute.

The two Demiurgically engendered parts of the complex that results in human rationality are the two chief projects that the Demiurge performs in the *Timaeus*. They are exemplary of his other formative activities. In each case, the Demiurge introduces a standard or paradigm into the phenomenal realm; he introduces some of the ideality of the Ideas into the phenomenal realm. His aim is not just to copy Forms correctly, but to replicate some of their function as Forms as well.

The Demiurge's making of a model or standard for our rational capacities turns out, for our modern minds, to be the strangest bit in the Platonic cosmology: The supreme God, who may or may not be a soul himself, creates a giant, thoroughly rational soul and stretches it through the entirety of the organized material realm, making the universe into a single rational living creature, a World Animal—a World Soul in the World Body. Plato gives a complicated, much debated argument for why there is only one world and how its singularity is tied up with its animality. But his overall point is as clear as it is odd to us. We will only be able to get rid of the vestiges of our gyrating discombobulated and discombobulating infant souls, if we have a model or standard for rational capacities. Having a single model eliminates possible confusions that might arise if there were more than one 'model'. So if there can be just one true model, that is a good thing. In the case of a model soul, it *is* possible for there to be just one, and so God makes just one. We come to have the developed capacity for reason when we model the circuits of our souls after the perfectly circular circuits of the rational World Soul. It is only then that we are capable of making true judgments about the most important matters and lead our lives correctly. As contributor Anthony Long puts it, "Plato's World Soul, so far as we can determine, was a largely original concept, intended by him as a major scientific break-through."

What of the required *content* of our rationality? One can't think about nothing. And as we will see later, we cannot think rightly or even at all about the blooming buzzing confusion. And for most of us, access to Forms is not in the cards. Yet we are, if stumblingly, rational. How so? The Demiurge comes to the rescue with the invention of . . . time. Time? Time provides us both a general model or standard for our understanding of the world and a specific mode of access to the higher reaches of intellectual content. The Demiurge makes time by setting, to the extent possible, the heavenly bodies in regularly repeating circuits. We are able to use these circuits as clocks, as *standards* or measures of time. At one point, Plato simply equates the regular circuits with time, which elsewhere he defines as motion that moves according to number. With clocks or standards more generally, we are able to make precise numerical judgments ("The train arrived at 6:01pm"), not merely relative comparisons that one thing is more or less or even the same as another ("The baby was born before the train arrived, but at the same time the news report started, whatever time that was"). It is in this capacity—to be able to make precise numerical judgments—that time provides us the highest grade of true opinion of which we are capable while staying within the heavens—that is, without access to either the intelligence of the Demiurge or the intelligibility of the Forms.

More particularly, it is from time that we learn number. It is for this reason that time is said to have been created. By learning number, we are set on the way up the path of higher education as laid out in *Republic* VII, where the orderly progression through the study of arithmetic, geometry, stereometry, astronomy, and harmonics is the course to reach dialectics and unhypothetical knowledge.

The core project of the Demiurge is to create two earthly standards—the rational World Soul as conveyed by the World Body and time viewed as a cluster of clocks.

The first movement of the *Timaeus* draws to a close with an elaborate account of vision, the very means by which we lowly but potentially rational creatures access these reason-generating standards—the heavens, their numbered motions, and their collective rationality.

The second movement of the *Timaeus* is cued by a problem left over in the furniture of the universe as it stood before the Demiurge began intervening into the world. The problem has *something* to do with the blooming buzzing confusion of the phenomenal realm. If the phenomena are in a universal flux, if, that is as Plato holds, earth, air, fire, and water are not eternal, inalterable, indivisible Democritean atoms, but transform into each other ceaselessly and in every moment, then how can we identify something as being any one of these rather than some other type of thing? It, whatever it is, say, water, may as well be and be called fire or air as water. Put generally, if each thing is transforming at every moment into every sort of thing, then we are not capable of saying what type of thing anything is.

The flux, which engines the resistance that the world presents to the Demiurge's projects here, draws into doubt its intelligibility for everyone. In order to solve this problem, Timaeus says that he has to invoke an additional stick of cosmic furniture, which like the Demiurge, Forms, and flux, existed before the orderly heavens were formed. This additional thing is called the Receptacle of all becoming. It is something in which or across which the flux of the phenomena takes place. Indeed it is also called "place" or "space"—the single Greek word for both is *chôra*. The Receptacle is chiefly characterized through a series of metaphors. It provides a place for sitting. It is a nurse, foster-mother, or (simply) mother—in contrast to the Forms, which are analogized to a Father, and to the phenomena, which, to complete the extended nuclear-family metaphor, are analogized to offspring. It is like a waxy substance that can receive impressions or a perfume base. In both of these cases, the relevant salient feature of the analogy is made explicit by Plato—the base or substrate must be perfectly characterless, lest it impose its properties onto the things it receives. One would not use as a base for a rose scent an unguent that smells of musk. The efficient perfumer would want to have on hand a base, like case, that would take on and then release any scent while contributing nothing of itself to the odor of the product. It is a vehicle for scent, but does not enter into the scent. Each phenomenon is necessarily in the Receptacle, but then it is necessarily not in them, since "in" is an asymmetrical relation. The receptacle is all receiving, receives all characteristics, and so must itself be characterless. It facilitates the presence of the phenomena, but is not part of that presence.

That said, there have been critical storms going clear back to the Academy over what metaphysical function or functions the Receptacle has. But of late, a consensus of critics, including several writing on the Receptacle in this volume, is forming up around the view that Plato hypothesizes the Receptacle of all becoming in order to explain the status of phenomena as (insubstantial) images of the Forms. Phenomenal objects in the *Timaeus* have the same metaphysical status as phenomenal objects in the central books of the *Republic*, where they are famously analogized to shadows on the wall of a cave and to reflections on water or in mirrors. In all these cases of images, but unlike photographic images or marble statues, the image, in order to exist, requires both the persistence of its original and a medium across which it can flicker.

The problem that was left over from the first part of Timaeus' speech was that flux draws the intelligibility, even existence, of the phenomena into doubt. Flux makes the phenomena self-contradictory. At one and the same time and in the same respect, a thing in flux is both fire and not-fire. But now, with the phenomena understood as images appearing in a medium, the phenomena can be 'saved' and the problem solved. For now in their second aspect as images, the phenomena can be accurately described by reference to the Forms of which they are instances. They are saved from utter unintelligibility—and from utter non-existence as well.

As images, they do not fully exist; they are not freestanding beings. Their existence is dependent on both the persistence of Forms and the existence of space. And yet they are there to be pointed at; they are not bottomless void, emptiness, nothingness. In the *Timaeus* at least, Plato's understanding of existence is basically locative. To exist is to be somewhere on pain of being nothing at all. The Forms and space fully exist because neither of them is dependent upon anything else. They are freestanding, there to be pointed at independently of anything else. Still, since what we see of the Receptacle is not the Receptacle itself, but the dream-like images in it, it is not fully *knowable* in the way the Forms are. If we see Forms head on, as it were, we see them as they are. They are self-revealing and incapable of deception. In contrast, we are said to know the Receptacle by a sort of bastard reasoning. In our cognition, the Receptacle is a product of hypothetical inference, not direct acquaintance. These dream-like images must be somewhere, what that somewhere is is the Receptacle of space.

Still, lots of controversy continues, including in the pages of this collection, over the nature and status of the Receptacle, especially over whether it makes sense to think of the Receptacle, in the way Aristotle did, as a *material cause*, as that *out of which* the phenomena are (made) and which persists through the changes of a phenomenon. An additional metaphor given for the Receptacle is that it is like gold out of which geometrical shapes can be ceaselessly remolded. What is the salient detail here? The out-of-which claim? Or the ceaseless-remolding claim?

Finally, there is controversy over the last metaphor that Timaeus gives for the Receptacle. He says that it shakes like a winnowing basket that separates kernels of grain. More particularly, the Receptacle is said to be shaken by the phenomena in it and, in turn, to shake them. Is this shaking to be read literally? Nearly all critics now, including all the contributors to this collection who weigh in on the subject, take the claim that the Receptacle shakes at face value, even though this seems to collide directly with the repeated claims that the Receptacle contributes no content to its contents. Motions characterize, even define, many things in the Receptacle. In the *Sophist*, there is a Form of motion. Its instances are in the Receptacle. How can all these claims be squared? To address these sorts of worries, God invented scholars.

Another consensus that is forming and that registers in this volume has to do with the characterization of the primary bodies (earth, air, fire, and water) in the pre-cosmic Receptacle. The background: In the Demiurgically ruled world, each primary body is equated with one of the five possible Platonic solids, that is, the five types of stereometric bodies that have both regular faces and regular vertices. So, for instance, the octahedron is a Platonic solid, but the double tetrahedron (or triangular hexahedron) is not, because some of its vertices have three sides coming together, others four. Plato views the regular 'solids' as made up of just their depthless faces. A particle of earth is an empty cube with sides that can and sometimes do come totally unhinged. Fire is an empty tetrahedron, whose sides of equilateral triangles can and do come totally unhinged. And so on with the icosahedron of water and octahedron of air. Primary bodies come unhinged as the result of their crushing and cutting each other in the rough and tumble of the phenomenal flux.

Since instances of the last three (fire, air, water) are all made of equilateral triangles, when their triangles come unhinged, they can recombine either as the type of particle they formed before (fire recombines as fire) or as one of the other two primary bodies with triangular faces (fire recombines, with additional unhinged triangles, to form air or water). This recombinant geometry is how Plato explains the resolution of the primary bodies into each other, a phenomenon that Plato thinks needs to be saved on any explanatory model of the physical world. The endless resolution of the four primary particles into each other essentially characterizes the flux of the phenomena. But how can all these claims be compatible with the theo-physics of the first part of the discourse, even if we acknowledge, as Plato does, that the atomic account is inadequate because it necessarily leaves earth, with its square sides, outside the primary bodies' cycle of resolutions.

Here is the puzzle more precisely: if order is the exclusive product of the Demiurge and the geometrical orderings of the Platonic solids are necessary to explain the pre-cosmic flux of the world before the Demiurge's interventions into it, then we seem to have a contradiction. The contradiction can be avoided if the primary bodies are viewed as existing in less than fully geometrized forms in the pre-cosmos: they are geometrical enough to produce the inter-body resolutions of the flux, but not so perfect that they can't be improved upon. And indeed later in the dialogue, we hear of the weak and warped triangles from which some primary bodies are constituted. Further, even at their introduction, the primary bodies are said to have "traces" of their natures prior to the interventions of the Demiurge. What these traces are are foreshadowings of the fully geometrical natures that they will have when the Demiurge does intervene; they are approximations to perfect instantiations of their Ideal geometries (the Form of fire, of earth, etc). That phenomenal earth, air, fire, and water exist as mathematical entities is a direct result of their Forms casting images of themselves across the medium of space. But they are imperfect tetrahedrons, octahedrons, etc. The dispersion of the geometrical, though imperfect, images of the primary bodies occurs without help from the Demiurge.

The emerging critical consensus is that the primary bodies do indeed exist in their geometrized form in the pre-cosmos. See the essays by Alan Code and Verity Harte. That the primary bodies are geometrized in the pre-cosmos has two important consequences. First, it turns out paradoxically that some order is a precondition of disorder. Underlying the flux of the phenomena is the geometry of the primary bodies. Their basic geometry is not dependent upon the Demiurge. This, in turn, explains why the *Timaeus* is not framed as a teleological argument for the existence of god. It gives no argument from design. God is simply presumed, not argued for. Depending on one's metaphysical sympathies, one might argue from geometrical order to Forms, holding that orderly mathematical objects can only exist if there are Forms of them, but in the *Timaeus'* view, one can legitimately claim that there is quite a lot of order in the world, necessarily so, independently of the Demiurge—even though that world is also properly called chaotic.

Second, from the geometric status of the primary bodies in the pre-cosmos, we learn more clearly about the manner in which the Demiurge goes about improving things. It is not by imposing order where there was none before, but rather it is the sort of ordering that takes something that falls away from a standard and brings it (more) fully into accord with it, a bit like straightening out a knife blade that has become bent. The Demiurge does not impose form on characterless matter. He improves things by tinkering and adjusting proportions and measures that already exist. If the World Body is running a fever, he lowers its temperature. But at each and every moment of the Body, whether fevered, chilled, or hale, it has a determinate temperature. At any moment, it is as 'formed' as it is at any other moment. If, as seems to be entertained in the cosmological myth of the *Statesman*, the World Soul eventually begins gradually to gyrate off center, the Demiurge brings it back on course, makes its rotations perfect again.

The Receptacle of space and the geometrized bodies of the *Timaeus* have fascinated Platonic scholarship. Six contributions to this collection have these topics as their points of departure—those of Donald Zeyl, Verity Harte, Alan Code, Stephen Menn, Ian Mueller, and Zina Giannopoulou. These topics have fascinated still others, not just physicists, classicists, and philosophers, but literary theorists and architects as well. In 1974, the literary theorist and litterateur Julia Kristeva wrote a germinal essay on Plato's Receptacle of space in her book *Revolution in Poetic Language*. The essay takes the shaking of the Receptacle literally and links it to Plato's many female metaphors for space—nurse, foster-mother, mother. The resulting position views the shaking not as a part of the workings of chaos, but as a distinctive generative principle, a source of creativity, a particularly female form of creativity, one which on the plane of meaning communicates by showing rather than telling, one that operates by signs and indicators rather than symbols, and which has certain parallels to the Freudian subconscious.

This cluster of Platonically inspired ideas has had a widespread and abiding afterlife especially within the Continental tradition—in linguistics, literary theory, psychiatry, and, as it turns out, architecture. The architect Peter Eisenman and the philosopher Jacques Derrida jointly created an architectural design, based on their understanding of Platonic space, for a garden within Paris' Parc de la Villette (general architect, Bernard Tschumi, 1982–1993) and produced an important testamentary book on the project, *Chora L Works* (1997). Architectural historian Anthony Vidler made the project a core of his 2005 memorial to Derrida, while architect and classicist Ann Bergren condemned the project as hopelessly confused, degrading to women, and having entirely missed the *Timaeus'* potentials. Both authors are represented in this volume with new essays tracking the positive influences of the *Timaeus* on modern architectural theory and practice. Additionally, Zina Giannopoulou's essay directly addresses Derrida's views on Platonic space.

The later reaches of the *Timaeus* have drawn far less attention than its opening two sections, those on the works of reason and the effects of necessity. The official program of the last third of the *Timaeus* sounds grand enough: it is to present a synthesis of reason and necessity operating cooperatively. But its content is deflationary when compared to what has gone before. The objects of the grand synthesis are largely just the bodily structures and processes of humans and other animals: the formation of the abdomen, marrow, hair, and sinews; the mechanisms of respiration and digestion; diseases involving air, phlegm, and bile—topics like that. Admittedly, this is not sexy stuff compared to god, time, and space. But all of the biology is built off of the chemistry of the primary particles, and so even when the text seems playful or wacky in its details—it is, after all, based on an atomic story that Plato knows will, at the end of the scientific day, not remain on the table of possibly true theories—it contains a suggestive reductionist account of biology, the model that predominates in contemporary science: if we remove talk of both souls and values from the discourses of nature, then biological properties (cell division, leaves turning red in the Fall, etc.) can be exhaustively analyzed into chemical properties, which are exhaustively reducible to properties of physics. Plato will not let us get strongly emergent or supervenient properties, like consciousness, mind, and free will, on the cheap. These things will not easily percolate up from Democritean atoms and the void, and they certainly will not bubble up from Plato's geometrized particles and the Receptacle. For Plato, it is physics *and* God that do the explaining in the realm animate beings with functions and goals. If a sum is greater than its parts in the physical realm, that is God's doing. There are things still to think about in the third part of the *Timaeus*, but, not surprisingly, none of the contributors to this volume focus on it.

A Reader's Guide to the Collection

To help readers find their way through the collection, I here provide précis that give the basic views and hint at the argumentative structure of each essay. I have lived long enough through the post-modern era to know that a wholly impartial representation of anything is impossible. I only hope that I have not seriously misrepresented the contributing authors' views. The abstracts:

The Big Questions

Anthony Leggett's essay "Plato's *Timaeus*: Some Resonances in Modern Physics and Cosmology" suggests that the enduring impact of the *Timaeus* for physics and cosmology lies chiefly in the questions Plato raises rather than in the specific answers he gives to them, though some of his accounts of physical structures remain intriguing, suggestive, even inspiring to current thought. Plato was asking the right questions. Not dead-end questions like, what is substance? or what is *a* substance? But questions like, did the universe have a beginning and does the universe exist in time or is time a result of the nature of the universe? Is our universe unique? On a literal reading of the *Timaeus*, Plato gave the right answers to these questions: our universe had a beginning, but time derives from the structures of the existing universe. Plato was right to see that units or measurements of time require orderly objects and conditions. And Plato sides with the majority of modern cosmologists in holding that our world is one of a kind. Plato's views on the relations among necessity, space, and mind are suggestive of contemporary worries over what it is about the universe that is fixed by basic background conditions and what about it is the product of arbitrary initial conditions.

The biggest question, though, is why the universe exists at all. Plato's answer, that it was created because a cosmic craftsman thought it would be a good thing to have around, is far out of favor with most contemporary cosmologists, but Leggett views as no less problematic some of the alternatives offered by modern physics, including the suggestion that our universe is just one of those things that happens from time to time. Plato would very much like things to turn out such that the universe is arranged with the specific aim of making intelligent life possible. Leggett ends his essay wondering, in somewhat the opposite direction: if quantum mechanics is the whole truth of the physical universe, as most physicists assume, then is there any determinate realization of the universe in the absence of observation? And if not, then, given that the universe is determinate, "observation by what or whom?"

God and Related Matters

Anthony Long's sweeping essay "Cosmic Craftsmanship in Plato and Stoicism" traces the development of Greek theology from the Presocratics through the Hellenistic era. Heraclitus turns out to be far more central in this development than is usually thought. Though Heraclitus did not conceive of the world as the creation of a divine craftsman, he did view the world as imbued with a divine principle—*logos* (account, discourse, ratio)—or divine element—fire—that governs the world by governing itself according to determinate measures and proportions, and so makes of the world a *cosmos* or orderly system. Human excellence is achieved when this system is echoed in each person as psychological balance and internal control.

Plato holds to Heraclitus' basic account of the physical world as a rational and balanced structure, but transforms his impersonal *logos* into the purposive intelligence of a divine craftsman who resides outside the physical world, but who is a supremely benevolent agent and has personal attributes—"a divinity, in other words, more similar to the providential god of Judaism and Christianity than anything in the preceding Greek tradition." Unlike the Judeo-Christian god, though, Plato's Demiurge makes things by reference to an eternal model exterior to his mind and by means of arithmetical and geometric instrumentalities shaping amorphous materials not of his own making. In addition to the general project of leading chaos into order, a process effected in significant part by his infusing the physical world with a rational soul, the Demiurge makes it possible for humans to become rational, in order that they might complete the project of making the world a thoroughly rational *cosmos*. Humans become rational by imitating the rationality of God.

The Stoics return god to the material world as a pantheistic principle, described as a craftsman, but one that does not use an external model and for whom materials offer no resistance. This god creates on a biological model by seeding himself into the world and seeing his DNA, as it were, develop throughout the material world, which acts as a nurturing ground for his "spermatic" principles. The goal of the Stoic god in forming mankind is to extend a share of his own rationality to each individual, with a view to forming an overarching community or city of which god himself is the constitutional monarch. So though for both Plato and the Stoics, god is craftsmanly, rational, providential, and benevolent, their gods differ markedly in their ontological status, instrumentalities, and ends.

Allan Silverman's exploratory essay "Philosopher-Kings and Craftsman-Gods" suggests a closer link is to be found between theoretical reason and practical reason, contemplation and action, in Plato's *Republic* and *Timaeus* than in Aristotle's *Nicomachean Ethics* and *Metaphysics*. For Silverman, reason's access to the Good motivates its possessor to produce more good and is probably necessary for his or her doing so. In the *Republic*, the philosopher descends from the world of Forms to the workaday world "with the aim of making more good, not at the cost of his own happiness, but simply because he has the opportunity of making others better." In the *Timaeus*, the view that knowing the Good entails doing good is most clearly found in the portrayal of the Demiurge's motivation for framing the orderly universe as flowing automatically from his goodness and lack of jealousy. The same linkages are assumed to hold for human creativity as well.

Charles H. Kahn's programmatic essay "The Place of Cosmology in Plato's Later Dialogues" offers an outline for a general understanding of the late Platonic dialogues that is unitarian in its thrust. Kahn argues that the new developments of the late dialogues (*Phaedrus, Sophist, Statesman, Philebus, Timaeus, Laws*) are an extension of the metaphysical dualism of the middle period dialogues (*Phaedo, Republic*), not a rejection of them. Once the *Phaedo* establishes the need for Platonic Forms and exposes the explanatory failures of purely physicalistic systems, Plato, in the late dialogues, can use the theory of Forms to take many of the physicalists' ideas and subordinately re-incorporate them back into a coherent account of the phenomenal world. The Presocratics, exiled from respectability in the *Phaedo*, are redeemed with light from the theory of Forms. The chief vehicles for this re-incorporation are a new concept of the soul understood as self-moving motion and the new ontological principles of limit and the unlimited, which, when blended by reference to Platonic Forms, put a break on the Heraclitean flux. Though written broadly within the tradition of the American unitarian interpretations of Plato (those of Paul Shorey and Harold Cherniss), Kahn's essay makes certain nods toward finding Aristotelian elements in late Plato.

Matthias Vorwerk's essay "Maker or Father? The Demiurge from Plutarch to Plotinus" explores the Middle Platonists' varying treatments of Plato's description of the Demiurge as both a maker and a father—in order to understand what Plato himself might have meant by this somewhat puzzling double designation. Fathers typically produce natural objects of the same type as themselves, while makers, at least in the obvious cases, produce artificial objects, which in consequence are different in kind from themselves. Drawing on Middle Platonic conceptual schemes, Vorwerk concludes that in the *Timaeus* the Demiurge is a father in relation to the cosmos taken as a whole, which is a living being, but he is a maker in relation to the constituent or material parts of the cosmos.

Thomas M. Robinson's wide-ranging essay "Plato on (just about) Everything: Some Observations on the *Timaeus* and Other Dialogues" spans from debates about the *Timaeus* that took place within Plato's Academy to contemporary debates about cosmology and justice in general. Robinson defends a literalist reading of the creation account: the orderly world is not eternally old; it had a beginning. But Robinson also defends the status of the Demiurge as distinct from the rational World Soul. Even if the Demiurge himself is a soul, his rational nature, unlike the World Soul's rationality, is non-contingent. Robinson suggests that modifications of Plato's cosmology worked in the *Statesman* myth draw Plato's views intriguingly close to some features of Big Bang theory and that modifications of Plato's social philosophy worked in the *Laws* draw Plato's views on distributive justice intriguingly close to those found in John Rawls' *A Theory of Justice*.

Space, Place, and Motion—The Receptacle of Becoming

Donald Zeyl's essay "Visualizing Platonic Space," by pressing Plato's meta-phors that imply that space is malleable and fluid, treats Platonic space as a medium or field for receiving images. Phenomenal objects are configurations in space, but are not each permanently fixed to a particular bit of space. While they each at every moment fill a particular region of space, they are capable of moving through space in the way that one and the same wave glides through different expanses of water as it moves toward the shore. The wave is both made of water and moves through water. On this account, the geometrized primary particles (earth, air, fire, and water) are analogous neither to granules nor to empty boxes. In all these ways, then, Plato gives a coherent account of how phenomenal objects may both appear in space and move through space.

    Verity Harte's essay "The Receptacle and the Primary Bodies: Something from Nothing?" offers a general reading of the relations among Forms, Demiurge, and Receptacle on which Plato avoids the charge that he tacitly has his Demiurge create, as though by magic, phenomenal objects from out of nothing. Pressing Plato's metaphors of Space or the Receptacle as a medium for receiving impressions (like a wax tablet), Harte holds that Plato's geom-etrized primary bodies (the tetrahedron of fire, the octahedron of air, etc.) are configurations *of* space, but are neither configurations *in* space (viewed as a container) nor configurations made *out of* space (in the way a sculpture is made out of bronze). The geometrical shapes are impressed, not embossed. Further even in the pre-orderly world, the primary bodies as images of Forms exist in their geometrized shapes—either in slightly irregular versions that the Demiurge then regularizes or in regular but transient shapes that the Demiurge then stabilizes. Given all this, then, if in addition one also rejects Aristotelian presumptions of what it means to be a thing (i.e., to be like a bronze sculpture), then Demiurgic intervention into the world is not a case of making something from nothing.

Stephen Menn's essay "The *Timaeus* and the Critique of Presocratic Vortices" views the development of Presocratic philosophy not as a smooth arc of ideas rising either toward Plato's *Timaeus* or Aristotle's *Physics,* but as a series of oppositional moves launched by later philosophers against earlier. Plato's critiques of earlier writers can be marshaled into five types, of which Menn's essay addresses two: the earlier writers' resort to narrative at the expense of demonstration and their failure to give teleological explanations. The bulk of the essay tracks the latter line of critique. Specifically, Menn contends Plato tacitly holds the view that Anaxagoras' reason-initiated centrifugal separations of physical kinds cannot give an adequate account of animal life. The criticism is shown to echo the earlier critique of Anaxagoras by Empedocles, a critique which is generalized by Plato into his attack on all the Presocratics. So while Plato's account of vortex-explanations might initially seem to be incidental in the *Phaedo* and *Timaeus,* it is actually the starting-point of his criticism of Presocratic physics and thus the starting point of his own physical project in the *Timaeus.*

Ian Mueller's essay "What's the Matter? Some Neoplatonist Answers" looks at various ways in which important figures of late antiquity—Proclus, Pericles of Lydia, Simplicius, and Philoponus—understood Plato's description of the Receptacle, his description of pre-cosmic disorder, and his geometric account of the four elements and their changes into one another (earth being excluded from such change). As one expects with philosophers of late antiquity, these men approach the *Timaeus* with a commitment to some (but not always the same) form of Aristotle's theory of so-called prime matter and his account of elemental change as a qualitative change of a material substratum in which all four elements participate. The different understandings range from one in which Aristotle's view replaces Plato's (Pericles) to one in which the two views are allegedly harmonized (Simplicius).

Zina Giannopoulou's essay "Derrida's *Khôra*, or Unnaming the Timaean Receptacle," analyzes and critiques the leading postmodern attack on Platonism, an essay by Jacques Derrida that attempts to trigger an implosion of Platonic dualism by appeal to purportedly contradictory elements and effects of Platonic 'space' or *khôra*. Derrida argues that Plato's need to introduce a third thing, as it were, 'between' Forms and phenomena, shows that the dualism of Forms and phenomena is itself unsustainable. He further holds that the very vehicle for this mediation, space, is an unuseful jumble of overripe metaphors. Against these positions, Giannopoulou first argues that the diverse metaphors that Plato uses for space, far from being an incoherent mess, cluster under three general concepts: containment, nurture, and (resting) place, and that in turn these concepts can be subsumed under the still more unifying concept of hosting. Further, though space has no internal properties either sensible or intelligible, it has exactly the external properties (imaged as malleability, adaptability, and durability) that allow it to serve as the necessary medium for the reception of sensible images of Forms and so, far from undercutting Plato's dualism, space makes the dualism of Form and phenomena possible.

Aristotle's Timaeus

Thomas K. Johansen's essay "Should Aristotle Have Recognized Final Causes in Plato's *Timaeus?*" aims to show that Aristotle was neither a careless nor a forgetful reader when he accuses Plato of appealing only to formal and material causes, but never final causes, in his accounts of the formation of substances. At first blush, it seems that final causes, as the goods for which things come into being, are at the core of Plato's project in the *Timaeus*, since it is both with an eye to them and for their sake that Plato's craftsman god builds the orderly world. But if, in keeping with Aristotle's views in the last book of the *Metaphysics*, mathematical concepts provide neither necessary nor sufficient explanations for the goodness of good things and if Plato's Demiurge only ever uses mathematical concepts (numbers, proportions, triangles) as the models for his interventions into the world, then Platonic formal properties can never also serve as final causes.

Alan Code's essay "Aristotle on Plato on Weight" argues that Plato's account of weight based on the geometrical properties of the primary bodies (earth, air, fire, water) is more coherent in its own terms than it is usually taken to be and that it is immune to Aristotle's core criticisms of it. On the most plausible interpretation of Plato's account of weight, it turns out that the fundamentally geometrical and numerical basis of the primary particles exists even within the pre-cosmos. The fundamental entities of the universe are numbers and geometries. The Demiurge improves upon the geometrical features of earth, air, fire, and water, but does not create geometrical features where none existed before. The ordered world is not an imposition of form onto characterless matter; the ordered world is not the imposition of quantity onto quality. Geometry is fundamental.

Reason and Myth

In 2005, Myles Burnyeat published in the new journal of ancient philosophy and science, *Rhizai*, a seminal paper, "ΕΙΚΩΣ ΜΥΘΟΣ [EIKÔS MYTHOS]," which argues that when Timaeus says that his cosmogonic discourses about the phenomenal world consist of "'likely' arguments" or "'likely' myths," he does not mean that they are "*merely* likely stories"—either ones whose truth is constrained by the status of phenomenal objects being likenesses of Platonic Forms or ones that could be improved upon through the acquisition of fuller knowledge by means of progressive science. For Burnyeat, *eikôs* here—usually rendered in translations as "likely" or "probable"—is primarily normative and aspirational rather than descriptive or metaphysical, and so most often in the *Timaeus* is better translated as "good," "appropriate," "rational," or "reasonable" and has as its primarily use the valuation of the practical reasoning of (divine) agents. The overall effect of this interpretation is to disengage the bulk of the *Timaeus* from the concerns about metaphysical dualism that dominated the central books of the *Republic* and to push the *Timaeus* in the direction of Aristotle's *Nicomachean Ethics*.

Gábor Betegh's essay "What Makes a Myth *eikôs*?" is a defense, by elaboration, of Burnyeat's position. Betegh declines to give the weight that Burnyeat does to the purportedly quasi-religious overtones of the 'exegetical' nature of myths about the phenomenal world as offering grounds for barring such myths as being likely simply in virtue of being about likenesses. But he argues that the general argumentative context of the discussion has this very effect. For Betegh a "likely account" *(eikôs logos)* is one that reveals a likeness *as* a likeness, while a "likely myth" *(eikôs mythos)* is a likely statement in a narrative form that also gives an account of how the likeness came about through the practical reasoning of a (divine) agent. In this way, a "likely myth" gives an aetiological explanation of an image, something that the mere appeal to an image as a likeness could not do. Betegh goes on to show a similar arrangement of explanations operates in other Platonic myths.

Alexander Mourelatos' essay "The Epistemological Section (29b–d) of the Proem in Timaeus' Speech" defends the traditional reading of the meaning of what for Plato constitutes a "likely story." Mourelatos first gives a detailed analysis of the proem, drawing attention to overlooked elements of its logical, syntactical, rhetorical, and stylistic components. In light of this analysis, he argues that the degree of truth of statements does after all for Plato depend upon the ontological status of their referents and, in a highly original move, also argues that, when Plato speaks of accounts of the phenomenal world that are no less likely than any others, he is referring to the possibility that any number of theories can 'cover' the same finite set of data. And so, on this account, Plato's views look both back to the possibility of multiple explanations of phenomena found in Xenophanes and forward to the methods of progressive modern science, in which conflicting hypotheses may be simultaneously entertained until disconfirming data make some of them untenable.

Time, Narrative, and Myth

Barbara M. Sattler's essay "A Time for Learning and for Counting: Egyptians, Greeks, and Empirical Processes in Plato's *Timaeus*" argues that while in the *Republic* rationality is denied to empirical processes, in the *Timaeus* empirical processes, both physical and cultural, can be in accord with reason. Unlike in the *Republic*, rationality in the *Timaeus* can encompass diversity and plurality; its key feature is regularity. On most traditional readings of the *Timaeus*, especially Neo-Platonic ones, *soul* is the vehicle for providing and maintaining the phenomena with such rationality as they have, but Sattler argues instead that rationality's earthly vehicle is *time*. For physical processes, what makes them rational through time is that time is motion that runs according to number. For human processes, rationality, chiefly practical rationality, has the complex temporal structure of decision making, in which past repositories of events provide possible models for future states of affairs, which, in turn, 'influence' present actions. The concept of reliability fuses the two senses of time—physical and human—into one.

Kathryn A. Morgan's suggestive essay "Narrative Orders in the *Timaeus* and *Critias*" declines to follow the recent critical trend toward upgrading the degree of intelligibility found in the phenomenal world of the *Timaeus*. For Morgan, Timaeus' narrative is a general account of how eternal patterns and models get realized in physical and narrative motion—imperfectly—and Critias' narrative is an account of how the unmoving patterns and models for Plato's ideal city get realized in quasi-historical action. Since according to Platonic principles an account images the degree of stability and structure of its referents, Timaeus' narrative about the phenomenal flux is necessarily choppy and inconsistent; perhaps even the question of whether Plato intends his creation story to be read literally or figuratively is unanswerable. And as far as human actions go, Critias recounts "a world in which Thucydides' hope that people could learn to recognize the processes of history because of their knowledge of a persistent element, the human thing, is vain."

Jon Solomon's illustrated essay "*Timaeus* in Tinseltown: Atlantis in Film" tracks the reception of Plato's Atlantis myth from the utopian literature of the Renaissance through Jules Verne to Blockbuster Video and your child's GameCube. The myth's uncanny juxtapositions of vivid detail and open texture make Plato's Atlantis story a DNA that can express itself in a dithering, even contradictory, array of representations. The Atlanteans were good guys in the Renaissance, only to turn sinister again in the industrial era. They pop up again as good guys in the 1985 movie *Cocoon* before settling into moral ambiguity in Disney's 2001 *Atlantis, the Lost Empire*. The myth's open texture invites 'scientific' infills to underwrite its 'authenticity', even as its strange, detailed geography and pageantry invite fantasy. The myth's cinephilic climax—the sinking of Atlantis paired with the cosmic destruction of Athens—has served as a booster rocket in the launch of the science-fiction genre. More specifically, the myth's linking of displaced nature and displaced life helped give birth to the monster and the space alien: *Undersea Kingdom* (1936); *Siren of Atlantis*; *Five Maidens from Outer Space*; *Journey to the Center of the Earth*; *Atlantis, the Lost*

Continent; *Journey Beneath the Desert*; *Conqueror of Atlantis*; *Beyond Atlantis*; *Warlords of Atlantis*; *Raiders of Atlantis*; *Cocoon*; *Alien from L.A.*; *Atlantis, the Lost Empire*; *Atlantis, Milo's Return* (Disney, direct to video, 2003); and the first SpongeBob SquarePants made-for-television movie, *Atlantis SquarePantis* (2007) with DVD and Nintendo follow-ups.

And there's no end in sight for the frenzy of popular interest in the story. While this book is in press, Hollywood releases a remake of *Journey to the Center of the Earth*—in 3-D. In the West Village, upscale Hudson Furniture snags a "Shopping With" feature in the *New York Times* for its Atlantis Chandelier, great swags and cascades of nickel chain starting at $12,900. Meanwhile, on a man-made island in the Arabian Gulf, there opens a marine-themed luxury resort, Atlantis Dubai: "Imagine exploring the mysterious ruins of Atlantis, lost for thousands of years deep beneath the sea. Now picture looking up to see 65,000 marine animals swimming in placid waters around you. Visitors can live out their own Atlantean adventure in The Lost Chambers, the maze of underwater halls and tunnels under the Ambassador Lagoon."

Timaean Architecture—Timber Framing the Universe and Building Today

Anthony Vidler's multi-pronged essay "The Atlantis Effect: The Lost Origins of Architecture" tracks from the Renaissance to the present the influences of Plato's mythical accounts of the construction of the cities of Atlantis and Ur-Athens on how architecture has "envisaged its authority." Geometry has a lot to do with that authority, but geometry can go awry as in the clash of circular and rectilinear element in Atlantis' construction and so contribute to social and geopolitical disorder and destruction. As important to architecture's authority is the concept of god viewed as architect-builder taken from Timaeus' discourse, which is wedged between Critias' two accounts of Atlantis, but which hovers in their background: "The foundation of the *polis* (city) demands a replication of the cosmic construct—the establishment of territories through geometry, their definition according to classes of inhabitants, and the careful exclusion of non-citizens of the *polis* into the worldly equivalent of chaos. In sum, the work of architecture." Finally, the *Timaeus*, with its concept of place or space with creative potential points to the possibility of recovering an architecture that exists without the divisions of theory and practice, "form and function, idea and material, intelligible and sensible, art and *techne* (craft)," and so could help restore an era when architecture places humanity with the world rather than against it.

Ann Bergren's illustrated essay (with animations available at *www.platos timaeustoday.com*) on Plato and architecture "Plato's *Timaeus* and the Aesthetics of 'Animate Form'" finds resonances of the dialogue in the branch of contemporary architectural design called "animate form," particularly in the work of two chief practitioners, Greg Lynn and Elena Manferdini. But this Timaean 'influence' running into the architectural present does not have the unevolving architectonic structurings, the simple geometric orderings, wrought by the Demiurge, as its model and does not aspire to make aesthetic judgments by reference to standards, templates, perfect cases, or Forms. It rejects the triumph of structure over mere part. Rather it looks to the *Timaeus'* pre-orderly world, the world before the Demiurge's interventions, and to the suggestive, mobile traces of the elements found there as spurs to and generative materials for design. Such design will share "with the pre-cosmic *chôra* [space] the attributes of variegation, perpetual shape shifting, simultaneity of opposites" and transformative imitation. The loveliness of design so conceived will not lie in unity, measure, and proportion—the marks of Platonic beauty traditionally conceived (maybe even by Plato himself in the *Philebus*)—but will be found in an earlier Homeric concept of beauty, the marks of which instead are *daidalos* "elaborately crafted and detailed," *poikilos* "variegated, differentiated, and mutiplicitious," and *aiolos* "glittering, mobile, and animated."

Ever After, Ever Before

Sean Carroll's informal summary of his wonder-inspiring essay, "Time and Change in an Eternal Universe" leads us from our familiar patch of the universe to the outer limits of what is currently known about dark matter and dark energy, and then, in light of that knowledge, conjectures about how the rest of the story of the universe will unfurl. Local, intense, but widely scattered condensations of dark energy will cause other universes to hive off from ours spiraling both endlessly into the future and, like films running in reverse, beginninglessly into the past. What is is eternal without the benefit or need of gods. Grandeur does not require glory. Nor symmetry a protractor.

Publisher's Note

For a list of the links and to view animations referred to in the three illustrated chapters—18. "*Timaeus* in Tinseltown: Atlantis in Film" by Jon Solomon; 20. "Plato's *Timaeus* and the Aesthetics of 'Animate Form'" by Ann Bergren; and 21. "Time and Change in an Eternal Universe" by Sean M. Carroll—visit: ***www.platostimaeustoday.com***.

Acknowledgements

The contributors to this volume were all participants in an international, interdisciplinary conference at the University of Illinois (Urbana) held September 13 to 16, 2007 and titled "Life, the Universe, Everything—and More: Plato's *Timaeus* Today." In all but two cases, the contributions derive from papers presented at the conference. The conference had books sessions on Thomas M. Robinson's *Cosmos as Art Object* and Thomas K. Johansen's *Plato's Natural Philosophy*. But rather than trying to reproduce those sessions here, I have included original essays by these authors. I organized the conference jointly with Barbara Sattler, who during the year-and-a-half effort moved from the University of Illinois to Yale. I am very grateful to Kirk Sanders of the University of Illinois for having stepped in to assist during the run up to the conference and for his help in pulling this anthology together.

The diverse topics to be addressed by the conference resonated across the campus. Over fifty units contributed funds to it. In addition, half a dozen professors donated research money to the cause: William Calder, Debra Hawhee, Michael Moore, Richard Powers, David Sansone, Bill Schroeder, and Harry Triandis. The University's higher administration strongly supported the conference. Provost Linda Katehi served as the conference's honorary chair and funded major components of the conference. The Office of the Chancellor made a special contribution towards conference amenities. I'm particularly grateful for funding from the College of Liberal Arts and Sciences, the School of Architecture, the School of Literatures, Cultures, and Linguistics, the Center for Advanced Study, the George A. Miller Programs Committee, and International Programs and Studies, which provided assistance from the William and Flora Hewlett International Endowment. The conference was also successful in securing substantial external support: a grant from the John Templeton Foundation (#12445), a major donation from University alumnus, Robert D. Novak, and major underwriting by Parmenides Publishing and the HYELE Institute for Comparative Studies. Many thanks to each. I also thank Parmenides Publishing, as I did when it published my book *God and Forms in Plato*, for continuing to make the study of ancient philosophy an adventure. I thank Alexander Mourelatos for bringing Yip Harburg's "Necessity" to the conference's attention both conceptually and sonically. The conference's original seed money came from the Department of Philosophy under the chairmanship of Richard Schacht and the Department of the Classics under the chairmanship of Kirk Freudenburg.

Eliza Tutellier, Managing Editor; Jeff Crouse, Acquisitions Editor; and Karen Succi, Production Manager, at Parmenides Publishing deserve special thanks for carefully shepherding this project through editing and production, processes which for this book proved unusually complicated. It was originally designed to contain a DVD whose core was to be film clips illustrating the chapter "*Timaeus* in Tinseltown." This effort was thwarted by Tinseltown itself, with cascading effects on the rest of the volume.

The *Timaeus* conference was produced on a computer that regularly made grinding noises. I thank my husband, Robert W. Switzer, for keeping it and me going.

Notes on Contributors

Ann Bergren is Professor of Classics at the University of California, Los Angeles. She holds a Master in Architecture degree from Harvard University's Graduate School of Design. She is the author of *The Etymology and Usage of* peirar *in Early Greek Poetry: A Study in the Interrelationship of Metrics, Linguistics, and Poetics* and *Weaving Truth: Essays on Language and the Female in Greek Thought*.

Gábor Betegh is Professor of Philosophy at the Central European University in Budapest. He is the author of *The Derveni Papyrus: Cosmology, Theology, and Interpretation*.

Sean M. Carroll is Senior Research Associate in the Department of Physics at the California Institute of Technology. He is the author of *Spacetime and Geometry: An Introduction to General Relativity*.

Alan Code is Board of Governors Professor of Philosophy at Rutgers University. He is the author of two forthcoming books, *The Philosophy of Aristotle* and *Collected Papers on Aristotle's Metaphysics and Logic*.

Zina Giannopoulou is Assistant Professor of Classics at the University of California, Irvine.

Verity Harte is Professor of Philosophy and Classics at Yale University. She is the author of *Plato on Parts and Wholes: The Metaphysics of Structure*.

Thomas K. Johansen is Fellow in Ancient Philosophy at Brasenose College, Oxford University. He is the author of *Aristotle on the Sense-Organs* and *Plato's Natural Philosophy: A Study of the* Timaeus-Critias. He has brought out a new edition and revised translation of Penguin Classics' *Timaeus* and *Critias*.

Charles H. Kahn is Professor of Philosophy at the University of Pennsylvania. He is the author of *Anaximander and the Origins of Greek Cosmology*, *The Verb 'Be' in Ancient Greek*, *The Art and Thought of Heraclitus*, *Plato and the Socratic Dialogue*, and *Pythagoras and the Pythagoreans: A Brief History*.

Anthony Leggett is the John D. and Catherine T. MacArthur Professor and Center for Advanced Study Professor of Physics at the University of Illinois. His first degree was a BA in Greats at Balliol College, Oxford University. But he has chiefly worked on the theory of low-temperature physics and was a 2003 Nobel Prize winner for his work on the superfluid phases of the light isotope of helium. He was knighted by Queen Elizabeth II in 2005 and is the author of *The Problems of Physics*.

Anthony A. Long is Professor of Classics, Irving G. Stone Professor of Literature, and Affiliated Professor of Philosophy and of Rhetoric at the University of California, Berkeley. He is the author of various books on ancient philosophy, including most recently *Epictetus: A Stoic and Socratic Guide to Life* and *From Epicurus to Epictetus: Studies in Hellenistic and Roman Philosophy*.

Stephen Menn is Associate Professor of Philosophy at McGill University. He is the author of *Plato on God as Nous*, *Descartes and Augustine* and the forthcoming *The Aim and the Argument of Aristotle's* Metaphysics.

Richard D. Mohr is Professor of Philosophy and of the Classics at the University of Illinois. He is the author of *The Platonic Cosmology*; *Gays/Justice: A Study of Ethics, Society, and Law*; *Gay Ideas: Outing and Other Controversies*; *A More Perfect Union*; *Pottery, Politics, Art: George Ohr and the Brothers Kirkpatrick*; *The Long Arc of Justice: Lesbian and Gay Marriage, Equality and Rights*; and *God and Forms in Plato*.

Kathryn A. Morgan is Professor of Classics at the University of California, Los Angeles. She is the author of *Myth and Philosophy from the Presocratics to Plato* and the editor of *Popular Tyranny: Sovereignty and Its Discontents in Ancient Greece*.

Alexander P. D. Mourelatos is Professor of Philosophy and of Classics at The University of Texas at Austin. He is the author of *The Route of Parmenides* and editor of *The Pre-Socratics: A Collection of Critical Essays*. Among his published articles, four that discuss Plato's conception of astronomy and of the mathematical sciences bear on the *Timaeus*.

Ian Mueller is Professor Emeritus of Philosophy at the University of Chicago. He is the author of *Philosophy of Mathematics and Deductive Structure in Euclid's Elements* and the translator of eight volumes in the Ancient Commentators on Aristotle series for Cornell University Press, covering Alexander of Aphrodisias on *Prior Analytics* 1.8–2.46 and Simplicius on *De Caelo* 2–4.

Thomas M. Robinson is Professor Emeritus of Philosophy and of Classics at the University of Toronto. His books include *Plato's Psychology, Contrasting Arguments: An Edition of the Dissoi Logoi, Heraclitus' Fragments: A Text and Translation with a Commentary*, and *Cosmos as Art Object: Studies in Plato's Timaeus*. With David Gallop, he jointly edited the University of Toronto Press' book series on Presocratic philosophy.

Barbara M. Sattler is Assistant Professor of Philosophy at Yale University. She and Richard D. Mohr conceived and organized the conference "Life, the Universe, Everything – and More: Plato's *Timaeus* Today."

Allan Silverman is Professor of Philosophy at the Ohio State University. He is the author of *The Dialectic of Essence: A Study of Plato's* Metaphysics.

Jon Solomon is Robert D. Novak Professor of Western Civilization & Culture and Professor of the Classics at the University of Illinois. He is the author of *Ancient Roman Feasts and Recipes – Adapted for the Modern Kitchen, The Ancient World in the Cinema, Ptolemy's Harmonics: Translation and Commentary, The Complete Three Stooges: The Official Filmography and Three Stooges Companion*, and, with Robert C. Solomon, *Up the University*.

Anthony Vidler is the Dean of the Irwin S. Chanin School of Architecture at the Cooper Union. His books include *The Writing of the Walls: Architectural Theory in the Late Enlightenment, The Architectural Uncanny: Essays on the Modern Unhomely, Warped Space: Art, Architecture, and Anxiety in Modern Culture*, and *Histories of the Immediate Present: Inventing Architectural Modernism*.

Matthias Vorwerk is Associate Professor of Philosophy at the Catholic University of America. He is the author of *Plotins Schrift "Über den Geist, die Ideen und das Seiende" (Enneade V 9 [5]): Text, Translation, Commentary*.

Donald Zeyl is Professor of Philosophy at the University of Rhode Island. He is the author of *Plato* Gorgias*: Translation and Introduction* and *Plato* Timaeus*: Translation and Introduction* and is the editor of Greenwood's *Encyclopedia of Classical Philosophy*.

1

Plato's Timaeus: Some Resonances in Modern Physics and Cosmology

Anthony J. Leggett

There are a few isolated passages in the *Timaeus* which an advocate might claim foreshadow modern scientific ideas. For example, 37c–38d seems to anticipate the concept of the "block" Universe as formulated by modern philosophers of science, and 52b similarly the Kantian notion of space. The "triangles" of 53d–57c might be regarded as a quasi-molecular theory of matter, and 67b makes a striking comment about the relation of frequency to perceived pitch. But I suspect much of this is coincidence. Overall, Plato's speculations on the nature of the physical world do not have much in common with the answers given by modern science.

Rather it is his *questions* that often have a modern resonance, and it is these which I shall address in this talk. In this context, the most interesting passages are probably 27d–38b, on the isotropy and uniqueness of the Universe and the nature of time, 47c–52d on *nous* (reason) versus *anankê* (necessity), the idea of the *hypodochê* (usually translated as "receptacle"), sameness and difference, kinematics versus dynamics, necessity versus contingency, and finally, the discussion from 69a onward about the relation of the physical Universe to human existence and perceptions. Just about all these issues are still alive, either explicitly or implicitly, in modern physics and cosmology.

We may as well start at the beginning. At 28b, Plato asks "Has [the Universe] always been? Was there no origin from which it came to be? Or did it come to be and take its start from some origin?" And he gives his own answer: "It has come to be." Interestingly, this would not have been the answer given by physicists and astronomers in the nineteenth century or indeed in the first three decades of the twentieth: for them, the Universe had indeed "always been," and would always be in the future. However, as is well known, in 1929

31

Edwin Hubble made a revolutionary discovery: the light we receive from nearby galaxies shows the famous "red shift," which is almost universally interpreted as evidence that they are receding at a speed proportional to their distance from us; in other words, the Universe is expanding uniformly, like the surface of a balloon which is being inflated. If one combines this information with the equations of general relativity, which are usually believed to govern the behavior of space, time, and matter on the cosmic scale, one is almost inevitably led to the conclusion that as we go back in time, the Universe becomes both very dense and very hot, until we eventually reach a point at which the laws of physics as we know them seem to make no sense—the (in)famous "hot big bang." As far as is known, neither the possible existence of an "inflationary" epoch in the later stages of the hot big bang, nor the recent discovery that the expansion has been accelerating, change this fundamental conclusion. Thus, according to our modern understanding, the Universe has indeed "come to be."

As to the possible futures of the Universe, according to our current understanding there are three possibilities, each corresponding to a different large-scale geometry, namely, (a) it will expand forever, eventually at a constant rate ("open" Universe), (b) it will expand forever, but at an ever-decreasing rate ("flat" Universe), (c) it will reach a maximum radius and then re-contract, ending in a "big crunch" ("closed" Universe). Which of these is actually realized depends on the Universe's current mass density, at present a very poorly known quantity. However, this uncertainty does not affect conclusions regarding the past.

The "hot big bang" cosmology raises a number of obvious questions, some of which certainly occurred to Plato. First, what was "before" the Big Bang? There are three obvious answers: (a) nothing, (b) a previous Universe, causally connected to ours, and (c) a previous Universe, causally disconnected from ours by a sort of "document-shredding" process at the Big Bang. Our current understanding of the laws of physics at the relevant scale does not allow us to say with confidence which, if any, of these answers is correct (or for that matter if they even really make sense).

A second obvious question, which resurfaces in the famous controversy two thousand years after Plato between Leibniz and Newton's disciple Clarke, is: Does the Universe exist in time, or does time derive its very meaning from the existence of the Universe? At 37c, Plato puts his finger on one aspect of the problem: "For before the heavens came to be, there were no days or nights, no months or years." In modern terms, we might ask: how do we actually define a unit of time? The standard modern definition is in terms of the frequency of the light emitted by a particular transition of the "atomic clock" constituted by a cesium atom; however, according to our present understanding no cesium atoms existed until the first supernova explosions, millions of years after the Big Bang. To measure time before this, we could perhaps resort to a clock derived from the fundamental element, hydrogen; but even hydrogen did not exist before the "recombination epoch," about 300,000 years after the Big Bang. At even earlier times, we could in principle imagine defining a unit of time via the mass of some elementary particle, say, an electron, since according to quantum field theory, this mass (m) defines a corresponding time (T) via the relation $T = h/mc^2$ where c is the speed of light and h Planck's constant; however, under the very dense and hot conditions of the early Universe, where particles are constantly fusing and mutating into one another, it is not clear that even the concept of a unique electron mass retains its meaning. Fundamentally, as Plato notes, the measurement of time requires not just the existence of matter but its existence under certain fairly well-defined conditions.

One possible way of getting around this difficulty in the early states of the Big Bang is simply to assume the truth of the equations of general relativity and to define the time (relative to the time of the Big Bang) by their solution. That is, a given energy density (we assume in the present context that we have an independent way of defining this quantity, though that is not entirely obvious) corresponds *by definition* to a given time. But now it is clear that this definition is somewhat arbitrary. Let's consider the question: Did the Big Bang really occur at a finite time in the past (roughly fourteen billion years ago)? According to this definition, yes. But no fundamental principle prevents us rescaling the definition of time, for example by setting $t_{new} = t_o \ln(t_{old}/t_o)$, where t_{old} is the "conventional" time, measured from the hot big bang, and t_o is some arbitrary value of t_{old}, say, that at which 50% of the hydrogen is recombined. With this definition the Big Bang occurred infinitely far in the past! (I am told that this point was made by E. A. Milne more than sixty years ago.)

Quite apart from questions regarding its measurement, what is the status of "time"? Is it a primitive concept, on the same footing as space, as Plato seems to suggest in 37a–b and as the modern "block Universe" scenario assumes? Or is it derivative (or as the currently fashionable buzzword would put it, "emergent") from the relations of more primitive, "timeless" events, as seems to be the view espoused by the modern practitioners of "loop quantum gravity"?

Is "our" Universe unique? Plato's answer was yes, and most but not all modern cosmologies agree. Other Universes, if they exist, might be distinguished from ours by their location in time or in space, or perhaps in other ways, for example by existing in different "dimensions." Once again we cannot say for sure . . .

Yet another question that still puzzles modern cosmology is: Why is the Universe so smooth? This is indeed usually regarded as one of the major mysteries concerning the Big Bang.

Finally, the most obvious question (or as some would argue, pseudo-question) of all: *why* the Big Bang, or more generally, why does the Universe exist at all? Plato raises this question, and answers it by positing creation by a cosmic *dêmiourgos* ("craftsman"). This kind of answer is not one that is particularly popular with modern cosmologists, but it is not clear that some of the answers given are any less problematic: for example, can one make any sense of the idea that the Universe is born from, literally, nothing by a quantum fluctuation (or in the words of E. P. Tryon, "I offer the modest proposal that our Universe is just one of those things that happen from time to time")? We clearly stand at the very edge of our understanding.

As a sort of footnote to the above discussion, it is worth noting one modern concern that is completely absent in the *Timaeus*, namely the issue of the "arrow of time." Its absence is not surprising: until the work of Newton in the seventeenth century, and that of Maxwell in the nineteenth, there was no reason at all to question the idea that the microscopic laws of physics encode a unique sense (direction) of the flow of time, so that the problem simply did not arise. From a modern point of view, however, it seems likely to be intimately connected with some of the other problems raised above, such as the extreme smoothness of the Universe.

I now turn more briefly to the second extended passage in the *Timaeus* (47c–52d) which has strong echoes in modern physics and cosmology. Three concepts that are ubiquitous in this passage are *nous* (mind), *ananke* (necessity), and *hypodochê* (receptacle). Several distinctions seem implicit here: in modern terminology we could call them the opposition of necessity and contingency, of kinematics and dynamics, and of general laws and particular initial conditions. Here I think Plato is wrestling with a dilemma that has equally occupied some contemporary thinkers such as Lee Smolin: those distinctions certainly seem to make sense for particular parts of the Universe, but is it obvious that they make sense when applied to the Universe as a whole?

One specific difficulty in trying to interpret this passage in modern terms is: Is the *hypodochê* a *physical* entity (in which case it is tempting to make the connection to the modern idea of the "vacuum"), or is it rather an underlying *scheme*? If the latter, we could perhaps point to a modern parallel in the general structure of Lagrangian field theory, which would then be in some sense enforced on us a priori (in Plato's language, the result of *"ananke"*) while the specific types of elementary particles actually realized, and their interactions, are contingent (the effect of *nous*). Indeed a central concern of modern high-energy (elementary particle) physics is whether the so-called Standard Model, which contains at present seventeen *a priori* undetermined ("contingent") parameters, is the final story, or whether we shall discover that some or all of these parameters are fixed by "necessity." This in turn relates to the question: which aspects of the behavior of a physical system are "natural" and which stand in need of explanation? As emphasized by, among others, the historian of science Thomas Kuhn, most of the major revolutions in the history of physics are characterized by a shift in the answers to this question, and there seems no reason to believe that we have reached the end of this line.

Finally, let me turn to the last third of the *Timaeus*, which repeatedly raises, explicitly or by implication, the question of the possible role of "anthropocentricity" in physics. There are two intriguing connections to modern concerns here. First, in 41d–47c and 69a onward, Plato raises the question: Is the Universe designed so as to support human life and consciousness? And answers it with an emphatic yes. Such a view, dominant for a large part of recorded human history, was equally emphatically rejected by the eighteenth-century (post-Newtonian) Enlightenment, but has made a curious comeback in recent times in the guise of the so-called Anthropic Principle in cosmology. The observation underlying this principle is that the physical conditions for the genesis and evolution of human life, and thus *a fortiori* of human consciousness, are extremely delicate: a very small change in any one of a large number of different parameters would make anything resembling life as we know it totally impossible. In its weakest form, the Anthropic Principle is little more than a list of coincidences; in its strongest (quasi-teleological) form it states in effect that the reason the fundamental constraints of physics have the values they do is to permit the existence of human life. A "medium" form that many contemporary physicists find quite attractive is what is sometimes called the "multiverse" scenario: there are many (perhaps an infinite number of) possible and perhaps even actual Universes (in time, space, other dimensions . . .) each characterized by its own set of "fundamental" constants, and it is not an accident that we live in this particular one, since only here are the constants fine-tuned to permit human life!

A second intriguing echo of Plato's questions concerns the (in)famous quantum realization (or as it is more commonly called, "quantum measurement") problem. Consider a generic experiment, in which a set ("ensemble") of microscopic entities (say, for definiteness, atoms) can proceed from a source A to a destination E by either of two routes, B or C. If we "inspect" to see which route is followed, then each atom chooses *either* route B *or* route C. However, if we do not "inspect," then the existence of interference effects at E rather strongly suggests that it is *not* true that each individual atom "chose" either one route or the other; apparently, neither alternative is definitely "realized"! Now quantum mechanics describes this situation by assigning "probability amplitudes" A_B and A_C to the choices B and C respectively, and most interpretations of the formalism assert that when both A_B and A_C are simultaneously non-zero, then neither choice B nor choice C is uniquely realized.

However, as Schrödinger pointed out in a famous 1935 paper, the formalism of quantum mechanics, when suitably extrapolated, leads to a description of the *everyday world* in which the amplitudes for two different outcomes, distinguishable, as it were, by the naked eye, are simultaneously non-zero! (In his example, the amplitude is simultaneously non-zero for a cat inside a closed box to be alive and for her to be dead.) So, if quantum mechanics is the whole truth about the physical Universe, as most physicists assume, is there any real-ization in the absence of "observation" (inspection)? And observation by what/whom? Was the state of the Universe definite before there were any human beings around to inspect it? This question is perhaps the most contentious in the whole of modern physics: while, needless to say, Plato did not have avail-able the basis for its formulation (quantum mechanics was far in the future when he wrote!), it is intriguing that discussions of it continue to bring up, at least by implication, many of the profound issues concerning the relationship of mankind to the Universe which he raised nearly 2,500 years ago.

2

Cosmic Craftsmanship in Plato and Stoicism

Anthony A. Long

My purpose in this paper is to explore the background and underpinning of the Platonic and Stoic ideas of divine craftsmanship, and to compare these two theological cosmologies. I am particularly interested in the ancient genealogy of powerful ideas that we have inherited but whose original content was shaped by a culture radically different from our own. The Greek idea of divine craftsmanship was principally prompted by quite specific developments in four intellectual domains—science, psychology, politics, and ethics. For the past one hundred and fifty years science and theology have been running on separate tracks. But in the Greek tradition they were unitary, as of course they largely were before Darwin and modern physics.

I start with the following outline. Greek conceptions of a supreme cosmic divinity and Greek notions of rationality and a well-ordered society originated and matured in tandem. Notions of rationality preceded the fully fledged idea of a world-crafting deity, but once this being was explicitly conceived as a perfect rational agent, its cosmological activities, as for instance its causal influence on astronomical regularities, influenced ideas and ideals of human rationality and a good society.[1] Plato pioneered the remarkable proposal that it is our human project to become as like as possible to God, presupposing a deep and quite novel connection between divine and human goodness.[2] That

---

1 No Greek philosopher was literally a monotheist, but the divine craftsman of Plato's *Timaeus* is represented as the supreme divinity, and likewise the Stoic Zeus. Hence I write God and Demiurge upper case when referring with one of these words to either of these two deities.

2 Recent discussions include Julia Annas, *Platonic Ethics Old and New* (Ithaca: Cornell University Press, 1999), ch. 3; David Sedley, "The Ideal of Godlikeness" in Gail Fine, ed., *Plato 2* (Oxford: Oxford University Press, 1999), pp. 309–328; Gábor Betegh, "Cosmological

connection underwrote the Platonic and subsequently Stoic idea that God's macrocosmic rationality should serve as the model for an ideally well-ordered soul or person, whose undeviating adherence to the rule of reason would be a microcosmic reflection of the world's order.

The Pre-Platonic Background.

The Greeks had many theological beliefs long before any explicit thoughts or expressions of rationality emerged. Those beliefs included the idea that the Olympian gods are responsible for the general workings of the world. As early as Homer and Hesiod, Zeus was taken to be a divine monarch and patriarch whose virtually unchallengeable rule gives the world in general a more or less stable structure. The mind and justice of this archaic Zeus, vaguely conceived though they were, foreshadowed more articulate concepts of cosmic order; for subordinate gods as well as humans could not overstep determinate boundaries without retribution.[3]

All theologies, whatever their truth may be, are human projections, psychologically speaking.[4] What we project is primarily what we already know, and also what we would like to believe and approve, and what we possibly fear. Like all human artifacts too, theologies involve analogy and model building, using the known (in the early Greek case monarchical and aristocratic social order) as a guide to the unknown. In the world as we observe it, many things, especially living things, have obvious beginnings and endings. Not surprisingly then, most cosmological myths picture the world itself as having a beginning, by analogy with our experience of birth. So too with the early Greek universe and its divinities. The world's continuing existence, on the other hand, and the immortality of its gods are projections that overstep the obviously known.

In the Greek mythological tradition, human beings and Olympian gods are anatomically and psychologically similar. The main distinguishing marks of the divine are immortality, freedom from such human vicissitudes as illness

---

Ethics in the *Timaeus* and Early Stoicism," *Oxford Studies in Ancient Philosophy* 24 (2003), 273–302; A. A. Long, "Eudaimonism, Divinity and Rationality in Greek Ethics," *Boston Area Colloquium in Ancient Philosophy* 19 (2004), 123–142; J. M. Armstrong, "After the Ascent: Plato on Becoming Like God," *Oxford Studies in Ancient Philosophy* 26 (2004), 171–184; and T. A. Mahoney, "Moral Virtue and Assimilation to God in Plato's *Timaeus*," *Oxford Studies in Ancient Philosophy* 28 (2005), 77–92.

3 See H. Lloyd-Jones, *The Justice of Zeus* (Berkeley: University of California Press, 1971), especially pp. 84–87, and Jean-Pierre Vernant, *The Origins of Greek Thought* (Ithaca: Cornell University Press, 1982), pp. 108–110.

4 Ludwig Feuerbach is the earliest modern thinker who gave currency to this proposition in *Das Wesen des Christentums* (1841), translated by George Eliot as *The Essence of Christianity* (New York: Harper & Row, 1957).

and aging, and uncanny motive power over the parts of the world that fall within the domain of each divinity. When the earliest Greek philosophers began to reflect on the origin and present structure of the world, they rejected the anthropomorphic features of the gods; but they retained immortality and motive power as properties of their new theological powers, while demystifying their behavior by relating it to empirical processes like heating and cooling.[5] Immortality and motive power, together with the abandonment of anatomical anthropomorphism, remain basic attributes of the divine for Plato, Aristotle, and Stoics. But in these later philosophers perfection of mind or rationality is God's primary attribute, making God the paradigm to which the human intellect should seek to conform itself.

An early start in that direction might seem to have been made by Xenophanes, who was the first Greek philosopher to credit his "greatest god" explicitly with an all-controlling mind, an intellect that he also characterizes as immobile and able "effortlessly to shake all things" (DK 21 B 24–26). If, as some testimony maintains, Xenophanes identified this divinity with the heavens or even with the whole world, he will have been a forerunner of Stoic pantheism and may have influenced Plato's conception in the *Timaeus* of a world that is "an ensouled and intelligent creature" (30b7–8).[6] However, Xenophanes manifested his skeptical tendencies by characterizing his supreme god as "quite unlike mortals in body or in thought" (B 23); and there is no evidence that he attributed any cosmogonical functions to this being.

Enter the extraordinary thinker Heraclitus. Criticizing Xenophanes among other authorities (DK 22 B 40), Heraclitus pioneered the notion that nature is a law-governed system of reciprocal changes between fire and other elements.[7] His expression for this system is *logos*. This term would soon become the standard Greek word for reason and rationality, but at the time of Heraclitus the primary meanings of *logos* were "account," "discourse," and "ratio." We may say, for ease of exposition, that Heraclitus sought to provide a rational account of a rationally structured world, but Heraclitus was not in a position to say that

---

5 For general background, see Werner Jaeger, *The Theology of the Early Greek Philosophers* (Oxford: Oxford University Press, 1947); G. E. R. Lloyd, *The Revolutions of Wisdom* (Berkeley: University of California Press, 1987), chs. 1–2; and Lloyd P. Gerson, *God and Greek Philosophy: Studies in the Early History of Natural Theology* (London: Routledge, 1990), ch. 1.

6 See J. A. Palmer, "Xenophanes' Ouranian God," *Oxford Studies in Ancient Philosophy* 16 (1998), 30–33.

7 I think it is a mistake to assimilate Anaximander's celebrated conception of cosmic justice and retribution *(dike)* to a notion of a law *(nomos)* of nature, as Heraclitus (uniquely among early Greek cosmologists) virtually does (B 114); see my discussion in M. Gagarin and D. Cohen, eds., *The Cambridge Companion to Ancient Greek Law* (Cambridge: Cambridge University Press, 2005), pp. 416–419. In this way Heraclitus inspired the Stoic Cleanthes' cosmological Hymn to Zeus, see my remarks in *Stoic Studies* (Berkeley: University of California Press, 1999), pp. 47–48.

as straightforwardly as later Greek thinkers could express this thought. What Heraclitus did have available to him were such concepts as structure, measure, proportion, balance, and rhythm.[8]

His cosmic *logos* includes all of these ideas, and because of that it comprises much that we and the later Greek philosophers associate with rationality. In addition, and very importantly, he associates the *logos* and his elemental fire with divinity. Heraclitus' fiery divinity governs the world by governing itself according to determinate measures and proportions.

From our theological perspectives it is difficult to make sense of a divine governor who is not also, by virtue of that status, the world's creator. Heraclitus, though, did not conceive of the world as the creation of a divine craftsman. He claimed emphatically that "this cosmos" is an everlasting process of the measured changes of fire (B 30). Where exactly, then, does divinity fit into this account? Heraclitus seems to construe god as a cosmic intelligence that manifests itself in the succession of diurnal and seasonal changes, the regularity of physical processes, and the unity of opposites (B 32, 67, 102). In spite of the gap he set up between conventional human judgments and the divine perspective on things ("to god all things are fair and just . . ."), Heraclitus found in nature analogies to human artifacts (like bow and lyre) that involve balance, measure, and proportion. Because we understand these concepts in their human application, he takes us to be capable of discovering their operation in the divinely governed cosmos itself.

Although Heraclitus did not prefigure divine craftsmanship and teleology, he did adumbrate a cluster of ideas that would become enormously potent in the later philosophical and theological tradition. These include first, the connection between the human faculty of rationality and the physical world as an orderly system; second, the selection of balance, measure, and proportion as key markers of rationality; and third, the ethical and psychological desirability of conforming one's own mind-set to the rhythms of the universe. In Heraclitus' philosophy *logos* is both a global force and a mental power. The cosmic order that he discovered—a universe governed by divine proportionality—also provided a startlingly new paradigm of human excellence as a microcosm of psychological balance and internal control. All of these points foreshadow the linkage that Plato and the Stoics were to elaborate between the rule of reason and divinity.

Looking back at his predecessors in his late dialogue *Philebus* (28c, 28d, 29d), Plato repeatedly makes Socrates say that all the wise or the men of old agree that the world is governed by *nous*, meaning intelligence or rationality. This can hardly mean that Plato took his predecessors to have anticipated his

---

8 For detailed discussion, see my paper "Heraclitus on Measure and the Explicit Emergence of Rationality" in D. Frede and B. Reis, eds., *Body and Soul in Ancient Philosophy* (Berlin: De Gruyter, 2009), pp. 87–109.

special theories concerning a divine craftsman or rational world soul. What Plato must mean here is that the Presocratic tradition in general took the world to be amenable to rational explanation because it is systematically structured as distinct from being random and chaotic.

Such a claim fits Presocratic cosmology very well. What would not fit that tradition would be a claim that the world owes its rational structure to the deliberate acts of a constructive, personalist, and supremely benevolent intelligence. Anaxagoras (nicknamed Nous) went some way in that direction, as did Diogenes of Apollonia (DK 64 B 3) in the next generation.[9] But their claims fell far short of what Plato took to be essential. Of his many theological and cosmological innovations, the biggest was his postulate that the world is governed by the purposive intelligence of a divine craftsman who is a supremely benevolent agent with personalist attributes—a divinity, in other words, more similar to the providential god of Judaism and Christianity than anything in the preceding Greek tradition.[10]

Plato's Cosmic Teleology.

How similar, however, is more similar? To come closer to grips with Plato's conception of divine craftsmanship and rationality, I need to discuss two things that strongly distinguish his philosophical outlook from that of traditional Christianity as well as his Greek predecessors—strong body/soul dualism, and the hold that mathematics exercised on his philosophical imagination.

Motive power, as we have seen, was a characteristic of the Olympian gods that the early Greek philosophers demystified when they identified their cosmic principles with such things as air or fire. Plato, however, taking air or fire to be lifeless *(apsycha)* phenomena could not accept their intrinsic properties as sufficient to account for cosmic order.[11] Like modern theistic defenders of I(ntelligent) D(esign), Plato refused to accept the idea that life could simply

---

9   For an excitingly original treatment of Anaxagoras, proposing that "teleological explanation started life in [his] doctrine of creationism," see David Sedley, *Creationism and its Critics in Antiquity* (Berkeley: University of California Press, 2007), ch. 1. Diogenes says (DK 64 B 3) that the world would not manifest "measures" (seasonal regularities, etc.) without "intelligence" (*noesis*), and that it is in general disposed "as beautifully as possible." Do these propositions make him "the first Greek philosopher who was overtly a telelologist," as T. Robinson has claimed in *Ancient Philosophy* 21:1 (2001), 175? I demur, see my note "Locating Diogenes of Apollonia," *Ancient Philosophy* 21:2 (2001), 476 and Sedley, *Creationism*, pp. 75–78.

10   Contrasting Plato's Demiurge with the Zeus of the *Prometheus Vinctus*, Gregory Vlastos wrote: "The more beauty and goodness outside of him, the better his unenvious nature is pleased. This is the noblest image of the deity ever projected in classical antiquity"—*Plato's Universe* (Seattle: Washington University Press, 1975. Reprint Las Vegas: Parmenides Publishing, 2005), p. 28.

11   See especially *Laws* X, 889b–d.

emerge from lifeless stuff. Physical elements, he proposed, behave as they are seen to do under the influence of a principle that, unlike them, is intrinsically self-moving. That principle he called soul, and he proposed that it pertains to the world in its entirety just as it pertains to all individual living beings (*Laws* X, 892a–899d).

World Soul is a concept so alien to our cosmological and theological ideas that we have great difficulty in approaching it as a serious contribution to making the universe rationally accessible and theologically satisfying. It looks at first glance to be an arbitrary imposition of animism, scientifically retrogressive by comparison with the mechanistic atomism of Plato's older contemporary, Democritus. In fact, Plato situates his most detailed arguments in favor of the World Soul in a context where he is determined to prove, against the likes of Democritus, that physical elements cannot be the world's first cause (*Laws* X, 889a–d). His World Soul, so far as we can determine, was a largely original concept, intended by him as a major scientific break-through. Stoicism took the concept over from Plato, and while it is not a feature of Aristotelian cosmology, Aristotle followed Plato in attributing the movements of the heavenly bodies to souls associated with these beings.[12]

All these philosophers were convinced that celestial motions are regular and systematic precisely because they are goal-directed. Soul offered itself as an explanation for this goal-directedness by analogy with its assumed functions and powers in the human body. As the motor of human agency, soul causes the body to move according to its deliberations, emotions, and wishes. Absent a soul, a body is inert. This observation prompted the belief that souls are ontologically distinct from the bodies that they animate, and that soul as such is either immaterial or at least distinct from empirical matter. Human souls, of course, make mistakes and frequently fail to act rationally, but they offered Plato the model for a principle of cosmic activity that would instantiate perfect rationality as its motivation and motive power.

Like the philosophers who followed his lead, he found seemingly incontrovertible evidence for such perfect rationality in the motions of the heavenly bodies, which never deviate from their circular course (even when they seem to do so, like the planets). More on this finding shortly. Plato was convinced that a soul's rationality or lack thereof is the sure indication of its desires and values. Far from being value-neutral, rationality for Plato implies goodness and the desire to be in the best possible state. David Hume famously objected that reason "is, and ought only to be, the slave of the passions."[13] Plato took exactly the opposite view. In his eyes, reason can only function properly when it is completely in charge of the passions, acting as desire's unqualified motivation.

---

12 See *On the Heavens* II.12, 292a20.
13 *Treatise on Human Nature*, part 3, section 3.

His case for the World-Soul in the *Laws* is largely based on the argument that the most rational motion is circular, and therefore requires a supremely rational agent (soul) as its cause. In the *Timaeus* the Demiurge, at the beginning of his creative work, manufactures the circles of that dialogue's World Soul according to an elaborate scheme of ratios (36a–d). These ratios generate the angles and speeds and proportions necessary to account for the uniform movements of the fixed stars and the deviant motions of the sun, moon, and planets.

As moderns, we are bound to find incessantly circular motion a very curious paradigm of rationality and good intentionality. Everlasting uniformity is completely at odds with the spontaneity, imagination, and capacity for divergent thinking that mark the rationality of the most intellectually gifted humans, Plato conspicuously among them. I have nothing to say by way of toning down this huge discrepancy. But it is not hard to understand why Plato, in his culture and with his paradigms, saw things quite differently.

First of all, there is the evaluative and metaphysical contrast, throughout his mature work, between the incorporeal realm of changeless, perfect, and intelligible reality, and the world of imperfect and changeable corporeality. Under this perspective, celestial movements, though properties of bodies, are the closest approximation to changeless reality because they are caused by incorporeal and purely rational souls. Secondly, in the mathematics and astronomy of his time he found a seemingly precise discourse for expressing the features of rationality I singled out when speaking of Heraclitus—ratio, balance, proportion, measure, harmony, and so forth.

Plato, as we have seen, was indebted to earlier accounts of a rationally structured cosmos, but because his explanatory ambition, unlike theirs, was teleological through and through, his cosmology is no less fundamentally an ethics and even a politics.[14] That teleological complexity, most conspicuously in the *Timaeus* and *Laws*, marks Plato as the world's first fully fledged theologian. The details of his theology are carefully qualified by metaphors and numerous caveats, and they are the subject of innumerable scholarly controversies.[15] Rather

---

14 These points are excellently made by Thomas K. Johansen, *Plato's Natural Philosophy* (Cambridge: Cambridge University Press, 2004); see especially his remarks on pp. 22, 190–197. See also Sarah Broadie, "Theodicy and Pseudo-history in the *Timaeus*," *Oxford Studies in Ancient Philosophy* 21 (2001), 1–28, especially 16–21.

15 It would strain the limits of this paper if I attempted to engage systematically with such classic questions as the relation between the World Soul of *Laws* X and the Timaean Demiurge. If pressed, Plato, I think, would identify the latter with the noetic faculty of the supremely virtuous and wise soul (*Laws* X, 897b7–8), which I take him to refer to later in that dialogue as Demiurge (902e5, 903c6), King (904a6) and Guardian (902a2, 7); for these references and further discussion, see Richard Mohr, *God and Forms in Plato* (Las Vegas: Parmenides Publishing, 2005), p. 198. In these later passages, the Athenian spokesman personifies divinity, as is appropriate to his theodicy, and adopts the metaphorical language of the *Timaeus* rather than the austere language he has previously used in expounding the World Soul. I

than engaging with these complexities here, I want briefly to analyze Plato's link between rationality and divine craftsmanship, asking what that striking image of divinity purports to tell us concerning the objective ends of human life.

Plato does not argue in the *Timaeus* from design to God, but from God to design. He starts from the premise that the observable world is as good as possible because it was made by an excellent divinity with precisely that intention (29e–30c). The questions Plato sets out to investigate are not the attributes of God but God's creative plan and the initial conditions for his craftsmanship. Unlike the biblical divinity, Plato's Demiurge does not say "Let there be light," and so forth. He bases his blueprint for the world on the paradigmatic "intelligible living being" (30c) that exist independently of himself. Nor does he manufacture the bodies of things out of nothing. Instead, he imposes geometrical structure on mindlessly moving and indeterminate "material"—the turbulent contents of the so-called "receptacle" or space—that also exists independently of himself (53ab). Such is the Demiurge's rationality, that he is able to "persuade" this material, also called "necessity," to play an accessory causal role to his benevolent intelligence—but only *as far as possible* (53b5). The pre-existence of mobile material sets physical constraints on the divine craftsman's workmanship (cf. 30a3, 37d2).

Most important, for our understanding of Plato's God, is the proposition that what motivates him to make the best possible world is the material chaos that initially confronts him (30a4–5). Here we may again draw a contrast with the Judaeo-Christian idea that the deity is an absolutely omnipotent creator who faces no pre-existing disorder. Here too we may find the distant legacy of archaic Zeus, who in Hesiod's *Theogony* defeats and controls the older generation of disorderly Titans. Arthur E. Lovejoy famously proposed that the Demiurge is conceived as "Self-Transcending Fecundity."[16] Plato, it is true,

---

agree with Richard Mohr (thanks to his correspondence) that the World Soul of the *Timaeus* is "never viewed as a maker, builder, compositor." But in the case of *Laws* X, that dialogue's World Soul is agreed to be "the cause of *all* things" (896d). I am not greatly impressed by the common objection (e.g., R. Hackforth, "Plato's Theism," in R. E. Allen, ed., *Studies in Plato's Metaphysics* [London: Routledge, 1965], p. 441), that the *Laws'* World Soul is a "created being" because I agree with Saunders' translation [in the Penguin edition] of the description of it at 967d as "far older than any created thing." I think Plato's point is that the *Laws'* World Soul, in virtue of its *nous* (reason), is the world's first cause and thus functions for that dialogue in the way that the Demiurge does in the *Timaeus*. The whole point of *Laws* X is to prove that the world is governed by intelligent divinity. If the virtuous World Soul of this dialogue were not precisely that being, the ensuing proof of its existence would completely miss the mark. I am therefore sympathetic to the positions adopted by such scholars as A. E. Taylor, *A Commentary on Plato's* Timaeus (Oxford: Oxford University Press, 1928), p. 82, and Harold Cherniss, *Aristotle's Criticism of Plato and the Academy*, I (Baltimore: Johns Hoplinks University Press, 1944), p. 607, to the effect that Plato's God is uncreated soul endowed with *nous* (reason).

16 *The Great Chain of Being* (Cambridge: Harvard University Press, 1936), ch. 2.

characterizes his divinity as "completely unbegrudging" and as "wishing all things to be as like himself as possible" (29e2–3). But there is no hint in the text of the *Timaeus* that creativity simply emanates from the Demiurge, as it will in due course emanate from the Neoplatonic One. As Sarah Broadie has convincingly objected to Lovejoy, the Demiurge is motivated by his judgment that order is in every way preferable to chaos.[17]

This judgment enables us to gauge the power and originality of Plato's craftsman image and the inter-entailment of his conceptions of goodness and rationality. Demiurge in its nominal or verbal or adjectival forms is one of Plato's favorite quasi-technical words. While he sometimes uses these words in relation to such humble crafts as cobbling, he applies them in the *Cratylus* (389a2, 390e1) to the exalted maker of names, whom he also calls a legislator. The semantic field of demiurgy, for Plato, ranges over all crafts. He takes any craftsman worthy of the name to be infallible in the sphere of his craft; and he characteristically associates demiurgy with the technical expertise necessary for rational and goal-directed creativity. The concept presupposes an ideal paradigm, an expert craftsman, and amorphous materials that the craftsman sets into appropriate order, following the formal structure of his paradigm.[18]

This is exactly the scheme we are offered as the image of God in the *Timaeus*. "God's wish," Plato says, "was to make the cosmos optimally resemble the most beautiful and most complete of intelligible things, and so he created a single visible living being, containing within itself all living beings of the same natural order" (30d). Why, we may ask, is the Demiurge motivated to make the visible cosmos a *complete* replica of his intelligible paradigm? Would his desire to bestow order on material chaos not be better served by restricting his creativity to the manufacture of items that best instantiate rationality, to wit—the celestial bodies and their associated souls rather than the complete animal and plant domains? One answer could be that the materials available to the Demiurge and the subordinate gods are necessarily limited in quantity and susceptibility to their craftsmanship, making it impossible for them to create more stars from material they actually end up using for terrestrial creatures. The materials are, though, sufficient to manufacture tokens of the intelligible Forms' rationality in the structures of all the living beings that the Demiurge and the subordinate divinities create, thus ensuring complete homology between paradigm and visible copy.

Prior to the world's creation, reality already contains supreme goodness and rationality by virtue of the intelligible Forms and the Demiurge himself. His creativity extends that goodness and rationality to the generated universe, *as*

---

17 Broadie, "Theodicy," pp. 10–16.
18 For further discussion, see Johansen, *Plato's Natural Philosophy,* pp. 83–86, and Sedley, *Creationism*, pp. 173–180.

far as possible. Throughout the *Timaeus* numerical proportion and geometrical symmetry are the principal concepts by means of which order and limit are bestowed on the universe. I have already referred to the ratios in the composition of the incorporeal World Soul. As to the world's physical constituents, the Demiurge imposes geometrical shapes on the pre-cosmic antecedents of the elements, making their structure and motions mutually harmonious, so enabling them to mutate into one another systematically.

In the *Timaeus* Plato offers us a description of divine craftsmanship in action. Yet, as we read on into the work's account of the human body and soul, we realize, remarkably, that quasi-demiurgic rationality and harmonics are actually being prescribed as the microcosmic goal of human life (cf. 89d4–90d). As rational self-movers, in virtue of being given a rational faculty of soul, we are also equipped, according to Plato, to conform our disorderly mental motions to the "thoughts and revolutions of the cosmos," and so become rational craftsmen of our own lives, and thus like God.[19] Yet, unlike the Demiurge, human beings are incarnate souls, with bodies that require the incorporation of irrational psychic faculties. Although the body we are given is wondrously shaped and proportioned with a view to serving the needs of a life that sets a premium on rationality, embodiment, like the material constraints on the Demiurge but to a far greater extent, necessarily limits human agency. Human beings, given their psychological and physiological complexity, face the strenuous task of imposing proportion and harmony on their mental and physical constituents. Thus human rationality, though a quintessentially divine gift, can only take command of the entire self if its affinity to cosmic order and intentionality is fully recognized and cultivated.

It should now be clear that Plato's model of divine craftsmanship concerns much more than world formation. Demiurgic rationality is the exercise of paradigmatic goodness. As such it stands as a model of virtue quite generally. In making best use of the available materials, the Demiurge serves Plato as theological underpinning for the civic excellence he imagines that Athens in the remote past displayed when its citizens singlehandedly overcame invasion from Atlantis. Sarah Broadie makes the essential point, where she writes in the article I already referred to: "If the creation story is not simply subordinate to the heroism story, then surely they are related as variations on the same theme: the overcoming of disorder" ("Theodicy," p. 18).

But, as Broadie also observes, there is the following crucial difference between the stories: while divine reason, because it is unembodied, can operate unhindered, human beings are assigned the very difficult task of liberating their own rationality from its bodily encumbrances. The human goal is to complete

---

19 See Sedley, "The Ideal of Godlikeness," pp. 316–321, and Long, "Eudaimonism," pp. 134–137.

the work of the Demiurge by making a specifically human contribution to the world's rationality. With this thought we are offered a remarkable theological reason as to why human beings are created in the first place.

Stoicism's Immanent Demiurge.

For further variations on the theme of cosmic craftsmanship in ancient philosophy, I turn to Stoicism. The antecedents of this Hellenistic school's cosmology and theology are complex. Its founding fathers were certainly inspired by Heraclitus, and also probably (though the extent is difficult to specify) by Aristotle. However, neither of these predecessors envisioned the world as the product of divine craftsmanship. That the Stoics did so is quite certain, and it is equally certain that Chrysippus, their leading thinker, drew directly on Plato's *Timaeus*.[20] *Demiourgein*, the verb corresponding to Plato's noun *demiourgos* and signifying "work as a craftsman," is one of the standard ways Stoic authorities described God's cosmological activity.[21] There is every reason to think that they encouraged their students to recognize this affinity to Plato's theological cosmology.

Craftsman, rational, providential and benevolent—these attributes are common to the Platonic and the Stoic God. When it comes to specifics, however, the Stoic Demiurge and the world that he generates turn out to be very different from their Timaean counterparts. One type of difference is literary. In writing the *Timaeus*, Plato took himself to be producing "a likely story" or myth. We are probably intended to take much of the work's scientific detail seriously if not quite literally, but Plato has invested his Demiurge with a personality and conversational style that the Stoics did not normally replicate.[22]

More significant than literary differences is the quasi-scientific nature of the Stoic Demiurge's cosmogonical functions, which includes rejection of Plato's incorporeal and independently existing Forms or archetypes. Like Plato, the Stoics attributed the structure of the world and its natural contents to divine agency and planning, but in their accounts of how their Demiurge operates

---

20 For Chrysippus' clear allusions to the text of the *Timaeus*, see Plutarch, *On Stoic Self-contradictions* 1052d=LS 46F (referring to *Timaeus* 33c7–d3) and Aulus Gellius 7.1.7= LS 54Q (referring to *Timaeus* 69b). References in the form LS are to A. A. Long and D. N. Sedley, *The Hellenistic Philosophers* (Cambridge: Cambridge University Press, 1987). For detailed discussion, see Gretchen Reydam-Schils, *Demiurge and Providence: Stoic and Platonist Readings of Plato's* Timaeus (Turnhout, Belgium: Brepols, 1999), especially ch. 1 and D. Sedley, "The Origins of Stoic God," in Dorothea Frede and André Laks, eds., *Traditions of Theology: Studies in Hellenistic Theology, its Background and Aftermath* (Leiden: Brill, 2002), pp. 41–83.
21 Diogenes Laertius 7.134.
22 There are exceptions, e.g., Epictetus, *Discourse* 1.1, but here the Zeus that addresses the reader is clearly a fictional conversationalist.

they largely eschewed metaphor or vague expressions such as Plato's statement that Intellect sought to "persuade" necessity (*Timaeus* 48a). We can take them to have reasoned thus: if the world has a cause that is not only intelligent but also intelligible, it had better act in ways that conform to observation and experience. According to these criteria, the Stoics inferred that only bodies can engage in causal interaction.[23] Therefore God himself cannot be bodiless but must be an *embodied* mind, acting directly in physical processes and giving form to matter by being present within it.

Plato's Demiurge gives the world a body and a soul, but the Demiurge himself remains apart from that creation.[24] The Stoic divinity does not make an artifact that is distinct from himself. He is, so to speak, his own product, making himself into the world by causing matter to become informed by his omnipresent intelligence. Does this pantheistic notion imply that there is no difference between God and the world? The answer depends on the perspective and the context of the question. If we pose it as a question about the world inhabited by us, God is taken to be present everywhere in the structures of animate and inanimate things alike. However, the Stoics were convinced that the world we inhabit had a beginning and will eventually end. From that perspective God has an identity that transcends the world because his existence, like that of matter, is eternal. In everlasting recurrence, God makes himself into the world and then, in a striking expression "withdraws into providence," bringing himself out of the world and ending it, in order to prepare for it anew.[25]

With inspiration from Heraclitus, the Stoics described God as a *fiery* intelligence, and they looked to the role of fire in technology as one of their models for God's demiurgic and self-transforming activity.[26] What that technology involves, however, has less to do with manufacturing than with biophysics; which brings us to what has been well called the Stoics' cosmobiology, and a further marked difference from Plato's idea of divine craftsmanship.[27]

The Stoic God's plan for the world is not a static paradigm, but a set of causal principles memorably and presciently called "seminal" or "spermatic,"

---

23 See the sources excerpted in LS, ch. 45.

24 The virtuous World Soul of the *Laws* is a closer analogue to the Stoic Demiurge, not only in its lack of personality but also in its being immanent in the world. The created world of the *Timaeus* is an "intelligent living being" *(zôion)*, and that description pertains to the Stoic cosmos in virtue of the presence of the Stoic divinity throughout as the world's soul (Plato, *Timaeus* 30c, Philo speaking for the Stoic Chrysippus, *De aeternitate mundi* 94).

25 For evidence and discussion, see LS, ch. 46 and my paper "World Conflagration and Everlasting Recurrence" in ch. 13 of my book *From Epicurus to Epictetus: Studies in Hellenistic and Roman Philosophy* (Oxford: Oxford University Press, 2006).

26 See Aëtius 1.7.33 (LS 46A) and Diogenes Laertius (LS 46B).

27 For cosmobiology, see David Hahm, *The Origins of Stoic Cosmology* (Columbus: Ohio State University Press, 1977), ch. 5.

which are equivalent to the creative mind of God at work.[28] In a quite literal sense, this divinity, to whom the Stoics gave the exalted name Zeus, fathers the world by endowing matter (allegorically construed as the female goddess Hera) with a kind of cosmic DNA or genetic program.[29] That program represents divine providence, but no less basically it represents fate or causal determinism. Having seeded the world, as it were, the Stoic divinity causes the world to evolve according to his predetermined formulae *(spermatikoi logoi)*.

Unlike the Platonic Demiurge the Stoics' craftsman God does not need to "persuade" necessity, because he incarnates necessity in the causal nexus that operates throughout the world.[30] That causal nexus, leaving no room for any undetermined happenings, was one of the Stoics' most powerful contributions to the concept of a rational cosmology. Yet, the causal nexus does not make their physical theory purely mechanistic, as it might appear to do, if taken in isolation from their theology. As the enactment of divine rationality and providence, the causal nexus is not only the way things necessarily had to be but also the way things optimally had to be. According to this theory, someone who fully understood the world's causality would be in touch with the benevolent mind of God.

Plato's Demiurge, in spite of all his power and benevolence, is constrained to some extent by material necessity. Not so the Stoic God. Matter *(hyle)* in this system is taken to be completely plastic and analogous to "wax" in its lack of intrinsic shape. It is thus accessible to every form that divine intelligence determines to be required in order for this to be the best of all possible worlds.[31]

Platonic and Stoic Demiurgy Compared.

I have provided only a lightning sketch of Stoic cosmology, but I hope it can serve as sufficient preparation for asking how the Stoics positioned themselves in regard to the teleology and rationality of the Platonic Demiurge. That divine figure, motivated by unbegrudging goodness, sets out to make the best possible world, first by generating a soul for the heavens and imposing mathematical order on pre-existing chaos; and second, by fashioning human beings with the "celestial" gift of a divine nature, in the form of a rational psychic faculty. With what motivation is the Stoic God credited and precisely how does his rational creativity manifest itself? For answering these questions in the absence of any

---

28 See Hahm, *Origins*, pp. 75–76, and references in n. 26 above.

29 Dio of Prusa 36.55 (*Stoicorum Veterum Fragmenta* 2.622) and Origen, *Contra Celsum* 4.48 (*SVF* 2.1074).

30 For a selection of texts on fate and the causal nexus, see LS, ch. 55.

31 Calcidius 292 (LS 44D).

complete Stoic text comparable to Plato's *Timaeus* we have only fragments to work with. Here is a brief statement of what I find.

The Stoics, as I already observed, named their cosmic divinity Zeus, taking that great name to signify "the cause of life," following the etymology proposed by Plato's Socrates.[32] This etymology plainly fits their cosmobiology. Moreover, it identifies the divinity so strongly with his procreative function that Lovejoy's word "fecundity," which he misapplied to the Platonic demiurge, is wholly apt in the Stoic case. No pre-cosmic disorder faces their Zeus, motivating his benevolent desire to introduce measure and proportion. The Stoic divinity is so bursting with life that he is not content to be alone for ever. His fecundity motivates him to generate a world of which he is the soul, and to whose particular beings he is the cause of life and life-giving elements.[33]

This divinity, unlike Plato's Demiurge, is not a mathematician but a chemist and biophysicist and nuclear engineer. We hear nothing in our Stoic sources concerning the divinity's arithmetical and geometrical activity, and much, instead, of his self-transformations and the mixing and vibrant motions of which he is the cause.[34] The world that he creates and makes himself into is a harmonious structure, but, because the matter with which he works is completely plastic to start with, he has no need to begin by restructuring it in terms of number, and shape, and proportion.

Turning now to rationality, I have already remarked on the causal nexus that the Stoic divinity plans out initially and then implements. This striking innovation transforms Plato's external and constraining necessity into the internal and unconstrained operations of the divine mind. Yet, causal necessity, it may seem, has no conceptual connection with a mind's rationality and benevolent intentionality. You can believe in determinism without believing in a divine creator. Indeed, you may well find these two ideas incompatible, especially if you think that determinism leaves no room for the kinds of choices that Plato's Demiurge requires human beings to make. I shall have to omit any detailed treatment of how the Stoics replied to this problem. It is clear, however, that in their eyes the causal nexus allows for human action to be "in our power," in the sense of its not being enforced by factors external to our own characters and our innate capacity to give or withhold assent.[35] In addition, the causal nexus exhibits the feature of rationality that most impressed them,

---

32 See Plato, *Cratylus* 396a–b and Diogenes Laertius 7.147.

33 In support of the Stoic God's "fecundity," I refer again to the school's allegorical deployment of the marriage of Zeus and Hera, with Hera likened to the matter impregnated by Zeus (references in n. 29 above).

34 For a selection of texts on the physical manifestations of divine activity, see LS, chs. 46–48 and 54.

35 See Susanne Bobzien, *Determinism and Freedom in Stoic Philosophy* (Oxford: Oxford University Press, 1998), especially ch. 6.3.5–7.

which was not mathematical proportion, balance, and limit, but coherence and consequentiality.

The Greek word that I refer to here is *akolouthia* ("following-upon-ness"). In Stoicism this term is importantly at work in all three of their divisions of philosophy.[36] First, in physics, it expresses the connection between antecedent events and their necessary effects, i.e., the causal nexus. Second, in logic, it names the relation of consequence that a valid conclusion has to the premises of a sound argument. And third, in ethics, it signifies actions that are in conformity with the normative nature of human beings. *Akolouthia* is a concept that identifies the ideal of rationality permeating Stoic philosophy as a whole. It asks us to take causality, logic, and ethics to share in the kind of coherence we formulate when we say that B follows A or A leads on to B. As cosmic mind, the Stoic divinity is the foundation of this multi-dimensional coherence.

But if this were all, it would not be clear why divine rationality is also well-intentioned and prescriptive, offering itself as the model for human action.[37] What is morally good about cosmic coherence? The Stoic answer is that it makes the world "like a well-ruled community," governed by irrefrangible laws.[38] Those laws are not only formulated by the divinity; they are also, as Seneca states, *always* followed by him.[39] Though omnipotent, the Stoic Zeus acts as a constitutional monarch, conforming himself to the prescripts of rational coherence. The Stoic world is the city of God.

We can now see that divine craftsmanship in Stoicism is much more directly political and anthropocentric than in Plato's conception. The chief lesson of the *Timaeus*, we have seen, is for human beings to cultivate their rationality, taking celestial motions as their model for trying to achieve mental balance and harmony. Plato politicized the human mind with his injunctions to put reason rather than passion in charge of our lives, but he did not conceptualize the created world as a polity. The Stoics took that bold step, calling the world "the habitation, as it were, of gods and human beings and the things that have come into being for their sake," and treating all the world's contents as generated

---

36 See my discussion in A. A. Long, ed., *Problems in Stoicism* (1971, London: Athlone Press, 1996), pp. 95–96.

37 Obedience to God and kinship with God are among Epictetus' constant themes; see my discussion in *Epictetus: A Stoic and Socratic Guide to Life* (Oxford: Oxford University Press, 2002), pp. 156–172, 184–189. Epictetus is the Stoic philosopher with the most fully elaborated account of how human beings stand and should stand in relation to divinity.

38 See Malcolm Schofield, *The Stoic Idea of the City* (Cambridge: Cambridge University Press, 1991), ch. 3.

39 *De providentia* 5.8: "Although the actual creator and ruler of the universe wrote the decrees of fate, he follows them; he obeys for ever, but gave orders only once . . . The craftsman cannot alter his material; this is its condition" *(ille ipse omnium conditor et rector scripsit quidem fata, sed sequitur; semper paret, semel iussit . . . Non potest artifex mutare materiam; hoc passa est).*

for our sake.[40] This was another way of saying that the project of the Stoic God is to generate a world in which the seeds of divine rationality and coherence are directly extended to human beings, equipping them, subject to their own understanding and volition, to function as a community in the law-governed ways he himself embodies. Much more directly than Plato, Stoicism sought to give cosmic craftsmanship an exact counterpart in the human ideal of a rational and socially cooperative craft *(techne)* of life.

* * * * *

To conclude: basic to the concept of cosmic craftsmanship in both philosophies is the proposition that human beings exist because a supremely creative and benevolent intelligence has deemed it good to fashion a world containing beings with a potential likeness to itself. Evidence of that providential intellect is available to us in the physical world's orderly structure. This evidence prompts the further proposition that orderly structure, as manifested in psychological and ethical integrity, should be the prime desideratum of any mind that fully recognizes its rational capacities and social identity. Cosmic order is the model for a well-ordered soul whose voice to itself can function as the human vehicle of divine craftsmanship. Thus far there is substantial agreement between Plato and Stoicism.

But when we ask about the practical and emotional effectiveness of their theological cosmologies, large differences begin to emerge. The Platonic Demiurge does his best, but he is constrained by his corporeal materials. So too are we, as we are also constrained by our psychological complexity. Straddled between incorporeal rationality and bodily motions, our dualistic nature presents us with a managerial task that is extremely demanding but whose difficulties and achievement are encouragingly reflected in the wonderful cosmological work performed by the Demiurge himself.

In Stoicism, by contrast, the divinity is faced with no externally limiting constraints. He makes the best possible world without qualification. The embodiment he confers on human beings is derived, like their souls, from himself.[41] With consummate ease, it seems, he makes himself into the world. Yet, the craftsmanship human beings are required to exercise, to make themselves godlike, is taken to be so demanding that everyone in fact falls short, with no known human being as yet having achieved fully fledged Stoic wisdom. Why

---

40 Eusebius, *Praeparatio evangelica* 15.15.305 (LS 67 L). For discussion, see Schofield, *The Stoic Idea*, pp. 64–67. Eusebius continues: "It must be believed that the God who administers the universe exercises providence for human beings, since he is beneficent, kind, well-disposed, just, and has all the virtues."

41 The human soul is sometimes described in Stoicism as an "offshoot" *(apospasma)* of God, e.g., Epictetus 1.14.6.

does their omnipotent and benevolent divinity make things so difficult for us, so distant from him in spite of our common share of rationality?

I ask an absurdly large question at the end of this paper. Among the many things that help to furnish some answers, I think the most relevant idea is the absolute perfectibility implicit in the Stoic concept of rational coherence. Nothing external, including our bodies, necessarily inhibits human beings from sharing in divine perfection. We are endowed with that potentiality, and are thus far like the divinity. But the gap between potentiality and actuality is absolute because rational coherence and the excellence it constitutes do not admit of degrees.[42] Rather than asking us, like Plato's Demiurge, to negotiate our unavoidable psycho-somatic complexity, the Stoic divinity sets human beings the extraordinary project of conforming their own rational faculty to his rational coherence. The offer of this worldly perfectibility and the exponential difficulty of accepting the offer go hand in hand.

At this point Stoicism moves beyond its Hellenic sources and becomes the tributary of a mightier theological stream. Jesus is reported to have told his disciples: "Be ye perfect, even as your father in heaven is perfect" (Matthew 5.48). Stoicism anticipates and echoes Jesus' imperative, which has always embarrassed sin-obsessed Christian theologians. The stock charge against Stoicism among Christians has been its shamelessly "arrogant" proposal that we can, in principle, perfect ourselves (really become godlike) by our own efforts if and only if we never deviate from the voice of reason.[43] What the Christian critics failed to understand is that the voice of Stoic reason (if it really is that, and not some beguiling pretender to the office) actually is the voice of God, and accessible to us because that is what we hear when we exercise our own rationality correctly. The "holy spirit" of Christian doctrine—the *hagion pneuma*—had a pre-Christian gestation as the divine offshoot of the Stoic's cosmic craftsman.*

---

42   See Stobaeus 2.99, 3–8 (LS 59N), id. 2.113, 18–19 (LS 59O), Diogenes Laertius 7.101 (LS 60O).

43   See for instance Pascal, *Discussion with Monsieur de Sacy*, cited in Long, *Epictetus*, pp. 263–264.

*Besides the *Timaeus* conference at Champaign-Urbana, I presented versions of this paper at the following universities: Princeton, Toronto, Indiana, Texas at San Antonio, and Yale. I thank my audiences at all these institutions for their comments, from which I have benefited in more ways than I can possibly register in this printed version. It is a pleasure to thank Richard Mohr for including me in his Champaign-Urbana line-up.

3

Philosopher-Kings and Craftsman-Gods

Allan Silverman

In seeking a Model of Mind, it seems best to start with what seems best, the divine. Plato and Aristotle—and here I will be concerned mainly with the former—accept that the divine is the best being that there is. This way of formulating the problem is fraught with controversies. For instance, the use of 'being' here stands in contrast to 'Being', whose capital letter signals that Forms are in play. So, while the divine mind might be the best being, it may or may not be a Being, i.e., a Form, and even if a Being, it may or may not be the best Being, for Plato signals at least in the *Republic* that the best of all is the Form of the Good. (Aristotle, in denying Forms, doesn't have this problem, though he might well have others.) Even harder to fathom is the relation of this best being to the good, in Plato's case to the Form of the Good; in Aristotle's case to the way the focal account of being and the focal account of good converge on the same primary actuality.[1] I also think, somewhat more controversially, that both believe that there is a divine being who is nothing other than a mind. Thus in Aristotle's case we worry about the mind of the prime mover. In Plato's case, the concern will be with the Demiurge of the *Timaeus*. I stipulate the identity of the *Demiurge* and *nous*, and I am prepared to treat the Demiurge and *nous* and the cosmic world soul as one phenomenon.[2] Finally, I accept that both Plato and Aristotle think that being like the divine as much as possible is

---

1   On the Good and its relation to the Divine, see Aristotle, *Metaphysics* 12.7–10. On the Form of the Good in Aristotle, *Nicomachean Ethics* 1.6.
2   This is controversial, not least because it involves how one stands on the question of whether Plato believes in the creation or not. I think that the account is 'for the sake of instruction', though obviously I cannot defend that claim here. Given my reading of the *eikôs mythos*, I think nothing turns on identifying the world-soul and the Demiurge.

one way of expressing the nature of human happiness and that striving to be like, or better, *modeling ourselves* on, the divine mind is one way of expressing what we humans do in trying to realize our happiness, whether or not we are aware of our striving to be so. I am especially interested, however, in the (self-) understanding of those who are aware of this striving to be like god, both how they incorporate being like the divine in their life-plans and how they (re-) incorporate their assimilation with the divine, should they achieve it, into the rest of their lives. Plato and Aristotle seem to part company over the activity, or more controversially activities, of their respective divine minds. The nature of the activity is hard to determine, whether we look in Plato or Aristotle. The passages are few and their meaning is difficult to make out.[3] In both we find a divine mind engaged in an activity of reason, indeed the best activity of reason. However, we can draw very different conclusions from the way in which the divine mind seems to exercise its reason in the two authors. Only in Aristotle do we find a divine mind that only contemplates, i.e., engages in *theoria*, as something distinct from another activity of reason, namely *phronesis*, and only somewhat late in his career do we seem to find it in Aristotle. It is this difference, the difference between practical and theoretical reason, that I want to explore in this paper, to see what lessons we can draw about the ways in which each thinks that a human being can be as divine as possible. This will require, at a minimum, some remarks about the nature of these activities and about their objects. I am sure that the following is only a prolegomenon.

My focus will be on the *Timaeus,* but maybe the best place to start today is the end of Book Five of the *Republic*. Plato and the *Republic* begin from Socrates' question: how ought one to live? Broadly speaking, Socrates believed philosophy or rational inquiry could answer the question, and, given his inquiry into or assumptions about human nature and the human soul, for Socrates the answer lies in a state of the rational soul, a state of knowledge. In Plato's hands matters become more complicated. In Book Four of the *Republic* he develops the account of the tripartite soul and of a psychologically harmonious condition in which reason rules the other parts. But at its end we have not learned in virtue of what kind of knowledge does reason manage to unify the soul. Book Five's third and greatest wave, that philosophers must be rulers and rulers philosophers, marks the beginning of the answer to that question.[4] Plato starts by differentiating the lovers of sights and sounds from philosophers. He advances the claim that there are things that completely are, the Forms, and

---

3 Moreover, the descriptions of the divine activities abound with language frequently found in their discussions of the human virtues, and rational and desiderative capacities, not surprisingly since we start from what is more familiar to us, our activities.

4 See especially B. A. O. Williams, *Ethics and The Limits of Philosophy* (Cambridge: Harvard University Press, 1985), chs. 1 and 3.

things that are and are not, the ordinary objects of the material world and their properties, and he assigns two powers set over these objects.[5] Knowledge is set over the former and is always true, belief is set over the latter and is true and false (*Republic* V 472b–480). In the three great metaphors of Sun, Line and Cave, as well as passages in especially Books Six and Seven, we find a more fine-grained range of objects and powers of the rational soul, and learn that among the objects of knowledge the Good has a special place, not least in that only in coming to know the Good can one in the strictest sense have achieved knowledge.

The objects of line and cave are comparably easy to characterize and distinguish from one another, with the profound exception of the objects of the first segment of the intelligible portion of Line, discursive thought or *dianoia*. Harder to understand are the different powers, the transitions between them, and the claim that powers have their own exclusive objects, implying that there is no belief about Forms and no knowledge of the material world.[6] What transformation(s), reflective or otherwise, takes one from belief, or *dianoia*, to knowledge? And once acquired, what does knowledge do to or for your other powers? Or, more practically, what does one do with knowledge? On the one hand, it seems that the best activity the philosopher can engage in is to (continue to) contemplate the Good and the other Forms. There is much to say about what this might mean. To the extent that the Knowledge of the Good is the last to be gained (*Republic* VII, 517c), perhaps one can know other Forms prior to achieving knowledge of the Good. Or, it might be that one can achieve knowledge of the Good prior to knowing all the Forms. If we know the Good and only some Forms,—let us say the Forms of the Virtues, along with what come to be called 'the greatest kinds'—then we can see what the philosopher might be doing when continuing in contemplation: he will be pursuing knowledge of other Forms. But then it can also be said that without knowledge of the Good, one lacks knowledge of any Form. This requires care, lest we land ourselves with the conclusion that actually the Good must be the Form known first, since it is required in order to know anything. For those who are holists, it might mean that after a long exercise in the sciences (and much else, including state administration), one comes to know the Good along with

---

5   On alternative ways of construing the relation between Knowledge, Belief and what they are about, see Gail Fine, "Knowledge and Belief in *Republic* 5–7," in G. Fine, ed., *Plato 1* (Oxford: Oxford University Press, 1999), pp. 215–246.

6   A strong reading of this passage maintains that in acting upon and in this material realm, one never exercises knowledge only belief. A weak(er) reading allows that some kind of knowledge might be available in this world, not least because this seems to best justify why the philosopher is best suited to rule. On either reading, however, the philosopher enjoys much better epistemic conditions than those who lack knowledge, and better even than some who have knowledge of the scientific but not philosophical variety.

and as it were simultaneously all the Forms. But then it would seem that the philosopher knows all that there is to know, that there is nothing left for him to contemplate. In this circumstance, should it be realized, it is appropriate to wonder what the philosopher does next.

These worries are independent of the special nature of the Good in Plato's theory. That is, the same worries about holism would arise were the One to be the master Form. But the emphasis on the special role of the Good suggests that there is more to the worry than holism. Plato's ontology relies on three distinct but related items: unchanging Forms, the objects of mind, i.e., the intelligibles; physical becoming, the objects of belief and the senses; and rational souls, intermediaries not only capable of grasping the intelligibles but also capable of acting on and bringing about changes in physical becoming, ideally as a response to their understanding of Forms. When it comes to assessing or understanding the very intelligibility of the Forms, and *a fortiori* in assessing what rational minds do in understanding the intelligibles, modern philosophers, as well as Ancient scholars influenced by Aristotle's division of practical from theoretical wisdom, tend to see the relations between Forms or intelligibles primarily in terms congenial to logicians, mathematicians and scientists, in terms of formal relations between concepts or relations between beliefs, or the regulation of beliefs. Here ethical Forms are either ignored or, while allowed to be central in our considerations of how we are to live or act in the material world in which we live, are accounted for through alternative means, e.g., through a focal analysis or analogically.

The onus of the distinction between theoretical and practical wisdom falls on those aspects of our lives that involve acting on affairs in this world, on deliberating about what to do, especially about what to do to achieve a goal or end, and perhaps most especially about what to do to achieve our ends as agents. It is practical in so far as we aim to bring about changes in others, the physical environment, and ourselves. Theoretical reason is, *ex hypothesi*, limited to changes in beliefs or other (representational) cognitive states, conceived to be independent of desires and not concerned with actions or items that can change. On this account of the objects of theoretical science, we do not in any way think about or act on particulars, or particular instances of the properties studied by the sciences. Ethical reflection, or the science of ethics, is not conceived to be a theoretical study on this account. Testing ideas, or collecting data and studying outcomes, seem excluded from theoretical reason's domain, eliminating on the surface at least explanation and prediction as part of theoretical science.

There does seem to be a difference between thinking about objects that can change and thinking about at least some objects that are necessary or unchanging. I am not sure that this is best conceived as the exercise of different kinds of reason, or reason acting or functioning differently, or just reason thinking about different things. I am also unsure that thinking in this manner is more leisurely, or in what sense the circumstances of leisure contribute to our ability or the occasions to think about whatever objects we do think about in this strict sense of theorizing. It seems as if the basic idea is that something is an act of *theoria* if one is not acting on others, other physical things or oneself, save for the reflective mental activity that is theorizing. In this regard everything other than the activity and object is a distraction.

The framework of the *Republic* not only resists this demotion, but also places the Good (and other ethical Forms) at the heart of the intelligibility of all Forms. This can and has been one reason to try to find a non-value aspect of the Good, roughly by treating it as a Form of Forms. More apposite, it is argued, are notions of order, structure and creation, the craftsman-like working up of 'ingredients' into excellent, well-ordered, interdependent wholes. Here, I think, we tend to overlook the role of the soul as mediator between the two so-called worlds, and in particular shrink from embracing the idea that thinking or reasoning is a dynamic process with its own standards and goals, a process that changes with changing circumstances, even while it preserves, to the extent possible, its gains, i.e., whatever knowledge it obtains. Perhaps Aristotle finds coherent a universe of intelligence and intelligible that is static and unchanging, an act or moment of contemplation, the unchanging vision of an unchanging vista. But this does not seem to me to be Plato's picture, not only because he explicitly promotes the Form of the Good, which is seemingly absent from Aristotle's realm of theoretical intelligibles, but because unlike Aristotle's pro-motion of mathematics and theology to the front ranks of theoretical inquiry, Plato accepts among the Forms the Forms of the Virtues as well as many that pertain to physical becoming (think of collection and division in the *Sophist* and *Statesman*).[7] Moreover, after discussing the five mathematical disciplines in which the twenty-somethings are to be trained, and even after spending their first five years of graduate school in dialectic, Plato insists that the would-be philosopher spend the next fifteen years in state-administration (*Republic* VII, 539e–540a). This stage is much the longest in the educational cursus and seems inevitably to redirect the synoptic gaze down from the objects of dialectic and the mathematical and astronomical heavens. Plato seems to think that serving in these jobs is in some way conducive to coming to knowledge of the Good. How are we to think about the objects of the science that they engage in at this stage? Since, in the chronological order of the fantasy, these folks will be working with mechanisms of the state created by older philosophers (i.e., the

---

7   See especially *Statesman* 258c–e, where Plato divides knowledge into two kinds, the prac-tical, such as carpentry, and the theoretical, such as mathematics. The latter simply furnish knowledge and do not involve, or are bare of, practical actions. The division in the *Sophist* 265 ff. is between acquisitive and productive crafts/skills.

founders), we can speculate that they will spend their time learning first how these mechanisms were designed and why, and then solving the problems that they are designed to address, e.g., court cases, decisions about trade and other relations between the *kallipolis* (the good, beautiful, just city) and its neighbors, whatever tax and revenue collection is needed to finance the activities of the military, religious and educational ministries, and overseeing the ministries. To think about the nitty-gritty details might incline one to conceive of the 'objects' of this part of one's life as dwelling in the bottom half of the line, as it were, unlike say the objects of the sciences studied for the previous ten, which occupy at least the third level. But this I think may not be right. Consider their activities instead as settling disputes and worrying about questions of distributive justice, and finally as learning to deal with the behaviors of the non-philosophical soldiers, educators, and craftsmen. Then, perhaps, we can say that these fifteen years are spent rather in the study of rhetoric, psychology, sociology and other social sciences.

Finally, Plato assigns to the rational part of the soul an essential desire for the Good. Now, it can be, and has been, argued that the natural desire of the rational part is not for the Good, but rather is only for Knowledge.[8] But in so far as knowledge has Forms for objects, and in so far as the Good has its position as the un-hypothetical first principle of the Forms, then it may be thought of as the ultimate focus of rational desire. In asking what one does with the knowledge of the Good, we might be asking whether the (rational) desire is satisfied with the mere acquisition, desiring perhaps to retain what one has. Or, is it that (also that?) in satisfying the thirst for knowledge we come to desire, in light of that knowledge of the Good (and the satisfaction of our desire), to make more good, though perhaps we can add that in making more good we are satisfying our desire to retain what we have striven to achieve. In so far as we are thus moved by the Good, given whatever circumstances we find ourselves in, we create or make things good, including in particular making others good.

While there is a sense in which Plato's remarks about Forms and knowledge resonate with the Aristotelian, or maybe better the post-Humean, conception, it seems totally belied by what philosophers actually do in the *Republic* and equally by what Plato himself is doing both in writing the *Republic* in the manner that he does and in general writing and teaching as he does. From within the *Republic*, it seems that the philosopher (sometimes) goes down to rule. Here the question might be with what attitude? I have argued elsewhere that the philosopher descends with the aim of making more good, not at the cost of his own happiness, but simply because he has the opportunity of making

---

8   See G. R. F. Ferrari, "The Three-Part Soul," in G. R. F. Ferrari, *The Cambridge Companion to Plato's* Republic (Cambridge: Cambridge University Press, 2007), pp. 165–201.

others better.[9] In this regard, the knowledge of the Good is such that he can do no more good for himself, for his soul is as well-ordered as it can be: thus knowing the Good entails being good. But secondly, it seems that in knowing the Good he desires to create or make more good: thus knowing the Good entails doing good, at least to the extent that the philosopher's reasons for action determine the goodness of his action. However, in descending to help others his best intentions may be thwarted by circumstances. Indeed, he may lack the ability, in some circumstances, to act on his knowledge.

But there are other ways to think about what the philosopher might do with her time. One possibility is that she teaches others, reproducing to the extent possible the path by which another can come to knowledge of the good. This takes the form of both lecturing and, apparently, writing. These creative products are at once the activities of reason in so far as it contemplates the good and, it would seem, directed at or intended for other individuals in the city.[10] An additional activity that might equally be reckoned among the contemplative would be the production of the very dialogues that Plato himself writes, including the *Republic* (and *Timaeus*). If these activities qualify as thinking about the Good because they are designed to bring about more good, it is incumbent to specify what strategy Plato is advocating to create more good. In the case of the *Republic*, this is generally taken to be the construction of the well-integrated *kallipolis*, whose aim is to produce the good for all the citizens of the state, to the extent that each class can be said to have a share in the happiness appropriate to each.[11]

---

9 Allan Silverman, "Ascent and Descent: The Philosopher's Regret," *Social Philosophy and Policy* 24: 2 (July 2007), 40–69

10 The latter invites, though it does not require, the audience to be either other philosophers or students enrolled in the school of philosophers. If it is limited to the former, then we find the philosophers cut off from all other individuals who occupy the city. To the extent that they are all philosophers, it seems hard to imagine what they would have to say to each other. If we expand the group to the limited few, we then need a *horos* or mark that allows us to segregate those who would be philosophers from the rest. The reading of the *Republic* becomes a matter of controversy on this score. The idea that we can identify a group is fed by the sequence of classes that constantly weed out individuals, thus requiring an explanation not only of what those who remain are doing, but also what happens to those who drop out. The specter of Leo Strauss looms in the background here, since the aim of contemplation becomes to make more of it in the narrow sense of encouraging a few elites to carry on the tradition. The epistemic story of how to find those few who, *ex hypothesi* are capable of philosophy, also needs to be told.

11 Now, there are different ways in which to read the aim of the philosophers, though they share the idea that he goes down to make more good. The difference between contemplating and acting in the world need not then be in its aim, but in the ways in which this is to be realized. The use of fantasy is one way in which Plato thinks creativity in writing can make more good. If this is a product of knowing the Good, the way in which the fantasy achieves its aim seems critical. The *Republic* has been read as a fantasy blueprint, a series of steps which if followed will, Plato thinks, produce the best state. In this respect, the blueprint speaks of a

The *Republic's kallipolis* and its construction is of course a fantasy, an exercise in utopian thinking which may (or may not) be the activity of theorizing. I think that the production of philosophical treatises is an exercise of *theoria*. (On the other hand, the idea that this is a leisurely activity seems to me questionable.) What kind of fantasy it is, a blueprint or an exercise in escape, is an open question. Here the details matter less than the moral, namely with what motive does Plato approach the authoring of his dialogues, the philosopher approach rule, and the *Demiurge* approach his creation.

Generally speaking, I take the aim of the *Timaeus* to be not simply to present a Craftsman whose making of the world is a fiction designed to offer us insight into the metaphysical structure of a cosmos that was never made. Even more important is its lesson in soul construction, where the 'craftsman-like' activities of the Demiurge in fashioning the cosmos according to a pattern (Pattern) is the model for our own activity of fashioning our souls in the appropriate way. (The cosmos has a model or Form, namely the World Animal Itself, as does all but one of its 'parts', namely a Form of Soul.[12]) The realm of Forms itself has a structure and hence so too does the cosmos, and this structure is to be viewed by us as a system of truths, including primarily what might be best thought of as practical truths, whose concern is the fashioning of raw materials to serve a purpose, namely the filling out of the parts of the cosmos. In so far as these truths and this structure is for the sake of instruction, we in turn can take as the moral that we are to emulate or imitate the Demiurge in so far as we are to discover practical truths as to how one ought to live, and thus that we are to treat the 'raw materials' of everyday becoming as well as our souls themselves as instrumentalities in the craft of living, i.e., as material for living well.

This decidedly practical reading of the Demiurge and the moral of the *Timaeus* is at odds with other interpretations. Consider what I will call a Plotinian account, as presented by Sedley.[13] (I do not mean to enroll Sedley as supporter of this reading.) On this account of the aim of the philosopher,

---

set of steps that will produce philosophers and the *kallipolis*, should it but be carried out. The purpose of the fantasy is to guide the would-be philosopher/ruler through the process. That is, the audience for the fantasy is limited to those who would think of their job as ruling and who have the requisite means to effect the changes at their disposal. This strikes me as doubly curious. In the first place, it assumes that, in this regard, Plato thinks that he can foresee a series of changes in circumstances in the material world which can be viewed as leading predictably to an outcome. The idea is thus at odds with his general skepticism about such interventions. Second, it suggests that there is a ready-made but limited audience for the *Republic*, one that is both intellectually and politically capable of reading and acting upon its recommendations.
12   This is controversial and requires a discussion, not provided here, about the nature of nous, soul, the demiurge and the prospects of there being Forms of Soul, Motion and Nous.
13   David Sedley, "The Ideal of Godlikeness," in Gail Fine, ed., *Plato 2* (Oxford: Oxford University Press, 1999), pp. 309–328.

we are encouraged to regard the assimilation doctrine as describing a purely intellectual assimilation to a higher being. The moral virtues, on this account, are a mere political expedient in the interests of a well-run society.[14] Sedley finds strong support for this devaluing of the political and moral virtues throughout the *Timaeus*, but especially at 90c–d: "Moral virtue, the harmony of the three soul-parts, is recommended in passing at the outset, but supreme happiness is located not there but in the godlike state of the rational soul-part taken in isolation."[15] Now Sedley recognizes that the world-soul explicitly concerns itself with becoming as well as being. Moreover, he is certainly cognizant of the Demiurge's interest in practical or creative activities, namely the creation of the cosmos and our place in it. However, Sedley draws attention to a series of remarks in the *Timaeus* and elsewhere that suggest that at some level, Plato wants to claim that our true self or our truest self is the rational soul, not the tripartite soul of which it is a part working in harmony, and holds out the prospect that we are to identify ourselves with this rational part alone.[16] But this is but the first step in the reading. For Sedley takes pains to show that the argument of the *Timaeus* isolates the rational soul as the locus or perhaps as nothing more than the circular motions which share a likeness with the motions of the world-soul with which they are kindred. The goal of each of us, note that it is each of us in the *Timaeus* not some limited number of us, as the argument of the *Republic* seems to imply, is to return these motions to their natural courses. They are initially disrupted by birth and at birth, and then discombobulated by the sensory streams coming in through the sensory faculties (42e–44c). We can help them regain their natural and regular circular motion by nourishing them in the proper way:

"Now for everybody there is one way to care for every part, and that is to grant to each part its proper nourishments and motions. For the divine element in us, the motions which are akin to it are the thoughts and the revolutions of the whole world. Everyone should take a lead from these. We should correct the corrupted revolutions in our head concerned with becoming, by learning

---

14   This reading gains some support from remarks within the *Republic* itself, both at 518d–e and in the discussion of the demotic virtues at 500d.

15   Sedley, "Godlikeness," p. 323.

16   Compare Waterlow (Broadie) and Korsgaard on identifying with reason and identifying with the constitution ruled by reason. Sarah Waterlow, "The Good of Others in Plato's *Republic*," *Proceedings of the Aristotelian Society* 72 (1972–1973), 19–36, especially pp. 21–22; Christine Korsgaard, "Self-Constitution in the Ethics of Plato and Kant," *The Journal of Ethics* 3 (1999), 1–29, especially p. 15 and n. 10. A crucial difference between Korsgaard and Waterlow (and others) is that her agent identifies not with reason but "with her constitution, and it says that reason should rule" (p. 15). Compare Waterlow: "For while Plato fully acknowledges the conceptual priority of agent to actions, there is for him something prior again to the agent, namely reason itself . . ." (p. 36).

the harmonies and revolutions of the whole world, and so make the thinking subject resemble the object of its thought, in accordance with its ancient nature; and, by creating this resemblance, bring to fulfillment *(telos)* the best life offered by the gods to mankind for present and future time" (*Timaeus*, 90c–d, after Sedley).

Three remarks on this passage. First, the clear message is that we should concern ourselves not with becoming, but with other better matters if we are to return our rational motions to their proper course. *Genesis* here is not birth, but the realm of becoming. This echoes the theme laid down at the outset by Timaeus that the Demiurge's model was something that is, not something that has come to be (*Timaeus* 28a–b). To emulate him in this regard, by looking at something that is, restores our rational motions. But this can be read in two ways. One treats it as a blanket prohibition, both for the would-be philosopher and for one who has resettled the circles of his soul, from at any time concerning himself with becoming. Thus even after order has been restored, the philosopher would still dissociate from becoming, whether because of the threat of disturbing his soul, or because he is drawn to the more attractive study of what is. But it can also be seen as a recommendation to the *aspiring* philosopher to fix his attention on the Forms and the principles of the Demiurgic construction of the cosmos. Here we hear echoes of the *Republic* and other dialogues that exhort us in the same direction. Only by turning away from becoming to face a different direction can we become happy. But this implies nothing about our actions or interests, once we have achieved knowledge of the good. It is open what we then do.

Second, the *Timaeus* encourages the philosopher/physicist to study astronomy and to seek to understand the mathematical physics that lies behind the cosmic cyclical motions.[17] The study of these motions and the reasoning behind them leads to the correct circular motions in our soul; indeed the circular motions of the heavens seem to exert an almost attractive force on the motions of reason causing them to move in a manner more similar to the cosmic motions, i.e., more cyclically. But these heavenly orbits are part of what is created, admittedly the best part of the cosmos. It is doubtful that we are to stop with these cosmic motions. For instance, there is the object(s) that is the model for the cosmos. Now the end point of this line of reasoning is to understand not just the nature of the model that always is, but also the creative and reflective activities of the *Demiurge* in using or working from this model. Foremost among these activities is the celestial bodies and their motions, but

---

17 To the extent that we are to be chary of thinking that these mathematical constructions are the best and only way to build a cosmic order, we should be equally chary of thinking that the *kallipolis* is the best and only way to create a state.

the whole of the cosmos and the principles of its construction are what the restored circular motions of reason think about.

Third, Sedley infers from his reading that "What we are urged to share with the world soul, then, does not include practical reasoning."[18] If I follow, the implicit assumption is that when we are concerned with becoming in any form, we are engaged in practical reasoning. Now the very enterprise Timaeus and company are engaged in, namely physics, is concerned with becoming. We can wonder whether the *eikôs mythos* that is Timaeus' account is itself a bit of practical reasoning, and hence not something that Plato would have us engage in at any point. Or we can view the relation between physics and philosophy differently, allowing one to be a part of the other once we are properly appreciative of the nature of the model and the Demiurge's activity. In this case, not only will there be a difference in our practical reasoning, since we are better informed about the nature of the cosmos and its constituents with which we interact everyday, but we will continue to study the physics of the cosmos in order to better understand the nature of the model and the Demiurgic activity. At a minimum, we will continue to consider whether the mathematics, i.e., triangles, is the best available.

Among the many conditions Plato lays down on understanding his physics, let me draw attention to a few. First, whatever approach we take to the teleology, there is an element of necessity or contingency or what is not under the control of intelligence, in the physical system, i.e., in the cosmos. We have to account for this in our physics and therefore in thinking about how to live our lives. Second, Plato (still) insists that there are Forms; I have argued traditional Forms—that serve as the model for what is created.[19] For those who think that 'rational deconstruction and reconstruction' is the instruction for which the myth is constructed, our account of the cosmos must be consistent with and governed by the essential natures of the Forms, whether these are only mathematical or not. Finally, a third constraint flows from the nature of the Demiurge, namely that he is good and that he creates. Let me pause a moment on both. That he might not create is not a possibility entertained by Plato. But in a logical sense, perhaps, can one not ask whether it is possible for the Demiurge not to bring the cosmos into being? Here we might think through some scenarios having to do with the recalcitrance of the material to do what he wants, or complex systems tending to have some incompatible demands or virtues, or what have you. But I don't mean this. These seem to me challenges to be overcome or recognized, should he act on his desire to create. I am worried about the question of whether the Demiurge just does not act—is

---

18 Sedley, "Godlikeness," p. 323.
19 Allan Silverman, *The Dialectic of Essence* (Princeton: Princeton University Press, 2002), pp. 246–284.

that possible for the Demiurge? Plato suggests that it is not. "Now why did he who framed this whole universe of becoming frame it? Let us state the reason why: He was good, and one who is good can never become jealous of anything. And so, being free of jealousy, he wanted everything to become as much like himself as was possible" (*Timaeus* 29e). Whatever the logical possibility, Plato's Demiurge acts, that is creates, because he is good, and he does so ungrudgingly and seeking to bring order, beauty and the good to his creation.

We might then ask whether we are to think of him as antecedently or afterwards aware that the outcome of his creation is something good but not completely good, not completely under his control, that there is some random factor that makes contingency ineliminable from the world? The answer to this again seems to me to be yes. So, the constraint is that the Demiurge acts, for the sake of the good, to bring about the physical cosmos, which he understands will include randomness, the precise occurrences of which he will not be able to anticipate. In so far as the Demiurge is us, we know all this, too. Thus when we consider what we are to do, we are entitled to think that when we act we should act with the same expectations and aims, namely for the best, knowing that we cannot press this all the way down. However, when we come to deal with the contingent and random, as surely we will, we are now equipped to understand how it arises from the ordered and what means, physically, I mean, are available to us to bring order to the cosmos.

The foregoing only scratches the surface of a number of issues pertaining to what might be thought of as 'the way down' the divided line and the transformations of the rational as well as the other parts of the soul effected by coming to know the good. One critical issue is whether the ruler can now be said to know things about the physical world, and whether the form such knowledge takes is the same as knowledge of the Forms. But regardless, it would seem from our reflections on the *Timaeus* and Demiurgic activity, that the mere fact that one's reason, once informed by knowledge of the Good and the other forms, is directed at contingent affairs is no reason (pun intended) to think that some kind of knowledge with a distinctive structure is at work. If I am right that Plato never intends us to hive off the practical from our model divine mind, it is because he is committed to the theses that knowing the Good entails not only being good, it also entails doing good, in whatever circumstances one finds oneself in, to the extent that doing good is possible. Such an exercise of reason is to model oneself on the divine mind.

Burrowing deeper would take us, for instance, to Aristotle and an inquiry into his reasons for separating *phronesis* (practical reasoning) from *theoria* (theoretical reasoning). I'll close then with some programmatic remarks about some of the possible differences between these two faculties. We act generically on other souls, the physical or material world, or on reason itself. These different objects are or might be complemented by an account of different faculties and/or different ways of thinking deployed by the same faculty. When Aristotle eventually splits from Plato over a separate faculty that is not a species of *theoria*—when he looks for a distinctive excellence of the *to doxastikon* (the thing that opines) that qualifies as *phronesis* as opposed to *doxa* (opinion)—the typical reason is a difference in objects, namely changeable contingent objects versus unchanging objects, though even here the objects of physics are problematic, since they too are for the most part and because we might wish to include sciences such as psychology and biology among the theoretical. A second, related, rationale has to do with desire: either theoretical wisdom involves no desires or a different kind of desire from the desire that is involved in practical wisdom and deliberation. So, for instance, one might be able to think theoretically about the objects of mathematics without engaging desire. More problematically one might be able to think about the Good, or about God, without engaging desire, or at least the same kind of desire that is engaged when one is thinking about one's own good or (inclusive) a good achievable by you. (Here, I think, Plato simply disagrees.) Finally, at least for the purpose of this paper, and again relatedly, one can look to the difference between universals and particulars, or universal judgments and particular judgments. Here I have in mind Aristotle's effort to argue that one can achieve practical virtue and develop practical wisdom without engaging in *theoria*, or perhaps without the exercise of theoretical wisdom. I am not sure that Aristotle can maintain this position in the face of Platonic objections. In the end, I suspect that the difference between them boils down to a difference in their model for a divine mind. Aristotle's account of the divine mind seems at the end of the day driven more by his account of actuality in the physics and metaphysics. Plato's model derives from reflection about our own mind. No surprise there, since he too tried to learn from his teacher what we should make of ourselves.

4

The Place of Cosmology in Plato's Later Dialogues

Charles H. Kahn

I am concerned here with the project of natural philosophy in Plato's later dialogues. My aim is to locate the cosmologies of the *Timaeus* and *Philebus* within a more general movement of thought, a movement that begins in the *Phaedrus* and comes to a conclusion in the 10th book of the *Laws*.

It has often been noticed that Plato takes a more positive view of the study of nature and change in his later dialogues. But this development has often been seen as evidence that Plato had abandoned the classical theory of Forms, where knowledge in the strict sense was limited to eternal, unchanging Forms. On the contrary, I propose to interpret the new concern with nature not as a rejection but as an expansion of the classical theory, a reshaping of the meta-physical epistemology of the *Phaedo* and *Republic* to include a philosophy of the natural world. Plato's fundamental contrast between unchanging Being and perishable Becoming remains intact; it is emphatically reasserted in both the *Philebus* and *Timaeus*. Furthermore, dialectic or the highest form of knowledge remains attached only to Being that is eternally stable and unchanging. What is new in the later dialogues is the application of this theory to the natural world, that is, to a positive account of the realm of change and becoming—what we might describe as the overcoming of Heraclitean flux.

Perhaps the most dramatic statement of the new point of view is the famous passage in the *Sophist* where the philosopher is compared to a child who, when forced to choose between two good things, demands "both!" Similarly, for knowledge to be possible, the philosopher must insist that Being include both what undergoes change and what is unchanging (249b–d). This extension of the concept of Being, and hence of knowledge, to the realm of nature is also reflected in the novel terminology of the *Philebus*, in those paradoxical expressions for

69

genesis eis ousian ("becoming into being," 26d8) and *ousia gegenêmenê* ("being that has come-to-be," 27b8–9). As in the *Sophist* so in the *Philebus*, the notion of Being has been deliberately expanded to include the subject of change. At the same time, the old preference for stability has not been given up: the truest beings, *ta ontôs onta*, remain those monads or Forms that are exempt from coming-to-be and perishing. This extension of the notion of Being to include Becoming raises many questions, to which we must return. For example, how can cosmology, as the study of Becoming, remain distinct from dialectic as the study of eternal Being, and yet take as its object natures that are stable enough for scientific study? But before exploring these new problems posed by the cosmologies of the *Philebus* and *Timaeus*, I want to sketch the larger movement of thought within which this more ramified notion of Being takes shape.

We can best chart the new approach if we begin from the baseline represented by Socrates' narrative in the *Phaedo*. There Socrates reports why he gave up the study of natural philosophy, despite his enthusiasm for the teaching of Anaxagoras that *nous* (reason, understanding) was the cause of cosmic order. Socrates was disappointed with the mechanistic accounts offered by Anaxagoras, where he had expected to find a rational explanation of natural phenomena in terms of what is good or best. So Socrates turned instead to seek the truth of beings—the truth of *ta onta*—in dialectic, that is, in the study of *logoi* (99e). Plato's resort to dialectic, as a substitute for Presocratic naturalism, was designed to redefine the entire enterprise of philosophy. But the *Phaedo* narrative does not mean that Plato had given up his interest in natural philosophy. The myths of the *Phaedo* and *Republic* X reflect his abiding concern with issues in astronomy and cosmology. But in neither of these dialogues is there any sign of a constructive theory of nature and change. Thus the mathematical studies of the guardians in the *Republic* are recommended for their pedagogical or spiritual value, not as an introduction to physics but as preparation for the transcendental dialectic that gives access to the Forms. Mathematics in the *Republic* is designed to turn the mind upwards, away from sensory Becoming to a noetic grasp of eternal Being.

The picture begins to change in the *Phaedrus*, which is in some respects the first of the "late" dialogues. Although the classical theory of Forms reappears in the myth of a chariot ride to an extra-celestial vision, the *Phaedrus* also presents a new view of the psyche as a principle of motion, and a new view of dialectic as philosophical analysis, that is, as division and collection. Both of these innovations point the way to doctrines of the later dialogues. The new view of the psyche as *archê kinêseôs* is fully exploited only in *Laws* X. On the other hand, the new view of dialectic pervades the later works. Beginning in the *Phaedrus* and continuing, for example, in the *Statesman* and *Philebus*, dialectic is conceived as the general method of rational inquiry, the source of all scientific knowledge (*Phaedrus* 266b, *Philebus* 16c2; cf. *Statesman* 284d, 285d6). At the same time, since dialectic remains the pursuit of essences and definition, the new conception of dialectic will entail a new conception of Forms. But that becomes clear only in the *Sophist*, where dialectic is characterized as the knowledge of which forms blend with one another and which do not. Once it is conceived as division and collection, this new view of dialectic naturally implies the network of interrelated forms that is outlined in the *Sophist*. But this implication is not developed in the *Phaedrus*. There Socrates connects dialectic not with the theory of Forms but with the philosophy of nature. Scientific rhetoric, he insists, conceived now as applied dialectic, requires philosophy in general and philosophy of nature in particular: "If Phaedrus does not adequately pursue philosophy, he will not be an adequate speaker on any topic" (261a). "All the great arts require idle speculation and natural philosophy" (*adoleschia kai meteôrologia physeôs peri* 270a1). It was because of his contact with Anaxagoras and the doctrine of cosmic Mind that Pericles became a great orator. The method of investigating nature is common to scientific rhetoric and Hippocratic medicine (270b1). Both rhetoric and medicine must be capable of studying natures generally, analyzing the nature of the body (for medicine) and that of the soul (for rhetoric), but also "the nature of the whole *(hê tou holou physis)*," that is, the nature of the universe (270c2). (Thus speaks Socrates in the *Phaedrus*.)

The contrast here with the *Phaedo* could not be more striking. Instead of turning away from natural philosophy to study the art of *logoi*, this new conception of scientific *logoi* requires the study of natural philosophy as indispensable preliminary training. Rather than construing dialectic as an alternative to Presocratic naturalism, dialectic is now presented as an art that includes the study of nature as a special case. The *Phaedrus* thus opens the path leading to the *Philebus*, *Timaeus*, and *Laws* X. Instead of abandoning cosmology, as in the *Phaedo*, and treating astronomy only as a branch of pure mathematics, as in the *Republic*, the Plato of the late dialogues will reclaim for his own philosophy all the territory studied by his Presocratic predecessors. Thus in the survey of different views of Being in the *Sophist*, Plato makes clear that not only Anaxagoras but also Heraclitus, Parmenides and Empedocles are to be counted as participants in the same discussion. And the *peras* (limit) and *apeiron* (unlimited, indefinite) of the *Philebus* make a similar point for continuity with the Pythagorean tradition. In these dialogues we can see that Plato is systematically reappropriating the subject matter of his Ionian and Italian predecessors. The appropriation is most fully developed, of course, in the *Timaeus*. Within the external framework of a dialogue, the *Timaeus* has the literary form of a Presocratic treatise, "beginning with the origin of the cosmos and ending with the nature of human beings" (27a). This was the pattern established already in Hesiod's *Theogony* and apparently followed by most Presocratics. *Laws* X provides a kind of coda or postscript to the *Timaeus*. For *Laws* X shows in one extended argument how the study of nature has been reclaimed for Platonic philosophy, and thus purged of the materialist and mechanist tendencies that distorted Anaxagoras' cosmology, the tendencies that came to a head in Democritus' theory of a world produced by chance collisions between lifeless bodies moving at random through infinite space.

It is in the context of this broader movement of thought concerning the philosophy of nature, leading from the *Phaedrus* to the tenth book of the *Laws*, that we can best consider the specific similarities and differences between the cosmologies of the *Philebus* and *Timaeus*. First of all, we need to recognize that these are not two alternative theories designed to cover the same ground. So much is obvious from the contrast in scale. Whereas the cosmology of the *Timaeus* occupies the entire dialogue—66 Stephanus pages out of 76 (omitting only the proem, which belongs more properly to the *Critias*)—the cosmological section of the *Philebus* is only a small fraction of the whole work (8 Stephanus pages out of 56). This quantitative inequality reflects a major difference in function. Whereas the cosmological narrative of the *Timaeus* is a self-standing piece—Plato's contribution to *peri physeôs historia* (investigation into the nature of things)—the corresponding section of the *Philebus* is largely subordinated to its role in a macrocosm-microcosm analogy. The cosmic blending of Limit and Unlimited serves in the *Philebus* as paradigm for the mixture of knowledge and pleasure in the good human life. We note, however, that this macro-microcosm parallelism is not perfect. Although pleasure belongs to the kind of the Unlimited, its competitor, knowledge, belongs not to the counterpart principle of Limit but to the fourth principle which is the Cause of blending between the first two. This lack of symmetry is due to the fact that the cosmology of the *Philebus* serves a secondary function as part of Plato's reappropriation of natural philosophy. Socrates in the *Phaedo* had abandoned cosmology because Anaxagoras was not able to provide a teleological account of nature. That is why in the *Philebus* Socrates must insist that knowledge and understanding (*nous*) be recognized as cosmic *cause*, as the source not of Limit per se but of the successful blend of Limit and Unlimited. It is because of this teleological role of *nous* that the cosmology of the *Philebus* can be read as a preparation for the *Timaeus*. It is essential to Plato's project in these two late dialogues that he resurrect the Anaxagorean conception of Nous as the explanatory cause of natural order.

In the *Timaeus* Plato will redefine the Anaxagorean principle of a cosmic Mind by fusing it with the more mythical notion of a cosmic Maker or artisan. The fundamental idea of the *Timaeus* (as of *Laws* X) is the conception of the natural world as a work of art. We meet this notion of a cosmic Maker or demiurge in occasional references in the *Republic* and elsewhere, including texts in Xenophon.[1] This notion of a cosmic artisan must have been a common theme

---

1   *Republic* 507c5, 530a; cf. 597d2; Xenophon, *Memorabilia* I.iv.7; cf. IV.vii.6.

before Plato, although pre-Platonic documentation is hard to find. (Perhaps in Pherecydes? In Empedocles the cosmic work of Aphrodite is compared to that of a craftsman.) The Greek model for cosmogony is more typically biological, and even sexual (as in the figure of *erôs* in Hesiod.) The notion of the creation of the world by an artisan god or Maker, so familiar from creation stories in other traditions, was probably developed in early Greek texts now lost. In any case it is in the *Philebus* that this conception is given an explicitly philosophical form, by the identification of causation with making: "It is necessary that everything that comes-to-be comes to be through some cause *(aitia)* . . . But the nature of a doer/maker *(to poioun)* differs only in name from a cause, so that the doer/maker and the cause can rightly be said to be one . . . And again the thing that is done/made *(to poioumenon)* and what comes to be *(to gignom-enon)* differ only in name" (26e–27a). This identification of cause with maker is made more plausible in Plato's text by the word-play on the double meaning of *poiein* (to do and to make). But this word-play serves only to articulate the philosophical thesis asserted by Socrates in the *Phaedo* and developed now in the *Philebus* and *Timaeus*: a rational explanation must take the form of an action-explanation, the activity of an agent, showing how what is done aims at a good outcome. This reflects the distinction, made in the *Phaedo* and reformulated in the *Timaeus*, between an explanatory cause and a necessary condition, that is, between a rational explanation and its mechanical instrumentation (*Phaedo* 98c–99c, *Timaeus* 46c–e).

This identity between causing and making in the *Philebus* gives explicit justification for what is taken for granted as the starting-point of cosmogony in the *Timaeus*, namely, that the principle of causality implies the rational action of a maker or demiurge (*Timaeus* 28a). This is of course no trivial assumption. The reinterpretation of *nous* as cosmic artisan is the key move that permits Plato in the *Timaeus* to satisfy the demand for a teleological explanation that remained unsatisfied in the *Phaedo*. We are not in a position to claim that the cosmological section of the *Philebus* was written to prepare for the cosmology of the *Timaeus*, since we do not know the order of composition. But we can say that a natural reading order will place the *Philebus* first, since it is concerned to deal explicitly with such problems, whose solution is taken for granted in the *Timaeus*. An equally striking case is the assumption of a world soul, an *anima mundi*, which is carefully argued for in the *Philebus* but very briefly introduced in the *Timaeus*. The conception of the universe as *empsychon*, alive and hence "ensouled," was implied from the beginning in the Presocratic use of microcosm-macrocosm analogies. But what is implicit in this Presocratic tradition becomes explicit in *Philebus* 30a–c, where Socrates argues (1) that our *psychê* (soul) must be derived from a world soul, just as the elements of our body are derived from corporeal elements in the cosmos, and (2) that the causal action of *nous* in the cosmos could not exist without a cosmic soul. (The second argument has a partial parallel at *Timaeus* 30b.) This second argument connects the notion of world soul with the teleological interpretation of nature, and thus prepares the way for the thesis of *Laws* X, where psyche as source of motion *(archê kinêseôs)* is presented as the ruling principle of nature. The world soul of the *Philebus*, like that of *Laws* X, seems to absorb the functions of the demiurge. On this point the *Timaeus* goes its own way, with a sharp distinction between the Maker and the world soul. One might suspect that the sharpness of this distinction is due in part to the literary form of a creation myth, with a personified Maker. But there may also be a philosophical reason for Plato to maintain a distinction between the principle directly responsible for cosmic self-motion and a higher principle of cognition alone, that is free from all motion and change.

What is common, then, to the cosmologies of *Philebus* and *Timaeus* is the teleological account of natural becoming, construed on the model of artistic making. What is distinctive of the *Philebus* is the introduction of Limit and Unlimited as the two principles whose combination will produce a successful blend. Distinctive also is the normative element in the notion of blending. The *Philebus* cosmology does not aim to explain all phenomena but only positive outcomes, like health, virtue and harmony (26b). (There is no negative principle resisting rational control, like Ananke (Necessity) in the *Timaeus*. The Unlimited is simply privative and neutral, like matter in Aristotle.) This restriction to good mixtures derives from the primary function of the cosmic scheme, which is to serve as paradigm for the successful blend of knowledge and virtue in a good life. Hence the *Philebus* offers not a general account of coming-to-be but a partial theory designed for a special role. There are, nevertheless, some significant parallels with the more comprehensive theory of the *Timaeus*. Both schemes take as their explanandum the realm of natural becoming, and offer an explanation on the basis of a pair of fundamental principles plus the agency of a rational cause. Thus at a certain level of generality, the four principles of the *Philebus*—Limit, Unlimited, their combination, and the cause of combination—might seem to correspond respectively to Form as father in the *Timaeus*, to Receptacle as mother, Becoming as offspring, and Demiurge as maker. But these parallels can be misleading as well as enlightening, since the differences are at least as important as the similarities.

We note, first of all, that in the *Philebus* only the notion of the Unlimited is analyzed in any detail (24a–25c), and it does not have the explicitly spatial structure of the Receptacle. As Socrates himself points out (25d7), no comparable account is given of Limit. The principle of Limit is simply described as equality, duality, and "every relation of number to number or measure to measure" (25a7–b1). In other words, Limit is represented by mathematical ratios imposed upon the qualitative flux of the Unlimited. Hence what corresponds to Limit in the *Timaeus* is not the archetypical Forms as a model for creation, for these lie outside the realm of Becoming and do not enter as ingredients into any phenomenal blends. What corresponds to Limit in the scheme of the *Timaeus* is only the principle of mathematical form, represented by numerical ratios in the construction of the world soul and by triangles in the construction of the world body. It is these mathematical structures, and not the transcendental Forms, that serve (like Limit) as immanent form organizing the passive matter of the Receptacle. So there is no direct parallel between Forms in the *Timaeus* and Limit in the *Philebus*.

There is a better fit between the Receptacle and the Unlimited, since these two passive principles both involve a flux of qualities that receive what definiteness and stability they possess from the intervention of the active principle. Here again, we can see the scheme of the *Philebus* as a kind of preparation for the *Timaeus* (and ultimately for Aristotle's notion of matter). I suggest that the Unlimited can be best understood as a first Platonic reshaping of Heraclitean flux in the direction of a constructive theory of Becoming. In the *Cratylus* and *Theaetetus*, Plato had shown that the principle of unrestricted flux cannot provide a coherent account of anything. (A kindred thought is expressed at *Sophist* 249b8–d2: no *nous* without stability.) It will be the task of the *Timaeus* to incorporate a concept of elemental flux within a positive theory of nature.

The blend of Limit and Unlimited in the *Philebus* can be seen as a first step in that direction, combining the "Heraclitean" principle of opposites, flux, and indefiniteness with a "Pythagorean-Eleatic" principle of order and stability—just the principle that is missing from the flux of *Cratylus* and *Theaetetus*.[2] It is this "blending" of the notions of change and stability, of Becoming and Being, that is implicitly entailed by the rejection of unrestricted flux in the two earlier dialogues. It is this new blend of Being and Becoming, called for in the *Sophist*, that is reflected now in the paradoxical terminology cited earlier from the *Philebus*: *genesis eis ousian, ousia gegenêmenê.*

In such a blend, where will the structuring principle come from? Ultimately, of course, from the Forms. But they are not mentioned in our cosmological text from the *Philebus*. (The Forms appear in the *Philebus* only as a puzzle, in the problematic monads of 15ab, but not in the positive cosmology of Stephanus pages 23–27.) Instead, we have the description of Limit in terms of ratios. For readers of the *Statesman* it should come as no surprise that the structure of Becoming is to be provided by mathematics. For the notion of *metrikê* (the science of measures) as normative mathematics, with its principle of "due measure" *(to metrion)*, is presented in the *Statesman* as the basis for all art and science, all *technai* (crafts, expertise, 284d). It is in this teleological conception of mathematics that provides the central theme common to the cosmologies

---

2   The notion of flux is, of course, only one ingredient in the description of the Unlimited, but its presence there is unmistakable: see 24d2–5.

of *Philebus* and *Timaeus*. This is the notion that the realm of becoming is structured and made knowable by principles that are mathematical in form: numerical ratios and geometric figures. Hence mathematics is the tool by which the Demiurge produces good results. It is in this sense that Plato appears as a "Pythagorean" in both dialogues.

There would be no point in listing all the topics (including the transcendental Forms) that are treated in the *Timaeus* but are lacking in the cosmological section of the *Philebus*. For the *Timaeus* offers a comprehensive cosmology, while the *Philebus* does not. But the *Philebus* does present one problem that is absent from the *Timaeus*. For the latter dialogue scarcely mentions dialectic, whereas the *Philebus* discusses dialectic twice, in two passages that are not obviously compatible with one another. On the one hand, dialectic as division and collection is presented as the general method of rational inquiry (16c2). Hence the discussion of cosmology is introduced as a direct application of this method (23c–27b). On the other hand, a later passage in the *Philebus* draws a sharp distinction between cosmology and dialectic, on the grounds that dialectic takes as its object eternal, unchanging beings, whereas cosmology is concerned with matters of change and becoming (59a–c; cf. 57e–58a).

Does Plato present two different notions of dialectic in the *Philebus*, one that is purely methodological and applicable to any subject matter, and another kind of dialectic that takes as its object only eternal beings?[3] A comparable question is posed by the terminology of *eidos*, *idea*, and *genos* (form, character, kind), which appears both in the account of dialectic (*idea* 16b1,7; *eidos* 18c2) and in the statement of the cosmology (*eidos* 23c12–e2; *genos* 25a1, 26d1, d2, 27a12; *genna* 25d3; *idea* 25b6). For this is exactly the same terminology used for the doctrine of Forms in the *Parmenides*, and again in the *Sophist*, where such forms are explicitly recognized as the object of dialectic (*Parmenides* 135c2, *Sophist* 253d–e). Do we have here *eidos* and *idea* used to refer to two different notions of form, corresponding to two conceptions of dialectic, only one of which entails the metaphysical commitment to eternal beings exempt from change? How can dialectic, when applied to cosmology, remain a concern with eternal objects?

Here, if Plato is to have a consistent conception of dialectic, we must provide him with a view that is at best implicit in the texts. There must be a sense in which, insofar as dialectic is an exercise of *nous*, its objects are all *noêta*—intelligible through and through. It is, as it were, the function of *nous* to see things *sub specie aeternitatis*. So to this extent its objects are all eternal beings, existing in unchanging logical space, in the *noêtos topos* (intelligible realm) of *Republic* VI. For the *Philebus* (by implication), as for the *Republic*

---

3 This question is posed by Dorothea Frede, and answered in the negative. See *Philebus* (Indianapolis: Hackett, 1993), pp. lx–lxiii.

and the *Timaeus*, it is the inhabitants of this space that are the *ontôs onta*, the true Beings.

On the other hand, many if not all of the objects of dialectic also admit a reference to their changing and perishable homonyms. In this respect, terms like *eidos* and *genos* are ambiguous. Gisela Striker has pointed out that, from the point of view of post-Fregean logic, terms like *genos* operate both as concepts and as classes; as classes they contain perishable individuals as members, but unlike classes, they are not uniquely identified by their extension.[4]

Thus terms like *genos* and *eidos* may be used to refer to the rational form or kind in question, as a definite nature or *ousia*, an eternally unchanging object of cognition. But the term *genos* can also be used to refer distributively to the perishable specimens of this kind. For example, the word *anthrôpos* can designate the form or concept of human nature (Man itself), but it can also apply to its perishable homonyms, individual human beings. It is in this latter sense that cosmology takes as its object things that come to be and perish. In fact, according to the *Timaeus*, the cosmos itself is an individual *zôon*, a living thing that has come into existence and that in principle might perish.

This referential ambiguity in the terminology of dialectic is a suggestion of my own, following Striker. As far as I can see, this interpretation is not directly supported by any text. But something of this sort seems to be required, if Plato is not to have two incompatible notions of dialectic in the *Philebus*.

To conclude. It is only in the *Timaeus* that the theory of Forms as a model for Becoming, and mathematics as a principle of rational structure, are both systematically applied to the world of nature. Thus, in the cosmology of the *Timaeus* Plato has extended his own philosophy to occupy the field of natural phenomena studied by the Presocratics. Thus in the long, uninterrupted speech of Timaeus we have in effect a treatise in the genre of *peri physeôs historia*, an investigation of the nature of things. Plato has incorporated the Presocratic enterprise into his own philosophy in such a way as to offer a successful competitor to the materialistic worldview of the atomists, and this achievement was destined to shape cosmological thinking for more than a millennium.

---

4   Gisela Striker, *Peras und Apeiron*. Hypomnemata 30 (Göttingen: Vandenhoeck & Ruprecht, 1970), pp. 36–37.

5

Maker or Father? The Demiurge from Plutarch to Plotinus

Matthias Vorwerk

In one of the most famous passages of the *Timaeus* Plato writes: "To find the Maker and Father of this All is difficult, and, having found him, to explain him to all is impossible."[1] The context of the quote seems to show that it is the divine craftsman, the Demiurge, who is named Maker and Father of the cosmos.[2] This conclusion is supported by further references in the dialogue, which qualify the divine craftsman as "the Father who engendered" the cosmos[3] and the "Demiurge and Father" of the created gods.[4] However, ancient Platonist interpreters of the *Timaeus* started to wondered what precisely the meaning of the terms "Maker" and "Father" were and how exactly they applied to the Demiurge. Moreover, they tried to understand systematically how the Demiurge is related to the ideas and in particular to the Idea of the Good of the *Republic*. The answers they gave to these questions had an impact on the

---

1 τὸν μὲν οὖν ποιητὴν καὶ πατέρα τοῦδε τοῦ παντὸς εὑρεῖν τε ἔργον καὶ εὑρόντα εἰς πάντας ἀδύνατον λέγειν. Plato, *Timaeus*, 28c3–5. All translations are mine unless stated otherwise.

2 He is the efficient cause by virtue of which the world of generation comes to be (ὑπ᾽ αἰτίου τινός, 28a4, c2; cf. 29a6: ἄριστος τῶν αἰτίων), the Demiurge (ὁ δημιουργός, 28a6, 29a3), the builder (ὁ τεκταινόμενος, 28e6).

3 Ὡς δὲ κινηθὲν αὐτὸ καὶ ζῶν ἐνόησεν τῶν ἀιδίων θεῶν γεγονὸς ἄγαλμα <u>ὁ γεννήσας πατήρ</u>, ἠγάσθη τε καὶ εὐφρανθεὶς ἔτι δὴ μᾶλλον ὅμοιον πρὸς τὸ παράδειγμα ἐπενόησεν ἀπεργάσασθαι, 37c6–d1.

4 λέγει πρὸς αὐτοὺς ὁ τόδε τὸ πᾶν γεννήσας τάδε—"Θεοὶ θεῶν, ὧν ἐγὼ <u>δημιουργὸς πατήρ τε ἔργων</u>, δι᾽ ἐμοῦ γενόμενα ἄλυτα ἐμοῦ γε μὴ ἐθέλοντος," 41a5–8; cf. 42e5–8: καὶ ὁ μὲν δὴ ἅπαντα ταῦτα διατάξας ἔμενεν ἐν τῷ ἑαυτοῦ κατὰ τρόπον ἤθει· μένοντος δὲ νοήσαντες οἱ παῖδες τὴν <u>τοῦ πατρὸς</u> τάξιν ἐπείθοντο αὐτῇ, καὶ λαβόντες ἀθάνατον ἀρχὴν θνητοῦ ζῴου, μιμούμενοι τὸν σφέτερον <u>δημιουργόν</u>.

use they made in their own metaphysical systems of the terms Maker and Father. Notably, Plotinus, the third century AD Neo-Platonist, seems to take issues with the phrase "Maker and Father" since he never even quotes it in the *Enneads*, but rather circumvents it by using the term "Demiurge" alone or in combination with "Maker." In this paper I will give a survey of some Middle-Platonic interpretations of the phrase "Maker and Father" that will shed light on the tradition that Plotinus is part of. Then, a discussion of central Plotinian passages will follow to determine Plotinus' understanding of the ontological position of the Demiurge and, consequently, the reason why he abandoned the traditional predicate "Maker and Father." Finally, possible implications for our reading of the *Timaeus* will be considered.

1. Some Middle Platonic Interpretations[5]

"Why is it that [Plato] addressed the Highest God as Father and Maker of all things?"[6] This is the topic of the second of the *Platonic Questions*, a collection of short essays on interpretive issues in the Platonic dialogues composed by the Middle Platonic writer Plutarch (+ c.a. 120 AD).[7] What puzzles Plutarch is not the fact that Plato calls the Highest God "Father"; every little child with at least a little bit of an education would know that Homer called Zeus "Father of men and gods" (πατὴρ ἀνδρῶν τε θεῶν τε).[8] Nor was it the name "Maker" that troubled him; the idea that the gods made, if not the cosmos, at least the human race was familiar since Hesiod's *Works and Days*: "The golden race of

---

5   For a recent survey of interpretations of the Demiurge from Plutarch to Porphyry see Jan Opsomer, "Demiurges in Early Imperial Platonism," in Rainer Hirsch-Luipold, ed., *Gott und die Götter bei Plutarch: Götterbilder– Gottesbilder –Weltbilder*, Religionsgeschichtliche Versuche und Vorarbeiten, 54 (Berlin and New York: De Gruyter, 2005), pp. 51–99; moreover Marco Zambon, *Porphyre et le moyen-platonisme*, Histoire des doctrines de l'Antiquité classique, 27 (Paris: Vrin, 2002), passim. An ancient review of interpretations is provided by Proclus, *Commentary on Plato's* Timaeus, I, 299, 13–319, 21.

6   Τί δήποτε τὸν ἀνωτάτω θεὸν πατέρα τῶν πάντων καὶ ποιητὴν προσεῖπεν; *Platonic Questions* 2.1 (1000E). I follow the text of Harold Cherniss (edited and translated, *Plutarch's Moralia: In seventeen volumes*. XIII, Part I, 999C–1032F, The Loeb Classical Library, 427 [Cambridge: Harvard University Press, and London: W. Heinemann, 1976], pp. 28–34). For a detailed analysis see Franco Ferrari, "Dio: padre e artefice. La teleologia di Plutarco in *Plat. Quaest.* 2," in Italo Gallo, ed., *Plutarco e la religione: Atti del VI Convegno plutarcheo, Ravello, 29–31 maggio 1995*, Collectanea, 12 (Napoli: D'Auria, 1996), pp. 395–409; moreover John Whittaker, "Plutarch, Platonism and Christianity," in H. J. Blumenthal and R. A. Markus, eds., *Neoplatonism and Early Christian Thought: Essays in Honour of A. H. Armstrong* (London: Variorum, 1981), pp. 50–63, here pp. 51–52; Zambon, *Porphyre*, pp. 91–95; Opsomer, "Demiurges," pp. 90–91.

7   See the introduction in Cherniss, *Plutarch's* Moralia, pp. 2–5.

8   *Iliad* 1.544 and passim; Plutarch alludes to this Homeric epithet himself: ὡς Ὅμηρος ἐπονομάζει, 1000F.

mortal men it was whom first / the immortals made (ποίησαν), the occupants of the Olympic houses" (v. 109–110).[9] What bothered Plutarch was the combination of both terms: "Maker and Father."[10] At a first, superficial reading one could understand the phrase "Maker and Father" as a hendiadys, i.e., as two terms expressing the same content. In that sense both a father and a maker are producers of something distinct from and independent of themselves. The question could be settled here, and that is what John Whittaker in his article "Plutarch, Platonism and Christianity" suggested:

> I doubt whether any modern scholar would regard Plutarch's quandary as a real problem. Today one would be inclined to suppose that Plato is using both terms—both maker and father—in a more or less figurative sense to express the relationship between the creator and the universe.[11]

However, taking a second, more careful glance, a significant difference appears between a father and a maker, between their respective modes of production, as well as between their products. Most notably, a father produces naturally and a natural being, while a maker produces artificially and an artificial being. Moreover, the product of a father is a living being, while the product of a maker is not.[12] Therefore, Plutarch is well justified to struggle with Plato's wording "Maker and Father."

In an attempt to explain Plato's choice of words, Plutarch suggests four possible interpretations:

1. The Highest God is Father of gods and men but Maker of irrational and inanimate beings. (1000E–F)
2. The term "Father" is used metaphorically. (1000F–1001A)

---

9 Χρύσεον μὲν πρώτιστα γένος μερόπων ἀνθρώπων / ἀθάνατοι ποίησαν Ὀλύμπια δώματ᾽ ἔχοντες. On the origins of the idea of divine creation see Willy Theiler, "Demiurgos," in Theodor Klauser, ed., *Reallexikon für Antike und Christentum*, III (Stuttgart: Hirsemann, 1957), cols. 694–711, here 696.

10 Note that Plutarch changes the sequence of the terms. While Plato speaks of "the Maker and Father," Plutarch in his paraphrasis calls the Demiurge "Father" and "Maker." This reversion of word order is not uncommon; for Plutarch see also *Table Talks* 8.1 (718A). John Whittaker (Alcinoos, *Enseignement des doctrines de Platon*, edited with introduction and commentary by John Whittaker, translated by Pierre Louis [Paris: Les Belles Lettres, 1990], p. xix) gives more examples, as early as Philo of Alexandria, and explains (p. xviii) that the reason is probably not a slip of memory but stylistic concerns. As the course of Plutarch's argument will show, he considers "Father" to be the nobler term and, therefore, might have put it first.

11 Whittaker, "Plutarch," p. 51.

12 Plutarch mentions some of these distinctions in 1001A–B.

3. God is both Father and Maker of the cosmos, because a father is a particular kind of maker. (1001A–B)
4. God is Father of the world-soul but Maker of the world-body. (1001B–C)[13]

The second interpretation, which understands Plato's use of the term "Father" metaphorically (1000F–1001A), is similar to the one that John Whittaker in the passage quoted above indicated. Plutarch points out that elsewhere in the dialogues Plato does, in fact, use 'father' metaphorically, e.g., in the *Symposium* where Phaedrus is called the "father of the conversation" (πατὴρ τοῦ λόγου, 177d5) or in the dialogue *Phaedrus* where the same Phaedrus is characterized as "father of beautiful children" (καλλίπαις, 261a2), namely because of his ability to inspire philosophical conversations, which become, as it were, his intellectual children;[14] and more examples could be added.[15] While the figurative sense is obvious in the passages from the *Symposium* and the *Phaedrus*, it is not in the case of the *Timaeus*; for it is, at least, conceivable that God produced the cosmos naturally and could, hence, rightly be called its father, as the third interpretation maintains. Plutarch does not seem to consider the term "Maker" to be metaphorical, as may be inferred from the fact that he does not include it in his discussion.[16]

The first interpretation, which claims that the Highest God is Father of gods and men but Maker of irrational and inanimate beings (1000E–F), is more scrupulous, as it presupposes that Plato chose his words carefully and intentionally when he called the Demiurge "Maker and Father." However, this interpretation approaches the issue not strictly philosophically. It is based on an exegesis of the well known Homeric epithet of Zeus "Father of men and gods" and takes it in an exclusive sense: The Highest God is Father of gods and men only, i.e., not of other beings, such as (a) animals and plants, which are irrational

---

13   It is not clear whether Plutarch is drawing upon existing interpretations as in some of the other *Platonic Questions* or developing from scratch possible alternatives; see Cherniss, *Plutarch's* Moralia, p. 5. Ferrari, "Dio," pp. 400–403 suggests a Stoic background for the third interpretation. This might also be true for the first interpretation if we compare SVF 2.1157; see below n. 19.

14   Cherniss, *Plutarch's* Moralia, p. 31, n. f. refers to the *Commentary on the* Phaedrus by Hermias for a similar interpretation: ἢ αὐτὸν τὸν Φαῖδρον καλὸν παῖδα <ὄντα> ἢ καλοὺς παῖδας τίκτοντα τοὺς λόγους (p. 222, 18–19 Couvreur).

15   See Fridrich Ast, *Lexicon Platonicum sive vocum Platonicarum index* (Leipzig: Weidmann, 1835–1838. Reprint: Darmstadt: Wissenschaftliche Buchgesellschaft, 1956), III, 66.

16   The question whether Plato used a certain word or phrase metaphorically was part of the standard interpretive technique employed by his exegetes according to Diogenes Laertius, *Lives of the Philosophers* 3.65; see also Heinrich Dörrie and Matthias Baltes, *Der Platonismus in der Antike: Grundlagen, System, Entwicklung*, III (Stuttgart-Bad Cannstatt: Frommann-Holzboog, 1993), nr. 97.1 with the commentary pp. 352–355.

living beings (ἄλογα), or (b) earth, water, air, fire, and their composites, which are inanimate beings (ἄψυχα). The gods that the Highest God engenders—he calls them, in accordance with the *Timaeus* (40d4), "engendered gods" (γεννητοὶ θεοί)—are, of course, the gods to whom the Demiurge entrusts the creation of all mortal beings.[17] Thus the following ontological hierarchy emerges:

1. the Highest God (ὁ ἀνωτάτω θεός),
2. engendered gods (γεννητοὶ θεοί),
3. human beings (or rational animals; ἄνθρωποι),
4. irrational beings (beasts and plants; ἄλογα),
5. inanimate beings (ἄψυχα).

According to the second interpretation, the Demiurge, identified with the Highest God, fathers both engendered gods and human beings, but makes irrational beings, i.e., beasts and plants, and inanimate beings. In support of this view Plutarch refers rather cryptically to the Stoic Chrysippus, who claimed that "one would not call the giver of sperm 'father of the placenta,' even though the placenta grows from the sperm."[18] The underlying idea seems to be that while both placenta and embryo originate from the father's sperm, only the embryo deserves to be called the father's offspring but the placenta, the after-birth, not. The reason is, it would seem, that the embryo will develop into a rational being as the father is, since it is of the same kind, while the placenta only serves to feed the embryo as long as it remains in the uterus. Similarly, then, engendered gods and human beings, as well as irrational and inanimate beings originate from the Highest God, but only gods and human beings are of the same kind as the Highest God, namely intelligent beings, while irrational and inanimate beings are not; they exist only for the sake of human beings, as the Stoics would say, to provide them food.[19] Therefore the term "Father" can be applied to the Highest God only with respect to engendered gods and human beings but not with regard to beasts, plants, and the elements. Of these he is Maker, not Father.[20]

---

17 Cf. *Tim.* 40d6–41d3.
18 SVF 2.1158.
19 See SVF 2.1157 (p. 333, 29–31 von Arnim): "Rational beings, which are superior, are similar to children that have been engendered, irrational and inanimate beings, however, to the placenta, which is created together with the child." (καὶ λόγον μὲν ἔχει τὰ λογικά, ἄπερ ἐστὶ προηγούμενα, παίδων γεννωμένων· τὰ δ' ἄλογα καὶ τὰ ἄψυχα χορίου συγκτιζομένου τῷ παιδίῳ). Note the distinction between 'engender' (γεννᾶν) and 'create' (κτίζειν), which corresponds with the distinction between father and maker. That the placenta supplies food to the embryo is stated in SVF 2.754.
20 Proclus, *Commentary on Plato's* Timaeus, I, p. 319, 15–17 reports a similar interpretation: "it is not the case, as some say, that the power productive of inanimate beings is that of a

The third interpretation (1001A–B) explores systematically the distinction between father and maker and the activities of engendering (γέννησις) and making (ποίησις). Making, Plutarch explains, is the more general term, while engendering is a particular form of making, even as coming to be (γένεσις) is a more general term, while being engendered (γέννησις) is a particular form of coming to be. Accordingly, all things engendered have been made in a general sense, but not all things made have been engendered. Hence, every father is, in a general sense, a maker of that which he engendered, but not every maker is a father of that which he made. To give an example: Sophroniscus was not only the father but also, in a general sense, the maker of Socrates, while Socrates was the maker but not the father of statues. Plutarch points out two criteria that distinguish engendering from making:

1.   The product of engendering is alive (ἔμψυχον).
2.   A part of the one who engenders—a principle (ἀρχή) or power (δύναμις)—is mixed into the nature of his off-spring (ἐγκέκραται) and determines it (συνέχει τὴν φύσιν); this nature of the off-spring is, as it were, a fraction and part (ἀπόσπασμα καὶ μόριον) of the father.[21]

In a word, engendering is the making of a living being.[22] As a living being, the product of engendering is connected to its father by a natural bond, namely by the unity of nature, while the product of craftsmanship is not; a house, a lyre, a statue are separated from their makers[23] insofar as they belong to another order of being, namely to the order of artificial being. It is important to note

---

maker, but the power productive of animate beings that of a father (οὐχ οἷον ἔνιοί φασι, τὸ μὲν τῶν ἀψύχων ποιητικόν, τὸ δὲ τῶν ἐμψύχων πατρικόν).” The difference between both interpretations is that the one reported by Proclus ascribes the term “Father” to the Demiurge with respect to all living beings, including beasts and plants, while Plutarch restricts it to the engendering of intelligent beings only, namely engendered gods and human beings. Surprisingly, this difference has been overlooked by Cherniss, *Plutarch's* Moralia, p. 31 n. b; Ferrari, “Dio,” p. 398; Zambon, *Porphyre*, p. 91–92; implicitly also by Opsomer, “Demiurges,” p. 90.

21   According to Proclus, *Commentary on Plato's* Timaeus, I, p. 300, 1–6, Porphyry introduced another distinction: a father produces entirely from himself (ἀφ᾽ ἑαυτοῦ γεννῶν τὸ ὅλον), while a maker receives the matter from someone else (παρ᾽ ἄλλου τὴν ὕλην λαμβάνων) (= fr. 40 Sodano [*Porphyrii in Platonis Timaeum commentariorum fragmenta*, edited by Angelo Raffaele Sodano (Naples: [s.n.], 1964)]); see Zambon, *Porphyre*, pp. 93–94. Plutarch could not make such a distinction, since he considers the soul to be the preexisting matter which the Demiurge brings into a rational and harmonious order; see 2.1 (1001C). The same holds if the third interpretation presented by Plutarch is of Stoic origin, as Ferrari, “Dio,” pp. 400–403 argues.

22   ἐμψύχου γὰρ ποίησις ἡ γέννησίς ἐστι.

23   ποιητοῦ . . . ἀπήλλακται γενόμενον τὸ ἔργον.

that Plutarch does not distinguish between engendering and making as opposite forms of coming to be, but subsumes engendering under the category of making as a specific form of it; that is, he does not limit the term making to artificial production. This conception is crucial to his explanation of Plato's Demiurge as "Maker and Father."

The cosmos, Plutarch continues, is not comparable to a created or crafted product of making, but contains life and divinity, i.e., it is a rational living being.[24] If the cosmos is a living being and shares in the divine nature, then its mode of production is comparable to that of other living beings, which have also been engendered and share in the nature of those who engendered them, i.e., in the nature of their fathers. Since the cosmos has been engendered by the Highest God, the Highest God consequently is its Father. But Plutarch concludes that the Highest God "is rightly called both Father of the cosmos, which has come to be a living being, and Maker."[25] The conclusion follows from both of Plutarch's preceding considerations taken together: Although the cosmos is not the product of artificial production, since it is a living being, the Highest God can be called not only its Father but also its Maker, because a father is also a kind of maker, namely a natural maker, and engendering is also a form of making, namely natural making. However, if a father is a kind of maker and engendering a form of making, then the Highest God is both Father and Maker of the cosmos.

In a fourth and final interpretation (2.2 [1001B–C]),[26] Plutarch specifies more precisely what it is that the Highest God engenders. It is not the world-body that God engenders. Following a literal understanding of the *Timaeus*,[27] Plutarch presupposes that matter exists coeternally with God as mere indefiniteness and indeterminacy; it is then shaped and ordered by God with proper limits and forms (πέρασιν οἰκείοις καὶ σχήμασι) in the manner of a craftsman imposing form on matter. The world-soul, however, is God's work by virtue of its intellectuality, rationality, and harmony (νοῦ μετασχοῦσα καὶ λογισμοῦ καὶ ἁρμονίας). These God mixes into the nature of the soul, which, like matter, preexists in an unordered state before the creation of the cosmos. By virtue of

---

24 Inferring from the *Timaeus*, one might say that its life is manifested in the motions of the planetary spheres, which are caused by the world-soul, while its divinity consists in its singularity, unity, and self-sufficiency, by which it imitates the paradigm; cf. 30c2–31b3, 34a8–b9, 36d8–e5, 37c6–39e2.

25 ὁ θεὸς . . . εἰκότως ἅμα πατήρ τε τοῦ κόσμου, ζῴου γεγονότος, καὶ ποιητὴς ἐπονομάζεται, 1001B.

26 This may be finally Plutarch's own; see Ferrari, "Dio," p. 403; Zambon, *Porphyre*, p. 93, 95. However, as Plutarch himself states, the previous interpretations do agree with Plato's teachings (τούτων δὲ μάλιστα τῆς Πλάτωνος ἁπτομένων δόξης); the fourth is not intended to replace but to complement them (εἰ κἀκεῖνο λεχθήσεται πιθανῶς).

27 For a short account of this interpretation see *Platonic Question* 4.

its participation in the divine nature the world-soul "is not only the work of God but also a part of him," as Plutarch puts it;[28] i.e., it is not separated from its maker as an artifact is. In other words, God is not only the efficient cause of the soul as a craftsman is of his product (οὐδ᾽ ὑπ᾽ αὐτοῦ [sc. μόνον]) and as he is of the world-body, but he is also its formal cause in a substantial sense (ἀπ᾽ αὐτοῦ καὶ ἐξ αὐτοῦ).[29]

Thus Plutarch resolves the problem of the double predication of the Demiurge as Maker and Father, which results from the distinct forms of production that characterize a maker (understood as a craftsman) and a father, in two steps:

1. He shows that both terms are partly homonymous, insofar as a father is a particular kind of maker (understood as a producer in general, not a craftsman).
2. He explains how exactly both terms apply to the Demiurge as creator of the cosmos. The Demiurge is Maker of the cosmos in a general sense; both world-body and world-soul are his product (ἔργον), as he gives order to both. More specifically, he is Maker of the world-body like a craftsman, because he is ontologically separated from his product; but he is Father of the world-soul, because it shares in his nature and is a part of him (ἀπόσπασμα, μόριον, μέρος).

Other Middle Platonists were less meticulous than Plutarch in their interpretation of the phrase "Maker and Father." In the two expositions of Platonic philosophy that survive from the second century AD—the *Didascalicus* by Alcinous (*The Handbook of Platonism*, as John Dillon translates the title)[30] and the *De Platone et eius dogmate* by Apuleius ("Plato and his Philosophy")[31]— neither author distinguishes systematically between the term "Father" and the term "Maker." Like Plutarch, they identify the Demiurge with the Highest

---

28 οὐκ ἔργον ἐστὶ τοῦ θεοῦ μόνον ἀλλὰ καὶ μέρος.

29 See Ferrari, "Dio," pp. 404–408. Heinrich Dörrie ("Präpositionen und Metaphysik," *Museum Helveticum* 26 [1969], 217–228, reprinted in *Platonica minora*, Studia et testimonia antiqua, 8 [Munich: Fink, 1976], pp. 124–136, here p. 222 [p. 129]), interprets ἐξ οὗ as indicating an emanation of the soul. However, this emanation can only refer to the rational nature of the soul, not to the soul as such.

30 Alcinous, *The Handbook of Platonism*, translated with an introduction and commentary by John M. Dillon (Oxford: Clarendon Press, 1993); for the Greek text, with French translation and notes, see Whittaker-Louis, *Alcinoos*. On the Demiurge in Alcinous see Opsomer, "Demiurges," pp. 79–83.

31 *Apulée, Opuscules philosophiques (Du dieu de Socrate, Platon et sa doctrine, Du monde) et Fragments*, edited with translation and commentary by Jean Beaujeu (Paris: Les Belles Lettres, 1973).

God; Alcinous calls him the First God (ὁ πρῶτος θεός),[32] Apuleius the Highest God (*summus deus*, 1.11.204).[33] According to Alcinous, God is Father and Cause of all things (πατὴρ καὶ αἴτιος πάντων, 9.163, 13–14), or, alternatively, Father of all things (πατὴρ πάντων, 16.172, 5–6), Demiurge of all that is (τῶν ὅλων δημιουργός, 172, 7), Maker of the universe (τοῦ παντὸς ποιητής, 15.171, 21). Alcinous explains God's fatherhood by the fact that he is "the cause of all things and orders the heavenly intellect and the world-soul according to himself and his thoughts."[34] In fact, Alcinous describes the ordering of the world-soul in terms similar to Plutarch: God does not create the world-soul; he makes it in the sense that he awakens and turns its intellectual power toward himself, thus enabling it to receive from him the ideas, according to which it in turn orders the cosmos.[35] As in Plutarch, the world-soul is preexisting and receives its divine nature from God, who actualizes its intellectual power. However, while Plutarch carefully distinguishes between God as Father of the world-soul and Maker of the world-body, Alcinous does not; there is not a single instance where he uses the terms "Maker" and "Father" together.

Apuleius, on the other hand, is more faithful to Plato's text when in a paraphrasis he renders "Maker and Father" as "Producer and Builder of all things" (*genitor rerumque omnium exstructor*, 1.5.190) and later in the text as "Father and Architect of this divine orb" (*pater et architectus huius divini orbis*, 1.11.204).[36] However, just in continuation of the earlier passage (1.5.190) Apuleius concludes with a Greek quote: θεὸν εὑρεῖν τε ἔργον, "it is difficult to find God" (191). Apuleius substitutes the term "God" for Plato's "Maker and Father," because in this context he is speaking of God as a principle in general.

---

32 *Handbook* 10.164, 18–165, 4, especially 164, 22; 27; 31.

33 *Deorum trinas nuncupat species, quarum est prima unus et solus summus ille, ultramundanus, incorporeus, quem patrem et architectum huius divini orbis superius ostendimus*, 1.11.204. At 1.6.193 he calls him also First God (*primus deus*). See B. L. Hijmans Jr. ("Apuleius, Philosophus Platonicus," in Wolfgang Haase and Hildegard Temporini, eds., *Aufstieg und Niedergang der römischen Welt [ANRW]*, II 36.1–2 [Berlin and New York: de Gruyter, 1987], pp. 395–475, here 436–439) on Apuleius' concept of the Highest God.

34 πατὴρ δέ ἐστι τῷ αἴτιος εἶναι πάντων καὶ κοσμεῖν τὸν οὐράνιον νοῦν καὶ τὴν ψυχὴν τοῦ κόσμου πρὸς ἑαυτὸν καὶ πρὸς τὰς ἑαυτοῦ νοήσεις, 10.164, 40–42.

35 καὶ τὴν ψυχὴν δὲ ἀεὶ οὖσαν τοῦ κόσμου οὐχὶ ποιεῖ ὁ θεός, ἀλλὰ κατακοσμεῖ, καὶ ταύτῃ λέγοιτ᾽ ἂν καὶ ποιεῖν, ἐγείρων καὶ ἐπιστρέφων πρὸς αὐτὸν τόν τε νοῦν αὐτῆς καὶ αὐτὴν ὥσπερ ἐκ κάρου τινὸς βαθέος ἢ ὕπνου, ὅπως ἀποβλέπουσα πρὸς τὰ νοητὰ αὐτοῦ δέχηται τὰ εἴδη καὶ τὰς μορφάς, ἐφιεμένη τῶν ἐκείνου νοημάτων, 14.169, 35–41; cf. 10.164, 42–165, 4. Contrary to Plutarch, who interpreted the *Timaeus* literally and, hence, assumed a creation of the cosmos in time, Alcinous teaches a continuous creation; see 14.169, 32–35; on the whole passage Dillon, *Alcinous*, 123–126; Opsomer, "Demiurges," pp. 81–82.

36 Apuleius, *On Plato*. Cf. also *On the God of Socrates* 3.124: "the Father, who is the Ruler and Creator of all things (*parentem, qui omnium rerum dominator atque auctor est)*." Here Apuleius emphasizes the authority that according to Roman law belongs to a father.

However, the substitution indicates that Apuleius did not attribute any particular significance to Plato's wording, so as to refrain from changing it.[37] Like Alcinous, Apuleius understands the terms Maker and Father as synonyms for God. It is only in another work of his, the *Apologia*, that he more carefully distinguishes between Father and Maker. God, he says there, is "the cause, principle and first origin of all that is," but while he is "the Highest Producer of the soul," he is "the Maker of his cosmos;" he is a "Maker without laboring" and a "Producer without procreating."[38] The distinction presented by Apuleius corresponds with the one we found in Plutarch: God is Father of the world-soul, whose rational nature he engenders *(animi genitor)*,[39] and maker of the world-body *(mundi opifex)*. However, Apuleius emphasizes explicitly the analogous sense of the predication: God is neither a biological Father, who procreates physically *(sine propagatione genitor)*, nor an anthropomorphic craftsman, who sweats while working on his project *(sine opera opifex)*.[40] Interestingly, the relation of the terms Father and Maker seems to be different than in Plutarch: while Plutarch understands engendering as a specific form of making, Apuleius implies with his statement that God is "the cause, principle, and first origin of all of nature" that both engendering and making fall under the general category of causation, without the one being subordinate to the other. A father is a reproductive, a maker a creative cause.

With Numenius, a Platonist also of the second century AD, whose works are transmitted only in fragments, we find the first Platonist philosopher to separate the terms "Maker" and "Father" and to assign them to different principles.[41] In his work *On the Good* he writes that "Plato was aware that only

---

37 Alcinous has a similar contextual substitution. He paraphrases *Tim.* 28c3–5 in his exposition of Platonic ethics 27.179, 35–37: "[Plato] believed that it is neither easy to find the worthiest and greatest good (τὸ μὲν δὴ τιμιώτατον καὶ μέγιστον ἀγαθὸν) nor safe, having found it, to present it to all." See Beaujeu, *Apulée*, p. 257 n. 1.

38 *totius rerum naturae causa et ratio et origo initialis, summus animi genitor, aeternus animantum sospitator, assiduus mundi sui opifex, sed enim sine opera opifex, sine cura sospitator, sine propagatione genitor, Apologia* 64, pp. 72, 20–73, 3 Helm.

39 Apuleius uses *animus* and *anima* almost indiscriminately; see Hijmans, "Apuleius," pp. 455–56.

40 Neither Plutarch nor Alcinous understood Plato's terminology univocally. Apuleius is anticipating typical Epicurean ridicule of creationism; see Matthias Baltes, "Zur Nachwirkung des Satzes Τὸ μακάριον καὶ ἄφθαρτον οὔτε αὐτὸ πράγματα ἔχει," in Michael Erler and Robert Bees, eds., *Epikureismus in der späten Republik und der Kaiserzeit: Akten der 2. Tagung der Karl-und-Gertrud-Abel-Stiftung vom 30 September 3, Oktober 1999 in Würzburg*, Philosophie der Antike, 11 (Stuttgart: Steiner, 2000), pp. 93–108; Opsomer, "Demiurges," pp. 56–63.

41 Numénius, *Fragments*, edited and translated with notes by Édouard des Places (Paris: Les Belles Lettres, 1973). On his theology and the role of the Demiurge see E. R. Dodds, "Numenius and Ammonius," in *Les sources de Plotin: Entretiens sur l'antiquité classique, 5, Vandoeuvres-Genève, 21–29 août 1957* (Geneva: Fondation Hardt, 1960), pp. 3–32, here pp. 12–16; des Places, *Numenius*, pp. 10–14; Matthias Baltes, "Numenios von Apamea und

the Demiurge was known to men, but that the First Intellect, who is called Being Itself, is entirely unknown to them."[42] In relation to the Demiurge, the unknown First Intellect is "superior in dignity and divinity."[43] In this passage Numenius obviously connects the *Timaeus* with *Republic* VI, where the Idea of the Good is presented as the cause of the existence and being of the ideas (509b6–10)—and, by extension, of all that comes to be in accordance with them—while it itself transcends Being by virtue of its dignity and power (509b9–10). Hence, he calls the Idea of the Good "Being Itself," the Idea of Being, as it were. The account of the *Timaeus* is obviously different: there the Demiurge is the cause of the cosmos, which he creates as an image of the Paradigm, identified with the ideas (28c5–29b2; 30c2–31a1; 39e7–9). Middle Platonists like Alcinous had resolved the problem of the ontological relationship between the Paradigm and the Demiurge, which in the *Timaeus* are presented as separate entities, by locating the Paradigm within the Demiurge, i.e., in his intellect as his thoughts. Aristotle's notion of a First God who thinks his own thinking served them as a model.[44] Hence, two of the three principles of creation in the *Timaeus*—Demiurge, Paradigm, Matter—were reduced to one, as these Middle-Platonists made the Paradigm, the totality of the ideas, the content of the Demiurge's intellect. Moreover, they assumed that the Idea of the Good of *Republic* VI was identical with the Demiurge, since in the *Timaeus* the Demiurge is described as good (ἀγαθὸς ἦν) and his goodness accounts for his desire to create the universe (Tim. 28d7–30a2). Numenius, however, objected

---

der platonische Timaios," *Vigiliae Christianae* 29 (1975), pp. 241–270 (reprinted in Annette Hüffmeier, Marie-Luise Lakmann, and Matthias Vorwerk, eds., ΔΙΑΝΟΗΜΑΤΑ: *Kleine Schriften zu Platon und zum Platonismus*, Beiträge zur Altertumskunde, 123 [Stuttart and Leipzig: Teubner, 1999], pp. 1–32], here pp. 257–267 (pp. 19–29); John Dillon, *The Middle Platonists: A Study of Platonism 80 BC to AD 220* (London: Duckworth, 1977; revised edition with a new afterword, 1996), pp. 366–372; Michael Frede, "Numenius," in *ANRW* II 36.2, pp. 1034–1075, here 1054–1070; Zambon, *Porphyre*, pp. 221–239; Opsomer, "Demiurges," pp. 66–73.

42 ᾔδει ὁ Πλάτων παρὰ τοῖς ἀνθρώποις τὸν μὲν δημιουργὸν γιγνωσκόμενον μόνον, τὸν μέντοι πρῶτον νοῦν, ὅστις καλεῖται αὐτοόν, παντάπασιν ἀγνοούμενον παρ' αὐτοῖς, fr. 17, 1–5.

43 ἕτερος πρὸ τούτου νοῦς πρεσβύτερος καὶ θειότερος, fr. 17, 7–8.

44 See Alcinous, *Handbook*, 9.163, 14–15: "The idea is in relation to God his thinking (νόησις αὐτοῦ)," with 163, 32–34; 10.164, 27–31. Apuleius, *On Plato*, 1.5.190; 1.6.192–193 discusses the ideas only briefly, without specifying their exact relation to God; the same is the case with Plutarch, see Franco Ferrari, "Der Gott Plutarchs und der Gott Platons," in Rainer Hirsch-Luipold, ed., *Gott und die Götter bei Plutarch: Götterbilder–Gottesbilder–Weltbilder*, Religionsgeschichtliche Versuche und Vorarbeiten, 54 (Berlin and New York: De Gruyter, 2005), pp. 13–25, here 20–23. For a brief account of these Middle-Platonic interpretations see Opsomer, "Demiurges," pp. 51–56, with further references; Heinrich Dörrie and Matthias Baltes, *Der Platonismus in der Antike: Grundlagen, System, Entwicklung*, V (Stuttgart-Bad Cannstatt: Frommann-Holzboog, 1999), nr. 128 with the commentary pp. 262–277.

to both the identification of the Idea of the Good with the Demiurge and of the Demiurge with the Paradigm. He argues that to be good is not the same as to be the Good and that, if the Demiurge is good, he is so only by participation in the Good, which thereby becomes "the idea of the Demiurge."[45] While Numenius distinguishes between Idea of the Good and Demiurge, he identifies Idea of the Good and Paradigm.[46] Continuing as Alcinous did to assimilate the first principle to Aristotle's self-thinking intellect, Numenius conceives of the Idea of the Good as the First Intellect;[47] its very goodness depends on its wisdom.[48] Accordingly, the First Intellect is superior in dignity (πρεσβύτερον) to the objects of its thinking even as the Idea of the Good is superior to the other ideas, since Intellect is the cause (αἴτιον) of its objects and the Idea of the Good the cause of all other ideas.[49] The causal relationship between the first principle and the ideas does, however, not result in an ontological separation, as it will later in Plotinus. The first principle does not transcend Being in the sense that it is not a being itself; it is rather the highest form of Being, from which all other beings are derived, the principle of Being that is naturally connected with Being.[50] It rides, as it were, on top of it.[51]

As a consequence of his diverging interpretation of principles in the *Republic* and the *Timaeus*, Numenius had to reconsider the scope of demiurgic activity. If the Demiurge of the *Timaeus* is only a secondary principle dependent on the first, then his activity is derivative and requires explanation. It is in this context that Numenius draws upon the phrase "Maker and Father." According to the testimony of Proclus, he identifies in the *Timaeus* three Gods "and calls the First Father, the Second Maker, and the Third the Work—for the cosmos is according to him the Third God—to the effect that his Demiurge becomes two, the First God and the Second, while the created work is the Third."[52] The

---

45 ὡς δὴ τοῦ δημιουργοῦ ἰδέαν οὖσαν τὸ ἀγαθόν, ὅστις πέφανται ἡμῖν ἀγαθὸς μετουσίᾳ τοῦ πρώτου τε καὶ μόνου, fr. 20.

46 Fr. 22.

47 <ἀγαθοῦ> ἰδέα ἂν εἴη ὁ πρῶτος νοῦς, ὢν αὐτοάγαθον, fr. 20, 11–12; cf. fr. 17.

48 Καὶ μὲν δὴ τὸ φρονεῖν, τοῦτο δὴ συντετύχηκε μόνῳ τῷ πρώτῳ, fr. 19, 4–5.

49 Εἰ δ' ἔστι μὲν νοητὸν ἡ οὐσία καὶ ἡ ἰδέα, ταύτης δ' ὡμολογήθη πρεσβύτερον καὶ αἴτιον εἶναι ὁ νοῦς, αὐτὸς οὗτος μόνος εὕρηται ὢν τὸ ἀγαθόν, fr. 16, 1–3. It is not entirely clear how exactly Numenius conceived of the First God as intellect, since he seems to attribute thinking proper to the Second God; see fr. 22 (below n. 57) with Dodds, "Numenius," pp. 14–15; Frede, "Numenius," pp. 1062–1063; Zambon, "Porphyre," pp. 229–230. For a detailed interpretation of fr. 16 see Dörrie-Baltes, *Platonismus*, V, pp. 265–269.

50 τὸ ἀγαθὸν οὐσίας εἶναι ἀρχή, fr. 16, 5; αὐτοάγαθον, σύμφυτον τῇ οὐσίᾳ, 9–10; ἡ δ' οὐσία μία μὲν ἡ τοῦ πρώτου, ἑτέρα δ' ἡ τοῦ δευτέρου, ἧς μίμημα ὁ καλὸς κόσμος, 15–17.

51 ἐποχούμενον ἐπὶ τῇ οὐσίᾳ, fr. 2, 16.

52 Νουμήνιος μὲν γὰρ τρεῖς ἀνυμνήσας θεοὺς πατέρα μὲν καλεῖ τὸν πρῶτον, ποιητὴν δὲ τὸν δεύτερον, ποίημα δὲ τὸν τρίτον· ὁ γὰρ κόσμος κατ' αὐτὸν ὁ τρίτος ἐστὶ

First God, however, is not the Demiurge of the cosmos, but "the Demiurge of Being" (ὁ τῆς οὐσίας δημιουργός), while the Second God is "the Demiurge of Generation" (ὁ δημιουργὸς ὁ τῆς γενέσεως). As the Second God imitates the First, so is the world of generation an imitation of the world of being.[53] Thus Numenius implies that the Second God imitates the creative power of the First, to the effect that he produces the cosmos as an image of the ideas, which themselves had been produced by the First God. It is by virtue of their creative power that both the First and the Second God are Demiurges, one the Demiurge of the intelligible cosmos, as it were, the other of the sense-perceptible cosmos.[54] However, since the products of the First and Second God differ, their modes of demiurgic activity do also: "The First God does not need to create; the First God ought rather be regarded as the Father of the creating God (i.e., the Demiurge);" he is not engaged in any work like a king, while the Second God traverses the cosmos to govern it.[55] The main distinction Numenius seems to be intending is that the First God remains with himself on his ontological level, while the Demiurge descends to a lower level, namely that of matter. Thus the First God preserves his indivisible unity, while the Second does not: in ordering matter and creating the cosmos he is divided and becomes two— the higher part remaining with the intelligible, the lower descending into the cosmos, presumably as world-soul, hence constituting the Third God.[56] When Numenius says that the First God "thinks with the help of the Second" and

---

θεός· ὥστε ὁ κατ᾽ αὐτὸν δημιουργὸς διττός, ὅ τε πρῶτος θεὸς καὶ ὁ δεύτερος, τὸ δὲ δημιουργούμενον ὁ τρίτος, Proclus, *Commentary on Plato's* Timaeus, I, p. 303, 27–304, 3 = fr. 21, 1–5. Dillon, *Middle Platonists*, p. 367 believes Proclus is misunderstanding Numenius regarding the distinction of Demiurges, in spite of fr. 16; see below. Another—more dramatic, as Proclus remarks—series of predicates he used was "Father, Son, Grand-Son (πάππον, ἔγγονον, ἀπόγονον)," *On Plato's* Timaeus, I, p. 304, 3–5 = fr. 21, 5–7.

53 Fr. 16, 6–8.

54 The term intelligible cosmos (νοητὸς κόσμος) occurs only in fr. 41, 6 where it is not cited directly from Numenius, but it was common since Philo of Alexandria; see Matthias Vorwerk (edited, translated and commentary), *Plotins Schrift "Über den Geist, die Ideen und das Seiende", Enneade* V 9 (5), Beiträge zur Altertumskunde, 145 (Munich and Leipzig: Saur, 2001), pp. 133–134; David Runia, "A Brief History of the Term *kosmos noetos* from Plato to Plotinus," in John J. Cleary, ed., *Traditions of Platonism: Essays in Honour of John Dillon* (Aldershot: Ashgate, 1999), pp. 151–172.

55 Fr. 12, 1–3; 12–14.

56 Fr. 11, 11–15; cf. fr. 15; 22. According to fr. 52, 64–75 there are two world-souls, a beneficial and an evil one (*unam beneficentissimam, malignam alteram*, 66), the latter being identical with matter; the former would be world-soul proper, which derives from the Second God (*rationabilis animae pars auctore utitur ratione ac deo*, 73–74). As Plutarch, Numenius seems to have accepted a creation of the cosmos in time; cf. fr. 52, 2–14. On the Third God as world-soul see Dodds, "Numenius," p. 14; Dillon, *Middle Platonists*, pp. 374–375; Frede, "Numenius," pp. 1055–1057, especially 1067; Zambon, *Porphyre*, pp. 230–231; Opsomer, "Demiurges," p. 73, with further references.

that the Second "creates with the help of the Third," he does not imply an ontological descent in the case of the First God, as the First remains on the level of Being when thinking with the help of the Second, but he does in the case of the Second, as the Second descends from the realm of Being into the realm of Generation when creating with the help of the Third.[57] In fact, the Second God is according to Numenius a double creator: not only does he create the cosmos, he also creates, in a sense, himself, namely his own idea or being, by imitating the First God (fr. 16). This conception of the Second God as double creator provides a key to understand the distribution of the terms Father and Maker to two different principles. The First God is the Father and not the Maker of the Second God, because apart from generating him he is not involved in his formation. Rather, the Second God constitutes himself, once generated, by imitating the Father or, in other words, developing by himself into the image of his Father, just like a son develops naturally into the image of his biological father. Moreover, there is a community of nature between the First and the Second God, who both are intelligible beings, even as there is a natural connection between a biological father and his biological son. The relationship between Second and Third God, on the other hand, differs significantly. The Second God is involved with the Third God, as he orders the cosmos. The Third God does not constitute himself as the Second does, but is ordered by the Second, very much like an artifact is formed by a craftsman. Finally, the First God is, like a father, completely autonomous in producing his offspring, i.e., he does not need to look for a model to produce. The Second God, however, does look at the First, namely at the ideas, to order the cosmos, again like a craftsman.[58] Hence the Second God is more appropriately called "Maker."

Numenius advanced beyond other Middle Platonists by introducing a Second God who mediates between a transcendent First God and the cosmos. Due to the recognition of another principle he was led to assume that the phrase "Maker and Father" in the *Timaeus* did not refer to the Demiurge as a single being, as Plutarch, Alcinous and Apuleius did, but rather denoted two different Demiurges:

---

57 Νουμήνιος δὲ τὸν μὲν πρῶτον κατὰ τὸ "ὅ ἐστι ζῷον" τάττει καί φησιν ἐν προσχρήσει τοῦ δευτέρου νοεῖν, τὸν δὲ δεύτερον κατὰ τὸν νοῦν καὶ τοῦτον αὖ ἐν προσχρήσει τοῦ τρίτου δημιουργεῖν, τὸν δὲ τρίτον κατὰ τὸν διανοού μενον, fr. 22.

58 Cf. fr. 18, where the Second God is compared to a steersman, who looks to the stars to direct the course of the ship; similarly does the Second God look toward the First, so as to order the cosmos according to the ideas. Note that in this fragment the relation between steersman and ship, i.e., between Second God and cosmos, is described in similar terms as that between First God and Being: the steersman "sits high on a bench" (ὑψίζυγος . . . ἐφεζόμενος, fr. 18, 2–3) upon the ship, while the First God "rides upon Being" (ἐποχούμενον ἐπὶ τῇ οὐσίᾳ, fr. 2, 16). See Baltes, "Numenios," p. 257 (18) n. 66.

1. The First God, identified with the Idea of the Good and the Paradigm, is the Demiurge of Being. He is the "Father" because of his transcendence over the cosmos.
2. The Second God, identified with the Demiurge of the *Timaeus*, is the Demiurge of Generation. He is the "Maker" because of his direct involvement with the cosmos.

Thus Numenius abandons the interpretation proposed by Plutarch, according to which the Highest God is Father of the world-soul but Maker of the world-body. He still implies a distinction between the mode of production of a father and that of a maker, but this distinction emphasizes more the degrees of involvement with the product. When Numenius states that the Demiurge is well known but the First God unknown (fr. 17), he is not falling into a contradiction with his interpretation of *Timaeus* 28c3–5, but rather assumes that Plato was making a general statement about the metaphysical causes of the cosmos, including both the First and Second God as Father and Maker, after which he then turned to describe the activity of the Maker only.[59] Also the Idea of the Good in *Republic* VI is described as difficult to find (506d8–507a5), which could have inspired Numenius to emphasize that the First God is unknown, especially since the Idea of the Good is called Father too (506e6).[60]

2. Plotinus

Nowhere in the *Enneads* do we find Plotinus quoting the phrase "Maker and Father," in spite of the fact that he addresses the role of the Demiurge several times.[61] In the only obvious reference to *Timaeus* 28c3–4 Plotinus speaks of "the Maker of this All" (ποιητὴν . . . τοῦδε τοῦ παντός, 5.9 [5] 5.20), dropping the term "Father," or of "the true Maker and Demiurge" (ποιητὴν ὄντως καὶ δημιουργόν, 5.9 [5] 3.26), substituting "Demiurge" for "Father."[62] One

---

59   In the following line the Demiurge is named "the Builder (ὁ τεκταινόμενος, 28c6)," i.e.,, a kind of craftsman. Proclus, *Commentary on Plato's* Timaeus, I, 304, 7–8; 13–22 criticizes Numenius both for reversing the order of the terms Maker and Father and for separating them.
60   Differently Baltes, "Numenios," p. 264 (26); Opsomer, "Demiurges," p. 68.
61   On Plotinus' interpretation of the Demiurge see Jean-Michel Charrue, *Plotin, lecteur de Platon* (Paris: Belles lettres, 1978), pp. 123–139; Jan Opsomer, "A Craftsman and His Handmaiden. Demiurgy According to Plotinus," in Thomas Leinkauf and Carlos Steel, eds., *Platons* Timaios *als Grundtext der Kosmologie in Spätantike, Mittelalter und Renaissance* [*Plato's* Timaeus *and the Foundations of Cosmology in Late Antiquity, the Middle Ages and Renaissance*], Ancient and medieval philosophy, 34 (Leuven: Leuven University Press, 2005), pp. 67–102, with further references.
62   *Timaeus* 41a7 the Demiurge in his speech to the created gods calls himself "Demiurge and Father" (Θεοὶ θεῶν, ὧν ἐγὼ δημιουργὸς πατήρ τε ἔργων), a phrase that Plotinus does

might suspect that Plotinus is quoting carelessly,[63] perhaps because he does not attribute any significance to the distinction between Maker and Father, just as Alcinous and, partly, Apuleius had not done. However, as a review of some other Plotinian passages will show, the omission of "Father" in the quote is intentional. With Numenius[64] and contrary to Plutarch and his other Middle-Platonic predecessors, Plotinus does not identify the Demiurge with the Highest God, a self-thinking intellect who contains the ideas as the objects of his thinking in himself. But he also diverts from Numenius' interpretation of *Republic* VI, namely that the Idea of the Good, Numenius' First God, is an intellect that is, while not coextensive with the ideas, somehow conjoined with them and nevertheless transcendent. Plotinus understands the Idea of the Good as absolutely transcendent, since it is "not a being, but yet beyond being" and, consequently, not an intellect.[65] This reasoning leads to an innovation in the hierarchy of divine beings, as Plotinus distinguishes three metaphysical principles, the hypostases of the One or the Good, Intellect, and Soul, which he claims to have been implied by Plato himself (5.1 [10] 8.1–14; see below).

Plotinus cannot accept that the Demiurge, or any intellect, is the first principle because of the multiplicity that the ideas introduce into the intellect. The issue is not only the multiplicity of the ideas, each of which is distinct from the other, but also the duality of the ideas and the intellect, who thinks them.[66] The first principle, however, so Plotinus argues for example in *Ennead* 2.9 [33] *Against the Gnostics*, must be absolutely simple, in order to be first; otherwise it would require yet another principle to explain its unity.[67] Therefore, the Demiurge and the Paradigm cannot be the first principle. This leads to another issue Plotinus has with the Middle-Platonic interpretation. A first principle, which is absolutely simple, cannot be a being, because all being allows for a distinction between being and form, or being and being something. Therefore, the first principle can only be the One, insofar as the One, absolutely speaking,

---

not quote either. Also in the myth of the *Statesman* the God is called "Demiurge and Father" (273b1–2).

63 For cases of careless quotations of Plato in the *Enneads* see H.-R. Schwyzer, "Plotinos," in *Paulys Realencyclopädie der Classischen Altertumswissenschaft*, XXI.41, edited by Konrat Ziegler (Stuttgart: Druckenmüller Verlag, 1951), col. 550, 41–55.

64 According to Porphyry's *Life of Plotinus*, Plotinus lectured on Numenius in his classes (14.12) and was even accused of plagiarizing him (17.1–6).

65 οὐκ οὐσίας ὄντος τοῦ ἀγαθοῦ, ἀλλ᾽ ἔτι ἐπέκεινα τῆς οὐσίας, *Rep.* 509b8–9. Plotinus frequently expands the phrase to "beyond intellect and being" (ἐπέκεινα νοῦ καὶ οὐσίας); see 1.6 [1] 9.36–39; 5.1 [10] 8.6–8; 6.8 [39] 16.34; 1.7 [54] 1.19–20, and John Whittaker, "ΕΠΕΚΕΙΝΑ ΝΟΥ ΚΑΙ ΟΥΣΙΑΣ," *Vigiliae Christianae* 23 (1969), 91–104.

66 See 5.6 [24] *On the fact that that which is beyond Being does not think, and on what is the primary and what the secondary thinking principle.*

67 2.9 [33] 1.1–12; cf. 5.4 [7] *How that which is after the First comes from the First, and on the One*, especially 1.5–21.

transcends the duality of being and form—it is not first being and then one, as Plotinus puts it, it is simply One beyond being.[68] If the One and the Good are identical as they both transcend multiplicity and being, then the Idea of the Good can be identified neither with the Demiurge nor with the Paradigm. No other place is left for the Demiurge but the second after the One or the Good beyond being. Thus, the first principle of the Middle Platonists, the Intellect that thinks the ideas, is demoted by Plotinus to the second rank, while a new first principle is introduced: the absolutely simple One beyond being.[69]

That Plotinus is aware of the novelty of his metaphysical system of three hypostases can be inferred from the fact that in *Ennead* 5.1 [10] *On the Three Primary Hypostases* he defends himself against the accusation of being an innovator. "These teachings," he says,

> are not new (μὴ καινούς), and they have not been formulated now but long ago, however not explicitly (μὴ ἀναπεπταμένους); my present teachings are merely interpretations of those earlier ones and they prove that these doctrines are old with the help of references to the writings of Plato himself (μαρτυρίοις . . . τοῖς αὐτοῦ τοῦ Πλάτωνος γράμμασιν, 5.1.[10] 8.10–14).

The references to Plato, which Plotinus presents in support of his metaphysics, are taken from two pseudo-Platonic letters, from the *Timaeus*, the *Republic* (8.1–10), and the *Parmenides* (8.23–26). Plotinus starts with *Letter* 2.312e (8.1–4). In this passage Plato, or whoever the author was, talking about "the nature of the first principle" (περὶ τῆς τοῦ πρώτου φύσεως, 312d7) states that "all things exist around the King of all things and for his sake, and he is the cause of all noble things; the secondary things are around the Second and the tertiary around the Third."[70] Whatever the author of these lines meant to say, Plotinus extracts from them three principles: a First King, a Second and a Third that he then identifies with the One or the Good, Intellect, and Soul respectively. To this end he first distinguishes between the One or the Good and Intellect, referring this time to the 6th Platonic *Letter* (8.4–5), which speaks of "the God and Ruler of all things, of those that are and those that will be, and

---

68 2.9 [33] 1.4–5; cf. 5.4 [7] 1.5–10; 6.9 [9] 5.29–34; Plato, *Parmenides* 139b4–e6 is in the background.

69 There is one passage in Numenius' fragments where the First God seems to be named the One (fr. 19, 12–13: τὸ ἀγαθὸν ὅτι ἐστὶν ἕν). However, since Numenius qualifies the Good as an intellect and as being, it is not equivalent to Plotinus' One. Note also that Plotinus prefers the expression "the Good" instead of "Idea of the Good," obviously because "idea" implies being; see 5.1 [10] 8.8–9 with n. 75 below; Schwyzer, "Plotinos," col. 552, 5–8.

70 περὶ τὸν πάντων βασιλέα πάντ᾽ ἐστὶ καὶ ἐκείνου ἕνεκα πάντα, καὶ ἐκεῖνο αἴτιον ἁπάντων τῶν καλῶν· δεύτερον δὲ πέρι τὰ δεύτερα, καὶ τρίτον πέρι τὰ τρίτα, 312e1–4.

the Father and Lord of the Ruler and Cause."[71] The Cause, Plotinus explains, is Intellect, since Plato identifies Intellect with the Demiurge. In fact, in the *Timaeus* the Demiurge is called both cause—"the best of all causes" (29a6)— and intellect.[72] Plotinus continues that Intellect, i.e., the Demiurge and Cause, "makes the Soul in that mixing-bowl" (8.5–6).[73] Plotinus interprets the Soul that the Demiurge mixes in the bowl as an hypostasis of its own, since from the same bowl both the world-soul and the souls of individual living beings are taken; i.e., the Soul mixed in the bowl but not yet joined to the world-body or individual bodies is undescended and part of the intelligible realm as Intellect and the One are. The world-soul and individual souls, however, have descended into their respective bodies, but they are not cut off from their source, the hypostasis Soul. Accordingly, individual souls are not parts or products of the World-Soul, but, as it were, its minor siblings.[74] Finally Plotinus identifies "the Father of the Cause and Intellect" with the Good (8.6–9). He quotes from *Republic* VI 509b the phrase "beyond being," which describes the transcendence of the Idea of the Good beyond all other ideas, and infers that the Good is also beyond Intellect, because being, intellect, and idea are in some way synonymous.[75] Hence, when Plato says "beyond being," he says implicitly "beyond the ideas" and "beyond Intellect." Thus Plotinus believes to have shown with the help of Platonic references that the metaphysics of three hypostases, which he teaches, is not an innovation or an infidelity toward Plato, but actually an accurate interpretation of Plato's own metaphysics. He concludes that "Plato knew that Intellect derives from the Good and the Soul from Intellect" (8.9–10), and provides as final evidence the distinction in the *Parmenides* between a One, a One-Many, and a One-and-Many, corresponding with One, Intellect, and Soul (8.23–27).[76]

---

71 τὸν τῶν πάντων θεὸν ἡγεμόνα τῶν τε ὄντων καὶ τῶν μελλόντων, τοῦ τε ἡγεμόνος καὶ αἰτίου πατέρα κύριον, 323d2–4. Perhaps Numenius had already used the same passages from the 2nd and 6th *Letters*; see fr. 15, 4–5 and fr. 12, 2–3. 13–14.

72 *Timaeus* 39e7. Also the distinction between "the things made through Intellect" (τὰ διὰ νοῦ δεδημιουργημένα) and "the things coming to be through Necessity" (τὰ δι' ἀνάγκης γιγνόμενα, 47e4–5) points towards an identification of the Demiurge with an intellect.

73 See *Timaeus* 35a1–36b6; the mixing-bowl is mentioned 41d4.

74 Cf. 4.3 [27] 1–8, especially 7.8–12; 4.8 [6] 8.

75 Cf. 5.9 [5] 8.1–7. Plotinus probably has *Sophist* 248e–249d4 in mind; see 6.7 [38] 8.22–32; 39.28–34.

76 Plotinus interprets the first three hypotheses in Plato's *Parmenides* (137c4–142a8; 142b1–155e3;155e4–157b5) ontologically; for the details see Michael Atkinson (translation and commentary), *Plotinus: Ennead V. 1, On the Three Principal Hypostases* (Oxford: Oxford University Press, 1983), pp. 196–198. According to E. R. Dodds' famous article "The *Parmenides* of Plato and the Origin of the Neoplatonic 'One'," *Classical Quarterly* 22 (1928), 129–142, it was primarily the *Parmenides* that inspired Plotinus; but the fact that Plotinus refers to the

The analysis of this short Plotinian text provides an explanation for the fact that throughout the *Enneads* the phrase "Maker and Father" is never used to designate the Demiurge. The term "Father" is reserved for the first hypostasis, the One or the Good, who is not the Demiurge of the *Timaeus*, as it transcends Being and Intellect.[77] It is the second hypostasis, the Intellect, that is the Demiurge; Plotinus even calls him the "true Maker and Demiurge" (5.9 [5] 3.25–26).[78] The reason for the emphatic "true" is twofold: both One and Soul can be makers. In 3.8 [30] 11.33–39 Plotinus draws a comparison between someone who, admiring the beauty of the sense-perceptible cosmos, wonders who its Maker is, and someone who, beholding the beauty of the intelligible cosmos, searches for its Maker (ποιητήν). Obviously, the One is the cause of the intelligible cosmos, but it is only in analogy to the Demiurge of the sense-perceptible cosmos that he is called a Maker, even as Numenius called his First God the Demiurge of Being, without identifying him with the true Demiurge, the Demiurge of Generation. This interpretation is supported by the fact that in the same sentence Plotinus refers to the One as "he who engendered such a child, the Intellect" (ὁ τοιοῦτον παῖδα γεννήσας νοῦν); the notion of the One as Father supersedes that of a Maker. Similarly, Plotinus can refer to the Soul as Maker. The higher part of the Soul does not descend into matter but its lower part does, in order to create the cosmos in accordance with the forms it receives from the higher part. This lower part of the Soul is the "lowest Maker" (ποιητὴς ἔσχατος).[79] However, the Soul is not the master craftsman, so to speak, but only his helper,[80] as it receives the principles for creating from Intellect. Hence, also Soul is not "the true Maker and Demiurge,"

Parmenides only after deriving the three hypostases from other Platonic texts may speak against this assumption.

77 Cf. 5.8 [31] 1.3–4: "his Father, the one beyond Intellect" (τὸν τούτου πατέρα καὶ τὸν ἐπέκεινα νοῦ). Plotinus uses the term Father also for Intellect in relation to soul, e.g., 5.1 [10] 1.1–2; 2.37–38; see Atkinson, *Ennead* V. 1, pp. 1–2, and for further references J. H. Sleeman and Gilbert Pollet, *Lexicon Plotinianum* (Leiden: Brill, and Leuven: Leuven University Press, 1980), cols. 828, 55–829, 29.

78 Plotinus is careful to reject any anthropomorphic connotations of the term; see 5.8 [31] 7.1–28.

79 See 2.3. [52] 18.8–16; Opsomer, "Craftsman," pp. 90–91; 97–98. The same distinction between two levels of Soul that are involved in creation is made in 5.9. [5] 3.24–37, where the role of the Intellect as the "true Maker and Demiurge" is emphasized; see Vorwerk, *Plotins Schrift*, pp. 91–94. Proclus, *Commentary on Plato's* Timaeus, I, 305, 16–20, reports similarly that Plotinus identified the Demiurge both with the transcendent Intellect and with the intellect of the world-soul.

80 Cf. 5.8 [30] 7.15: ψυχῆς διακονησαμένης.

the only Demiurge is Intellect, and, quite appropriately, Plotinus never refers to either the One or the Soul as Demiurge.[81]

In conclusion, Plotinus does not understand the terms Maker and Father as mere synonyms. While he uses Maker for all three hypostases, he reserves Father mostly for the One, thus following the distinction we found already in Plutarch that a Father is a particular kind of Maker.[82] The One, however, is not the "Maker" of the *Timaeus*, i.e., the Demiurge; the true Maker is Intellect. Hence, Plotinus also follows Numenius in distributing the terms "Maker" and "Father" to different principles. Unlike Numenius, who could refer the term "Demiurge" to the First God as the cause of the ideas, Plotinus refrains from predicating the term "Demiurge" of the One, to emphasize, it seems, its absolute transcendence. The One does not need Intellect to think, as Numenius' First God needs the Second; it does not think at all. The *Timaeus*, if we follow Plotinus' interpretation, is then not about the first principle, the First or Highest God, but about the second principle, the Second God. The question the *Timaeus* wants to answer is not "What is the origin of all of reality?," i.e., of all of being. The question rather is "What is the origin of this world, the cosmos?"[83]

3. Conclusion

This short survey of various interpretations of the phrase "Maker and Father" from Plutarch to Plotinus reveals an intensive engagement of Platonist

---

81   Against Denis O'Brien ("Origène et Plotin sur le roi de l'univers," in Marie-Odile Goulet-Cazé, Goulven Madec, and Denis O'Brien, eds., ΣΟΦΙΗΣ ΜΑΙΗΤΟΡΕΣ = *Chercheurs de sagesse: hommage à Jean Pépin*, Collection des Études Augustiniennes, 131 [Paris: Institut d'Etudes Augustiniennes, 1992], pp. 317–342, here 329–331), who argues that the Neo-Platonist Origen rightly criticizes Plotinus for introducing several "Makers." Origen's work is lost, but its title is preserved by Porphyry, *Life of Plotinus*, 3.32: "Only the King is Maker" (Ὅτι μόνος ποιητὴς ὁ βασιλεύς).

82   Hence, Plotinus does not understand the term "Father" as merely explanatory to "Maker," as F. M. Schroeder ("Representation and Reflection in Plotinus," *Dionysius* 4 [1980], 37–59, here 41) suggests.

83   The discussion about the Demiurge of the *Timaeus* continued in the history of Platonism, as is documented by Proclus, *Commentary on Plato's* Timaeus, I, 299, 13–319, 21. See also Theiler, "Demiurgos," cols. 702–704; Werner Deuse, "Der Demiurg bei Porphyrios und Jamblich," in Clemens Zintzen, ed., *Die Philosophie des Neuplatonismus* (Darmstadt: Wissenschaftliche Buchgesellschaft, 1977), pp. 238–278; Jan Opsomer, "Proclus on Procession and Demiurgy in the *Timaeus*: A Neoplatonic Reading of the *Timaeus*," in M. R. Wright, ed., *Reason and Necessity: Essays on Plato's* Timaeus (London: Duckworth, 2000), pp. 113–143; John Dillon, "The Role of the Demiurge in the *Platonic Theology*," in A. Ph. Segonds and C. Steel, eds., *Proclus et la Théologie platonicienne: Actes du Colloque International de Louvain 13–16 mai 1998, en l'honneur de H. D. Saffrey et L. G. Westerink*, Ancient and medieval philosophy, 26 (Leuven: Leuven University Press, and Paris: Les Belles Lettres, 2000), pp. 339–349.

philosophers not only with Plato's philosophy in general but with his very words. Plutarch was the first to inquire about Plato's intention in calling the cause of the cosmos "Maker and Father." He distinguished between making and engendering as different forms of production, but assigned both to the Highest God as Demiurge of the cosmos, namely engendering with regard to the creation of the world-soul and making with regard to the creation of the world-body. This distinction occurs also in Apuleius but not in Alcinous. Apuleius, however, understood making and engendering as two different kinds of coming to be, while Plutarch considered engendering to be a specific kind of making in general; hence, making could mean either production in general or artificial production in particular. It was Numenius, who first divided the phrase "Maker and Father" and applied "Maker" to the Second God, whom he identified with the Demiurge of the *Timaeus*, the Demiurge of Generation, while he applied "Father" to the First God, the Demiurge of Being, who is, as it were, the Demiurge of the *Republic*, the Idea of the Good. Plotinus followed Numenius, insofar as he referred "Father" to the One or the Good, the first hypostasis, but considered only Intellect, the second hypostasis, to be the "Maker" proper; in a general sense, however, he could use the term "Maker" also for the One as well as for the Soul, accepting the classification of production found in Plutarch.

The question one might want to ask is: How does this help us to understand the *Timaeus* better? Do all of these interpretations find some justification in the *Timaeus*? It is obvious that Plato in the *Timaeus* did not apply the terms Father and Maker separately to distinct metaphysical entities, as we saw at the beginning of this paper. Nor did Plato reserve these terms and the related activities of engendering and making to the Demiurge only. He ascribes the same activities to the created gods, as the Demiurge speaks to them: "create and engender living beings" (ἀπεργάζεσθε ζῷα καὶ γεννᾶτε, 42d2). Moreover, in 50d3 Plato calls the Paradigm Father, as it engenders the cosmos in the receptacle, which in turn takes the place of the mother. This passage may have encouraged Middle Platonists to conflate the Demiurge with the Paradigm, as both are called Father, and, in fact, the use of the term Father for both the Demiurge in 28c and the Paradigm in 50d may be a key to reconcile the two parallel accounts of creation in the *Timaeus*, the demiurgic and the biological one.[84] Plato also seems to distinguish, although not systematically, between engendering and making as two different forms of Demiurgic production. Throughout the *Timaeus* the production of the body, whether it be the world-body or the bodies of individual beings, is distinguished from the imparting of soul: First, the world-body is created, then the soul placed into it (34a8–b9);

---

84   See, for example, Thomas K. Johansen, *Plato's Natural Philosophy: A Study of the* Timaeus-Critias (Cambridge: Cambridge University Press, 2004), pp. 80–83.

first the bodies of living beings are created, then souls are placed into them (42e6–43a6). Only that which has soul, however, is the product of engendering, as Plutarch stated. Therefore, the Demiurge is rightly called "the Father who engendered" the cosmos (37c7),[85] since the cosmos as a whole is a living being.[86] But whenever the creation of either body or soul is described, terminology of artificial production prevails, such as making (ποιεῖν), crafting (δημιουργεῖν), composing (συνιστάναι), building (τεκταίνειν), producing (ἀπεργάζεσθαι). Thus, one could say that in the *Timaeus* the Demiurge is Father in relation to the cosmos as a whole, namely as a living being, but Maker in relation to its constituent parts, an interpretation that none of the Platonists suggested but that is inspired by their discussion of Plato's words.*

---

85 Similarly 34b8–9: "he engendered him as a blessed god" (εὐδαίμονα θεὸν αὐτὸν ἐγεννήσατο).

86 See Filip Karfík, *Die Beseelung des Kosmos: Untersuchungen zur Kosmologie, Seelenlehre und Theologie in Platons* Phaidon *und* Timaios, Beiträge zur Altertumskunde, 199 (Munich and Leipzig: Saur, 2004), p. 184.

*I am grateful to the Fondation Hardt pour l'étude de l'Antiquité classique in Vandœvres-Genève for three weeks of peace in August 2008 to finish this paper.

6

Plato on (just about) Everything: Some Observations on the Timaeus *and Other Dialogues*

Thomas M. Robinson

When I first began studying Greek philosophy, the *Timaeus* was a dialogue barely read by Greek philosophy scholars in the Anglo-American orbit. Now that it has become almost fashionable among them to read it, I am delighted to revisit it, knowing that this time around there might be a rather broader readership for some of my own particular heresies on the topic published over the years. Or perhaps I should say 'erstwhile heresies', since a number of these—to my surprise—appear to have secured for themselves over the years some modest degree of acceptance in the scholarly community.

Let us begin with the status of the so-called creation account in the dialogue. Is this account a 'myth' or not? (Plato himself, as is well known, on occasion (e.g., at 29d1) uses the word '*mythos*' to describe it.) And if it *is* a myth, what can be made of its description as *eikôs* (29d1), normally translated 'likely'?

I raise the question again in response to a thoughtfully argued and challenging piece by Miles Burnyeat, in which he suggests that 'myth' is indeed the correct translation of *mythos* here, and that *eikôs* is better translated 'appropriate' or 'reasonable' or 'probable' than 'likely'.[1]

I myself am not convinced that the translation 'myth' is correct in this instance. In so saying, I do not wish to deny that on occasion 'myth' would indeed be an appropriate translation of the word; all will turn on context whether it would or would not be.

As I understand it, a *mythos* is a story, in prose or verse, involving one or more divine or semi-divine beings. How it is viewed by its readership or audience will indicate whether they are likely to take it to be a 'myth' or not; the

---

1 M. F. Burnyeat, "EIKÔS MYTHOS," *Rhizai* II:2 (2005), 143–165.

story as such is a story, or account *(logos)* of an event or events purporting to describe something involving one or more divine/semi-divine beings, and in itself it carries no implications till the evidence of context gives us a further clue to its import.

A good example in our own language is the much-used phrase 'creation story'. To a believer this is a warm phrase accurately describing a genuine cosmic event. To an unbeliever it is a myth, a piece of make-believe. But each is happy to employ the same phrase, the first using the word 'story' to indicate fact, the second to indicate fiction.

The important point here is that we have in English a nicely ambiguous term, 'story', which does double duty very well. And so, I would say, does Greek with the word *mythos*, and Plato exploits its ambiguity here in the *Timaeus* to great effect. His account of the world's formation is a *mythos*, in that it involves one or more divine or semi-divine beings. But the context makes clear that it is not a *mythos* in the sense of '*only* a mythos', in the way that to an unbeliever the creation story is 'only a story' (or 'just a myth'). On the contrary, there is no indication that the story is to be taken in any way other than seriously. I carefully say 'seriously' at this stage rather than 'as a true statement'; we need to 'read on a bit further', as Harold Cherniss used to say, before we can either come to any conclusions as to Plato's intentions in this regard, or possibly even decide that no clear conclusions are reachable.

My reason for underlining the seriousness of Plato's claim (whatever its putative truth-content) is the way he seems content to use the words *mythos* and *logos* interchangeably; his 'story' *(mythos)* of the world's putative formation is also his 'account' *(logos)* (e.g., at 30b7) of the world's putative formation, at a point in time which is the beginning *of* time. And a *logos* of a creation is a rational statement, to be treated seriously even if it turns out, on investigation, to be false; it is not in itself silly or meaningless, as the 'myth' of creation is to many unbelievers.

For these reasons I would myself resist translating *mythos* here as 'myth'; it closes down our options when they should still be wide open. 'Story' is much safer as a translation, and we should continue to adopt it.

What about the supposed 'likelihood' of this story/account? Burnyeat has offered convincing reasons why the word we translate 'likely' in the phrases *eikôs mythos* and *eikôs logos* is on occasion perhaps better translated 'appropriate' or 'reasonable' or 'probable' (e.g., at 55d4). This seems to me a point well worth making. But is such an interpretation applicable in the present context?

I ask the question because Plato himself, almost as though he senses a misleading ambiguity which he does not wish his readership/audience to fall into, takes care to point out the analogy between the sensible world as an *eikôn* (likeness) of the eternal and the account of that world's status as *eikôs* (likely) (29c1–d3). And on the face of it, this is the perfect contextual guidance we need. Appreciating this yet misapprehending it, Cornford acts as though Plato's text had read *monon eikôs*—'merely likely', but this is to downgrade Plato's aim, and it is no surprise, in view of the move he has just made, to find Cornford finishing up with an interpretation that has Plato in effect arguing that his account of the world's formation is *un*-likely![2]

But nothing could be further from Plato's mind. His story/account of the world's formation is 'likely'! (At one point [44c7–d1] he goes on to call it 'particularly likely,' or 'especially likely'). Far being 'merely' likely, it is genuinely likely, in the way the sensible world is a genuine likeness of the eternal.

So again, while appreciating Burnyeat's well-taken point about the occasional use of the word *eikôs* to mean appropriate or reasonable or probable, I want to re-affirm that Plato's own stress, in context, of the parallelism between the noun *eikôn* and the adjective *eikôs* is still our best guide to interpretation of how we are to understand his account of the sense world's putative formation. And the account, it turns out, is a very good example of a *logos* that, stated at its weakest, will be 'no *less* likely than anybody *else's*' (29c7–8) and, stated at its strongest (something he calls '[a goal] to hold on to' [*antechomenois*, 44d1]) will be '*especially* likely' (*malista eikotos*, 44c7–d1).

In this likely account of the world's beginning the Demiurge is a major figure, and his status continues to be controversial, as he continues to be written off as simply a figure of speech for something else, like world soul (see, most recently, Carone), or reason within world soul (Cornford).[3] But these moves, it seems to me, continue to run into major difficulties.

Their *prima facie* strength lies in the fact that Plato does on occasion describe the Demiurge as 'Reason' (e.g., at 48a1–2), and that he further describes world soul as being wholly rational in its activities (36e4–5). The Demiurge, it is further argued, does nothing in Plato's account that cannot be said to be *done* by rational world soul or the reason within world soul, and he is consequently best described as being merely symbolic (Cornford, among many commentators).[4] So, following this argument, we in our turn can legitimately apply Ockham's razor to Plato's argument and affirm that, whatever he said, he *meant* that only one Reason, not two, fashioned (or is in an eternal state of fashioning) the universe and sustains it.

But this interpretation still fails to convince. While the same word, *nous*, is used for reason in world soul and the reason that is/characterizes the Demiurge, their nature as non-contingent in the case of the Demiurge and contingent in the case of world soul forever guarantees their difference in kind, whether or

---

2   F. M. Cornford, *Plato's Cosmology* (London: Routledge and Kegan Paul, 1937), p. 23.
3   Gabriela Roxana Carone, *Plato's Cosmology and its Ethical Dimensions* (Cambridge: Cambridge University Press, 2005), pp. 29–52; Cornford, *Plato's Cosmology*, p. 39.
4   Cornford, *Plato's Cosmology*, p. 37.

not we think that Plato, all appearances to the contrary, really thought of the world of sense perception as eternal (a topic to be discussed later). The same argument would obtain for world soul and the soul of the Demiurge if one were to maintain that he himself had a soul; the contingency of the one and the non-contingency of the other would continue to guarantee their difference in kind, whether world soul was eternal or not.

In saying 'whether world soul was eternal or not' I am of course far from suggesting that the matter is an open question. On the contrary, it seems to me clear that Plato's intention was to argue that both the world as we know it and its soul came into being a point in time which was the beginning *of* time, and I set out the alternate possibility merely *argumenti causa*, to illustrate how it in no way influences the more important point about non-contingency and contingency.

Given the attacks of Aristotle on the notion of a world formed in time that were soon to appear on the scene (*Physics* 251b), it must have been as big a temptation for his pupils then as it has been for many interpreters since to save Plato from himself by taking him to mean the very opposite of what he says, in order to bring him into line with Aristotelian orthodoxy. So, notoriously, it has been claimed by many and continues to be claimed today that, while saying clearly that the world of sense perception was temporal in origin, he actually meant that it was eternal.

But such talk is no favor either to Plato or to rational argument. A 'likely account' is just that, likely, not unlikely; and nothing seems more unlikely than that Plato would have said p ('it is temporal in origin') but actually meant not-p ('it is *not* temporal in origin'). Minor incoherencies in a philosopher's thought one may expect, but hardly an incoherency of so all-embracing a nature.

One way to deal with the matter is to deny that Plato ever said that the world of sense perception ever *did* come into being (the matter *composing* it, of course, is for Plato, as for so many of his predecessors, without temporal origin, but that is a quite different claim), and it is certainly true that, if this could be shown, then at least one obstacle to our reading of the *Timaeus* as an account of an eternal universe would be removed from the scene.

One way to do this is to argue that the famous asseveration '*gegonen*' ('it has come to be', 28b7) is simply a classic use of the perfect tense in Greek to indicate a present meaning. That Greek grammar allows for this possibility cannot be denied. But is it a probability in this particular context? Surely not (*pace* the shade of Proclus, who famously suggested it, and is supported on the point most recently by Carone, op. cit., pp. 32–33 and p. 205 n. 26). A mere paragraph earlier in the argument Timaeus had set out the terms of his discussion with a stark statement of what needed to be investigated, i.e., the question 'whether this world has always existed or took its origin from some starting point' (27c5). And his answer comes very quickly indeed: 'it *has* come into being!'

If there were any doubt about this, it is surely laid to rest by the structure of Plato's complete argument, which follows upon two striking questions:

'What is that which is forever and has no becoming? And what is that which comes to be and never is?' (27d6–28a1)

The natural answer, to any reader of the antecedent *Phaedo* or *Republic*, is 'any Form' and 'any sense object', particularly when the former is characterized in the next sentence as 'unchanging' and the latter as something that 'comes to be and passes away'. Many readers, beginning with Xenocrates in antiquity and running right up to the present,[5] accept the presence of an *aei* in the second question, so that it reads 'What is it that *forever* comes to be and never is', and, taking *genesis* in its other sense of 'process' or 'constant change' rather than 'beginning', have consequently found in the combined questions a reference to two contrasting universes, the eternal and unchanging world of Forms and the eternal but forever changing world of sense objects that is a central feature of the *Republic*. Their understandable conclusion has been that, 'at the top of the show', so to speak, Plato is warning us that he is not to be taken literally; he may go on to talk about the world as supposedly having an origin in time, but astute Platonists will know that what he is really talking about in his dialogue is the unchanging world of Forms and the ever-changing world of sense objects, neither of them having had any beginning in time.[6]

A variant on this is the view, based on a third sense of *aei* as meaning 'invariably' (always a possibility that has to be investigated), which concludes that Plato's two famous questions do indeed deal with *any* Form and *any* sense object (rather than the world of Forms and the world of sense objects), but that what they are really stressing is the invariance of the features characterizing each one. So a form is invariably found to be unchanging and not subject to *genesis* (flux), such that one can say truthfully that it invariably *is*; a sense object, by contrast, is invariably found to be in flux, such that one can say truthfully that it at no time *is*.

As I have argued elsewhere, following Whittaker,[7] the manuscript evidence for the presence of an *aei* in the second sentence is split, and we must look to internal evidence from the nature of the argument itself to try to decide whether it was ever present or not. And this evidence seems to me to clearly

---

5   For details, see T. M. Robinson, *Cosmos as Art Object* (Binghamton University: Global Academic Publications, 2004), pp. 1–2.

6   For a strong and articulate defense of this view, and of the non-literalist approach to the so-called 'creation myth' of the *Timaeus* in general, see Leonardo Tarán, "The Creation Myth in Plato's *Timaeus*," in John P. Anton and George L. Kustas, eds., *Essays in Ancient Greek Philosophy* (Albany: SUNY Press, 1971), pp. 372–407.

7   Robinson, *Cosmos*, p. 1; John Whittaker, "*Timaeus* 27d5 ff.," *Phoenix* 23 (1969), 181–182 and "Textual Comments on *Timaeus* 27c–d," *Phoenix* 27 (1973), 387–388.

favor its absence, once we examine Plato's complete argument, which can be put together as follows from Plato's affirmations at 28b7–c2:

a) A sense object is seeable, touchable, and has bulk.
But the world is seeable, touchable, and has bulk.
Therefore the world, too, is a sense object.

b) All sense objects come to be.
But the world is a sense object (see [a] above).
Therefore the world too has come to be.

c) What comes to be comes to be also does so thanks to the agency of some cause.
But the world has come to be *(gegonen)* [see [b] above].

Therefore it must have done so thanks to the agency of some cause.

Whatever one thinks of the worth of this argument, it seems clear that a supposed introduction to it in terms of the stability of the eternal world of Forms and the instability of the eternal world of sense objects is no introduction at all. It might conceivably have introduced an argument about the eternal world of stable Forms by contrast with a world of *un*stable *matter* that is also without beginning or end, but that is not the point he wishes to argue here (though he clearly believed it, 52d3–4). In the present context he has only one objective: to show that the world, as a sense object like all other sense objects, had a beginning in time and a cause other than itself.

A similar criticism can be made of attempts to read the two opening questions in terms of what invariably *(aei)* characterizes a Form and invariably characterizes a sense object, i.e., stability and instability respectively. What is claimed amounts to a perfectly accurate statement of the nature of Forms and sense objects as propounded in earlier dialogues like the *Phaedo* and *Republic*, and repeated later on in the *Timaeus* itself as a statement of the difference between the world of Forms and the world of basic matter, which as 'traces' *(ichnê,* 53b2) of the real has always existed. But it is totally out of place as a supposed introduction to the argument we have before us, where it is the supposed *eternality* of the world of sense objects that is being denied, not its instability. Whatever the theoretical possibility that *aei* can often mean in Greek something like 'invariably' or 'on every occasion that x is found' or 'throughout the entire period of existence of x', this usage does not seem in this particular context to make the best sense, or at any rate to make the best sense if we are to credit Plato with a coherent argument.

I use the word 'coherent' with care, since it is of course far from clear that the argument, for all its fame (in various guises) across the centuries, is going to work. That it coheres is clear enough: its form is, in Aristotelian terms, that of a first figure Darii syllogism. So its structural validity is unlikely to be cause for debate. But its soundness is another matter. While one might well concede that seeability, touchability, and the possession of bulk are necessary conditions of x's being characterized as a sense object, and even granting, *argumenti causa*, the highly improbable assumption that the universe is 'seeable' *in exactly the same sense* that the table in front of me is seeable (something absolutely necessary if the syllogism is not to collapse at once on the grounds of possessing an ambiguous middle term), the crucial addition to Plato's list to make his conditions *sufficient* as well as necessary is missing, and that is 'the possession of a physical context'. But there is, of course, no physical context for a universe which subsumes all space, and this crucial disanalogy alone ensures the collapse of the argument almost before it has begun.

Yet the argument must, it seems, be allowed to stand as Plato's argument, on grounds of hermeneutical generosity if on no other. It may be unsound, but at least it is valid; the competing versions of the argument, by contrast, are incoherent as well as unsound, in that in each of them the questions purportedly introducing them are irrelevant to the conclusion drawn.

What we are left with, however, is a claim that the world is a sense object in exactly the way the things we see around us are sense objects, with the necessary conclusion that it came into being in time, and at a point in time, it turns out, which is the first point *of* time. This makes Plato's position intriguingly similar, of course, in one important respect to the Big Bang theory, though no inference in favor of its overall soundness can be inferred from this. The Big Bang theory itself remains a theory, however plausible. And it also differs critically from Plato's account in that it does not assert the *prima facie* absurdity that the universe is a physical object in precisely the same way that my table is a physical object.

On the other hand, it is remarkable (and little noticed) that in Plato's account of space as well as time an analogy with the Big Bang theory can also be found. Timaeus talks of how space is in a constant state of moving its own contents and in its turn being moved by them (52e4–53a7). This is the only time that I know of in which a philosopher before the twentieth century has suggested that space, far from being some sort of container for things, or pure extension, or the like, was something that was itself eternally in motion, and that such motion was logically if not temporally the cause of the eternal motion of its own contents. For Anaxagoras, the world started spinning outwards from an initial dense cluster of matter, and is likely to spin still further out (fr. 12, DK), and it is tempting to see this contention as the earliest known analogy with the Big Bang theory. But the view is only really analogous to a well-known *metaphor* that attempts to describe what happened when things first went bang and has continued happening since; it is the best thing we can do, using a three-dimensional model, to describe an event still taking place, and very spectacularly, in four dimensions. Since Anaxagoras' universe consists of something expanding *into* space, rather than of space itself expanding and carrying its own contents with it, and also expanding in three dimensions not four, the supposed analogy with Big Bang theory is less strong than it might have at first glance appeared.

The Platonic view of space might at first sight appear even less close to the Big Bang view than was that of Anaxagoras, not least because there is no suggestion in Plato that the world reached its present state by any sort of expansion process. But the notion that space moves, and can move its own contents, is absolutely radical, and is something where Big Bang theorists will recognize that, in the *Timaeus,* an ancient cosmologist has come interestingly close to sharing a hypothesis they consider critical for their own theory. Add this to the notion, also advocated in the *Timaeus*, that time began with the birth of the universe of sense perception (38b6), and we have strong grounds for believing that his theory is comparable to Big Bang theory in two quite significant respects.

But we must return at this point to the role and status of the Demiurge. On the assumption that he is accurately describable as being for Timaeus either pure (non-contingent) Reason or non-contingent Reason within (similarly non-contingent) World Soul, in either case being radically distinct from World Soul, is there anything in the *Timaeus* to suggest, as Johansen has put forward as a possibility,[8] that Timaeus may have had in mind multiple demiurgic interventions in things, including future interventions, in much the same way modern astrophysicists hypothesize the possibility of multiple (possibly even an infinite series of) Big Bangs consequent upon each Big Crunch?

I myself find nothing in Plato's text to suggest it. Even if the imperfect tenses *egen* (if it is the correct reading; the Oxford text reads the aorist *êgagen*, 30a5), *êhyrisken* (30b1) and *synetektaineto* (30b5) do (though this is my own observation, not Johansen's) have a somewhat conative look to them, suggesting what an effort it was on the Demiurge's part to fashion the world we know, the strongest inference one can draw from this would still only be that the great Potter, after throwing and rejecting several imperfect pots, finally threw one that he was sufficiently satisfied with to keep, i.e., this present one.

But Plato does in fact come round eventually to the notion of multiple demiurgic interventions, in the myth of the *Statesman* (289d–274e), and it is worth pausing to examine what he says there.

In brief terms: in the beginning a good and rational Demiurge sets the spheroid universe spinning. Having reached the limit of its spin, like a spring tightening till it can tighten no more, the universe then reverses itself, and

---

8 Thomas K. Johansen, *Plato's Natural Philosophy* (Cambridge: Cambridge University Press, 2004), pp. 90–91.

spins backward till it reaches its original state of quiescence. At which point the Demiurge intervenes with another push, and the process starts all over again, possibly *ad infinitum*.

The affinities with Big Bang theory here are of course even more startling than those we detected earlier in the case of the *Timaeus*, and we need to look carefully at what has happened to Plato's thinking in the interval to make them so. What he has done is to finally pay attention to the Second Law of Thermodynamics in a way he had failed to do in the earlier dialogue. There, in an action not unsimilar to that of a *deus ex machina* in certain Greek tragedies, and one equally unsatisfying, the Demiurge simply by his own *fiat* determines that the universe, unlike all other spinning objects, will never cease spinning, and will never cease to exist as the universe; it cannot be destroyed, as Timaeus puts it, by anything other than the Demiurge himself (32c2–4), and this is clearly not contemplated as a possibility.

On the reasonable assumption that any new dialogue of the master would have been a subject of avid discussion in the Academy, it seems reasonable to think that one among many questions Plato would have faced upon completion of his *Timaeus* would have been why in that dialogue he had overridden a reality of nature he was fully acquainted with, and that is, that moving systems, including systems in circular motion, tend to run down? If the world really *is* a physical object just like all other physical objects, and is in circular motion, it too will tend to run down, and his cosmology would surely need to be fine-tuned to accommodate this fact.

A further problem that must surely have been voiced by first readers is the impression which the *Timaeus* leaves that the Demiurge, on either interpretation of the story of the world's formation, literal or figurative, and on the basic assumption that we are to take the difference between contingency and non-contingency seriously, seems to be portrayed as being either pure, unensouled intellect, or an intelligent soul that is not the soul of a body, positions which on the face of it fly counter to common sense.

To take these two objections in turn:

The accommodation, as it happens, gets made, and in very startling terms, and it comprises the cosmological part of the myth of the *Statesman*. Now, finally, the universe, like any other object in circular motion, is allowed to do what first readers of the dialogue, though certainly not contemporary proponents of the Big Bang theory, must have found near-incomprehensible, and that is, spin as long as its momentum from the initial demiurgic push allowed it to do so before spinning back to its original state of quiescence, where the whole process was started again with another demiurgic push, and so on possibly *ad infinitum*.

At a stroke, Plato has achieved an extraordinary thing, without the slightest sense, apparently (and understandably), of the possibility of such a thing as quadridimensionality, and that is, the notion that a finite universe will be subject to the Second Law of Thermodynamics while nonetheless never running down. And in so doing he comes the closest to contemporary astrophysical theory ever achieved by any Greek philosopher. Which is not of course to argue that the Big Bang theory is not itself subject to possible future collapse; like any other theory, it could well be discarded in light of further evidence, and its Platonic forerunner would fall with it. But the subtlety, sophistication and imaginativeness of what Plato has come up with in the *Statesman*, and its massive superiority to Aristotelian theory in the matter, must surely finally be acknowledged, whether it finally collapses or whether it goes on to fame as having at least seen something of what was necessary if progress in our understanding of how the world got to be this way was ever to be made.

As far as the second objection is concerned, in the same myth of the *Statesman*, Plato continues to speak of his Demiurge in terms suggesting he is a non-contingent entity but tries to accommodate himself in some measure to the objection by suggesting he is also co-extensive with the world. However, the move draws down upon him the further ridicule of Aristotle, since it seems to attribute size *(megethos)* to the Demiurge (*On the Soul,* 406a30 ff.), and in that sense to make him physical, and thus part of the universe he is supposed to be directing. At which point two possible lines of response lie open to Plato: either to adopt the line that in calling the Demiurge 'Intelligence' *(nous)* in the *Timaeus* he meant it, unequivocally, as '*nous* and nothing but *nous*, unensouled and unembodied', or thought of the Demiurge as himself ensouled. Certainly, Timaeus' comment at *Tim.* 30b3, which has all the appearances of the statement of a principle, makes it look as though he might just have meant it in this way, since the principle is clearly stating that if intelligence 'comes to be present' *(paragenesthai)* in something, what it comes to be present in will be a soul; but there is no mention of any need for the Intelligence that is the Demiurge to 'come to be present' in anything.

Whether he did mean the Demiurge to be taken as pure, unensouled Intelligence has divided commentators from the beginning, the Neo-Platonists for the most part suggesting that he did, most modern interpreters that he did not.[9] And the reason could well be that Plato himself never achieved full clarity in his own mind on the matter. But that is a topic that takes us too far from the *Timaeus* and *Statesman*, to which we must now return.

In the closing pages of the *Timaeus*, Plato mentions how humans were given sexual organs as the very last of their endowments, after a first generation

---

9   The strongest modern defense of the possibility that Plato thought of the supreme principle as unensouled *nous* seems to me that of Richard Mohr in his *God and Forms in Plato* (Las Vegas: Parmenides Publishing, 2005), pp. 189–195.

of life on earth spent without them (90e–91a). It takes little imagination to see his friends and pupils asking him why he did this.

Answers in terms of the goals of the ostensible goals of the *Timaeus* itself can of course be offered, and Cornford's suggestion is a plausible one: "Plato may wish to indicate that sexual passion is not the fundamental form of Eros, but an accidental appanage of our existence in time."[10] But the fact that the topic re-emerges in the myth of the *Statesman* suggests that Plato had given the matter further thought, and that something more wide-ranging in its implications than had appeared to be the case in the *Timaeus* was going on. In the myth Plato suggests that, after the destruction of the human race caused by each end to a cosmic cycle, a new human race came into being from the dead, and that "it was not part of a man's natural endowment in that era to beget children by intercourse" (271a), and it seems a natural inference that he would also, as a committed teleologist, have assumed that they did not yet possess sexual organs either, there being as yet no *telos* (the "begetting of children by intercourse") that would necessitate them.

One can reasonably ask again, What is going on here? In the *Timaeus* the human race came into being at the beginning of time fully formed in all respects but one: they had no sexual organs. Now, in the *Statesman* myth, the generation of humans following on each comic cycle comes into existence, not by demiurgic fashioning but by some sort of natural evolution, and at that time they, too, as purely 'earth-born' creatures, as we have just seen, did not reproduce sexually (271a) and were almost certainly for that reason presumed by him to have had no sexual organs. Plato himself offers no further detail on the matter, but a key to his thoughts might well lie in the possibility that he has begun to think that individual living things might evolve through natural cycles in a way the greatest of all living things, the universe itself, evolves through natural cycles, form at all times following function. How forward-looking such a notion is becomes clear the minute we compare it with the views Philip Henry Gosse put forward at the time of the celebrated 'belly button controversy'.[11]

In the turmoil created by the thinking of Darwin, Gosse took it upon himself to try to answer the question whether Adam had a belly button or not. Either of the two possible answers to the question caused problems. If he did not, then he was not fully human; humans have belly buttons. If he did, then God had built a lie into his very body, since the possession of a belly button was *prima facie* evidence that he came from human parents, and was thus not the first human after all.

Gosse himself opted to say that Adam *had* a belly button, and that this fact (along with the fact of millions of fossils lying in the earth suggesting a

---

10   Cornford, *Plato's Cosmology*, p. 356.
11   Philip Henry Gosse, *Omphalos* (London: Voorst, 1857).

history the universe has never had) is part of God's plan to test our faith. Plato, by contrast, just as committed as Gosse to the view that a god fashioned the world, but happy to accept the cyclical evolution of both the world and the living forms within it, takes the more straightforward view I have suggested above, that humans coming into existence by some force other than human procreation would be unlikely to have themselves possessed organs suggesting the power to procreate; however such organs came to be, they must have come later in the sequence of things.

With the myth of the *Statesman* Plato appears to have surpassed the thinking of the *Timaeus* in a number of ways, and it could well be considered the apogee of his speculation on the cosmos, the role of the divine within it, and, I have argued, the manner in which we ourselves got to be the creatures we are. But his thinking on these matters went considerably further as he grew older, and opinions set out in *Laws* X cannot be passed by in silence.

While the notions of a temporal beginning to the world had by this time vanished from the scene, thanks very possibly to ongoing criticisms by Aristotle, Plato's commitment to the control of the universe by his supreme principle, now described as 'the best soul' (or 'the best type of soul')—i.e., good, rational soul—remains firm, and this is in effect his new definition of godhead. Just how seriously he takes the matter to be is distressingly evident from the first moment, when he offers his 'proofs' of the existence of such a good and rational god or gods (886a–899d), and then has to deal with those who might fail to be convinced. Defining atheism in a broad enough sense to catch the maximum number of delinquents—it means denying either the existence of the gods, or that they care for us, or affirming that they are open to corruption (907b)—he goes on to institute the death penalty for contumacious atheism, defined as failure to abjure such atheism after five years of imprisonment (909a).

But Plato is not finished yet. Having lived long enough, like many another philosopher, to see many of his most deeply held beliefs ridiculed by a new generation—in this case a generation of people, especially young people, who have bought into an atomic theory of matter, and what they take to be its natural corollaries, materialism, relativism, and atheism—he is in a state of deep anger, and now offers us a distinction which will allow him to vent it. Some contumacious atheists, he admits, are, their atheism aside, otherwise good people. These will be put to death too, of course (909a), but that is *all* that will happen to them. The others, who combine their contumacious atheism with an immoral life, will be kept alive in absolutely solitary confinement, to maximize their suffering till the moment when they finally expire. Then, when they die, the state will guarantee their souls will endure torment even in the beyond, by ensuring that their bodies will be cast out beyond the borders of the state unburied (909b–c).

One could spend time speculating why Plato in old age has apparently become a *Creon redivivus*, but my present purpose is to see how his new cosmo-theology relates to the earlier *Timaeus* and *Statesman*. Here it seems clear that the essence of the earlier beliefs has in fact been retained, even though some of the detail has changed. Whether or not we think he ever believed in a Demiurge, and whether or not that Demiurge, if he believed in him, was seen by him simply as pure intellect or as the intellect of world soul, all can agree that in the *Timaeus, Sophist, Statesman,* and *Philebus* he believed in the governance of the world by a rational being which was providential in nature and characterizable as 'divine'. In the *Laws*, this supreme principle seems to be now, finally and unequivocally, said to be a rational *soul*, described as the 'best [type of] soul' or 'the best soul' (897b7, 897c7), and its relationship to the world is, thanks again very possibly to the criticisms of Aristotle, now, finally and unequivocally, stated to be an eternal one. But it is still the relationship of a non-contingent to a contingent entity, and the essence of Plato's view on the divine guidance of things has thereby been retained, even if the notion of the sense world's temporal origin has been abandoned. Whatever his concessions to various criticisms over the years, Plato holds firm to a number of basic commitments to the end, and his final thoughts can be said to be, on matters that really count, more or less consonant with earlier ones.

Which cannot be said of his second thoughts on two other topics, those of sexual relationships and of justice.

To sex, whether hetero- or homosexual, Plato always seems to have reacted with a certain *frisson* of disgust, so it is not wholly surprising to find him treating of both topics in fairly negative terms in his final dialogue. But what he actually says comes as a shock. If the activities of the ensouled universe are now to be the arbiter of conduct, as a famous passage of the *Timaeus* had first suggested (46e–47c) and as is now basically re-affirmed in the *Laws*, (838e–839a), Plato seems to have come round to thinking that homosexual practices in particular might have to be re-assessed. In the *Phaedrus* they had been something at best tolerated, and actively excluded from his vision of the truly good and virtuous life, in which homosexual couples would meet at the level of minds not bodies (256a–b). Though even there he affirms that couples who could not meet this exacting standard and also occasionally met as bodies too would, if they were also virtuous, still win a major reward in heaven (256b–e).

No longer. Using as his new criterion of goodness not just *Natura*, but *Natura qua* productive (838e–839a; cf. 636b–e, 836c) (an affirmation never made, or even hinted at, in any previous dialogue), he now, in the *Laws*, maintains that the only acceptable form of sexual conduct is heterosexual conduct, and that the only form of *that* conduct which is acceptable is one operating without let or obstruction within the confines of a legitimate marriage.

At a stroke the tolerance evinced in earlier dialogues has been overturned, and the refusal to desist from homosexual practices is now characterized as a major crime, to be punished by what many Greeks, to whom life in the *polis* was everything, would have considered a living death—deprivation of all civic rights (*atimia*, 841e).

Here, too, one could spend time speculating about the ways in which many of Plato's friends must have re-acted to this new stance, but, since no reliable evidence is available, we can simply pass on to the second topic, that of justice, and ask what second thoughts he might have had on this too. And here too the evidence of change is strong, and significant.

Whether we are talking of the civic justice described in detail in the *Republic* or the cosmic justice described in the *Timaeus*, the doctrine is the same: justice is a state of balance, within either organism, of reason, spiritedness and gut-desire, each doing what it should be doing and with reason in overall control. For the Plato of the *Laws* there has clearly been a major change of thinking on the matter. The first hint of this comes with our realization that the doctrine of tripartition has now finally broken apart, its *disiecta membra* lying scattered across the dialogue like the bits of a broken Humpty Dumpty. Once this becomes clear, it is less surprising to find a new doctrine of justice too, in terms now of relationships with others rather than of balance within an organism. But the second thoughts are in this case not really new thoughts, but rather a return to the more Socratic thinking of pre-*Republic* days.

Ironically, this relational view of justice is to be found even within the framework of the *Republic* (352c), but as the road *not* followed, however; despite its clear interest to Thrasymachus, and for that matter to Glaucon and Adeimantus, it is passed over in very short order in favor of a state-of-the-organism view that has gone on to become celebrated as 'the Platonic' notion of justice. Which is a pity, since on this point Plato's second thoughts are, it seems to me, a good deal more satisfactory than his earlier ones.

The new view is at base a view of 'justice as fairness' that will be readily recognizable to readers of John Rawls.[12] This is brought to the fore in a remark-able passage (later criticized on certain points by Aristotle, *Politics* 1266b), on the distribution of wealth and property in the 'second best' society that will be governed by the new Laws. It is a society where gross inequities of wealth will be forbidden; there will be no super-rich citizens, and no citizens living in abject poverty. There will be a basic quantum of property, x, which will remain fixed in value and will be the right of all citizens. Any citizen will be allowed to rise to a possession of wealth, goods, etc., up to a maximum of four times that basic value, anything above that maximum being ceded as an automatic

---

12   The classic statement of his views (later modified on various points) is to be found in John Rawls, *A Theory of Justice* (Boston: Harvard University Press, 1971).

datation to the state (744b–d). And by the same token anyone who has achieved more than the one quantum might also *fall back* from that level to that of one quantum again. (An idea that clearly worried Aristotle.)

In this society, as in that of Rawls, any rational agent will be satisfied, if things worked out that way, to live at the level of its least advantaged member, the possessor of the basic one quantum. And justice as fairness will be thus attained, regardless of the putative state of soul of any individual.

The *prima facie* good sense (and, let us say it, fairness) of these final thoughts on justice do a lot, it seems to me, to make up for the horrors of Plato's final thoughts on atheism and homosexuality. But any friend of Plato will still deeply regret that such horrors ever got voiced, and that they appear to be something that he once genuinely—if only for a short period before his demise—believed.

7

Visualizing Platonic Space

Donald Zeyl

I

The "reasonable myth"[1] that constitutes Timaeus' discourse is, as myths typically are, rich in visual elements. We are invited to become spectators of the process of formation of the universe. We see in our mind's eye the divine Craftsman gazing at his eternal model and plying his materials into conformity with that model. We watch him blending mixtures of indivisible and divisible Being, Sameness, and Difference, dividing the mixture into mathematically proportioned portions, and creating the grand soul-circles of the Same and the Different, sending them spinning in their opposing directions along their respective paths. We visualize the fixed stars moving consistently and predictably along the outer circle of the Same, while imagining the divided circle of the Different bearing along the diverse and seemingly unpredictable celestial courses of the planets. We are in the audience as we listen to the Craftsman solemnly charging the lesser gods to complete the work of creation. We try to visualize (not very successfully) what it is like for a beam of fire to emanate from the eye and coalesce with a beam of daylight fire transmitted from the object seen. We visualize the lesser gods encasing the immortal soul within a mortal human body, creating the mortal soul parts to mediate between them. The examples could go on.

---

1 I follow here an interpretation of the phrases *eikôs mythos* and *eikôs logos* proposed by Myles Burnyeat, "EIKÔS MYTHOS," *Rhizai* II:2 (2005), 143–165. The usage of both of these expressions draws attention variously to each of the two aspects of the discourse as narrative or story *(mythos)*, and rational argument inviting critical reflection *(logos)*.

The difficult and obscure passage on the "receptacle" and its role, including the formation of the elemental "bodies" and their interactions (48e2–58c4), invites similar visualization. The passage is rich in illustrations and analogies, and by paying careful attention to these elements as well as to the more discursive and conceptual accounts, we are meant to gain a clearer understanding of how this mysterious "third kind"[2] does its work.

In this essay I offer some proposals that I hope may illuminate what the role of the receptacle is and how we might visualize it as doing its work. My account will be relevant to the much-discussed question as to whether the receptacle serves as a material substratum, the stuff "out of which" spatio-temporal particulars are made up, or as space, the medium "in which" they make their appearances and from which they disappear. I hope to show how the receptacle can and does play both of those roles.[3]

It is initially plausible to expect the receptacle of the *Timaeus* to play both roles. First, we think that spatio-temporal particulars must be made up of *something*. They cannot be mere constellation of properties, mysteriously bundled together and even more mysteriously capable of maintaining that bundling as they move through space. And they cannot be made up of space, if space is sheer emptiness. Moreover, they could not travel *through* space if they were somehow made up of (parts of) space, for spatial parts cannot (logically) travel through space. For these reasons the intuition that construes the receptacle as matter is very strong. And indeed the various analogies used to illustrate the role of the receptacle suggest that the receptacle serves as a material substratum. For what is the *gold* that underlies the various shapes that are molded into it but the material substratum to those shapes (50a4–b5)? And what is the odorless liquid into which various fragrances are introduced but the material substratum to those fragrances (50e4–8) or the malleable stuff upon which a variety of shapes are impressed the material substratum to those shapes (50e8–51a1; cf. *ekmageion*, 50c2)? On the other hand, one seeks in vain in the text of the *Timaeus* for any account of the receptacle in terms of *hyle* or equivalent term used by Aristotle and later thinkers to refer to matter. What we do find, on the other hand, is the unambiguous denomination of the receptacle as *chôra* (52a8, d2), and *chôra* is undoubtedly space. Moreover, we do not find anywhere the suggestion that the receptacle is that "out of which" spatio-temporal particulars are constructed,[4] but plenty of references to it as that "in which" they appear.

---

2   *Triton genos*, 48e4.
3   For a discussion of the various interpretive positions, see Keimpe Algra, *Concepts of Space in Greek Thought* (Leiden: Brill, 1995), chapter 3.
4   To the extent that spatio-temporal particulars are constructed "out of" anything, it is the four regular solids, which in their turn are constructed "out of" the two types of basic triangles, the true ultimate principles *(archai)* of the physical world (48c3).

It seems difficult if not impossible, however, to reconcile the roles of space and material substratum, and this is evident when we ask what it means to be a receptacle part. A spatio-temporal particular is a receptacle part that is temporarily characterized in a certain way.[5] Such particulars are capable of undergoing alteration and locomotion, sometimes but not always simultaneously. If a particular is a spatial part of the receptacle, there is no difficulty in understanding how it can undergo alteration over time, different combinations of characteristics manifesting themselves in the same part of space over time. But there is difficulty in understanding how it can relocate, since (as we have just observed) parts of space do not travel through space.

On the other hand, if a particular is a material receptacle part, there is no difficulty with either its change or its relocation. The same bit of matter takes on and sheds various characteristics over time, and travels from one part of space to another over time. But in that case, contrary to the text, we should think of the receptacle and its parts as being the material contained *in* space, and not *as* space itself. Is there a way of construing the receptacle as simultaneously the spatial matrix for all becoming and the material "filling" of that matrix? And how can visualization help understand what it might "look like" for a spatio-temporal particular to change and/or relocate over time?

II

As Timaeus begins the second division of his discourse to introduce the role of necessity (*anankê*, 47e4–5) in the economy of the formation of the world, he complains that the status of the four "elements" —fire, air, water, and earth—has been universally misunderstood. Contrary to prior and contemporary physical theory, these four are not the ultimate building blocks of the physical world. It will turn out that each consists of units that possess interchangeable parts, and it is these interchangeable parts—the basic triangles—that should be considered the ultimate principles (*archai*, 48c3) of all physical reality.[6] But to get to an account of these units and their parts, some preliminary questions need to be addressed. These questions will require the expansion of the metaphysical duality of changeless paradigms (the Forms) and their ever changing, generated and visible "imitations" or images, to include a third factor. While the Forms are self-subsistent, their images are not: they exist only by subsisting in something else (cf. 52c1–5). This mysterious "something else" is in itself neither

---

5   At 51b4–6 the text speaks of instances of visible fire as ignited "parts" of the receptacle (and so with water, etc.).
6   48b3–e1. Only fire, air and water share interchangeable parts. Earth, which does not, is excluded. See 54b5–d5.

intelligible nor visible. It can be apprehended only by what Timaeus describes as "bastard reasoning."[7]

When we observe our world carefully, we notice that air does not remain air, but changes into water, or fire, and that these changes happen in both directions. The elements, presumed to be enduring, do not in fact endure but change into one another. What is fire at one time undergoes successive changes over time, turning (apparently)[8] into each of the other elements at some time, and possibly back to fire.[9] Since each one of the four fails to endure over time and each turns into every other, none of them has a claim to being referred to by any one of the element names any more than by any other. What we observe as fire and thus refer to as *fire* changes into air, and thereby loses any claim to that name. In fact, there is no stable or reliable language by which to refer to any one of them (49b5). And what goes for the elements goes *a fortiori* for the compounds constituted out of them.

The observation of inter-elemental transformation and the problem of language to which that observation gives rise leads Timaeus to propose a solution. Just what that solution is remains controversial. In broad outline, I take it to be the following:[10]

Given that what we refer to as *fire* fails to endure as fire, we should not suppose that our reference to it is to something that is fire *in its own right* (*kath' hauto*, in Aristotle's terminology). None of the names of the elements (and their compounds) should be construed as functioning as a label that assigns some permanent identity to its referent throughout the course of its various changes. To refer to something in a manner that presumes to fix its permanent identity through change is to designate it as a "this," but nothing we observe in this fluid world of ours qualifies as a "this." The fleeting things under our observation should instead be designated as items that are "such," i.e., as temporarily having this or that quality, for a "such" designation does not assign any putative permanent identity to its referent; it rather makes clear that when we (correctly) refer to something as *fire* we are actually referring to a subject that is (at that

---

7   *Logismos nothos*, 52b2. In contrast with Forms that have intelligible natures apprehended through dialectical reasoning, the receptacle has no inherent nature and its existence is arrived at by some kind of "transcendental deduction" of the conditions necessary for the existence of ever-changing images of eternal Forms in a spatio-temporal world. The argument at 49a6–50a5 is such a deduction.

8   "So it seems" (49c6). Later, earth will be exempted from such inter-elemental transformation (56c8–d6).

9   Thus completing a "cycle" (49c6–7).

10   I follow here the reading and interpretation defended in Donald J. Zeyl, "Plato and Talk of a World in Flux: *Timaeus* 49a6–50b5," *Harvard Studies in Classical Philology* 79 (1975), 125–148. The syntax and semantics of 49d–50a remain disputed. For discussion, see Donald J. Zeyl, *Plato: Timaeus* (Indianapolis: Hackett, 2000), pp. lvi–lxiv.

time) fire-like. That same subject may (at another time) be water-like, and so on, at which time it is referred to as *water*. There is, then, a subject (or a set of subjects)[11] that, while having no specific identity of its own, appears at one time as fire-like and at another water-like, etc. Since that subject does endure over time without undergoing any change in itself over the course of its different manifestations as fire, water, or what have you, it alone is properly designated by the expression "this." That subject is the receptacle.

So construed, the receptacle plays the role of cosmic *substratum* or *hypokeimenon*, the enduring subject of change that Aristotle postulates in *Physics* I, 7. Any instance of water that we see, and in fact any sensible particular that our language permits us to characterize as one sort of thing rather than another, is in fact a part of the receptacle that is temporarily so characterized by virtue of its imitation of a certain Form (or combination of Forms). It is "in" that part of the receptacle that the Forms' imitations come to appear, and "from" which they disappear (49e7–50a1).

So far, to say that the receptacle serves as the substratum of spatio-temporal particulars is only to assign it a metaphysical role. It is not yet to say in what respect of its nature, as matter or as space, it serves in that role. The notion of a *material* substratum is familiar enough to us from Aristotle; that notion has become the common sense notion as well as the notion that is operative in modern science. What about the notion of a *spatial* substratum? That notion seems less familiar. But it is worth exploring.

What is it to be a spatio-temporal particular? One answer to this question might be: to be made up of some bit of matter; any particular throughout its existence is identified as that particular by the material bit that makes it up. But an equally good answer might be: to occupy a particular place or to be situated somewhere.[12] On the latter view, a particular is a part of space where a certain constellation of characteristics is manifested. What may make us somewhat resistant to this idea is that we tend to think of space as empty, and hence that a particular so conceived as equally empty. In our visualization a spatial particular—as opposed to a material particular—would seem to have no mass.

Rather than reject the notion of a spatial particular, perhaps we should reexamine the notion of Plato's receptacle as *chôra* or space. We think of space as mere extension and sheer emptiness. But there is no *a priori* reason to think of Platonic space in that way, and there are two good reasons not to. First, the analogy of the gold example (50a4–b5) and the straightforward description of space as a recipient of impressions and as subject to being "modified, shaped and reshaped by the things that enter it" (50c2–3) suggest that Platonic space is

---

11   In so far as it is divisible into parts, what is true of it as a whole is also true of its several parts.
12   52b4–5 and cf. Zeno's paradox of place, which trades on the assumption that to be is to be somewhere (DK 29A24).

something plastic or malleable. Second, the description of pre-cosmic space as being shaken by the powers within it and in turn shaking them (52e1–5) suggest that Platonic space is itself, and not just its contents, subject to motion. Sheer empty space on the other hand is neither malleable nor subject to motion.[13] These considerations commend a visualization of Platonic space as not empty but as *filled* space or, more specifically, as *matter-filled* space.[14]

It is plausible to suppose that the notion of a "field" (as in "visual field," "magnetic field") comes close to Plato's conception of *chôra*. Just as it is necessary for an object to be seen that it occupy a certain place within the seer's visual field, so for a spatio-temporal particular to exist (or come to be or pass away), it is necessary for that particular to be situated (*hedra*, 52b1) at a particular location within a physical field. The field itself would then be three-dimensional, unarticulated, characterless but malleable matter. Visualize not an empty box that contains, say, an apple; visualize rather an aquarium that contains fish and other aquatic organisms. The water in the tank is the filled, material field in which the fish lives and moves, and has its becoming and perishing.

However, even if the notion of filled space and of contents of such space can be made somewhat intelligible in this way, the aquarium visualization just suggested falls short. For a fish—so we think—is not made up of aquarium water: it has its own matter, distinct from that of the surrounding water. And as it swims around, it takes that matter "along" to all the places it visits. The fish is a material particular moving within a filled space, not a spatial particular. So the visualization misleads.

Sense can be made, however, of the notion of a spatial particular by importing another visualization. Visualize a wave, moving toward the shoreline. What is it that makes a particular wave, which at t_1 is 100 yards away from the shore and at t_2 50 yards away, *the same* wave? It is not that the wave at t_2 is constituted by the same bit of water that constituted it at t_1, for clearly the wave, as it traveled, did not take any water "along" with it as it approached the shore. At t_2, the water that made up our wave at t_1 makes up a different wave (or no wave at all).

The "wave analogy" suggests a different model for understanding the continuity of a spatio-temporal particular in locomotion. On this model what preserves the identity of a spatio-temporal particular is not the bit of matter that constitutes it, but the continuity of a configuration in the succession of filled places within the field that the particular occupies. Furthermore, this model

---

13   The notion of space being shaken by and shaking its contents is difficult to square with a conception of space as sheer emptiness. Some advocates of that conception dismiss the agitation of space as "literal" and search for a non-literal interpretation. See e.g., Richard Mohr, *God and Forms in Plato* (Las Vegas: Parmenides Publishing, 2005), pp. 124–132.

14   The notion of space as sheer emptiness makes it equivalent to a Democratean "void." Plato denies the existence of a void at *Timaeus* 79a1.

is consistent with the notion that the filling of this field is something material: it is water that constitutes the wave throughout its journey, even though it is not the same bit of water throughout. The wave needs a material substratum throughout its journey if it is to be a particular: no wave is at any time water-less. But it need not be the same part of that substratum that it "takes along" in order to be the same wave over time.

A spatial particular, like the wave in our visualization, is not non-material, but it is not the matter that makes it up at any given place that individuates it. Rather, it is individuated by the continuity of the constellation of characteristics manifested in a contiguous series of "places" that it occupies over the course of its existence.

Return again to the fish-aquarium visualization. Suppose, this time, that we are converted to Thales' point of view and come to think of the fish as itself made up of water: the fish *just is* the water at the place it occupies; that place is imprinted with a particular configuration of colors and outlines.[15] Now visualize the fish moving from place$_1$ to place$_2$. What we observe is a succession of water-filled places being imprinted with the same[16] configuration of colors and outlines. We could interpret this observation in either of two ways: (i) We could take the (common sense) "material particular" view, namely that the bit of water that constitutes the fish *itself* travels from place$_1$ to place$_2$; so that the matter imprinted at place$_2$ is identical with the matter that started out at place$_1$, and similarly imprinted throughout its passage. The fish takes its constituent matter "along." Or (ii) we could take the "spatial particular" view, according to which the bits of matter at place$_1$ and place$_2$ are indeed different, just because they are at different locations within the field. The matter remains where it is; what moves across the (stable) matter is just the configuration. The fish as it moves is then constituted by whatever water exists in the places it traverses. What gives the fish such continuity and stability as it has is just the continuation of the configuration of colors and outlines. My suggestion is that motion in Platonic space should be visualized as the second, not as the first.

Suppose now that its configuration of colors and outlines is the result of a series of "projections" from outside the aquarium. We are familiar with the work of movie projectors. Movie projectors create images on screens, which are two-dimensional surfaces. These projections consist of various configurations of colors and outlines. Imagine the possibility of coordinating a group of instruments like movie projectors that are able to project images into a suitable

---

15 Of course, were we able to "see" the internal skeleton, tissues and organs of the fish, we would see what we expect to see. But what applies to the fish as a whole would equally apply to these internal parts: they are constituted by water imprinted by configurations of colors and outlines as well.

16 We should, of course, allow for the fish's own motions of fins, tail, etc.

three-dimensional medium (rather than onto a two-dimensional screen). These projections would produce three-dimensional images in the medium, or "field." From one projector, say, the image would derive one of its colors, from another, another, from yet another projector its particular outlines, and so forth. And these projectors would be so coordinated that any one image projected into it could be observed to "travel" from one place within the field to another. Of course, as the image traveled, it would not be taking any part *of the medium* along with it, just as a two-dimensional image "traveling" across a movie screen does not take any part of the screen with it.

Let us return to our fish in the aquarium. If we now think of it as a three-dimensional image in water, the product of a projection into the water by realities outside the aquarium, we can understand what it means for the fish to move from one place to another. The fish is nothing other than a series of water places that successively come and cease to bear a particular configuration of colors and outlines, and it is *that configuration* that moves, not the water places into which that configuration is projected.

Now to return from *analogans* to *analogandum*. The account of Platonic space that I am trying to develop is that of a neutral three-dimensional material medium or field within which spatio-temporal particulars, as images of Forms, come into and pass out of being. These images are the products of the Forms' "projecting" their various natures into the field. Space as the material medium "receives" these projections.

So far, assisted by these visualizations, the account I have given is meant to illuminate how Platonic space can serve as the (primarily spatial, but also material) *hypokeimenon* for the images that subsist in it. But Timaeus' account of the receptacle goes further to include a description of the "pre-cosmic" condition of space and its contents, of the Craftsman's ordering of the regular solids that constitute the elemental bodies, as well as of the interactions among those solids. Can the account so far developed be extended to encompass these further episodes of Timaeus' story?

III

In the pre-cosmic state of the universe the receptacle is already a given. It is not manufactured by the Craftsman. We read that in that state the receptacle is "filled with powers *(dynameis)* that are neither similar nor evenly balanced" (52e2). What are these "powers"? They are described as powers that render every part of the receptacle itself unbalanced (e3), and cause it to "sway irregularly in every direction" (e3–4). The receptacle in turn is described as being shaken by "those things" *(hyp' ekeinôn,* e4) and in its reactive motion shaking them in turn. The latter phrase suggests that "those things" are the pre-articulated *contents* of the receptacle, the "traces" *(ichnê,* 53b2) of the ordered elements of fire, air, earth and water.[17] In that case, it is the lopsided constitutions of these various "traces" that appear to be responsible for the erratic motion throughout the receptacle, and it is by giving mathematically proportionate shape to (53b4–5) these "traces," transforming them into balanced entities (the four regular solids) that the Craftsman brings about cosmic order.[18] Thus it is the receptacle's contents—the aggregates of the pre-ordered configurations within the receptacle—that because of their irregularities move and possibly interact in a way so as to cause disorderly and erratic motion, and the receptacle itself, considered apart from those contents, reacts to that motion by causing them to move in yet more erratic ways.

A possible way to visualize the receptacle as malleable filled space that is shaken by and in turn shaking its contents is to visualize it as having fluidity. Imagine a container of liquid into which new liquid makes a forceful entrance—a modern hot tub, for example. Imagine further that this liquid "system" (again like a hot tub) is perpetually returning itself as an entering stream into itself. The entering stream creates a current within the surrounding recipient liquid. Every part of the recipient liquid is "shaken" by the entering stream, but the current of that entering stream is also itself "shaken" by the reactive motions of the recipient liquid. Because of the imbalance of its constituent parts, this liquid system is in perpetual agitation—a "shaking machine" (*organon seismon parechon*, 53a4). The shaking that is contributed by the receptacle itself has the effect of (roughly) stratifying the contents by mass into distinct regions—an effect similar to that of a winnowing sieve (52e5–53a2).

In the pre-cosmic state, the shaking that goes on is depicted graphically (52d4–53a2), giving the impression that it is extremely convulsive. Return to the two-dimensional movie screen analogy proposed earlier. We should now imagine images projected not onto a stable screen, but onto a sheet flapping in the wind or on some other "shaking" surface. The images that now appear are chaotic, only accidentally resembling what would be projected onto a stable screen— "traces" thereof as it were. Similarly, in terms of the three-dimensional aquarium analogy, instead of thinking of a perfectly placid body of water typical of a modern aquarium, let us imagine the water in it churning, as in a hot tub. Continue to imagine our fish as an image, the product of outside "projectors"

---

17 Significantly, the preface to the account of the receptacle speaks of "the very nature of fire, water, air, and earth *before the coming to be of the heaven*, and their properties *(pathê)* they had *before this* (sc. ordered world)" (48b3–5, emphasis added).

18 What are these "traces" of fire, etc.? "Presumably they are collections of corpuscles consisting of various accidental combinations of irregularly shaped surfaces, combinations that fall far short of the artfully constructed polyhedra to be described later, but coincidentally resembling them in some ways and, to that extent, behaving like them in tending to appear in different regions of the Receptacle" (Zeyl, *Plato: Timaeus*, lxvii). Mohr, *God and Forms*, pp. 111–117, defends a similar view.

casting their projections into the now agitating medium. The image now will be helter-skelter, barely recognizable as a fish—perhaps no more than a "trace" of a fish, as it were. And the movements of this fish-trace from one place to another are simply the internal agitating movements of the water—currents, say, within the water, that "bear"[19] it along.

Malleability and fluidity—properties required for the receptacle to do its work[20]—reinforce the interpretation of space proposed here as not sheer emptiness, but as filled. Moreover, they are properties of Platonic space in both its pre-cosmic condition and in the ordered cosmos. In bringing order to the pre-cosmic elemental "traces" the Craftsman does not alter the nature of space as such, or diminish its susceptibility to agitation. That susceptibility remains within the unalterable aspect of necessity *(anankê)*—an aspect that neverthe-less can be persuaded to serve the ends of intellect *(nous)*. But by ordering the disordered contents of space, rendering the irregular particles into the four regular solids, the Craftsman does much to eliminate the imbalance of these contents: he brings about a state of near-uniformity, thereby greatly reducing (but not totally eliminating)[21] the erratic motions. In consequence, the reactive agitation of space is correspondingly reduced; while remaining malleable and fluid, space no longer displays the same degree of instability.

The Craftsman begins his work by "selecting"[22] the two ultimate types of right-angled triangles: the half-equilateral scalene and the isosceles. Out of the former he constructs the tetrahedron, the octahedron and the icosahedron—the basic particles respectively of fire, air, and water—and out of the latter he constructs the cube—the basic particle of earth. Each of these particles has its own "region" *(topos)* of the spatial field into which it tends to move by virtue of its particular constitution: thus the tetrahedra that constitute fire are the light-est, and thus have the tendency to move furthest away from the center—the natural "above" (cf. 62c3–63e8); the cubes that constitute earth are the heavi-est, and have the tendency to move toward the center—the natural "below."

---

19 It is remarkable how frequently the verb *pherein* (at e.g., 48a7) and its passive *pheresthai* (e.g., *peripheromenon* at 49e5) are used in describing the relation of the receptacle to the mov-ing images within it.

20 It goes without saying that the possession of these properties by Platonic space does not contradict the required characterlessness of the receptacle.

21 It should be remembered that as part of the physical world the elemental particles are not perfect instances of the geometric constructions they exemplify (the latter being Forms). They are neither eternal nor indestructible. Consequently, there will be a residual imbalance in each one individually, as well as in their compounds. They will continue to evoke the reac-tive "shaking" of the receptacle even in their ordered state, and the consequent "winnowing" persists in that state as well. See 57c2–6.

22 *Prohaireton*, 54a2; cf. b2, c1.

These orderly motions disturb the receptacle much less than their pre-cosmic counterparts, provoking a much-reduced reactive agitation on its part.

What does it mean for the primeval irregular particles, or the reconstituted regular particles, to exist *in* space? Both "field" and "filling" are necessary if such particles are to exist. The nature of space as three-dimensional "field" permits, indeed requires, that anything that is to exist "in" it be a three-dimensional object or an aggregate of three-dimensional objects. Thus the particles can and indeed must be three-dimensional.[23] The nature of space as matter permits, indeed requires, any three-dimensional entities within it to be "filled," that is to be stuff bounded by surfaces. It is impossible for solid corpuscles to consist of nothing more than triangles, since mere geometric configurations of empty space do not have bulk or mass.

IV

Finally, the story must be filled out with an account of how change and/or movement of the ordered elemental particles and their compounds in general are possible. The account will focus on a given ordered elemental micro-particular, and I shall assume that the same account applies to compounds, which are aggregates of such micro-particulars.

There are two alternative accounts with which I should like to contrast mine. The first is that of geometric particles as material particulars, and the second that of such particles as spatial but immaterial particulars. On the first, a particle is a discrete bit of matter with a geometrically configured surface of one of the four types. On the second, the particle is just a discrete bit of empty space, and the geometric configurations "wrap" that space. A crucial component of any account of the motion of particles and their aggregates is a visualization of "cutting and crushing," the mechanism that underlies inter-elemental trans-formation (56c8–57c6). According to this account, particles with sharper angles to their triangular surfaces tend to "cut" those with less sharp angles, break-ing up the latter into (possibly) a greater number of particles of another kind, while particles with less sharp angles tend to "crush" the sharper-angled ones, causing a plurality of the latter to coalesce into a lesser number of the former.

Suppose, first, that elemental particles are material particulars, configura-tions of matter moving about in (otherwise empty) space. They are granule-like solid bits, and their geometric surfaces are not "wrappers" that contain them, but just their surfaces. As they move through space, they "take along" the bits of matter of which they are composed. Should a particle be cut by another par-ticle with sharper angles, it splits up into two or more particles, and its matter is accordingly divided. On the other hand, should it and some other particle

23   They are to have "depth," *bathos*, 53c5–6.

be "crushed" so that they coalesce, two distinct bits of matter unite to become one new one. On this account we should not visualize triangular surfaces as such becoming disconnected from one another and recombining with others; we should visualize triangularly surfaced bits of matter breaking apart from or coalescing with each other, always to form other triangularly surfaced bits.

The difficulty that this visualization presents is that it construes the receptacle not as space, but as movable matter contained in (empty) space. The particles are not configurations *of* space but configurations (of matter) *in* space. This ignores Timaeus' account of the receptacle as itself space *(chôra).* Whatever the particles are, they should be understood as configurations *of* space, not as configurations of matter *in* space.

The second account, by contrast, understands the particles as indeed configurations of space and not of matter in space. On the assumption that the space they configure is non-material, the geometric "solids" enclose nothing but discrete parts of empty space.[24] They are solid only in so far as they are three-dimensional constructions, but not in the sense that their sides are surfaces *of* anything. They are wrapper-like enclosures that move about, and in the processes of cutting and crushing their triangular sides come apart from each other and reassemble themselves with other compatible sides to constitute new and different configurations. For this to be possible these sides must consist of ultra-thin membranes that when assembled enclose a part of empty space. But if so, questions inevitably arise as to what such membranes are made of, how thin they can possibly be, i.e., whether their thickness is a divisible or an indivisible magnitude, raising the spectre of a Zenonian paradox.[25] Questions also arise about the intelligibility of detached sides momentarily floating about (an interval during which they aren't "sides" of anything) between configurations, and what guarantee there is that such detached sides will reattach with others to form new particles, and why there should be no residue of unattached sides floating about.[26]

The second account, when visualized, seems absurd. An empty particle is—in terms of our previous visualization—like a waterless wave. In addition, this visualization, while rightly representing the particles as configurations *of*

---

24   "[T]he triangles are simply two-dimensional plane figures which when forming regular solids enclose vacancy or empty space." Mohr, *God and Forms,* p. 117.

25   DK 29B1.

26   It is significant that the description of intertransformation among fire, air and water contains no suggestion of temporarily detached triangles (56d6 ff.). That suggestion does appear to be present in the description of the "cutting" of earth by fire (56d1–6), where a simple earth particle must yield to cutting without being transformed into particles of another kind. It is difficult to assign sense to that earth particle's "drifting about" (*pheresthai,* d2) even while its constituent right-angled triangles "refit themselves" (*synarmosthein auta hautois,* d4–5) to form an earth particle again, but it is not clear what other description might be available.

space, still requires a space *in* which the configurations are to travel if they change location at all. For all relocations involve movement in space.

The account proposed here of geometric particles that are configurations of filled, malleable, liquid space yields a visualization that (in contrast to the first account above) is true to the receptacle's nature as space and (in contrast to the second) allows the particles to be configurations of a material substratum, and not just wrappers of empty space. Recall the aquarium fish visualization suggested earlier, and construe a given geometric particle as itself a micro-particular. As that micro-particular moves through its medium from one place to another, it is nothing but a particular configuration of a series of contiguous matter-filled places. This configuration does not "take along" in its journey any of the matter at any one place. As with the wave, the configuration moves without the matter moving with it.

But this account has to be elaborated in two ways. First, given that the matter-filled medium is not totally static, there is some residual instability in space itself and thus some movement of the configuration that is not attributable to its own "natural" motion due to its constitution. Second, what surrounds our micro-particular at any of its locations is not undifferentiated material space, but material space that is itself thoroughly configured throughout.[27] Thus if our micro-particular is, say, a particle of water moving through a region of air, the succession of places it enters are air places that are being reconfigured as water places, and the succession of places it exits from are re-reconfigured as air places. Since the mechanism of cutting and crushing is the recognized mechanism of reconfiguration, we should imagine that the reconfiguration of adjacent filled places is accomplished by this means.

We can now transfer this model to the behavior of mid-sized objects, given that such objects are clusters of geometric solids. Such objects can change without moving, move without changing, or move and change simultaneously. Both of these behaviors can be visualized at the micro-level as reconfigurations of matter-filled space by means of cutting or crushing. Return once again to the fish swimming in the aquarium. On our previous visualization the fish is a series of configurations of colors and outlines; the motion of the fish is just the locomotion of these configurations in the water-medium. We can now visualize what it is for these configurations to change or move about. The particular color-and-outline configurations occurring at any one place are themselves

---

27   The absence of a void (79a1) entails, on this interpretation, that space is exhaustively configured into particles of fire, air, water, and earth. On the view that the elementary particles are material granule-like bits, this presents a problem for motion, since such bits will require unoccupied space to move into. On the view defended in this paper, there is no similar problem: here it is not granules of matter that displace others, but places within space that accept different configurations over time.

functions of the behavior of the geometric particles that come and cease to configure contiguous places within the filled medium in the manner described.

I have not included in this account any mention of *soul* as the source of regular, law-like motion in the universe. I take it that in terms of the chronology of the "reasonable myth,"[28] soul is associated with intelligent and thus orderly motion, and therefore absent from the pre-cosmic state of things; the erratic motion of that state is attributable only to the irregular configuration of the "traces" together with the fluid and volatile nature of the receptacle. The introduction of soul is concomitant with the regularization of the traces to constitute the regular solids. Clearly in the ordered world, soul has a directing role in the movements of observable spatio-temporal particulars, but significantly soul is not mentioned in Timaeus' account of motion in that world; that account is purely mechanistic (57d7–58c4). It is reasonable to suppose that the account there depicts the more nearly regular behavior of the receptacle and its contents in contrast with the pre-cosmic conditions described earlier, yet still without the presence of soul. Presumably the presence of soul has the effect of rendering the motions of the universe still more regular, and certainly purposeful, to the extent that necessity is persuadable by intellect. Nevertheless, the integration of the causal efficacy of soul with the mechanistic account presents a difficulty inherent in psychophysical dualism that the discourse does little to address.

If something like this account is both intelligible and consistent with the text, there is good hope that the *Timaeus'* account of the receptacle is after all coherent, and can stand as a philosophically respectable treatment of space/matter. We shall not be compelled to take the view that Plato's receptacle is hopelessly incoherent, a bad job which was abandoned in favor of the (allegedly) more sophisticated treatment of *apeiron* in the *Philebus*.[29]

---

28   The characterization of the discourse as a "reasonable myth" (see note 1) renders suspect the ancient and still contemporary dispute as to whether the discourse should be taken literally or metaphorically (on this see Zeyl, *Plato: Timaeus*, pp. xx–xxv). In attempting to get beyond the myth to the "real" account both interpretations fail to respect the actual mythical character of the discourse.

29   See Kenneth Sayre, "The Multi-layered Incoherence of Timaeus' Receptacle," in Gretchen J. Reydams-Schils, ed., *Plato's* Timaeus *as Cultural Icon* (Notre Dame: University of Notre Dame Press, 2003), pp. 60–79. As long as the chronological relation of the *Timaeus* to the *Philebus* remains uncertain, no developmental argument along the lines proposed by Sayre is reliable.

8

The Receptacle and the Primary Bodies: Something from Nothing?

Verity Harte

I. Framework: Providing Context for and Identifying Questions to be Addressed

Partway through Timaeus' account of the demiurge's construction of the cosmos, he backtracks to complicate somewhat his picture of demiurgic activity. At the outset of his account, Timaeus had described how the requirement that the cosmos be as fine as it can be mandated the construction of the body of the cosmos by means of four types of material: earth, fire, water, and air. Nothing was said about the origin of the four materials used in the body's construction: neither that they have nor that they lack such an origin. This omission was not striking. We were already aware that the demiurge did not start his act of construction from scratch; he began with an already existing inheritance[1]—all that is visible, being in a, then, disorderly condition (30a4–5). This inheritance he set about putting in order, including the construction of the cosmic body. Thus, it was natural to assume that the four types of material he used were simply included in his inheritance. This assumption was only encouraged by the fact that earth, air, fire, and water—one or more of them—are, by the tradition of the period, the candidate elements: the persisting material substrate of the world.

Partway through his account, Timaeus corrects this assumption. Earth, air, fire, and water are not elements (48b5–c2). They too were subject to a demiurgic act of creation (see especially: *genesin* at 53b8). In preparing to describe this creation, Timaeus adds to the dual framework of intelligible paradigm

---

1   So one might reflect *paralabôn* at 30a4. Unless otherwise identified, all references are to Plato, *Timaeus* in John Burnet, ed., *Platonis Opera* IV (Oxford: Clarendon Press, 1902).

and perceptible image, a third item: the so-called 'receptacle of all becoming' (49a5–6). In this receptacle were 'traces' of earth, air, fire, and water even prior to any demiurgic act of creation (53b2). By explaining and describing the nature and condition of earth, air, fire, and water prior to the creation of the cosmos (cf. 48b3–5), Timaeus prepares the way for his subsequent description of the demiurge's creation of the earth, air, fire, and water from which he creates the body of the world. This creation is effected by the demiurge shaping[2] the four materials by means of forms and numbers (53b4). The material of each type is constructed as one of four regular, geometrical solids: the pyramid (for fire); the octahedron (for air); the icosahedron (for water); the cube (for earth).

In this paper, I shall offer one possible picture of the relation between the primary bodies and the receptacle in which were found their pre-cosmic traces, a picture broadly similar to one that I have presented elsewhere.[3] I shall then consider one possible objection to this picture: that, on this picture, Timaeus has the demiurge conjure up something from nothing.[4] I will end by considering what may be said in response to this objection.

II. Some Prior Questions Regarding the Demiurgic 'Creation' of Earth, Air, Fire, and Water

Before getting to the picture, however, I want to address some prior questions. The demiurge is explicitly credited with the *creation* of earth, air, fire, and water (see, especially, *genesin*, in addition to *diataxin*, at 53b8). But there are questions as to how best to understand what manner of creation this is. In what sense does the demiurge *create* earth, air, and so on? In so doing, what exactly is it that he creates? And what are the conditions in which this creation occurs?

The demiurgic creation of earth, air, fire, and water is not what we might call a "Book of *Genesis*" creation; when the Book of *Genesis* tells us that God created 'great whales' or 'cattle' or 'man',[5] the creation occurs in a context in which nothing resembling a whale or a man already exists. But the demiurgic creation is not like that: there are, after all, 'traces' of earth, air, fire, and water, independent of the demiurgic creation.

But what is a trace? Not, I take it, a smidgen: a little bit of fire or earth. Ordinarily, a trace—or its Greek equivalent, an *ichnos*, a track or a footprint—is some residue or marker indicative of the presence of that of which it is a trace. It is not a small portion, or miniscule version, of the person or animal of which

---

2   So *dieschêmatisato* at 53b4.
3   Verity Harte, *Plato on Parts and Wholes: The Metaphysics of Structure* (Oxford: Oxford University Press, 2002), § 4.4.
4   The objection is put by Kathrin Koslicki in her review "Verity Harte: *Plato on Parts and Wholes: The Metaphysics of Structure*," *Journal of Philosophy* 101 (2004), 492–496.
5   Genesis I.21, 24, 27 (King James Version).

it is a trace. Traces have two connected aspects. The first is *heuristic*: a trace can be used, especially by an expert, to identify and locate the item of which it is a trace. Typically, it can be so used because of the second, *causal* aspect of traces: the presence of a trace is a causal consequence of the prior presence of that of which it is a trace.[6] Ordinarily, these two aspects will be related in a straightforward manner. A hunter can use the traces of a deer to identify and locate the deer because these traces were caused by the prior presence of the deer. But the *Timaeus* example is not so straightforward. The traces of earth and fire and so on cannot be a causal consequence of the prior presence of what the demiurge has yet to create. If they are a causal consequence of anything,[7] then, they must be a causal consequence of the existence of Forms of earth and of fire and the rest, whose existence Timaeus endorses by the oddly democratic means of casting his vote (51d3 ff). The traces can, nevertheless, play a heuristic role as regards the earth, fire, and so on of the demiurge's creation, as well as regarding the Forms. Since the demiurge already has knowledge of Forms, what the traces may indicate, when used as heuristics, will be a question more for us readers of the *Timaeus* than for the demiurge.

The existence of Forms makes clear that, although there is something that the demiurge creates, he is not responsible for it being the case that fire is what it is. He is not responsible for the formal nature of fire. What fire is, and, hence, what *is fire*, is something determined by the Form of fire. But, then, what is it that the demiurge does create? The demiurge creates the earth, air, fire, and water to be used in his construction of the perceptible body of the cosmos. In his perceptible inheritance, there are traces of material of these four types. The demiurge organizes and shapes his perceptible inheritance so as to ensure the existence, not of mere *traces*, but of the actual material needed for his construction: material that conforms to the nature of the four appropriate material types. Just as one would expect of a craftsman, the demiurge ensures that materials of the appropriate type are available and ready for the use he will make of them.

What the demiurge is responsible for, then, is the existence of organized, perceptible bodies of earth, air, fire, and water ready for use. At least he is responsible for this, subject to two further qualifications.

The first qualification concerns the perceptibility of the materials the demiurge creates. Individual such items of earth, air, fire, and water are not in

---

6 Among several other Platonic reference to traces, the heuristic aspect seems prominent in: *Phaedo* 115b9, *Cratylus* 393b3, *Republic* 365d2, 410b1, *Philebus* 44d7, *Theaetetus* 187e2, *Laws* 951b7; the causal in: *Gorgias* 524c5, *Republic* 430e9, 432d3, 462a6, 553a10; and perhaps a combination in *Sophist* 226b2, *Phaedrus* 266b7 (quoting *Odyssey*), 276d4, *Statesman* 290d5, 301e4. An explicit combination of the two is found at *Theaetetus* 193c4. I am grateful to M. M. McCabe for direction to many of these various references.

7 It is not clear the traces of the *Timaeus* must be a causal consequence of something. Their existence—and their heuristic value as traces—could be a brute fact that is left unexplained.

fact perceptible, according to *Timaeus* 56b7–c3.[8] They are not perceptible "on account of their smallness." They can, however, be perceived en masse, when bulked together. Thus, it is fair to say that the materials that the demiurge creates are of a perceptible sort. Their imperceptibility as individual items is not the, in principle, imperceptibility to which Forms, for example, are subject.

The second qualification regards these materials' claim to be bodies. That each is a body seems undeniable; it is a fact that Timaeus takes to be evident to all (53c3–6). And, as Sarah Broadie has observed,[9] in the *Timaeus*, corporeality is closely bound up with being perceptible. The complication is just how any one sort of material could be perceptible and corporeal, given what Timaeus has elsewhere said. When describing the construction of the body of the cosmos, Timaeus linked corporeality to being both visible and tangible (31b4), and being both visible and tangible was said to require the presence of both fire and earth. This is a puzzle that I will set aside.

III. The Primary Bodies and the Receptacle: One Possible Picture

I turn now to my picture of the relation between the primary bodies that the demiurge creates and the receptacle in which he found their pre-cosmic traces.[10]

Begin with the four primary bodies that the demiurge creates. Each is identified as a geometrical object, one of four regular solids. As such, each is a configuration of space, in three dimensions. I stress that each is a configuration *of* space, as distinct from a configuration *in* space. Configurations *in* space have the space they are in as a separate container. The regular solids could be configurations *in* space, like objects in a container, if they were made of some material distinct from that which contains them; one could make them out of paper, for example. However, the regular solids that the demiurge constructs are identified with earth, air, fire, and water, and these are the material constituents of everything bodily. So it is hard to see what (other) material these regular solids could be made up of. Further, there is nothing in what Timaeus says that suggests that the regular solids are made of some sort of material, unless space itself is that material.[11] This latter is certainly possible, but should not be misunderstood. Since the regular solids that the demiurge constructs

---

8   At least they cannot be *seen;* perhaps this need not be taken to generalize across the other senses.

9   In an important, and influential, contribution to the Laurence Seminar on the *Timaeus*, which took place in Cambridge in May 1993.

10   It is not my intention to try to defend this picture here in all its details, nor against all possible objections. For further discussion, see Harte, *Parts and Wholes*, § 4.4.

11   The regular solids are made of plane surfaces, which are in turn made up of triangles. But this does not alter the point I want to make. These items too are configurations of space, now in two, rather than three, dimensions.

are configurations of space, space as such—the three dimensions considered in abstraction from any specific configuration—may be viewed as the matter of the four configurations. But, if we do so view it, we should not be misled into thinking of space as *bodily stuff*.[12] Viewed as configurations of space, this picture of the primary bodies can complement Timaeus' account of the receptacle; the receptacle is explicitly described as being space, but is described in ways that have made several readers think of it as matter.

Next, then, consider the receptacle. What is the relation between the receptacle, which Timaeus introduces and characterizes by way of preparation for his account of the construction of earth, air, fire, and water, and these four material bodies that the demiurge creates? In his construction of these materials, as elsewhere in the *Timaeus*, the demiurge's activity consists largely in the imposition of structure, typically, structure of a mathematical sort. Timaeus' description of the receptacle is, I suppose, a description of the material condition of the pre-cosmos, in abstraction from that structure which the demiurge imposes.

There are several, long-standing difficulties as regards the correct interpretation of the receptacle passage. But there are, I think, a number of things that may be said without generating too much controversy. First, the receptacle is identified as that in which earth, air, fire, and water come to be present and, in doing so, make their appearance therein; and it is that from which, in turn, they disappear (49e7–50a1). The receptacle is thus a vehicle of some sort for the appearance of earth, air, fire, and water. Second, these appearances of earth, air, fire and water in the receptacle are imitations of the Forms of earth, air, fire, and water (50c5). There are, thus, three components involved in Timaeus' story: (i) Forms; (ii) imitations of Forms—appearances of earth, fire, and so on; and (iii) the receptacle, identified as space at 52a8.

Identification of the receptacle as space comes relatively late in Timaeus' story. Prior to that—and, in addition to describing the receptacle as a nurse (49a6) and a mother (50d3)—Timaeus has used three different images when describing the character and role of the receptacle.

In a first image, he asks us to envisage a person forming all the various shapes from gold and never ceasing forming different shapes, one after the other (50a5–b5). In this image, I take it, the gold stands in for the receptacle; the shapes for the appearance of fire and so on within it; the ceaseless replacement of one shape by another for the apparent continuing cycle of inter-transformation of the four materials, which Timaeus used as a datum from which to begin his account of the receptacle. (This datum and its consequences are the principal arena for controversy.)

---

12 Especially given the *Timaeus*' own picture of corporeality: cf. above.

In Timaeus' second image, he describes the receptacle as "lying by nature as an impress [or: mould] for everything" (50c2), "moved [or: changed] and *shaped* by the things that enter into it" (50c2–3, my emphasis). His third and final image begins by departing from the talk of shapes and shaping, comparing the receptacle to the odourless base of perfumed ointments (50e5–8). Like such a medium, the receptacle must itself be free from the characteristics that, as a medium, it will display. Timaeus then provides a second illustration of this point, and one that returns to the recurring theme of shape: "those who set out to take impressions of shapes in soft materials, do not," he says, "allow any shape to be apparent therein; by levelling the materials out they make them as smooth as possible" (50e8–51a1).

What might we say about the receptacle based on these images, taken together? The dominant conception that arises from the images is of the receptacle as medium, in which imitations of Forms occur.[13] The occurrence of Forms in the receptacle is analogous to the way in which an impression occurs in wax or other, soft materials. This should be contrasted with the way in which an object may be said to be *in* a container. A medium, unlike a container, does, in some sense, take on and display the impressions it receives, but it does so without altering its character. As in the first image, an impression made upon wax—or softened gold—may be said to be formed 'from' the gold, for it is the configuring of the wax or gold as a result of the impression that produces an observable triangle, for example. The triangle so produced is not, however, made out of wax or gold;[14] it is not a waxen or golden triangle. Rather, the wax or gold is the medium informed by the impression it receives. We may think of this medium as the matter of the impression, but, if we do, we should not thereby think of it as the stuff of which the impression is made.[15] Running through all three images, the central example of this process of being impressed is that of a medium that displays shape by being itself shaped.

This allows for the following picture of the relation between the primary bodies and the receptacle. The receptacle is a medium, identified as space. This is the sort of medium we would expect in light of the identification of the primary bodies as four regular solids. Each such solid is a configuration of space. Space, abstractly conceived, is the (unstructured) medium informed by the specific geometrical configuration of each regular solid. Like the media

---

13   Cf. Richard Mohr, "Image, Flux and Space in Plato's *Timaeus*," *Phoenix* 34 (1980), 138–152.

14   Cf. Mary Louise Gill "Matter and Flux in the *Timaeus*," *Phronesis* 32 (1987), 34–53.

15   The analogy most likely to mislead on this point is the first, I think, because it is tempting mentally to substitute the gold of this analogy for some pliable material, like plasticene, and envisage the process as forming shapes made out of this material by manual manipulation. But this substitute image fails to respect two key facts: (i) gold is a metal, albeit a soft one; and (ii) the shapes that are to be formed 'from' or 'out of' it are two-dimensional.

of Timaeus' three images, the receptacle functions as a medium by taking on some, specific, shape; however, the shapes taken on by the receptacle are in three dimensions.

With this picture in mind, we are in a position to answer three important questions as regards the receptacle and the imitations of Forms occurring within it.

First, the receptacle is portrayed as a medium, which, being a medium, is itself free from the spatial configurations that it will take on. However, Timaeus makes clear that, even prior to any demiurgic activity, the receptacle has the appearance of certain material features. How does it do so?

What Timaeus says is that, prior to the activity of the demiurge, "the part of [the receptacle] which is made fiery appears on each occasion as fire; the part which is moistened appears as water," and so on for each of the four, primary materials (51b4–6). Notice that it is a part or region of the receptacle that is made fiery and appears as fire. This identification of specific parts or regions of the receptacle is parasitic upon that (portion) of space being somehow configured.[16] We must, then, suppose that, even in the absence of demiurgic activity, the receptacle is somehow configured.

This brings us back to the subject of traces, and to a second question: how should we understand the claim that earth, air, fire, and water have "certain traces of themselves," despite being said to be "disposed in the manner likely for everything when god is absent" (53b2–4)?

On the assumption that the receptacle is somehow configured, even prior to the demiurge's activity, there are two ways to answer this question. On either option, the configuration of some portion of the receptacle accounts for its appearance as fire, or as earth. The choices are (i) suppose that, by some pre-cosmic accident, portions of the receptacle take on precisely those configurations which the demiurge imposes, but do so only fleetingly or in some other unstable fashion; or (ii) suppose that, in the absence of the demiurge, portions of the receptacle are configured in ways that closely resemble, but do not precisely correspond to, the configurations of the regular solids. I do not know how to decide between these two options, though the second fits better with the results of my reflections on what, ordinarily, seems characteristic of traces.

This brings us on to the third question, which concerns the role played by Forms in these appearances of fire and so on in portions of the receptacle. What makes a pyramid or pyramid-like configuration of a region of the receptacle a trace of fire, as opposed to a trace of water? To this, the short answer—anticipated earlier—is: by its being (or being like) an imitation of the Form of fire,

---

16 The idea, then, is that spatial individuation—spatial location—will here be a relative, not an absolute matter. On the requirements for regionalization of the receptacle, cf. Allan Silverman, "Timaean Particulars," *Classical Quarterly* NS 42 (1991), 87–113.

and not of water. But what *makes* this an imitation of the Form of fire, as opposed to that of water? When Timaeus later explains the perceptual features of earth, air, fire, and water, and the varieties and compounds thereof, he ties their perceptual character to the geometrical character of the respective regular solids (e.g., 61d5–62a5 on fire). If the geometrical character of the relevant solids is responsible for the perceptual character of the four materials, then it must be the geometrical character of the portion of the receptacle in question that is responsible for its appearance as fire, and not water. [17]

Here, then, is the completion of my picture of the relation between the primary bodies and the receptacle. The regular, geometrical configurations that the demiurge imposes upon the receptacle are the means by which he instantiates the Forms of earth, air, fire, and water. Individual such items of earth, air, fire, and water imitate Forms through their geometrical construction; they are configurations of space, whose perceptible, and other,[18] properties are parasitic upon their geometrical structure.

IV. Something from Nothing?

This, then, is the picture. Now the objection: does it not seem as if Timaeus is trying to get something from nothing? The objection matters, because, *if* Timaeus is trying to get something from nothing, then this is a problem. And a problem unanswered should call into question the picture on which it arises.

It is easy, I think, to see why the objection arises. After all, the rabbit out of the hat is the robustly material, phenomenologically rich, earth, air, fire, and water; and the resources of the magician are just: space and geometry. The objection may come in a number of different guises, some more challenging than others.

First, one might object that the regular solids are not very solid; they are mere configurations of empty space. This objection has, I think, a diagnosis. It is tempting—I find—to provide oneself with a visual image of the regular solids, at least in one's mind's eye. One might imagine the solids made out of straws for their edges or with faces of paper. Imagined thus, the solids are hollow, so the question of their solidity or lack of it arises. But models of the regular solids, so imagined, are configurations *in* space, where space acts as their container. They are not, as in my view, configurations *of* space, where

---

17   As Stephen Menn points out to me, this view goes nicely with the fact that the Greek term, *ichnos*, commonly refers to a track or footprint, that is, to something whose *shape* constitutes it as trace). *Ichnos* can, however, also identify the spoor of an animal (cf. LSJ s.v. *ichnos*).

18   As Sarah Broadie points out, the geometrical character of earth, air, etc. explains the ways in which they do (and do not) transform into one another, their motion, the existence of various different forms of each, etc. Sarah Broadie, "The Contents of the Receptacle," *The Modern Schoolman* 80 (2003), 171–190.

space—rather than straw or paper—is the medium that takes on and displays the configuration in question. Viewed as configurations *of* space, the regular solids are not empty, not empty of space, that is, for they are three-dimensional.

Still, the objector rejoins: how can *space*, even when configured three-dimensionally, be productive of the phenomenal character of fire or of earth? I have already suggested that Timaeus does make a systematic attempt to tie the features—phenomenal and otherwise—of the four primary bodies to the geometrical character of the solids in question. So, for example, fire is both the lightest and the most mobile of the four primary bodies. It is most mobile through having the least number of faces and hence the sharpest edges or points; it is lightest through having the least number of like parts, being made of the smallest number of elementary triangles, with the least number of faces (56a6–b2). This geometrical sharpness of fire is responsible, in turn, for the phenomenology of its sharp, cutting feel (61e1–2).

But this is the magic to which the objector objects. Perhaps, then, it is a *mistake* to take the configuration of the solids to be literally *constitutive of* the features in question? Perhaps configuration works in an environment that is independently imbued with potentially phenomenal character as a result of the action of Forms?

This takes us back, once again, to the pre-cosmic traces. It might seem natural to respond to the objection that Timaeus is trying to create something from nothing by remembering that this is not a Book of *Genesis* creation: the Demiurge of the *Timaeus,* unlike the God of *Genesis*, did not start from scratch. In the receptacle, there already exist things connected to earth or to fire: those pre-cosmic traces. Perhaps these have, in themselves, some phenomenal character related to that of earth or of fire.

But this line of response will not be sufficient on my understanding. It would be sufficient if the phenomenal character of earth or of fire occupied configured regions of the receptacle without being constituted by them. (This is a view that has its defenders.[19]) But it is not much help to the objector, if, as on my view, any phenomenal character of the pre-cosmic traces would *itself* have to be constituted by their geometrical character. To the objector, this looks like getting something from nothing *all along*.

My own line of response, then, to the fundamental objection is to attack its presuppositions about what is involved in being *something*, from a Platonic point of view. My strategy is to follow my story through. Let me combine the results of my picture of the relation between the primary bodies and the receptacle with a return to some of the points that emerged from the question of *what* it is that the demiurge creates.

---

19   Silverman, "Timaean Particulars," for example.

The demiurge makes it the case (as I think) that portions of the receptacle *are* perceptible earth, air, fire, and water, and not merely traces; he does so by imposing the relevant geometrical configuration; in Timaeus' words, by shaping them by means of forms and numbers (53b4–5). On this view, the reality of something *being fire* comes precisely from the formal mathematical shaping the demiurge imposes, a fact that goes hand in hand with the view that the *being* of Fire—its formal nature—is constituted by something essentially intelligible, and not perceptible. Ultimately, it is to this intelligible being that the traces direct us. Thus, the impression that we have here a case of something from nothing is rooted in an un-Timaean picture of the nature of what 'somethings' there are. While it may be a mystery to us how geometrical entities could be responsible for the phenomenal character of our interactions with the materials they constitute, the link that Timaeus has drawn between corporeality and perceptibility, and his geometrical analysis of corporeality strongly suggest that this is indeed how the story is meant to go.*

*My thanks to the audience in Illinois for helpful discussion and to M. M. McCabe and Barbara Sattler for additional comments.

9

The Timaeus *and the Critique of Presocratic Vortices*[1]

Stephen Menn

Harold Cherniss, in his essay "The Characteristics and Effects of Presocratic Philosophy,"[2] says that the history of Presocratic philosophy has to start from Aristotle and Theophrastus, but that those authors are telling a teleological story of the gradual anticipation of Aristotelian philosophy, and make anachronistic use of Aristotelian concepts in interpreting the Presocratics. For this reason, says Cherniss, while the historian remains dependent on Aristotle and Theophrastus, he must be aware of their biases and must correct for them as far as possible by using other evidence, where possible our (generally short) verbatim quotations from the Presocratics. Now you might think that this attitude would lead Cherniss to a strongly anti-teleological reading of Presocratic philosophy, with each thinker interpreted purely for himself and not as part of any larger story of progress. In fact, however, what Cherniss says is that Presocratic philosophy is a series of partial anticipations, not of Aristotle, but of the *Timaeus*, which he describes as a kind of *summa* of Presocratic natural philosophy.[3] Setting aside for now the question of whether this is the right way to read the Presocratics, one might question whether this is the right way to read the *Timaeus*. One

---

1 This is a shorter reworking of the results most relevant to the *Timaeus* of a longer paper now in draft, "Anaxagoras, Empedocles, Leucippus." I am able to give more detail and more supporting argument there.

2 Originally published in *Journal of the History of Ideas* 12 (1951), 319–345; reprinted in Cherniss's *Selected Papers,* Leonardo Tarán, ed. (Leiden: Brill, 1977), pp. 62–88. I will cite the original pagination, which is given in the reprint as well.

3 Thus the last sentence of the essay: "In the *Timaeus* Presocratic philosophy had its resurrection and transfiguration, the parts that were meaningless made meaningful in a whole that is far more than their mere summation," p. 345.

might have thought that the *Timaeus* was not a *summa* of Presocratic natural philosophy, but a critique of it, and an attempt to rival it; most obviously, the *Timaeus* seems to criticize the failure of Anaxagoras' promise to provide teleological explanations, and, more generally, to criticize anyone who takes the "accessory causes *[synaitia]*" of things for their real causes. However, there could be some truth in both the *"summa"* and the "critique" descriptions: Plato wants to do better than the Presocratics by standards that they themselves should accept, wants to carry out their programs of explanation better than they themselves were able to do, so it's not surprising if the *Timaeus* takes up some Presocratic themes or styles of explanation. In some cases, Plato wants to show that he can take this style of explanation further than his predecessors did; in other cases, he is exploring some type of causal explanation to find its limits, to show what it can't explain.

Let me note three key examples of explanatory themes that Plato takes up, not just from the Presocratics in general, but from nameable individual Presocratics. Most obviously, he takes over from Anaxagoras the project of explanation through *nous* (reason, intelligence), and, connected with this, the idea that *nous* is immediately causally responsible for the rotation of the heavens. Also, he takes over from Empedocles the idea of a providential divinity, Empedocles' Love or Plato's demiurge, who is responsible for fitting unlike and even opposite things together in precise numerical proportions, and for arranging parts in teleologically organized wholes, in such a way as to produce harmony or peace or friendship between the different components; this is supposed to be necessary, above all, in order for living things to exist. (This is a properly Empedoclean theme, and is not in Anaxagoras, who is not interested in causes that bring unlike things together, but only in causes that separate things out of a mixture and thus sort like to like; Anaxagoras has no interest at all in harmony or proportion.) Finally, Plato takes over from Democritus the idea that what might seem to be irreducible material differences, say, between fire and earth, are instead explained by differences in the geometrical shape of the smallest particles of each kind of body; and, connected with this, that there is a shaking motion, which both Democritus and Plato compare to a winnowing fan (Democritus B164, *Timaeus* 52e6–53a1), which is responsible for sorting particles of similar shapes together, and is thus responsible for heavy bodies' falling and light bodies' rising.

Now to understand Plato's attitude to these and other themes of Presocratic philosophy, we need to put them into the context of his critique of the Presocratics. I'll list schematically five main points where he sees himself as criticizing, not just individual thinkers, but all or almost all of the Presocratics. Most obviously, he criticizes their failure to provide teleological explanations: a few Presocratics promised these, but even they generally failed to deliver. Second, he criticizes Presocratic physics as merely narrative, and it is true that most Presocratic physics tries to explain particular phenomena by fitting them into a grand cosmogonic narrative. Plato thinks that such a narrative does not define, does not grasp essences of things and therefore cannot proceed to demonstrations, and that it therefore fails to be scientific, unlike dialectic and mathematics.[4] This is not just a critique of Presocratic physics, but of all physics, and Plato thinks that the *Timaeus* too can be no more than a narrative, a *mythos*, but he will try at least to make it a "likely" or *eikôs mythos* (*Timaeus* 29d2), and more so than the Presocratics had been able to achieve. Third, and connected with this, Plato, and his demiurge, will make use of a higher discipline, dialectic: the *mythos* can be *eikôs* only because the world itself is a likeness of something whose essence can be grasped by dialectical definition. To put it another way, it is not sufficient to posit *nous*, as Anaxagoras does; we must also posit a corresponding realm of intelligibles *(noêta)*. Fourth and again connected, Plato and the demiurge will make use not only of dialectic but also of mathematics: the demiurge in ordering the world makes use of principles from at least arithmetic, geometry, harmonics or mathematical music theory, and mathematical astronomy (perhaps we should add mathematical optics, 46a2–c6), and this is the reason why the world is, at least in some parts and to some extent, mathematically intelligible; by contrast, the Presocratics except for Philolaus had generally not been interested in integrating mathematical astronomy into their cosmogonic stories. Fifth, Plato thinks that the Presocratics have understated the role of soul in the cosmos: soul is prior to body and is the bearer of rationality into the sensible world, above all through introducing rational patterns of motion; and so the demiurge, besides giving the world numerical proportions and bringing it into the likeness of a Form, also gives it a rational soul and makes it into a living thing.

These points will all be familiar enough; I'll concentrate here on the first two, and here I think it will help to compare Plato's attitude with Aristotle's. On teleology, Aristotle basically agrees with Plato's criticism of Presocratic physics. On narrativity, again, Aristotle agrees that Presocratic physics is narrative, not definitional or demonstrative, and thus that it fails to be scientific. But unlike Plato, Aristotle thinks that this does not hold of physics as such, but only of bad physics (including the *Timaeus*), and that it is possible to construct a scientific physics which will proceed from definitions that grasp the form or essence of natural things; but these will be not mathematical or dialectical definitions but properly physical definitions, which means that they will grasp the *natures*

---

4   On the difference between the kind of account that can be given of the cosmos (and temporal things generally) and the kind of account that can be given of their eternal paradigms, see *Timaeus* 27d5–29d3. Because physics, unlike mathematics, is non-defining and non-demonstrating, Plato excludes it from the curriculum of the rulers of the ideal state in *Republic* VII.

of natural things, where a nature is a disposition to a characteristic natural *motion* which is the goal of the natural thing. Not all motions which happen to natural things are natural—a stone can be thrown upward—but Aristotle thinks that motions contrary to nature should be explained as causal byproducts of natural motions, and that they are brief interruptions; only natural motions can be eternal or regular. I have spoken elsewhere[5] of Aristotle's project of *denarrativizing* physics. In many of his particular physical treatises, he tries to explain phenomena that would more traditionally have been explained as part of a cosmogonic narrative; Aristotle replaces the narrative, chronological order with a logical or causal order of explanation. In *On the Heavens*, in particular, he explains things that would traditionally have been explained through a cos-mogonic vortex, namely the rotation of the heavens and the separation of heavy and light bodies, with heavy bodies moving down or toward the center, and light bodies up or away from the center. Aristotle rejects these vortex-explanations, not just because he thinks the world is eternal and so rejects any cosmogony, but because if something moves as it does because it is caught in a whirlpool, its motion will be violent and contrary to nature. Rather, the motion of the heavens must be explained through heavenly bodies' having a distinct nature which inclines them to motion around the center, while heavy and light bodies likewise have natures which incline them to motion away from or toward the center. Plato agrees with some but not all of this. He agrees that the math-ematically precise motions of the heavens could not have arisen from a vortex; rather, the heavens are moved in circles because this is the perfect motion, the motion "most in accord with *nous* and wisdom" (*Timaeus* 34a2–3), and most immediately because it is implanted in them by a rational soul. Aristotle agrees that the heavens are moved in circles because this motion is most perfect, and that it is implanted in them by *nous* and (apparently) by soul; but he thinks that this is not enough, that the heavenly bodies must also have a nature that inclines them to circular motion, that if they were made (as the *Timaeus* says) of fire and therefore were naturally inclined to motion away from the center, their motion around the center would be violent and painful for the soul and could not be eternal (*On the Heavens* II, 1, 284a27–35). Plato will not be both-ered by this, because he defines fire and the other simple bodies (so far as he defines them at all) by geometrical shapes and not by their presumed natural motions, and he explains the characteristic motions of heavy and light bodies by something like a vortex, the shaking of the receptacle which sorts bodies of each type together, but does not bring them to any teleologically determined natural place (52e1–53a7, 57b7–c6, 63b2–e8). Thus Plato keeps a vortex sub-ordinate to *nous*, while Aristotle banishes vortices altogether.

---

5   In my article "Aristotle" in the *Encyclopedia of Philosophy*, second edition, Donald Borchert, ed. (Detroit: Macmillan, 2006).

To understand Plato's treatment of vortices, we have to go in more depth into his attitudes, not just to Presocratic philosophy as such, but to particular Presocratics; and here too it will be helpful to compare Aristotle. Plato in the *Phaedo* has his character Socrates, as he describes his own pursuit of wisdom (especially 96a6–99d2), start by studying crude natural philosophers who used only material-cause explanations, and then turn to Anaxagoras, who promised explanation through *nous* (which Socrates thinks must be teleological explanation through the good), but who then disappointed Socrates by failing to deliver on this promise. Aristotle in *Metaphysics* I, 3–7 builds on this passage of the *Phaedo* and tries to fill it out into a whole history of philosophy, or more precisely a history of the aspirations to wisdom and their disappointment. Aristotle starts with early philosophers who used only material-cause explanations (I, 3, 983b6–984b8), then turns to Anaxagoras who, "in saying that *nous* is present, as in living things, so in [the whole of] nature as the cause of order and all arrangement, appeared like a sober man in comparison to those who had spoken at random before him" (984b15–18); then Anaxagoras of course disappoints. Aristotle has close echoes of the *Phaedo* in his description of Anaxagoras' promise and failure (though he also has significant differences of interpretation from Plato, which I'll pass over here).[6] He fills out the story by including other philosophers, Parmenides and Democritus and most importantly Plato himself in this history and in this critique, but the one I want to concentrate on at the moment is Empedocles.

Aristotle represents Empedocles as being very similar to Anaxagoras. Anaxagoras introduced a good principle as a cause of motion and order, and Empedocles added a bad principle as a cause of motion and disorder; Empedocles is somewhat better than Anaxagoras, "he makes more use of his causes than [Anaxagoras], but not enough, nor does he attain consistency in them" (I, 4, 985a21–23), and ultimately he falls victim to very similar criticisms. (Empedocles is also preferable to Anaxagoras in that he uses only four material principles, rather than infinitely many, so explicitly *Physics* I, 4 188a17–18. This is good not just because having fewer posits is always preferable, but because it forces him to give formal-cause explanations instead: where for Anaxagoras the difference between blood and bone is an irreducible material difference, Empedocles explains it through different numerical proportions of earth, water, air, and fire, *Metaphysics* I, 10, 993a17–22 [not explicitly mentioning Anaxagoras].) The only important differences that Aristotle sees between Empedocles and Anaxagoras, apart from the issue of material principles, are that Empedocles has two opposing moving principles, and, connected with that, that he sees an alternation between

---

6   With *Metaphysics* I, 3, 984b15–19 compare *Phaedo* 97b8-d4; with *Metaphysics* I, 4, 985a16–21 compare *Phaedo* 98b7–c2. For more discussion see my "La sagesse comme science des quatre causes?," in *Aristote: Physique et métaphysique*, Maddalena Bonelli, ed. (Paris: Vrin, forthcoming).

the rules of Love and Strife, whereas for Anaxagoras, once *nous* has begun to act, it never ceases to rule (an issue on which Empedocles is preferable, *Physics* VIII, 1, 252a5–22). Aristotle is clear on how he sees the chronological relationship between Anaxagoras' philosophy and Empedocles': Anaxagoras was the first to posit a moving and ordering cause,[7] and "Empedocles, in contrast with the earlier thinkers, was the first to introduce a *division* of this kind of cause, positing not a single principle of motion but different and contrary ones" (*Metaphysics* I, 4, 985a29–31). Empedocles therefore wrote later. If Empedocles wrote before Anaxagoras, he would have to have been one of the drunken people who spoke at random before Anaxagoras introduced *nous* (I, 3, 984b15–18, cited above), and indeed this is what many modern scholars have taken Aristotle to think;[8] but the fact is that Aristotle sees Anaxagoras' *nous* and Empedocles' Love as very similar kinds of cause (he often speaks of "*nous* or Love," as if the differences were minor), and that wherever he gives contrasting evaluations of the two philosophers he prefers Empedocles. When Aristotle, in a list of different philosophers' opinions on the material principles, justifies listing Anaxagoras last by saying that Anaxagoras, "being prior [to Empedocles] in age *(hêlikiâi)* but posterior in works *(ergois)*, says that the [material] principles are infinitely many" (I, 3, 984a12–13), he must mean in calling Anaxagoras "posterior in works" not that his works are superior, nor that while born earlier he wrote later than Empedocles, but rather that Anaxagoras' works are inferior (which is unquestionably what Aristotle thinks on the immediate issue, Anaxagoras' view that there are infinitely many material principles by contrast with Empedocles' view that there are four).[9]

The impression we would get from Aristotle is that Empedocles took over Anaxagoras' description of a moving and ordering principle, the source of goodness in the world; that for some reason he renamed it Love instead of *nous*; and that he decided to complement it with a contrary moving and disordering principle to account for the manifest evil in the world (so I, 4, 984b32–985a4). But there is something wrong with this story. The effects which Anaxagoras attributes to *nous*—the vortex and the consequent separation and sorting of

---

7 Apart perhaps from shadowy figures like Anaxagoras' fellow-citizen Hermotimus, from whom Aristotle has no writings, or from poets who may have obscurely hinted at such things: see Aristotle's extended scholarly parenthesis *Metaphysics* I, 3, 984b18–I, 4, 984b32.

8 And they have taken the description of Empedocles as "the first to introduce a *division* of this kind of cause" to be putting him, not after Anaxagoras, but after Anaxagoras' murky poetic precursors.

9 And so Alexander of Aphrodisias interprets the passage in his paraphrase, *In Metaphysica* 27,28–28,1. For fuller argument and a survey of scholarly opinion, see my "Anaxagoras, Empedocles, Leucippus." There are good parallels for "posterior" in the sense of "inferior," none for "posterior" in the sense of "more sophisticated, thus superior."

like to like—are effects which Empedocles attributes not to Love but to Strife.[10] It would be truer to say, not that Empedocles takes over Anaxagoras' good principle and complements it with an evil principle, but rather that he takes the effects that Anaxagoras attributes to *nous*, attributes them to an evil principle, and then supplies a good principle to counteract or complement its effects. And presumably the main reason he would do so is that he sees, correctly, that the effects of a vortex—separation and the sorting of like to like, whether we attribute these to *nous* or to Strife—are not sufficient to account for the formation of the world as we inhabit it, and in particular for the formation of living things: there might be *bone* as a material, but not *bones* as functioning parts of animals. Empedocles would therefore introduce Love to explain the bringing of unlike things together that is needed for the formation of living things and the other good features of the world.

To put my cards on the table, I think Aristotle is right that Empedocles has read Anaxagoras and is trying to respond to him, and I think Empedocles is motivated above all by the need to give an adequate explanation of the formation of living things.[11] What I want to suggest here is that Empedocles' critique of Anaxagorean vortex-explanations gave the model for the critique which Plato develops in the *Phaedo* and *Timaeus* and which Plato will turn against all Presocratic physicists including Empedocles (and which Aristotle will in due course turn against the *Timaeus* as well). And, beyond that, I want to suggest that Empedocles gave Plato a model not just for critique but for physics as such, that there is a sense in which the project of the *Timaeus* is essentially Empedoclean in a way that it is not essentially Anaxagorean (despite the unmistakably Anaxagorean promise of explanation through *nous*): namely, that it is *oppositional* physics. That is: we wish to criticize a type of physical explanation favored by some earlier philosopher or philosophers. We don't deny that the kinds of causes they describe are really acting in the world, but we deny that they are sufficient to account for the world we inhabit. We develop this critique in the form of a narrative, describing the kinds of causes favored by our predecessors and letting them do their utmost; we then try to show that the world they would produce if they governed unchecked is not the world we inhabit, but a chaos incapable of sustaining living things.

---

10   Empedocles makes Strife responsible for the separation of the elements in many places, notably B17. A vortex is the immediate mechanism of separation notably in A49, so presumably it is caused by Strife. There is an immediate connection between Strife and a vortex in the Strasbourg Empedocles papyrus a(ii)3–4, Alain Martin and Oliver Primavesi, *L'Empédocle de Strasbourg* (Berlin: De Gruyter, 1999), pp. 132–133, and the apparent vortex at d8, pp. 146–147, is likewise the result of Strife. Apparently the ultimate fate of all living things, and their punishment for breaking up the harmonious unity of the Sphairos, is to be centrifuged to death in the Strife-induced vortex which will separate out each element to its own region of the cosmos. But the reconstruction of text and sense in these lines is conjectural.

11   Again, for full discussion and defense see my "Anaxagoras, Empedocles, Leucippus."

For Empedocles the cause in question is Strife, and it would produce the world of total strife, with all four elements completely separated from each other, and so none of the mixtures which are necessary for living things; Love must then be brought in first to bring earth, water, air, and fire together in definite numerical proportions so as to produce blood and bone and the like, and then to fit these together in teleological structures to produce living things including us. For Plato, the causes favored by earlier philosophers fall under the head of Necessity, and if it governed alone it would produce the chaos of the pre-cosmic Receptacle. *Nous* must be brought in, first, to impose the shapes which distinguish earth, water, air, and fire (if it did just this and left the rest up to Necessity, the shaking of the Receptacle would sort these out into, presumably, four great masses, but would not produce composite bodies or at least not teleologically determined composite bodies, and in particular not living things). Then *nous* must be brought in again, "persuading" Necessity (48a2–5, cf. 68e1–69a5), in order to produce sublunar living things. The comparison between Empedocles' world of total strife and Plato's pre-cosmic Receptacle was made already by Plutarch (he says that in Empedocles' reign of Strife, when the elements were wholly separate and each "moving with their own self-willed motions," "they were as, according to Plato, 'everything is from which god is absent' [*Timaeus* 53b3–4], that is, as bodies are when *nous* and soul have departed," *On the Face in the Moon* 926F), and perceptively, since these extreme states of the world have similar structural functions in the two stories.

There are certainly important differences between Empedocles and the *Timaeus*, most strikingly that Empedocles does not dispute that Strife and the vortex are able to produce the gross structure of the cosmos, i.e., the rotating heavens and the separation of the four cosmic masses; he only denies that they can produce living things. Plato, of course, cannot say that Necessity can produce the gross structure of the cosmos but cannot produce living things, since he thinks that the cosmos is a living thing, indeed the most perfect of living things: if Strife cannot produce even a fish, it certainly cannot produce a cosmos. This difference is connected with a deep divergence between Empedocles and Plato in their attitudes toward the heavens. For Plato, the heavens are the most rationally governed part of the sensible cosmos, immortally living, where the activity of the world-soul is most manifest; while Necessity has some role, subordinate to *nous*, in the governance of the sublunar world (including sublunar living things), it seems to have no role at all in the heavens, and Plato describes *nous'* works in the heavens before he has introduced the "wandering cause." For Empedocles, by contrast, Strife tends to inhabit the outer regions of the world. Strife reaches the greatest extent of its reign when it penetrates all the way to the "center of the vortex"; when Love has begun to reconquer the world, it establishes a domain around the center where it can rule or at least share the rule with Strife and where it can produce living things, while Strife is forced outward toward the heavens, which continue to be dominated by Strife's vortex and where there are no living things; when Love has completely pacified the world, Strife will be forced even further out, beyond the heavens, where it will lurk and wait for its chance to break in again (for all this see Empedocles B35). Empedocles does not deny that the cosmos can become a single great living thing, but for Empedocles this happens only in the Sphairos, in the distant past and the distant future, while for Plato it is a present reality. To put it another way, for Plato the worlds of Love and Strife, or *nous* and Necessity, do not alternate in time (perhaps Necessity dominated in the past, but if so, it will not return); rather, they are two aspects of a single state of the cosmos, with *nous* predominating, and completely dominant in the heavens. And the key to the difference is that Plato, unlike Empedocles, has been persuaded by mathematical astronomy that the motions of the heavens are too mathematically perfect to be the result of a vortex (so especially *Laws* XII, 966e2–967d2). He therefore follows Anaxagoras in attributing the motion of the heavens to *nous*, although for Anaxagoras this is apparently a single rotation, while for Plato it is a plurality of harmoniously cooperating rotations (the "motion of the Same" accounting for the daily rotation of the whole heaven, the divided "motion of the Other" accounting for the zodiacal motions of the seven planets, *Timaeus* 36b6–d7). But Plato entirely breaks Anaxagoras' connection of *nous* with vortices and with separation and the sorting of like to like. Rather, Plato attributes to *nous* what Empedocles attributes to Love, the bringing of unlike things together in harmonious proportions and the assembly of parts into teleological wholes and in particular living things. There seems to be an especially Empedoclean reference when the demiurge produces love or friendship *(philia)* by bringing earth, water, air, and fire together in continued proportion (32b3–c4). When Plato does bring in something like a vortex to explain the motions of heavy and light bodies, he attributes it not to *nous* but to Necessity. Here what Plato describes is not so much an Anaxagorean vortex as a Democritean vortex, complete with Democritus' simile of the winnowing-fan (Democritus B164, *Timaeus* 52e6–53a1, as noted above). The reason, I think, is that Plato wants to exhibit the operations of Necessity in their purest form. While Anaxagoras' vortex is circular and produced by *nous*, Democritus' vortices arise spontaneously from the random rectilinear motions of atoms colliding with each other; Democritus thinks that these will be channeled into something like circular motion when they are confined inside the "membrane" of interlocking atoms that surrounds a cosmos, and will then produce the sorting of like to like and cosmic order (Diogenes Laertius IX, 31–33, attributed to Leucippus). Plato agrees that the random shaking of the Receptacle will produce a sorting of like to like, but denies that it can produce cosmic order, life, or the rotations of the heaven.

    I do not mean to suggest that, either for Empedocles or for Plato, Love and Strife or *nous* and Necessity are purely antagonistic. Strife, by separating out pure earth and water and air and fire, provides the materials which Love can bring together in harmonious proportions to produce blood and the like, and then to produce living things (we could put this in Hesiodic terms and say that while the love and thus the mixture of heaven and earth are needed for any further living things to be generated, their strife and thus their separation are needed for there to be room for anything else to emerge). Likewise for Plato, the shaking of the Receptacle produces the raw materials, and also the impulses to motion, which *nous* will "persuade" to serve the ends of living things. The idea of a teleological nature contriving to make the natural impulses of earth, water, air, and fire serve the higher ends of a living whole is also in Aristotle. But Aristotle, following out Plato's ideal of teleological explanation, his claim that "*nous* ordered all things," and his idea that the causality of *nous* should come about through persuasion rather than violence, rejects the violence which Plato seems to retain in the *Timaeus*: the violence which the demiurge employs in constructing and rationalizing the world soul (Plato actually speaks of the demiurge "fitting together by violence" the circle of the different into the world-soul, 35a8) and in imposing its circular motion on a world composed of earth, water, air, and fire, the violence of the original creation in time (including stamping the shapes of the regular polyhedra on earth, water, air, and fire) which begins the narrative, and the violence of the shaking of the Receptacle. In Aristotle the narrative form of the critique of earlier physics disappears, as do vortices, as does narrative as such, replaced with an attempt at causal demonstration for-the-most-part from the natures of earth, water, air, and fire, the heavenly bodies and the *nous* that moves them, and the souls which are the architectonic natures of living things. But to understand the formation either of the *Timaeus* or of Aristotle's physical treatises, we should go back to Empedocles' narrative critique of vortex-explanation.

To return to Cherniss. If—*if*—there is a teleological development in Presocratic natural philosophy, leading either to the *Timaeus* or to Aristotle, it is not a straightforward story of something striving to attain its natural form. Rather, it is a development of critique. Anaxagoras' attempt to explain the world through *nous* called forth Empedocles' critique and Empedocles' attempt to surpass him, above all in the teleological explanation of living things as the products of divine craft; Empedocles in turn calls forth deeper rethinkings of the critique which will apply against a broader range of philosophers including Empedocles himself, and thus he also calls forth attempts to outdo him as he outdid Anaxagoras. Or, to put it another way, each philosopher takes over the ideas and impulses of earlier thinkers, and tries to make them cooperate in the service of allegedly higher ends.

10

What's the Matter? Some Neo-Platonist Answers

Ian Mueller

In this essay I want to say a very few things about Neo-Platonist interpretations of the *Timaeus* relating to the receptacle and the geometric characterization of earth, water, air, and fire. The starting point of my reflections was translating Simplicius' commentary on books 3 and 4 of Aristotle's *On the Heavens*, and much of what I say is based upon that. But I will also be invoking a passage from his commentary on Aristotle's *Physics* and some material in John Philoponus and Proclus. I begin with some remarks about Simplicius' basic conception of what we call Aristotle's criticisms of Plato. At the beginning of his extensive discussion of Aristotle's objections to Plato's geometrical chemistry, Simplicius says:

> The disagreement between the philosophers <Plato and Aristotle> is not substantive, but Aristotle pays attention to those who understand Plato superficially and frequently raises objections against the apparent meaning of what Plato says and what can be understood in a worse way, and he seems to be refuting Plato. (Simplicius, *On Aristotle's* On the Heavens, 640, 28–31)[1]

Simplicius' point is not that Aristotle is a superficial reader, but that he raises objections to the surface meaning of what Plato says in order to prevent other

---

1 *Commentaria in Aristotelem Graeca*, VII (Berlin: Georg Reimer, 1894). John Philoponus speaks much the same way in commenting on Aristotle's criticism of Plato's treatment of the soul in the *Timaeus*; see, e.g., Philoponus, *Commentary on Aristotle's* On the Soul, *Commentaria In Aristotelem Graeca*, XV (Berlin: Georg Reimer, 1897), 125, 29–31.

people from espousing those superficial readings.[2] In connection with another passage in *On the Heavens* in which Aristotle connects Plato's association of the cube with earth to earth's stability Simplicius refers to Aristotle's earlier criticism[3] of Plato for allegedly saying that the earth has a winding motion around the pole:

> It is worth pointing out that Aristotle does know that Plato thinks the earth is steady, since it was Plato who said that it is a cube because it is stable and remains fixed. Consequently when in the preceding book he asserted that the earth is said by Timaeus to be wound and move <around the pole>, he was confronting those who understand Timaeus' words in this way. (Simplicius, *On Aristotle's* On the Heavens, 662, 31–663, 2)

So, Aristotle knows and shares Plato's true view, and his criticisms are all directed at the superficial readings of Plato made by others.[4]

1. Simplicius

Simplicius begins his discussion of Aristotle's criticisms with a brief characterization of what he takes to be the fundamental Platonic theory of the elements of the geometrical chemistry of the *Timaeus*,

> which says that solid figures are proximate elements of . . . fire, air, water, and earth, bodies which we call elements but which, as Plato says [*Timaeus* 48b3–c2], are not even to be ranked as syllables but are even more composite than syllables, since they are composed of the solid figures, pyramid, cube, and the others, these figures

---

2   Cf. Henry J. Blumenthal, "Neoplatonic elements in the *de Anima* Commentaries," *Phronesis* 21 (1976), 65, and for a more general discussion of Neoplatonist understanding of the "harmony of Plato and Aristotle" see Ilsetraut Hadot, "Aristote dans l'enseignement philosophique néoplatonicien," *Revue de Théologie et de Philosophie* 124 (1992), 407–425, and for its development, the same author's *Studies on the Neoplatonist Hierocles*, translated by Michael Chase, *Transactions of the American Philosophical Society* XCIV, 1, pp. 5–14. For a rejection of Simplicius' approach to apparent disagreement between Plato and Aristotle see Philoponus, *Against Proclus* (Hugo Rabe, ed., *Ioannes Philoponus, De Aeternitate Mundi contra Proclum* (Leipzig: B. G. Teubner, 1899); reprinted, Hildesheim: Georg Olms, 1984; English translation: Michael Share, trans., *Philoponus,* Against Proclus *on the Eternity of the World 1–5* (Ithaca: Cornell University Press, 2004), 29, 2–8.

3   *On the Heavens*, 2.13.293b30–32, on which see Simplicius' commentary at 517, 3–519, 11.

4   In reading Simplicius it is important to bear in mind that in many cases he simply reports Aristotle's criticisms without trying to show why they are directed at superficial readings. In this circumstance, a modern philosopher can easily get the impression that Simplicius really thinks a criticism is appropriate and telling.

are composed of planes, and the planes are composed of matter and form. (Simplicius, *On Aristotle's* On the Heavens, 638, 20–25)

In the last words we see at work the standard Neo-Platonist view that Plato's chemistry is built on top of a broadly Aristotelian view of the physical world in which the fundamental "elements" are matter and form, a theory which Plato is taken to have adumbrated in the well-known and difficult description of the receptacle at 48e2–52d1 of the *Timaeus*.[5]

Simplicius goes on to expound the geometry of Plato's chemistry, stressing the fact that it rules out the possibility that there could be any interchange between earth and the other simple bodies, whereas the other three do change into one another. When Plato introduces this limitation on interchangeability he says (*Timaeus* 54b6–7), "We should now be more specific about what was previously said in an unclear way." Simplicius commends Alexander of Aphrodisias for recognizing that "earlier <Plato> had hypothesized that all these things are composed of the same matter and said they change into one another, but later instead of matter he directly hypothesizes different triangles for them and no longer accepts that they come to be from one another" (Simplicius, *On Aristotle's* On the Heavens, 640, 5–8). Simplicius continues by stating Alexander's objection to this way of looking at things:

> If . . . matter, according to Plato, is given form by the triangles and bodies are generated from them, why would it not be possible that the matter which underlies earth be subsequently given shape by the triangles which give form to water and air and fire? (Simplicius, *On Aristotle's* On the Heavens, 640, 9–12)

Simplicius' immediate response to Alexander (Simplicius, *On Aristotle's* On the Heavens, 640, 12–19) is not as clear as one might like, but he subsequently restates it in a clearer form, which shows that he thinks Plato "really" did think there was total interchange among the elements. There Simplicius first cites

---

5 Simplicius' confidence that Plato holds the matter/form theory is undoubtedly buttressed by his idea that Plato is only recounting Pythagorean ideas formulated in the post-Aristotelian pseudepigraphic work *On the Nature of the Cosmos and of the Soul* ascribed to Timaeus of Locri (Text and German translation: Walter Marg, ed. and trans. *Timaeus Locrus, De Natura Mundi et Animae*, Philosophia Antiqua, No. 24 [Leiden: E. J. Brill, 1972]); English translation: Thomas Tobin, ed. and trans., *Timaeus of Locri, On the Nature of the World and the Soul* (Chico: Scholars Press, 1985). Before describing the geometrical chemistry briefly Timaeus says (32), "The principles of things which come to be are matter as substratum and form as the *logos* of shape. What is generated from these are the bodies earth and water, air and fire. The generation of these is a follows. Every body is composed of planes, and a plane is composed of triangles . . . ."

a passage—*Timaeus* 50b10–c6—from the description of the receptacle[6] to show that Plato believes that "things made from the same matter change into one another with the matter enduring through the change" (Simplicius, *On Aristotle's* On the Heavens, 643, 29–30) and then says:

> In order that Plato not be thought to disagree with himself nor Aristotle to disagree with Plato, what was said just a little while ago should be said again: according to Plato, earth changes into the other simple bodies and changes from them insofar as it is composed from the same matter, first matter, but insofar as it is composed directly from the isosceles <right> triangle, it is unchangeable. For so long as the triangles keep their own specificity, earth cannot come to be from the half <equilateral> triangle nor the other simple bodies from the isosceles <right> triangle. But when the triangles themselves are broken up[7] and re-combined and given shapes, then what was previously an isosceles—either the whole or a part of it—becomes a half-triangle and the coming to be of earth from the others (and of the others from it) is made manifest since there is a resolution of the triangles down to their matter. And if this didn't happen the doctrine of matter which is entirely without form and receives the forms of everything would be empty *(mataios)*. (Simplicius, *On Aristotle's* On the Heavens, 644, 7–18)

What, then, is the relationship between the Aristotelian account of elemental change as qualitative change in a substratum, expressed most fully in *On Coming to be and Perishing*, and the Platonic/geometric one? Roughly speaking, the Platonic one goes deeper:

> For because Plato explains the differences between the qualities heat, cold, dryness, and moistness on the basis of difference of figures, it is prima facie clear that he is seeking other principles of

---

6   "It is always receiving all things, but it does not ever in any way take on any form which is similar to the things entering it; by nature it lies as a matrix which is changed and given shape by the things entering it, and because of them it appears different at different times. And the things which enter into it and depart are copies of the things which always are and are modeled after them in a way which is difficult to describe . . ." (*Timaeus* 50b10–c6). A further quotation by Simplicius of part of this passage is of some interest. He writes, "For matter 'is always receiving all things, and it does not ever in any way take on any form which is similar to any of the things entering it', so that it does not reproduce the forms bestowed on it badly by also displaying its own appearance. These things are written about matter in the *Timaeus*." (Simplicius, *On Aristotle's* On the Heavens, 658, 5–8)

7   *Katathrauesthai*, a verb used by Plato at *Timaeus* 56e5 in connection with the dissolution of fire.

the coming to be of these four bodies, fire, air, water, and earth, principles which are prior to the qualities relating to heat, cold, dryness, and wetness and are found in differences in <the category of> quantity because these differences are more akin to bodies. For as Theophrastus reports, Democritus said earlier that explanations in terms of heat and cold and such things are amateurish *(idiotikôs)*, since the soul yearns to hear another principle which is more appropriate to body than this sort of activity of what is hot. (Simplicius, *On Aristotle's* On the Heavens, 640, 32–641, 9)[8]

So, because Aristotle's account of elemental change remains at the level of quality, it does not reach prior quantitative principles which are more appropriate to bodies. For Simplicius Aristotle's account is not incompatible with Plato's and is certainly not false. Indeed, it is obviously true—it just doesn't go deep enough. However, in his characteristic fashion Simplicius also wants to invoke Aristotle as believer in the priority of quantity to quality, although what he says about Aristotle is nothing I would want to try to defend as an interpretation:

> Even Aristotle himself thinks that shapes come to be in matter prior to the other qualities. That he does so is clear from the fact that what he calls the second substratum is called qualityless body. And, as he demonstrates, shape and most of all shape when it has been limited, is made substantial together with three-dimensional body insofar as it is body. (Simplicius, *On Aristotle's* On the Heavens, 576, 6–10)

This quotation introduces us to some of the technical terminology used in later discussions of matter, 'second substratum' and 'qualityless body'. Neither of these terms is Aristotelian (or Platonic), although as this passage indicates, Simplicius is somehow convinced[9] that Aristotle used the term 'second substratum'. We get

---

8   In another passage Simplicius offers his account of the differences between Democritus' atomism and Plato's theory:
> But Plato's view is presumably different from Democritus' because it gives priority to something simpler than bodies, namely the plane, which is simpler than the atoms (which are bodies), and because it recognizes that symmetries and proportions are demiurgic of the figures, and because it treats earth differently <from the other elements>. (Simplicius, *On Aristotle's* On the Heavens, 576, 16–19)

9   See also Simplicius, *On Aristotle's* On the Heavens, 134, 10 ("which the Peripatetics call second substratum") and 599, 5–7 (perhaps referring to Alexander). Cf. 565, 22–25: "If Aristotle, too, thinks that qualityless body comes to be first from matter and form, and he says that it is finite and the substratum of qualities, how is it not necessary that it have shape and that shapes exist prior to qualities?"

a clearer sense of what this term means from what Simplicius says after an earlier citation of Theophrastus' report on Democritus. He says that he is describing the Pythagoraeans, but he is clearly offering an interpretation of the *Timaeus*:

> And in the same way the Pythagoreans ascend to planes, consider-
> ing figures and magnitudes to be causes of heat and cold . . . . For
> every body is immediately determined quantitatively in substance,
> but shape . . . has been taken from the genus of quantities, so that
> every body is a quantity which has been given a shape. For in itself
> matter is incorporeal, and the second substratum is a body which
> is in itself qualityless but which has been given form by a variety
> of figures; and the second substratum differs from mathematical
> body by involving matter and being tangible, touch apprehending
> it because of its bulk and not because of heat or coldness. And so
> they say that this second substratum, being painted with different
> figures, produces the elements which are more fundamental than the
> four elements: the elements which are more fundamental than earth
> are painted with the cubical figure, . . . and the other elements are
> composed from the other figures in this way. And they say that all
> the other powers <of earth, water, fire, and air> and their changes
> into one another follow from the difference among figures of this
> kind. (Simplicius, *On Aristotle's* On the Heavens, 564, 26–565, 12)

Thus, on Simplicius' understanding, Plato recognizes an incorporeal first mat-ter which takes on various three-dimensional shapes and becomes body, but body without qualities or the second substratum. In a way not specified clearly the second substrata produce the qualities which are emphasized in Aristotle's account of the simple bodies and their changes. This second substratum is like a mathematical body, except that it is material and tangible, although it lacks the qualities which Aristotle made fundamental to his account of change among the simple bodies, such as hot and cold. In this context the terms 'material' and 'tangible' seem more like abstract placeholders than conveyers of information about the second substratum. The second substratum is material because it "contains" prime matter. Simplicius denies that its tangibility involves its being hot or cold, and I doubt that it is either hard or soft; it simply shows the kind of "resistance" *(antitupia)* which the Stoics may have invoked to explain the difference between extension and body.[10]

---

10 Cf. A. A. Long and D. N. Sedley, *The Hellenistic Philosophers* I (Cambridge, England: Cambridge University Press, 1987), p. 273.

2. John Philoponus

In his diatribe *Against Proclus*, John Philoponus argues against the idea of an incorporeal first matter, referring to it as babbled about (*thruloumenos*, 404, 10) and mythical (*mutheuomenos*, 406, 8), and substituting for it the view that first matter, the ultimate substratum, is 'the indefinite three-dimensional' (*to aoriston trichei diastaton*, 405, 26)[11] or qualityless body, clearly something analogous to Simplicius' second substratum, but probably not, as we will see, exactly like it. Philoponus, who as a Christian does not consider Plato or Aristotle to be an authority figure, states the view he is dismissing in the following way:

> Plato and the most prominent of the earlier people declared that matter is incorporeal and formless . . . . And they say that quantity is first conjoined with this formless and incorporeal matter to produce the three-dimensional, which is qualityless and is called body without qualification *(haplôs)*. They hypothesize that the great and the small is the first differentia of this body without qualification. For that body in itself which is defined by only the three dimensions is a certain indefinite *(onchos)* bulk and is defined by the difference of the great and the small. (Philoponus, *Against Proclus*, 407, 23–408, 9)

> Just as animal cannot exist without one of its proper differentiae, so too the unqualified nature of body is indeed defined, as they say, by the three dimensions, and is different from the differentia of the great and small, but it is impossible for it to exist without one of these differentiae. (Philoponus, *Against Proclus*, 408, 26–409, 3)

> Next from these four elements coming together and being combined, composite bodies come to be. So they say that there is first and unqualified matter, which is incorporeal and formless, second there is the three-dimensional and qualityless body, which they also say is the second (after matter) substratum, and third and more proximate <to us> the four elements. (Philoponus, *Against Proclus*, 409, 18–25)

I wish to signal what I believe without anything like a sense of certainty is a difference between Simplicius' second substratum and Philoponus'

---

11   See Frans A. J. de Haas, *John Philoponus' New Definition of Prime Matter*, Philosophia Antiqua 69 (Leiden, New York, and Köln: E. J. Brill, 1997).

three-dimensional. Simplicius' characterization of the second substratum as "given form by a variety of figures" and "painted with different figures" suggests that the qualityless second substratum comes in definite shapes and sizes, of which the primary and perhaps only examples are Plato's fundamental solids. On the other hand, Philoponus speaks of the three-dimensional as indefinite, suggesting that it is something which needs to be given definite size and shape as well as qualities. I shall have more to say about differences between Philoponus and Simplicius in the next section.

3. Pericles of Lydia

In discussing interpretations of the *Timaeus*, Simplicius (*On Aristotle's* On the Heavens, 564, 10–13) tells us that Iamblichus thought that Plato was speaking "symbolically" when he gave his geometrical account of the simple bodies. I take this to mean that Iamblichus did not think the account was true when taken literally, although I believe we do not know whether Iamblichus had anything to say about the relevant physics.[12] However, Simplicius goes on to tell us that "more recent" Platonic philosophers did offer a reading of the *Timaeus* taking no account of its geometric aspect:

> Since the four elements are composites of matter and form and therefore do not satisfy the definition of a principle, they say that the qualities which are called affective,[13] heat and dryness and their opposites, coming to be first in matter (or qualityless body), also compose the four elements . . . . And if someone were to ask why fire heats and water cools, they would say "Because fire is hot, water cold." For they posit these things as principles and do not seek further for a cause beyond the principles. (Simplicius, *On Aristotle's* On the Heavens, 564, 14–24)

It can be inferred from things Simplicius says in his commentary on Aristotle's *Physics*[14] that one such later Platonist was Pericles of Lydia, the dedicatee of Proclus' *Platonic Theology*.[15] Simplicius is there concerned to refute the doctrine

---

12   I note that at 576, 3–4 of *On Aristotle's* On the Heavens, Simplicius himself invokes the possibility of a symbolical interpretation in connection with the non-interchangeability of earth with the other simple bodies, although he does not insist upon it.

13   The term 'affective quality' (*pathêtikê poiotês*) is taken from Aristotle's *Categories*, 8.9a18 ff. Simplicius regularly applies it to the fundamental properties of the four elements, heat, coldness, wetness, dryness.

14   *Commentaria in Aristotelem Graeca*, IX (Berlin: Georg Reimer, 1882), p. 227, 23 ff.

15   H. D. Saffrey and L. G. Westerink, eds. and trans., *Proclus, Théologie Platonicienne*, I (Paris: Les Belles Lettres, 1968), 1.1.5.6–7, where Proclus addresses Pericles as his dearest

that first matter is qualityless body, a view which he ascribes to the Stoics[16] among earlier people and to Pericles among later ones. In material which I shall assume is taken from Pericles, Simplicius gives three arguments for the view that first matter is qualityless body and then attempts to show that this view was held by both Plato and Aristotle. The arguments are, I think, framed in a context in which some version of the Stoic notion of qualityless body is accepted and the issue is whether it is, as Simplicius thinks, a so-called second substratum under which there is a first substratum or matter or whether, as Pericles thinks, it is first matter. My interest is not in these arguments, but in the textual considerations invoked to enlist the support of Plato,[17] both of which come from the pages in the *Timaeus* in which Plato describes the receptacle:

---

friend. Proclus also mentions him at 872, 19 of his commentary on Plato's *Parmenides* (Victor Cousin, ed., *Procli Philosophi Platonici Opera Inedita* [Paris: Aug. Durand, 1864], pp. 617–1258; reprinted, Hildesheim: Georg Olms, 1964; English translation: Glenn R. Morrow and John M. Dillon, trans., *Proclus' Commentary on Plato's* Parmenides [Princeton: Princeton University Press, 1987]). And in his life of Proclus (Henri Dominique Saffrey and Alain-Philippe Segonds, eds. and trans., *Marinus, Proclus ou sur le Bonheur* [Paris: Les Belles Lettres, 2001]; English translation: Laurence Jay Rosán, *The Philosophy of Proclus* [New York: Cosmos, 1949]), 29.16–19, Marinus says that Proclus took Pericles with him to the Athenian Asclepion in a successful attempt to cure a sick child.

16 It is well known that the Stoics' two fundamental principles are matter and god, matter being also called 'substance' (Diogenes Laertius, *Lives of the Philosophers* [Miroslav Marcovich, ed., *Diogenis Laertii Vitae Philosophorum*, I (Stuttgart and Leipzig: Teubner, 1999); English translation in the Loeb Classical Library], 7.134), 'qualityless', 'first' (see, e.g., Diogenes Laertius, 7.134 and 150), and perhaps 'body' (see Long and Sedley, *Hellenistic Philosophers*, I, p. 274). I quote Sextus Empiricus (*Against the Physicists* [in Hermann Mutschmann, ed., *Sexti Empirici Opera*, II (Leipzig: Teubner, 1914); English translation in *Sextus Empiricus* III in the Loeb Classical Library] 10.312):

> The Stoics made the coming to be of everything to be from a single qualityless body; for, according to them qualityless matter is a first principle of things and turns through everything; when it changes the four elements, fire and air, water and earth, come to be.

It is, of course, rather surprising to find an associate of Proclus adopting such a Stoic position.

17 Of the three "non-textual" arguments for qualityless body as prime matter, one is itself really textual: Aristotle and Plato are said to introduce matter on the basis of elemental change (Simplicius, *On Aristotle's* Physics, 227, 26–30). The strictly textual argument invoking Aristotle cites no specific text:

> If body accrued to matter and departed from it like any other form, it is clear that before body accrued to matter and after it departed, the privation of body, that is incorporeality, would apply to matter. And there would be a natural incorporeal substance. But Aristotle clearly does not think this, since he frequently says that natural things are bodies and involved with bodies. (cf. *On the Heavens* 1.1.268a4–6 and 3.1.298b3–4)

> Now the nurse of Becoming, having been made watery and
> fiery and receiving the characters *(morphas)* of earth and air . . .
> (*Timaeus* 52d4–6; Cornford translation)

> When the arranging of the universe was undertaken, at first fire
> and water and earth and air had some traces of themselves but
> were altogether disposed in the way that is likely for anything
> from which god is absent; these things being in this condition at
> that time the god first gave them shape with forms and numbers.
> (*Timaeus* 53a9–b5)

After quoting these passages "Pericles" says, "If the demiurge first put the forms
of the elements into matter, and the common substratum for these forms is
qualityless body, qualityless body would be matter." (Simplicius, *On Aristotle's
Physics*, 228, 8–10)

The first counterargument[18] by the believers in qualityless matter as primary substratum invokes the Timaeus' introduction of triangles:

> That Plato did not intend body to be the first substratum (which
> we call matter) would be clear from the fact that he first takes his
> plane <figures> as elements of body, obviously because they are
> more fundamental. And so he writes in the *Timaeus* [53c5–8]:
> "Every form of a body also has depth, and it is in addition abso-
> lutely necessary that depth be contained by the plane nature."
> And also for Plato body is three-dimensional . . . , and such a
> thing has number and figure as part of its substance. Both Plato
> and Aristotle say that matter in itself has none of these things,
> except that when it participates in forms, then it is changed in
> shape *(metaschêmatizesthai)* by forms and numbers. (Simplicius,
> *On Aristotle's* Physics, 228, 17–28)

Although Simplicius does not put forward this textual argument as his own, he
obviously accepts the conclusion for which it argues, and I am confident that
he accepts the argument itself. If this is so, the argument would be one indication that he associates the second substratum with the demiurge's imposition of
forms and numbers on what for Simplicius is formless and qualityless matter.
The fact that Simplicius associates three-dimensionality with definite size and
shape, suggests that he does not think of his first matter as three-dimensional
in the way that Philoponus does. Richard Sorabji has argued that Simplicius

---

18 For the most part the arguments for matter rather than body as prime subject are that
body has shape and size and matter does not.

assigns to Aristotle the view that first matter is 'indefinite extension' *(diastasis)*.[19] Although Sorabji does not claim that Simplicius holds the same view, I am confident that Simplicius holds in this case, as in most others, the same view as he ascribes to Aristotle. Given this assumption, I am moved to ask whether it is appropriate to call what is dimensionless 'extension'. If not, the term would seem inappropriate for Simplicius' idea of first matter, which would seem to be very close to that of Plotinus, who, as one author puts it, "denied to matter not merely a definite magnitude, but magnitude and extension altogether."[20] In this connection I would like to point out some other terms Simplicius uses for matter in *On Aristotle's* Physics: *ektasis* (extending out; 230, 23; 536, 25); *chusis* (diffusing out; 536, 26; 537, 26) or *echusis* (538, 1, 13); *diaspasmos* (scattering; 537, 37); *paresis* (slackening; 230, 23 and perhaps 538, 13; cf. *pareimenon (pariêmi)* at 230, 25); and *eklelumenon* (being spilt; 230, 25).[21]

4. Proclus

In his commentary on the *Timaeus* Proclus has the following to say about the phrase 'all that is visible' in the sentence (*Timaeus* 30a3–5) "The god took over all that is visible—not at rest but in discordant and unordered motion—and brought it from disorder into order":

> The words "all that is visible" show that this visible thing is corporeal, since it would not be visible if it were incorporeal and qualityless. Consequently these words do not refer to matter or to the second substratum; rather the words refer to what already participates in forms and has certain traces *(ichnê)* and reflections *(emphaseis)* of them and is "in discordant and unordered motion." For the presence of indistinct images of the forms imparts different motions to all that is visible, as Timaeus himself will say subsequently, and these images are illumined by all the divine orders prior to the demiurge, but before the creation the Paradigm

19   Richard Sorabji, *Matter, Space, and Motion* (London: Duckworth, 1988), pp. 7–22. I would like to thank Richard for discussing with me the complex question I am raising here, on which much more should be said. For another attempt to closely identify the views of Philoponus and Simplicius, see de Haas, *John Philoponus' New Definition*, pp. 120–131.

20   F. R. Jevons, "Dequantitation in Plotinus' Cosmology," *Phronesis* 9 (1964), 66.

21   I would also like to quote Lucas Siorvanes' words about a cousin of *diastasis*, *diastêma*, a word which is not used by Simplicius for matter but is his preferred term for understanding what place is: "The Neoplatonic *diastêma* has its context in the metaphysical theory of 'procession' *(proodos)* from the One to the Many. Being extends from unity and wholeness to plurality and particularity." (Simplicius, *Corollaries on Place and Time*, p. 17 n. 1)

especially illumines them with being itself. (Proclus, *On Plato's Timaeus*, 387, 8–19)[22]

What Proclus goes on to say shows that his main interest is in promoting the disordered condition of the *Timaeus* rather than matter as the cause of evil. This comes out in his invocation of the same passage in another work:

> Perhaps then disorder and evil happen not because of matter but because of what is "in discordant and unordered motion." For this is the "corporeal nature" that, as the Eleatic Stranger affirms [Plato, *Statesman*, 273b], is the cause of disorder for the lowest things of the universe; it cannot be matter, as there is motion in it, whereas, matter is by itself immobile. Nor is this first composite qualityless body (for it is visible, as Timaeus says, whereas what is qualityless is not visible), but with some reflection of all the forms, it is a brew of all forms so to speak. That is why this first composite by its motion produces disorder. For the traces of the different forms leading to one and another motion show that the whole motion is discordant. (Proclus, *On the Existence of Evils*, 34.14–24)[23]

For Proclus, then, what for Simplicius is first matter and for Pericles is unqualified body is qualified body, a body which receives traces of qualities as reflections from the Forms prior (in a logical, not a temporal, sense) to the intervention of the demiurge. Pericles does not appear to have distinguished between the stage at which the receptacle contains only traces of qualities and when it is arranged into a cosmos by the demiurge, and we do not know how he dealt with Plato's distinguishing between the two stages. Perhaps he thought the distinction was "symbolical," or perhaps he just could not make sense of the traditional notion of first matter as opposed to qualityless body.

My first quotation from Proclus contains his only use of the term "second substratum" in extant works, but it appears from a passage in his commentary on Plato's *Parmenides* that he accepted some version of the hierarchy first matter/second substratum/visible world. In the passage Proclus is describing one of many ancient attempts to identify the subjects of the various hypotheses of the second part of the *Parmenides*. According to it, "the fourth hypothesis is

---

22   Ernest Diehl, ed., *Procli Diadochi in Platonis* Timaeum *Commentaria*, I (Leipzig: Teubner, 1903).

23   H. Boese, ed., *Procli Diadochi Tria Opuscula*, (Berlin: De Gruyter, 1960), pp. 172–265; translation after Jan Opsomer and Carlos Steel, trans., *Proclus on the Existence of Evils* (Ithaca: Cornell University Press, 2003).

about body organized in some way, the fifth about unorganized body, the sixth about organized matter, the seventh about unorganized matter . . . ." (Proclus, *On Plato's* Parmenides, 1054, 3–7) According to Proclus,

> We could not say how organized matter differed from body, whether organized or unorganized. For if matter is organized when it becomes qualityless body, organized matter is the same as unorganized body, and if it takes on quality it is the same as organized body . . . . And how can the fifth hypothesis be about unorganized body? The fifth hypothesis explicitly concludes that, if the others do not participate in the One, they neither stand still nor move; but Timaeus described unorganized body as "in discordant and unordered motion." (*On Plato's* Parmenides, 1054, 12–25)[24]

I take it that Proclus is willing to recognize unorganized matter, that is, first matter. But he cannot accept the notion of an organized matter unless it is to be identified with qualityless body, Simplicius' second substratum, or with organized body, that is body as it exists in our cosmos. It is not clear to me how Proclus could possibly identify unorganized body with both qualityless body and with the body in discordant motion, since in the earlier passages he explicitly asserts that the body in discordant motion has qualities. I suggest that when Proclus says, "if matter is organized when it becomes qualityless body, organized matter is the same as unorganized body," he means by unorganized body the body which has not been given qualities at all, but has the extension and the resistance of the second substratum. If this is right, then we may have in Proclus a bifurcation above the level of first matter into a visible unorganized body in discordant motion (all that is visible) and an invisible unorganized body, which is the same as Simplicius' second substratum. I have no idea how Proclus might have tried to organize this bifurcation into a single hierarchy, if, indeed, he did try.

---

24 Text supplemented by the Latin translation of William of Moerbeke in Carlos Steel, ed., *Commentaire sur le* Parménide *de Platon/Traduction de Guillaume de Moerbeke,* II (Leuven: University Press, 1985).

11

Derrida's Khôra, *or Unnaming the Timaean Receptacle*[*]

Zina Giannopoulou

Jacques Derrida was deeply fascinated by Plato. From his response to Foucault's *Histoire de la folie* (1967) to *La Pharmacie de Platon* (1972) to *La Carte Postale* (1980) to *Khôra* (1980) and *Politiques de l' amitié* (1994), he dealt with issues of Platonic ethics, metaphysics, and epistemology from a deconstructive perspective.[1] Of all these works, "Plato's Pharmacy" and "*Khôra*" exemplify his most sustained engagement with Platonic philosophy. But whereas the former has received extensive commentary from classicists and philosophers, the latter has been relatively neglected.[2] When scholars of the ancient world turn to it, they mainly seek to reveal the ways in which the Timaean receptacle underwrites

[*]I am grateful to Charles Griswold, Julia Lupton, Steve Mailloux, Nick Smith, and Rei Terada for valuable criticisms and suggestions; to Allen Miller for allowing me access to his forthcoming paper on Derrida's *Khôra*; and to the editor, Richard Mohr, for his kind invitation to the *Timaeus* conference and his unfailingly incisive comments.

1 See Jacques Derrida, "Nous autres Grecs," in Barbara Cassin, ed., *Nos Grecs et leurs modernes*, (Paris: Seuil, 1992), pp. 262–267; Miriam Leonard, "'The 'Politiques de l' amitié': Derrida's Greeks and a national politics of classical scholarship," *Proceedings of the Cambridge Philological Society* 46 (2000), 45–78 and *Athens in Paris: Ancient Greece and the Political in Post-War French Thought* (Oxford: Oxford University Press, 2005), pp. 189–215; Paul A. Miller, *Postmodern Spiritual Practices: The Construction of the Subject and the Reception of Plato in Lacan, Derrida, and Foucault* (Columbus: Ohio State University Press, 2007), pp. 133–177.
2 For some notable exceptions see Catherine Zuckert, *Postmodern Platos* (Chicago: University of Chicago Press, 1996), pp. 235–243; John Sallis, *Chorology: On Beginning Plato's* Timaeus (Bloomington: Indiana University Press, 1999), pp. 91–124; and Drew A. Hyland, *Questioning Platonism: Continental Interpretations of Plato* (Albany: State University of New York Press, 2004), pp. 109–122. For a review of Hyland's book see Charles L. Griswold, "Reading and Writing Plato," *Philosophy and Literature* 32:1 (2008), 208–211.

Derridean deconstruction.[3] Beyond this broad academic circle, the *chôra* has influenced Julia Kristeva's approach to semiotics, Luce Irigaray's discussion of gender, Peter Eisenman's design of a garden for Le Parc de la Villette, Ann Bergren's work on architecture and gender, and Jeffrey Kipnis' interest in deconstruction and architecture.[4]

It is not hard to see why Timaeus' account of the *chôra* attracted Derrida's attention. As a third kind mediated by Forms and particulars, the receptacle was seen as a prime example of *différance*, the marginal and differential meaning that undercuts and destabilizes Plato's metaphysical dualism.[5] In *Phaedrus* the *pharmakon* "is the movement, the locus, and the play: (the production of) difference. It is the *différance* of difference. It holds in reserve, in its undecided shadow and vigil, the opposites and the differends that the process of discrimination will come to carve out."[6] The *chôra* serves a comparable function: by positioning itself between intelligibles and perceptibles and by refusing to be identified with them, it dismantles this "logic of exclusion" from within. It both shows up the polarity for what it is and invalidates it. Its deconstructive force manifests itself not only in the realm of metaphysical dualisms, but also in that of discursive binarisms, such as *mythos* vs. *logos*. The Timaean receptacle is for Derrida something like an uncompromising rebel lodged at the heart of a system in tension: its "third" presence calls attention to the limitations of the entire edifice and explodes the conceptual foundation that supports it.

The trouble that the *chôra* spells for the Platonic universe begins with its name. In "Plato's Pharmacy," Derrida explores the multiple uses and (mis)translations of another word, *pharmakon*, at once "drug" and "remedy," in order to problematize an important aspect of Plato's logocentrism, his deeply ambivalent attitude toward writing. He notes that "this regulated polysemy has allowed, by ineptness, indetermination or over-determination, but without

---

3 *Khôra* is the third part of the volume *On the Name*, T. Dutoit, ed., (Stanford: Stanford University Press, 1995). All quotations come from this edition. It was originally published in French as three separate booklets in 1993: *Passions*, *Sauf le nom*, and *Khôra* by Galilee.

4 Julia Kristeva, *La révolution du langage poétique* (Paris: Seuil, 1974); Luce Irigaray, *Speculum de l' autre femme* (Paris: Minuit, 1974); Jeffrey Kipnis and Thomas Leeser, *Chora L Works: Jacques Derrida and Peter Eisenman* (New York: The Monacelli Press, 1997); Ann Bergren, "Architecture Gender Philosophy," in J. Whiteman, J. Kipnis, and R. Burdett, eds., *Strategies in Architectural Thinking* (Cambridge: MIT Press, 1992), pp. 8–46; Jeffrey Kipnis, "Twisting the Separatrix," in Kipnis and Leeser, *Chora L Works*, pp. 137–360. See also Anthony Vidler, "A City Transformed: Designing 'Defensible Space,'" *Grey Room* 7 (2002), 82–85. Derrida uses the term *khôra* to refer to the receptacle and I shall respect his choice of transliteration when I refer to his notion of the receptacle. Otherwise, I shall use the latinized *chôra*.

5 Derrida makes the connection between *pharmakon* and *chôra* in "La pharmacie de Platon," *La Dissemination* (Paris: Seuil, 1972), pp. 184–186. All translations come from Barbara Johnson, ed., *Dissemination* (Chicago: The University of Chicago Press, 1981).

6 Derrida, "Plato's Pharmacy," p. 127.

contradiction, the translation of the same word by 'remedy', 'poison', 'drug', 'philter', etc." This multiplicity of definitions and translations has occluded "the plastic unity of this concept, its very rule, and the strange logic which links it to its signifier" in such a way that it has "been dispersed, masked, obliterated, struck with a relative unreadability, by the imprudence or empiricism of the translators, certainly, but first and foremost by the redoubtable and irreducible difficulty of translation."[7] As we shall see, a similar semantic indeterminacy or overdeterminacy besets the *chôra*. To be sure, Derrida's bafflement is neither capricious nor without precedent, occurring as it does already in Timaeus' account. In it, the introduction of the receptacle is signaled by an admission of its "difficult and obscure" (49a3: *chalepon kai amudron*) nature, followed by a reference to the "difficult to describe and marvelous" (50c6: *dusphraston kai thaumaston*) manner in which the Forms are imprinted on it, and culminating in Timaeus' acknowledgment of his "utter resourcelessness" (51b1: *aporôtata*) to make it intelligible, given how "exceedingly difficult it is to comprehend" (51b1: *dusalôtotaton*). Even after Plato's time, from Aristotle to the present, the question of the *chôra*'s nature has proved curiously intractable, so much so that Kenneth Sayre has proclaimed Timaeus' account "incoherent from start to finish, defying 'legitimate' (nonbastard) reasoning at every stage of development."[8]

In light of the many difficulties that bedevil our comprehension and description of the *chôra*, it is not surprising to hear Derrida wonder, "what of this place? It is nameable? And wouldn't it have some impossible relation to the possibility of naming?" (90–91). In this paper, I shall focus exclusively on the *Khôra*'s treatment of the receptacle's nameability. I shall argue that Timaeus' *chôra* is not as resistant to naming as Derrida thinks it is. Its formlessness and ability to receive all things without absorbing their features deprive it of neither existential nor nominal identity. *Chôra* correctly names the receptacle for its peculiar beingness consists in its hosting the particulars it receives. The *chôra* is true to its essence and name by functioning precisely as what its name connotes, i.e. space or place. Being and function coincide, and this coincidence makes naming both possible and meaningful. By overemphasizing stark linguistic polarities ostensibly endorsed by Plato, such as metaphorical vs. proper sense and *mythos* vs. *logos*, Derrida misses vital nuances, semantic ambiguities already embedded in the text which significantly weaken his claim to *chôra*'s unnameability. Such ambiguities certainly complicate the receptacle's relationship with naming, but do not render it impossible. In the end, one is tempted to think that Derrida's reading of the *chôra*'s name works through a strange

---

7   Derrida, "Plato's Pharmacy," p. 80.
8   Kenneth Sayre, "The Multilayered Incoherence of Timaeus' Receptacle," in Gretchen J. Reydams-Schils, ed., *Plato's* Timaeus *as Cultural Icon* (Notre Dame: University of Notre Dame Press, 2003), p. 61.

misreading of the text: strong binarisms are blithely attributed to Plato, allowing the *chôra* to function as salutary *différance*, the displaced difference that effectively explodes a system already bursting at the seams.[9] But the system is stronger than Derrida suspects, and the receptacle, far from undermining it, bolsters and supports it.

Let me begin with Timaeus' use of metaphors to describe the *chôra*. Even a perfunctory glance at the relevant sections of the dialogue shows that references to the *chôra* are couched in metaphors, images, and similes. Images of containment are the most prevalent: "imprint-bearer" (*ekmageion*: 50c2; cf. 50e8–9), "container" (*dechomenon*: 50d3; see also 53a3, 57c3), "winnowing basket" (*plokanôn*: 52e6), "receptacle" (*hypodochên*: 49a6; 51a5), "all-recipient" (*pandeches*: 51a7; cf. 50b6). Viewed functionally rather than descriptively, the *chôra* is compared to a "nurse" (*tithênên*: 49a6; 52d5, 88d6), a "foster mother" (*trophon*: 88d6), and a "mother" (*mêtri*: 50d3; see also 51a5). In addition, there are two words connoting location, namely "space" (*chôras*: 52a8; see also 52d3; 53a6) and "place for sitting" (*hedran*: 52b1). Finally, the receptacle has been viewed as a mirror, although it is not described as such in the dialogue.[10]

Derrida seems uncomfortable with this proliferation of metaphors. Those who deploy figurative language to describe the receptacle "ask themselves no questions about this tradition of rhetoric which places at their disposal a reserve of concepts which are very useful but which are all built upon this distinction between the sensible and the intelligible, which is precisely what the thought of the *khôra* can no longer get along with" (92). The objection here is that as a third *quid* that transcends the binary opposition between what is visible and subject to generation and what is intelligible and perpetually selfsame, the *chôra* cannot be expressed by words whose validity depends upon the viability of that opposition. Its notional idiosyncrasy defies the verbal apparatus of Platonic dualism. But it is far from clear how and why the metaphorical language of containment and nurture is rooted in an interpretative tradition that sanctions the polarity Derrida wishes to reject. The intelligibility of Forms, entities that lie outside of space and time, does not obviously require the use of spatial or nurturing imagery, and although perceptibles occupy space, successful references to them are possible without recourse to spatial language. Nor is the conceptual dichotomy between Forms and particulars ordinarily expressed in

---

9   Hyland, *Questioning Platonism*, 114, also doubts that the metaphysical dualism the *khôra* deconstructs is "Plato's doctrine," but puts his observation to a different use.

10   For the *chôra* as a reflecting surface see A. E. Taylor, *A Commentary on Plato's* Timaeus (Oxford: Clarendon Press, 1928), p. 348; Francis M. Cornford, *Plato's Cosmology* (London: Kegan Paul, 1937), p. 192 n. 4; p. 371; Edward N. Lee, "On the Metaphysics of the Image in Plato's *Timaeus*," *Monist* 50 (1966), 341–368; Richard Mohr, "Image, Flux, and Space in Plato's *Timaeus*," *Phoenix* 34 (1980), 138–152; and Mary-Louise Gill, "Matter and Flux in Plato's *Timaeus*," *Phronesis* 32 (1987), 34–53.

terms of space, and so interpretations of the *chôra* that avail themselves of spatial language need take no stance on the validity of Plato's metaphysical dualism.

But what if the concern is about the validity of the polarity between metaphorical discourse and precise denotation? Should the various references to the *chôra* be understood as figures of speech or as names that befit the nominata? Is the distinction possible or even desirable? Here is what Derrida says in this regard:

> "We shall not speak of metaphor, but not in order to hear, for example, that the *khôra* is *properly* a mother, a nurse, a receptacle, a bearer of imprints or gold. It is perhaps because its scope goes beyond or falls short of the polarity of metaphorical sense versus proper sense that the thought of the *khôra* exceeds the polarity, no doubt analogous, of the *mythos* and the *logos* . . . . The consequence which we envisage would be the following: with these two polarities the thought of the *khôra* would trouble the very order of polarity, of polarity in general, whether dialectical or not." (92; emphasis original)

The sentiment conveyed in this paragraph is that repudiation of metaphors does not legitimize use of appropriate names, because the *chôra* does not abide by the logic of this opposition. Nor is it comfortable with the entrenched distinction between *mythos* and *logos*, which Derrida sees as "analogous" to that between metaphorical and proper sense. If, as he thinks, logocentrism governs binarisms of this sort, the *chôra*'s recalcitrance to them questions the soundness of the logocentric system and exposes it for the sham conceptual construction that it is.[11]

Before I proceed to register objections against this view, it will be useful to glance at an interpretation of the dichotomy between *mythos* and *logos* that greatly influenced Derrida's own thinking on the matter. In *Mythe et societé en Grèce ancienne*, Jean-Pierre Vernant casts the opposition in the following way:

> "Thus myth puts into play a form of logic which could be called— in contrast to the logic of noncontradiction of the philosophers—a logic of the ambiguous, of the equivocal, of polarity. How can one formulate, or even formalize, these see-saw operations, which flip any term into its opposite whilst at the same time keeping them both apart? The mythologist was left with drawing up, in conclusion, this statement of deficit, and to turn to the linguists,

---

11   In "Plato's Pharmacy," he characteristically says, "metaphoricity is the logic of contamination and the contamination of logic," p. 149.

logicians, mathematicians, that they might supply him with the
tool he lacked: the structural model of a logic which could not
be that of binarity, of the yes or no, a logic other than the logic
of the *logos*."[12]

According to Vernant, mythic discourse thrives on ambiguities, tolerates
contradictions, and revels in indeterminacies, while argumentative discourse
or *logos* excludes the middle ground between contradictories. The logic of the
former rejects binarisms; that of the latter requires them. The relevance of this
quotation to Derrida's project is obvious: the *khôra* is the entity that "flips any
term into its opposite whilst at the same time keeping them both apart." As a
third entity between sensibles and intelligibles, "it oscillates between two types
of oscillation: the double exclusion *(neither/nor)* and the participation *(both this
and that)*" (91). By situating itself between Forms and particulars, it belongs to
neither one and yet is strangely akin to both.

The analogical relation between "proper vs. figurative meaning" and
"*mythos* vs. *logos*" is left unaccounted for, and in the absence of clarifications of
the relevant terms and the presuppositions that bring them together interpretations can at best be speculative. Even so, the contrast between the elements of
the analogy suggests not only that proper meaning is antithetical to figurative
meaning just as *mythos* is antithetical to *logos*, but also that proper sense is
endemic to *logos* but incompatible with *mythos*, just as metaphorical sense is akin
to *mythos* but foreign to *logos*. But these alliances and dichotomies are arguably
too crude. For why would one suppose that proper sense, ordinarily associated
with objective reality and truth, is alien to myth? From the fact that mythic
discourse casts truth in its own idiom and makes it serve its own message, it
does not follow that it is inherently incapable of locating and articulating it.
Nor is argument necessarily averse to metaphoricity. Although it obeys "the
logic of noncontradiction," it can still use metaphors for its own purposes.

Even in Plato, *mythos* and *logos* are not always as rigidly demarcated or as
sharply contrasted as Derrida assumes, and recent Platonic scholarship has done
much to bridge the gap that ostensibly separates them.[13] Within the confines
of *Timaeus*, the permeability of the seemingly well-defined borders between

---

12   Jean-Pierre Vernant, *Mythe et societé en Grèce ancienne* (Paris: Maspero, 1974), p. 250.
Derrida prefaces *Khôra* with this quotation, and I borrow it from him.
13   For a good study of this issue, followed by an extensive bibliography, see Luc Brisson, *Plato
the Myth Maker*, translated, edited, and with an introduction by Gerard Naddaf (Chicago
and London: The University of Chicago Press, 1998), pp. 91–113. Although the distinction
between the two terms is variously construed, *mythos* most often means nonfalsifiable speech
or story, while *logos* is falsifiable speech.

these two notions is evident.[14] Drew Hyland calls attention to Critias' description of his opening tale as a *logos*, despite its overtly mythic provenance, and to Timaeus' characterization of his cosmological account both as "likely myth" (29d2) and as *logos* (27c4).[15] Along these lines, in referring to the cosmological principles of the sensible world, Timaeus uses the term *eikôs mythos* ("likely story") three times and the term *eikôs logos* ("likely account") seven times.[16] His description of the *chôra* is preceded by an appeal to *eikôs logos* whose explanatory power is intriguingly stated as follows, ". . . I shall try right from the start to say about things . . . what is no less likely than any, more likely in fact than what I have said before" (48d2–4). Likelihood, no matter how strong, is not a characteristic of irrefutable argument, and so Timaeus' conjunction of *eikôs* and *logos* betrays uneasiness about the epistemic reliability of his account. Thus *logos* and *mythos*, as they are commonly understood, come dizzyingly together. Furthermore, the question whether Timaeus' speech is meant to be read literally, as the creative exposition of the fashioning of the world by the craftsman god, or figuratively, as the imaginative narrative of the principles underlying the cosmos which evinces a rather cavalier attitude toward consistency and accuracy, has been around for centuries.[17] Accordingly, both text and scholarly interpretation complicate our understanding of Plato's dualism in *Timaeus* and challenge the view that the *chôra* "troubles" it (92).[18] At almost every step the

---

14   For a most recent discussion of the interpretative challenges posed by the literary form of the dialogue see Paul A. Miller, "The Platonic Remainder: Derrida's *Khôra* and the *Corpus Platonicum*," forthcoming in M. Leonard, ed., *Derrida and Plato* (Oxford: Oxford University Press).

15   Hyland, *Questioning Platonism*, p. 111.

16   For *eikôs mythos* see 29d2, 59c6, 68d2; the word *eikôs* is dispensed with at 69b1. For *eikôs logos* see 30b7, 48d2, 53d5–6, 55d5, 56a1, 57d6, 90e8. For useful comments on this distinction see Brisson, *Plato the Myth Maker*, pp. 129–130 and Albert Rivaud, "Notice," in *Platon: Timée*, vii–ccv (Paris: Société d' Edition, 1965). See also Myles Burnyeat, "EIKÔS MYTHOS," *Rhizai* II:2 (2005), 143–165.

17   The controversy dates back to Aristotle and Xenocrates and has survived in modern times. For the literal view see Gregory Vlastos, "Creation in the *Timaeus*: Is It a Fiction?" in Reginald E. Allen, ed., *Studies in Plato's* Metaphysics (London: Routledge, 1965), pp. 401–419; R. Hackforth, "Plato's Cosmogony," *Classical Quarterly*, n.s. 9 (1959), 17–22; Richard Sorabji, *Time, Creation, and the Continuum* (Ithaca: Cornell University Press, 1983), pp. 272–275; Thomas M. Robinson, "Understanding the *Timaeus*," in *Proceedings of the Boston Area Colloquium in Ancient Philosophy*, 2 (Lanham: University Press of America, 1986). For the metaphorical view see Taylor, *A Commentary*, 66–70; Cornford, *Plato's Cosmology*, pp. 24–32, 34–9; Harold F. Cherniss, *Aristotle's Criticism of Plato and the Academy* (Baltimore: Johns Hopkins University Press, 1944), pp. 392–457; Leonardo Tarán, "The Creation Myth in Plato's *Timaeus*," in J. P. Anton and G. Kustas, eds., *Essays in Ancient Greek Philosophy*, vol. 1 (Albany: State University of New York Press, 1977), pp. 372–407.

18   Hyland, *Questioning Platonism*, p. 115, argues that Plato himself undercuts the being/becoming dualism by placing the good beyond being in *Republic* and *eros* between the divine (Being) and the mortal (becoming).

dialogue invites us to reconsider the value of received discursive polarities, and introduction of the receptacle into the metaphysical dualistic schema is but one of the ways in which this invitation is issued.

Derrida does not simply deny the ability of figurative language to convey the nature of the receptacle; in a surprisingly Beckettian move, he asserts the inability of language in general to pin down its obscure essence. "We would never claim to propose the exact word, the *mot juste*, for *khôra*, nor to name it, itself, over and above all the turns and detours of rhetoric . . . . Its name is not an exact word, not a *mot juste*. It is promised to the ineffaceable even if what it names, *khôra*, is not reduced to its name" (93–94). Here the word "*chôra*" appears to be lamentably deficient, a malapropism destined to communicative failure. In "How to Avoid Speaking: Denials," a somewhat similar sentiment is voiced, "if the *khôra* receives everything, it does not do this in *the manner* of a medium or of a container, not even in that of a receptacle, because the receptacle is yet a figure inscribed in it."[19] As an all-receiving entity, the *chôra* must be a receptacle, and yet, quite paradoxically, it does not function as one. A gap yawns between what the *chôra* is or does and how it does it.

Derrida derives justification for his belief in the essential inappropriateness of the word "*chôra*" from the following passage: "the same account [as that applying to gold] holds also for that nature which receives all the bodies *(kai peri tês ta panta dechomenês sômata phuseôs)*. We must always refer to it by the same term *(tauton autên aei prosrêteon)*" (50b5–7). The word *tauton* may be construed both adverbially ("in the same manner") and as an internal accusative ("by the same *prosrhêsis*, name or term of address"). Derrida adopts the former construal, on the grounds that it alone preserves *chôra*'s "singular impropriety, which precisely is nothing" (97), a "nothingness" that should not be called anything, because a nominal act would bestow upon it ontological concreteness. In so doing, he establishes a semantic distinction between "appellation"—which hosts a multiplicity of expressions without sacrificing the conceptual unity of the notion expressed—and "name"—which captures an essentially fluid signified by means of an arbitrarily unified and fixed signifier.[20] John Sallis transfers this distinction to the realm of translation: "to translate *chôra*, for instance, as place, is to say that both words have the same semantic correlate, the same meaning, translation consisting in the move from one word to the other by way of the common meaning. To grant the possibility of translation is, then, to grant the legitimacy of bringing an eidetic determination to bear on the *chôra*."[21]

---

19 J. Derrida, "How to Avoid Speaking: Denials," in H. Coward and T. Foshay, eds., *Derrida and Negative Theology* (Albany: State University of New York, 1992), p. 106 (emphasis added).
20 Derrida, "How to Avoid Speaking," p. 107.
21 John Sallis, *Platonic Legacies* (Albany: State University of New York Press, 2004), p. 33.

There are at least two concerns with Derrida's reading of this passage. First, having already declared the grave difficulty of ascertaining the "manner" in which the *chóra* receives all entities, he cannot, on pain of self-contradiction, endorse a translation that suggests not only that such a manner exists, but also that it is identifiably "the same." Secondly, it is true that Timaeus' "all-receiving nature" has up to this point been variously described, and so to privilege one "name" seems textually unwarranted. On the other hand, it is inadvisable to ignore the syntactical ambiguity of *tauton*, thereby whimsically simplifying an inherently complex idea. Rather than favoring one or the other construal, a synthetic approach recommends itself. Might the word "*chóra*" grasp the essence of the "third kind" by, say, articulating its *modus operandi*? If so, it would be the most appropriate "name" precisely because it would connote the "sameness of manner" in which the third *genos* (kind) operates, while all the other references to it would recast, literally or figuratively, this fundamental idea. As we have already seen, Timaeus' descriptions of the receptacle fall mainly within three conceptual categories, those of containment, nurture, and space. Strictly speaking, it is difficult to see "sameness of manner" here, but it is also equally difficult to detect an endless proliferation of signifiers, an anarchic cluster of metaphors meant to capture a distressingly elusive entity. For the concepts of containment and space evoke the notion of place, while the idea of sheltering or protecting, associated with the metaphor of nurse, is not alien to place, either.[22] It is tempting to say that *chóra* is, after all, the *name* most appropriate to the "third kind," for it serves as a common denominator, correctly identifying the receptacle's main function and also accommodating without strain any semantic surplus, whatever else this thing is over and above its "name."

Perhaps the most important reason for the unnameability of the receptacle is its lacking being. Here is what Derrida says about this issue:

> "*Khôra* is neither of the order of the *eidos* nor of the order of mimemes, that is, of images of the *eidos* which come to imprint themselves in it—which thus is not and does not belong to the two known or recognized genera of being. It is not . . . . *Khôra* is not, is above all not . . ." (95).

And a little later, he adds:

> "*Khôra* is neither sensible nor intelligible. There is *khôra*; one can even ponder its *physis* and its *dynamis*, or at least ponder these in a preliminary way. But what *there is*, there, is not" (96).

---

22 *Chôra* in Attic Greek has a range of meanings closer to those of our 'place' or 'location' than to the three-dimensional space of Cartesian physics.

The idea that the *chôra* is neither intelligible nor perceptible is hardly contestable. After all, Timaeus never tires of declaring its status as a *tertium quid*. But Derrida's sweeping claim that the receptacle lacks being ("it is not") because it does not belong to the two "known genera of being" is untenable, because it mistakenly attributes unqualified "being" to a genus, i.e., phenomenal entities, that can have it only in a qualified manner. "Mimemes" or "eidetic images" have "being" only insofar as they are copies of the Forms they exemplify. Their beingness, in other words, is derivative, and cannot be established independently of the sources that bestow it on them. Similarly, the existence of the *chôra* cannot be fathomed independently of that of the particulars whose coming-to-be requires and legitimizes its presence.[23] In *Timaeus*, "being" is hierarchically triangulated: particulars enjoy a kind of essence that is parasitic upon that of the Forms, and the receptacle's peculiar *ousia* is bound up with the particulars' derivative essence.

Before I move on, I would like to examine a little more closely Derrida's contention that the receptacle "troubles" the opposition between Forms and particulars. As a third kind, it hovers in an ontological twilight between them, and so, Derrida claims, dislodges the binary structure on which the entire edifice of Platonic metaphysics rests. But one might plausibly argue that by situating itself between the intelligible and the sensible world and by requiring for its articulation a "kind of bastard reasoning" between understanding and opinion (52b2), the *chôra*, far from undoing these inexorably fixed dualities, affirms and brings them into sharp relief, because the very intelligibility of the cosmological account requires a third kind. It is *necessary* to speak of the *chôra* (49a3–4), and this *triton genos* is itself the product of necessity. Although why this is the case is never made explicit, it is clear that *qua* wetnurse, the *chôra* necessarily sustains the particulars whose nature is necessarily grasped by reference to the Forms. As copies of the eternal Ideas, perceptible entities must inhere in something that exists to support their role as images. There must be a receptacle for any image *of* Forms to be *in* (52b3–4). The receptacle, then, contains, as it were, the necessity of the entire metaphysical system, thereby legitimizing it. This specification of the *chôra*'s function does not blithely negate its being a third kind, but rather underscores its centrality for a proper understanding of the other two. Properly conceived, the receptacle is less an instance of Derridean

---

23 Derrida wonders whether the *chôra* is not a being 'beyond being' *(epekeina tês ousias)*, a metaphysical category to which Plato assigns the Good in *Republic* 509b. The view seems implausible to me, unless we take the expression 'beyond being' to indicate, trivially, a realm 'beyond the Forms'. But even so, the question remains: how and why would the Good and the *chôra* be thought of as metaphysically comparable? See Jacques Derrida, "Tense," in Kenneth Maly, ed., *The Path of Archaic Thinking: Unfolding the Work of John Sallis* (Albany: State University of New York Press, 1995), pp. 73 ff.; and John Sallis, "Daydream," *Revue Internationale de Philosophie* 52 (1998), 397–410.

différance, the marginal meaning that calls into question Plato's dualism, than the foundation upon which this dualism rests.[24]

Another vital aspect of the *chôra*'s ontology—and one affecting its complicated relationship with naming—is its lack of agency and subjecthood. The comparison with mother and nurse casts it as "passive and virgin matter," notions traditionally associated with the feminine element. The receptacle's passivity is shown by the fact that it affords the space where the particulars gather, but does not hold them as its own; it receives them, but does not make them its permanent possessions. "*Khôra*," Derrida writes, "must not receive for *her own sake*, so she must not *receive*, merely let herself be lent the properties of that which she receives. She must not receive, she must receive not that which she receives" (98; emphasis original). This contradictory language suggests that the receptacle enables the activity of other entities without partaking in it; it is a mere facilitator, an inert tool. In this sense, the passive voice seems to be the modality best suited to its passivity. Derrida, accordingly, says that the nonbeing of the *chôra* can only "be declared," namely, "caught or conceived" in a net of verbal allusions to the notions of giving and receiving, but does not itself "*give* place by receiving or by conceiving." The receptacle, then, does not "give" or "catch" anything, but is helplessly caught in linguistic significations, all of which are destined to miss its inscrutable nature. It is "anything but a support or a subject," for it is an "inaccessible, impassive, 'amorphous' entity" (95). As we saw earlier, it is an existent that lacks determinate content: "*there is khôra; . . . . But what *there is*, there, is not*" (96). The absence of a proper point of reference is marked by the omission of the definite article in the following aphoristic proclamation, "there is *khôra* but the *khôra* does not exist" (97).

It is far from clear why activity must be linked with the notion of "giving." But even if one were to grant the connection, one may still contend that the reason why the receptacle does not "give place"—namely, does not act on something external to itself by positioning it in space—is that it is itself space. The act of giving is part-and-parcel of the *chôra*'s essence, an inseparable feature of its nature: the receptacle offers itself, makes itself available for the endless cycling of the phenomena. By giving itself, it receives, so that self-giving and receiving are inextricably bound together. From this vantage-point, the *chôra* emerges as a peculiar kind of agent: the passivity of its functioning as the inert recipient of all things presupposes the activity of its offering itself as such. This conceptualization of agency challenges Derrida's view that "the expression *to give place* does not refer to the gesture of a donor-subject, the support or origin

---

24   For an interpretation that sees Derrida as invested in excavating architectonics that are 'quasi transcendental' and, therefore, as interested in foundations, see Rodolphe Gasché, *The Tain of the Mirror: Derrida and the Philosophy of Reflection* (Cambridge: Harvard University Press, 1986), pp. 142–154.

of something which would come to be given to someone" (100). The *chôra is* the subject of the twin act of self-giving/receiving, just as it is, quite literally, a sub-ject or sub-stratum, "lying under" the phenomena it receives and envelops.

Furthermore, the association of the *chôra*'s passivity with its lacking permanent possessions or qualities is rather troublesome. It is true, of course, that in order to receive all forms, the receptacle must be formless, just as the base for a fragrant ointment must be as odorless as possible (50e5–8). And yet at any given moment it acquires the form of the particular it receives, thereby taking on, however transiently, its appearance: it visibly is what the particular is like (51b4–6). Its characterlessness is contrasted with the characteristics of the likenesses of the intelligible objects: they bear specific features *qua* imitations of the Forms, while it has none, since it is not an imitation of a Form (51a1–6). But while the *chôra* lacks characteristics of its own, it is a stable entity with an abiding power *(dynamis)*, the ability to receive the various sensibles and to adapt its nature to theirs. Its *dynamis* endows it with qualities one might reasonably call "her own." The comparison of the *chôra* with a lump of gold reveals what these are. As Richard Mohr observes, "gold is malleable so that it can receive and hold all shapes . . . yet it offers no resistance to the various shapes which it received so the shapes can constantly be molded and remolded, unlike, say, stone."[25] Malleability and adaptability are essential characteristics of the *chôra*, but so is durability, the power to receive and sustain the transient phenomena without dissipating into non-existence. This feature may also be connected with gold. Anne Freire Ashbaugh suggests that the reason why gold is chosen for the comparison "appears in the discussion of metals (*Timaeus* 59b–d). Here gold is described as a fusible variety of water that is quite dense because it is com-posed of fine, uniform particles that give the appearance of something shining *(stilbon)*. The offshoot of gold is *adamant* (*Timaeus* 59b), a hard material likely to remind us of something stable because it endures through many changes."[26] The receptacle is malleable, adaptable, and enduring, an all-receiving entity that becomes temporarily qualified, as particulars go in and out of existence, while itself remaining permanent.

The communication of this peculiar sense of permanence would seem to require linguistic stability. And in fact, we do encounter the notion that the *chôra* admits of a certain degree of verbal fixity at the end of a notoriously difficult

---

25   Richard Mohr, "The Gold Analogy in the *Timaeus*" in Richard Mohr, *God and Forms in Plato* (Las Vegas: Parmenides Publishing, 2005), p. 108. See also Edward N. Lee, "On the Gold-Example in Plato's *Timaeus* (50A5–B5)," in J. P. Anton and G. Kustas, eds., *Essays in Ancient Greek Philosophy*, vol. 1 (Albany: State University of New York Press, 1971), pp. 219–235. The same sentiment is conveyed by the characterization of the receptacle as plastic, impressionable stuff (50c2–6, e7–51a1).
26   Anne Freire Ashbaugh, *Plato's Theory of Explanation: A Study of the Cosmological Account in the* Timaeus (Albany: State University of New York Press, 1988), p. 121.

passage concerning the proper way of speaking about the elements. Before I examine what it tells us about the receptacle, let me briefly turn to its controversial account of the nature of the particulars. According to the traditional interpretation, phenomenal fire, for example, should not be called "this" *(touto)*, but rather "what is such" *(to toiouton)*.[27] To call it "this" or "that" would be to bestow on it a kind of stability and fixity, that it does not have. Phenomenal entities lack self-subsistence, as they always become something other than what they are at any given moment. Phenomenal fire can legitimately be called "fire" in the sense that it is *like* the Form of Fire, but inasmuch as it is not the Form, it is not "this," but merely "what is such." The alternative interpretation proposes that we should not say "this is fire," but rather say that "what is always such is fire." "Suches" are either "perpetually identical characteristics" or "recurrent, stable and determinate characters."[28] On this account, bits of phenomenal fire cannot be called "fire" at all, not even when they momentarily appear as fire, for they are indistinguishable parts of the phenomenal flux. On the traditional reading, then, transient particulars are *toiauta* ('suches') and thus subject to fleeting linguistic qualification, whereas on the alternative view, linguistic discourse is reserved for entities of a quite different sort, particulars being condemned to verbal indeterminacy. On neither account, however, are particulars securely pinned down by language.

Now at the end of this passage, Timaeus draws a crucial distinction between particulars and the receptacle. Whereas the phenomenal entities are almost unspeakable fugitives, "that *in* which *(en hô)* they each appear to keep coming to be and *from* which *(ekeithen)* they subsequently perish, that's the only thing to refer to by means of the expressions 'that' *(touto)* and 'this' *(tode)*" (49e7–50a2).[29] A little earlier, the reason for denying the particulars the qualification "this" *(touto)* was that they appear never to remain the same (49d1–3). At 49d7–e2, phenomenal water is not to be called "this" *(touto)*, because it lacks "a certain stability" *(tina . . . bebaiotêta)*. But then if the *chôra* can be referred to by means

---

27 This reading was first challenged by Harold F. Cherniss, "A Much Misread Passage of the *Timaeus* (*Timaeus* 49c7–50b5)," *American Journal of Philology* 75 (1954), 113–130; reprinted in Harold F. Cherniss, *Selected Papers*, edited by L. Tarán (Leiden: Brill, 1977), pp. 346–363. Since Cherniss offered his alternative proposal, the traditional reading has been defended by Norman Gulley, "The Interpretation of Plato, *Timaeus* 49D–E," *American Journal of Philology* 81 (1960), 53–64; and Donald Zeyl, "Plato and Talk of a World in Flux: *Timaeus* 49a6–50b5," *Harvard Studies in Classical Philology* 79 (1975), 125–148. For a more recent account of the controversy see D. P. Hunt, "'The Problem of Fire': Referring to Phenomena in Plato's *Timaeus*," *Ancient Philosophy* 18 (1998), 69–80.

28 For the former understanding of "suches" see Cherniss, "A Much Misread Passage," p. 118. For the latter see Edward N. Lee, "On Plato's *Timaeus* 49d4–e7," *American Journal of Philology* 88 (1967), 1–28.

29 In "How to Avoid Speaking," Derrida goes directly against the text when he says, "*Khôra* is not even *that* (ça), the *es* or *id* of giving, before all subjectivity," p. 106.

of such demonstrative pronouns, it must possess a kind of ontological fixity, a strange selfsameness, of which Derrida deprives it. Whether it is viewed as neutral stuff, in which various characteristics temporarily inhere, or as space in which things appear and from which they disappear, its abiding nature is to receive fleeting entities or characteristics, the results of the particulars' participation in Forms. And we are given no reason to think that this nature resists discursive fixity.

Derrida, however, overlooks or downplays the receptacle's ontological stability and insists that "with *khôra itself/herself,* if one could at all speak about this X (x or *khi*) which must not have any proper determination, sensible or intelligible, material or formal, and therefore must not have any identity of its/her own, must not be identical with herself/itself" (99). But from the fact that the *chôra* does not possess any material or formal determinacy one cannot infer that it is a mental posit resistant even to self-identification. As a bearer of particulars, the *chôra* has a functional identity and is a certain kind of entity, identical with itself and different from Forms and particulars. Like the Forms, it is self-identical and eternal, yet it remains impervious to reason (51a7–b2), and though it hosts sensible particulars, it cannot be apprehended directly through the senses. Distinct from both Forms and particulars but strangely like them in some respects, the receptacle is a *triton genos.*

Its "thirdness" is, indeed, vital to the structure of the Timaean universe and to Derrida's deconstructive project. We are indebted to the latter for uncovering and commenting on the receptacle's importance, its peculiar nature and function. But in his eagerness to see the *chôra* as the perfect illustration of the elusive *differance,* I think that Derrida exaggerates its ontological and discursive fluidity and offers a rather monolithic account of the nature of the polarity it transcends. I have here suggested that the *chôra* enjoys a peculiar kind of existential identity which is bound up with its being an "all-receiving" entity, and that its name reflects that identity. It is, therefore, a proper name, not a nominal approximation. Its featurelessness emerges when compared to the featured entities that populate it, but should not be construed as complete absence of qualities. For it is precisely by dint of permanent qualities such as malleability, adaptability, and durability that it can fulfill its function. Finally, instead of directing our attention at individual metaphysical entities and seeing the *chôra* as undercutting a rigid binary system of Forms and particulars, it is more fruitful to look at how the three kinds are ontologically interrelated: the particulars owe their existence to the Forms, and the *chôra* exists so that the particulars might exist. Like another Atlas, the Timaean receptacle supports the phenomenal world, and by so doing legitimizes Platonic metaphysics.

12

Should Aristotle Have Recognized Final Causes in Plato's Timaeus?

Thomas K. Johansen

'Yes', appears to be the obvious answer. The *Timaeus*, after all, is the work in which Plato attempts to show how a divine craftsman made the world in the best possible way. The world is as it is, it seems, because this is the best way for it to be. So, if we take as our rough notion of a final cause 'the good for the sake of which something is or comes about' it seems that not only are final causes at work in the *Timaeus*, they are fundamental to its account.

Aristotle's Criticism: Metaphysics *I.7*

Yet Aristotle fails to acknowledge final causes in Plato. In *Metaphysics* I, he surveys the various notions of 'cause' *(aitia)* that his predecessors have used. The survey is based on his own distinction between the 'four causes'. He finds that different philosophers have recognized different causes but nobody has properly understood them all. In particular, nobody seems to have properly articulated the notion of the final cause, that for the sake of which things are or come about. In his own words:

> **T1** "That for the sake of which actions and changes and movements take place, they assert to be a cause in a way, but not in this way, i.e., not in the way in which it is its nature to be a cause. For those who speak of reason and friendship class these causes as goods; they do not speak, however, as if anything that exists either existed or came into being for the sake of these, but as if movements started from these. In the same way those who say the One or Being is the good, say that is the cause of substance,

179

but not that the substance either is or comes to be for the sake
of this. Therefore it turns out that in a sense they both say and
do not say the good is a cause; for they do not call it a cause *qua*
good but only accidentally." (*Metaphysics* I.7 988b6–15, after
revised Oxford translation)[1]

Aristotle here refers to two different groups of philosophers to whom he
thinks the same criticism applies. It is clear from earlier chapters that he takes
Anaxagoras *(nous)* and Empedocles *(philia)* as members of the first group and
Plato and the Pythagoreans as belonging to the second.[2] Aristotle thus thinks
that Plato failed to make proper use of final causes. This paper tries to answer
why he thinks so, and to what extent he is justified, as far as the *Timaeus* is
concerned, in thinking so.

Let us start by being clearer about the general nature of Aristotle's criticism
and how it applies to the two groups before we specifically turn to Plato. We
find the following general pattern behind Aristotle's objection to both groups
of philosophers:[3]

> X is a final cause of actions, changes, movements, etc., only if, a)
> X is the cause of Y (actions, changes, movements, etc.), and b) X
> is good, and c) X *qua* good is the cause of Y.

> Intelligence, Friendship, the One or Being satisfies a) and b), but
> not c). Therefore, Nous, Friendship, the One, or Being is not a
> final cause.

The important criterion, then, on which all of the proposed causes fail to count
as final causes is c), they are not causes *qua* good. Compare the case of the
musician who builds a house. The musician is the cause of the house, because
it so happens that he is also a builder. It is the musician *qua* builder that builds

---

1 τὸ δ' οὗ ἕνεκα αἱ πράξεις καὶ αἱ μεταβολαὶ καὶ αἱ κινήσεις τρόπον μέν τινα
λέγουσιν αἴτιον, οὕτω δὲ οὐ λέγουσιν οὐδ' ὅνπερ πέφυκεν· οἱ μὲν γὰρ νοῦν λέγοντες ἢ
φιλίαν ὡς ἀγαθὸν μὲν ταύτας τὰς αἰτίας τιθέασιν, οὐ μὴν ὡς ἕνεκά γε τούτων ἢ ὂν ἢ
γιγνόμενόν τι τῶν ὄντων ἀλλ' ὡς ἀπὸ τούτων τὰς κινήσεις οὔσας λέγουσιν· ὡς δ' αὕτως
καὶ οἱ τὸ ἓν ἢ τὸ ὂν φάσκοντες εἶναι τὴν τοιαύτην φύσιν τῆς μὲν οὐσίας αἴτιόν φασιν
εἶναι, οὐ μὴν τούτου γε ἕνεκα ἢ εἶναι ἢ γίγνεσθαι, ὥστε λέγειν τε καὶ μὴ λέγειν πως
συμβαίνει αὐτοῖς τἀγαθὸν αἴτιον· οὐ γὰρ ἁπλῶς ἀλλὰ κατὰ συμβεβηκὸς λέγουσιν.
2 While Anaxagoras and Empedocles have different notions of the first principle, *nous* and
philia, respectively, it is likely that Aristotle is treating Plato and the Pythagoreans here as
having the same first principle, referred to alternatively as "the one or being." For Aristotle
also says that both Plato and the Pythagoreans held that the one and being were essentially
the same (*Metaphysics* III.4 1001a10–12).
3 Which, I take it, is why Aristotle introduced the second group by saying 'in the same way'.

rather than *qua* musician. Similarly Intelligence, Friendship, the One or Being may be causes, which are good, but they are not causes insofar as they are good. Rather, there is some aspect other than their goodness that works as the cause of the actions, movements and changes. In each case, the good is the cause only accidentally, not *per se*, as required of a final cause.

The next question, then, is why Aristotle thinks these thinkers do not employ their causes *as good*. If we take the first group first, Aristotle seems to rule out their causes as final because they were presented as origins of movement, that is to say, as efficient causes. Now one might think that this point requires that for a cause to count as final it cannot also be a cause in any of the other three ways which Aristotle recognizes. So if something is an efficient cause it cannot *ipso facto* be a final cause. However, it is clear that this is not Aristotle's view. As Aristotle says in the *Physics* the same thing often plays the roles of both efficient, formal and final causes in nature:

> **T2** "The last three often coincide; for the what and that for the sake of which are one, while the primary source of motion is the same in species as these. For man generates man . . . ." (*Physics* II.7 198a25–27)

Another, related, example is the soul. Aristotle says in *De Anima* II.4 that the soul is at once the final, formal and efficient cause of living beings. So it seems that it cannot be Aristotle's general view that something can only be a final cause if it is not also an efficient cause. By the same token, it seems clear that Friendship or Intelligence could in principle have worked both as a final cause and as an efficient cause.

Compare Aristotle's criticism of Empedocles in *Metaphysics* XII:

> **T3** "Empedocles also has a paradoxical view; for he identifies the good with friendship. But this is a principle both as a mover (for it brings things together) and as matter (for it is part of the mixture). Now even if it happens that the same thing is a principle both as matter and as mover, still being them is not the same. In which respect then is Friendship a principle?" (1075b3–6, after revised Oxford translation)

Aristotle makes it clear that he is not opposed to making the same thing, in this case Friendship, do the job of two different kinds of causes; what he minds is Empedocles' not distinguishing the ways in which Friendship works as an efficient and as a material cause. Aristotle thinks then that the same thing can play the role of several causes; the important thing, however, is that one articulates the distinctive roles of these causes.

I would suggest that the philosophers being criticized in **T1** are selected not only because they offer the sorts of principles that Aristotle thinks could also play the role of final causes, but also because they might reasonably be expected to play this role. Specifically these principles, amongst those offered by his predecessors, raise the expectation that they are causes for the good. In contrast, he would not mention in this context those philosophers who, he thought, only operated with material causes such as fire or water because such items do not seem likely candidates for final causes in the first place. In the case of Anaxagoras, meanwhile, we would expect Intelligence not only itself to be something good but also to work in order to bring about good things. Compare Socrates' reaction to Anaxagoras' Intelligence: 'I was delighted with this cause and it seemed to me good, in a way, that Intelligence should be the cause of all. I thought that if this were so, the directing Intelligence would direct everything and arrange each thing in the way that was best' (*Phaedo* 97c, translation by Grube with 'Intelligence' for 'Mind'). Aristotle echoes Socrates' hopes:

> **T4** "When one man said, then, that Intelligence was present—as in animals, so throughout nature—as the cause of the world and of all its order, he seemed like a sober man in contrast with the random talk of his predecessors. We know that Anaxagoras certainly adopted these views . . . . Those who thought thus stated that there is a principle of things which is at the same time the cause of beauty, and that sort of cause from which things acquire movement." (*Metaphysics* I.3 984b15–22)[4]

Aristotle recognizes that Intelligence raises the prospect of final causation. As he says here, Anaxagoras and others 'stated' that there was a principle which was at the same time the cause of beauty, that is, a final cause, and an efficient cause. They 'stated' it but they did not show it. Aristotle's criticism is much the same as Socrates: Anaxagoras, and others, may have talked about a principle of beauty or goodness, but they made little 'use' of it as a final cause.[5]

---

4 νοῦν δή τις εἰπὼν ἐνεῖναι, καθάπερ ἐν τοῖς ζῴοις, καὶ ἐν τῇ φύσει τὸν αἴτιον τοῦ κόσμου καὶ τῆς τάξεως πάσης οἷον νήφων ἐφάνη παρ' εἰκῇ λέγοντας τοὺς πρότερον. φανερῶς μὲν οὖν Ἀναξαγόραν ἴσμεν ἁψάμενον τούτων τῶν λόγων . . . οἱ μὲν οὖν οὕτως ὑπολαμβάνοντες ἅμα τοῦ καλῶς τὴν αἰτίαν ἀρχὴν εἶναι τῶν ὄντων ἔθεσαν, καὶ τὴν τοιαύτην ὅθεν ἡ κίνησις ὑπάρχει τοῖς οὖσιν·

5 See Aristotle, *Metaphysics* I.4 985a17–21: σχεδὸν γὰρ οὐθὲν χρώμενοι φαίνονται τούτοις ἀλλ᾽ ἢ κατὰ μικρόν. Ἀναξαγόρας τε γὰρ μηχανῇ χρῆται τῷ νῷ πρὸς τὴν κοσμοποιίαν, καὶ ὅταν ἀπορήσῃ διὰ τίν᾽ αἰτίαν ἐξ ἀνάγκης ἐστί, τότε παρέλκει αὐτόν, ἐν δὲ τοῖς ἄλλοις πάντα μᾶλλον αἰτιᾶται τῶν γιγνομένων ἢ νοῦν, echoing *Phaedo* 98b: Ἀπὸ δὴ θαυμαστῆς ἐλπίδος, ὦ ἑταῖρε, ᾠχόμην φερόμενος, ἐπειδὴ προϊὼν καὶ ἀναγιγνώσκων ὁρῶ ἄνδρα τῷ μὲν νῷ οὐδὲν χρώμενον οὐδέ τινας αἰτίας ἐπαιτιώμενον

Instead, the principle seems to have worked almost entirely as an efficient cause. Anaxagoras' Intelligence, then, from Aristotle's view-point, as from Plato's, bore the promise of introducing final causation. Similarly, we might expect Empedocles' Friendship both to be a good itself and to work as such to bring about good things in nature. For that is how friendship works in the human sphere, as we see from Aristotle's own discussion of friendship in the *Nicomachean Ethics*.[6]

Can a similar point be made about the second group of philosophers? These were philosophers who identified what Aristotle saw as the cause of substance, that is, the formal cause, but failed to make proper use of it as a final cause. We saw that we would expect the formal cause also to be the final cause in nature. We also saw that final causes are goods for the sake of which things come about. Given, then, that Plato also says that his formal cause, the One, is good—even that it is 'the good itself'—we can see why Aristotle thinks Plato's principle is a *prima facie* candidate for final cause. Of course, Plato's principle, like the others mentioned, disappoints. Aristotle is adopting the same argumentative strategy that Plato used in the *Phaedo* against Anaxagoras . . . this time against Plato himself!

The Relevance of the Timaeus

It is something of a puzzle how, if at all, Plato's *Timaeus* relates to Aristotle's criticism in **T1**. It is fairly clear that the criticism does not specifically address the *Timaeus*. The principle of the One or Being is not referred to in the *Timaeus*. The *Philebus* (e.g., 16c–18d) and *Republic* II–VII would be closer, though hardly exact, references. It may also be that Aristotle has in mind unpublished or 'unwritten' work by Plato, such as the so-called lecture "On the Good." However, the lack of a specific reference to the *Timaeus* does not mean that Aristotle is ignoring it or considers it irrelevant. Aristotle refers to the *Timaeus* elsewhere in discussions of Plato's causal theory.[7] He could hardly have expected his audience not to see the relevance of the *Timaeus* to his account of Plato's causal theory in **T1**. Indeed, I would put the point more strongly: given the prominence of the *Timaeus* in Plato's thinking about nature, any effective critique by Aristotle of Plato's causal theory would have to withstand reference to the *Timaeus*. Otherwise, Aristotle faces the charge which Harold Cherniss famously raised: Aristotle's denial of final causes in

---

εἰς τὸ διακοσμεῖν τὰ πράγματα, ἀέρας δὲ καὶ αἰθέρας καὶ ὕδατα αἰτιώμενον καὶ ἄλλα πολλὰ καὶ ἄτοπα.

6 Friendship is treated by Aristotle in the *Nicomachean Ethics* as a virtue or not without virtue (VIII.1) and as implying good will towards one's friends (VIII.2).

7 Principle of motion: *Metaphysics* 1071b32. Matter: *Physics* 209b11.

Plato was "evidence of careless reading or forgetfulness" of the *Timaeus*.[8] I would like to show in this paper that Aristotle was neither a careless nor a forgetful reader: his critique of Plato in **T1** can be justified also in the light of the *Timaeus*.

Now one way in which Aristotle's criticism has been defended in view of the *Timaeus* is the following: the *Timaeus* failed to recognize final causes for the same reason that the first group of philosophers in **T1** did, that is, their principles, while good, worked as efficient causes rather than proper final causes. This interpretation is initially attractive for at least two reasons. First, it offers a way of understanding what seems glaringly obvious to the reader of the *Timaeus*: that Plato adopted Intelligence as a basic causal principle and that he tried to show how this Intelligence arranged the world for the good. Second, it reflects in a quite precise way how Aristotle elsewhere conceives of the relationship between final and efficient causes.[9]

Here is, in outline, how such a reading can be developed. For Aristotle final causation operates in nature independently of conscious desires. When we explain an acorn's growth by reference to the goal of being an oak tree this does not imply that the acorn wants to be an oak tree. It cannot then be part of a basic concept of a final cause that the goal works as an object of desire. But when intelligence works so as to bring about a certain good, the goal is an object of desire.[10] But the desire is the efficient cause of the process. One criterion we can use to tell the two notions of an end apart is a temporal one: an end which is a genuine final cause comes after the process it causes while an end which works as an object of desire obtains at the same time as the process it brings about. For efficient causes are simultaneous with their effects, while that for the sake which comes later.

Now in the *Timaeus*, Plato presents the world as the product of god's beneficence. Here the goodness of the cosmos features in the account of the cause of the creation, but only insofar as it is the object of god's desire. So, it seems, the *Timaeus* presents the good only as a feature of the efficient cause of the cosmos and not as a final cause in its own right. The *Timaeus* cannot therefore be said to have presented a proper notion of final causation, at least as it operates in nature according to Aristotle.

---

8   Harold F. Cherniss, *Aristotle's Criticism of Plato and of the Academy,* I (Baltimore: Johns Hopkins Press, 1944), p. 454.

9   Two published works in particular lie behind my presentation of this interpretation: David Sedley's *Creationism and Its Critics* (Berkeley: University of California Press, 2007), and Monte Ransome Johnson's, *Aristotle on Teleology* (Oxford: Oxford University Press, 2006). I'm also greatly indebted to Robert Bolton's "Aristotle on the Beginnings of Teleology" (unpublished).

10   For helpful discussion of the distinction see David Charles, "Teleological Causation in the *Physics*," in Lindsay Judson, ed., *Aristotle's* Physics: *A Collection of Essays* (Oxford: Oxford University Press, 1995), pp. 101–128.

Timaeus' account of the eye illustrates the point.[11] At 46c–47d Timaeus makes the distinction between causes *(aitiai)* and contributory causes *(sunaitia)*. He illustrates the distinction through the example of the eyes. The processes by which vision occurs are causes only in the sense that they contribute to the good end which Timaeus designates the 'cause' *(aitia)*. The proper cause, then, is the good which the eyes serve, namely the regulation of the soul's motions which the perception of the heavenly bodies makes possible. Timaeus comes close to using the Aristotelian language of 'that for the sake of which'.[12] However, Timaeus makes it clear that this good is to be understood as the cause in the context of god's desire to bring it about. In this way, he can maintain consistency with his earlier claims that the real cause is an intelligent one (46d–e) and that it is god's desire to make the world as good as possible (29e–30a). The good seems then to work as a cause as an object of god's desire. So, in Aristotle's book, the good in the *Timaeus* would count as an aspect of the efficient cause rather than a final cause in its own right. Aristotle was therefore right not to recognize final causes in the *Timaeus*.

Now on this reading there is clearly an important difference between the *Timaeus*' and Aristotle's use of the good in explanations of natural phenomena. However, there are several reasons to resist the conclusion that it is *this* difference which motivates Aristotle's denial of final causes to Plato. And so even if Aristotle is aware of the relevance of the *Timaeus* to his argument in **T1**, he will not use this difference to justify his criticism of Plato. First of all, Aristotle made it clear in the previous chapter (*Metaphysics* I.6 988a8–16) that he thinks that Plato only recognized two causes, the formal and the material causes. So it would be odd if he now charged Plato with reducing the final cause to the efficient. Secondly, Aristotle is quite explicit in **T1** that his criticism is of those who make the One or Being the cause of substance, which is another way of saying the *formal* cause. So we should try to make sense of Aristotle's criticism in terms of the way in which Plato's formal cause raises the expectation of it also being a final cause. Third, the reading lands Aristotle with the awkward claim that conscious final causes are somehow not final causes. This is problematic given Aristotle's insistence in the *Physics* that 'some [of the things that come to be for the sake of something] are in accordance with intention

---

11 For a fuller exposition see my *Plato's Natural Philosophy* (Cambridge: Cambridge University Press, 2004), pp. 106–110.

12 47b–c: "Let us rather say that this is the cause of this to these ends: god devised sight and gave it to us so that we might see the revolutions of intelligence in the heavens and use their untroubled course to guide the troubled revolutions in our own understanding, which are akin to them, and so, by learning what they are and how to calculate them accurately according to their nature, correct our own straying revolutions by imitating the altogether unstraying revolutions of god." All translations of the *Timaeus* are from Desmond Lee, (revised by T. K. Johansen), *Plato's* Timaeus *and* Critias (New York: Penguin, 2008).

(prohairesis), others not, but both are in the class of things which are for the sake of something' (196b18–20).[13] Note, finally, that Aristotle in **T1** includes 'actions' *(praxeis)*, along with changes and movements, as the domain where his predecessors have failed to make proper use of final causes. So it would be odd if he meant to say that *praxeis* don't offer a proper subject for teleological explanation or that the failure to appreciate final causes was based on an assimilation of natural causation to intentional agency.

I think, therefore, that there are good reasons for not taking Aristotle to be accusing Plato of reducing the final to the efficient cause or an aspect thereof. We are better off following Aristotle's own directions: the problem is that Plato introduced formal causes which while they promised to work as final causes failed to do so.

Aristotle's Criticism, Again

I have already suggested a way in which Aristotle thought that the One as a mathematical principle might raise the prospect of being a final cause of beauty. But to see how Plato's notion of the One for Aristotle failed to live up to this promise, we need a fuller picture of the Platonic theory that he is targeting. In I.6 Aristotle presented the causal role of the One as follows:

> **T5** "Since the Forms are the causes of all things, he thought their elements were the elements of all things. As matter, the great and the small were principles; as substance, the One; for from the great and the small, by participation in the One, come the numbers. But he agrees with the Pythagoreans in saying that the One is substance and not a predicate of something else; and in saying that the numbers are the causes of the substance of other things, he also agrees with them." (987b18–25)[14]

Aristotle's here specifies the two causes used by Plato: the great and the small which worked as a material cause, and the One which served as the formal cause or cause of 'substance'. The great and the small by participation in the One give rise to number. These numbers are themselves understood as formal causes of other things, namely, of perceptible objects. Aristotle goes on to

---

13 Revised Oxford translation of τούτων δὲ τὰ μὲν κατὰ προαίρεσιν, τὰ δ' οὐ κατὰ προαίρεσιν, ἄμφω δ' ἐν τοῖς ἕνεκά του . . .

14 ἐπεὶ δ' αἴτια τὰ εἴδη τοῖς ἄλλοις, τἀκείνων στοιχεῖα πάντων ᾠήθη τῶν ὄντων εἶναι στοιχεῖα. ὡς μὲν οὖν ὕλην τὸ μέγα καὶ τὸ μικρὸν εἶναι ἀρχάς, ὡς δ' οὐσίαν τὸ ἕν· ἐξ ἐκείνων γὰρ κατὰ μέθεξιν τοῦ ἑνὸς [τὰ εἴδη] εἶναι τοὺς ἀριθμούς. τὸ μέντοι γε ἓν οὐσίαν εἶναι, καὶ μὴ ἕτερόν γέ τι ὂν λέγεσθαι ἕν, παραπλησίως τοῖς Πυθαγορείοις ἔλεγε, καὶ τὸ τοὺς ἀριθμοὺς αἰτίους εἶναι τοῖς ἄλλοις τῆς οὐσίας ὡσαύτως ἐκείνοις·

say, in the lines following **T5**, that Plato disagreed with the Pythagoreans by making the mathematical forms separate from the perceptible objects. The numbers have the status of intermediate forms. The One is then the formal cause of mathematical objects which directly are the formal causes of sensible objects.

Already *Metaphysics* I.9 (991b9ff) offers some criticism of the idea that forms understood as numbers can be causes. But we have to wait until *Metaphysics* XIII and XIV for extended discussion of the issue. And it is towards the very end of that discussion, in XIV.4 and 6, that Aristotle particularly addresses the role which the mathematical forms might play in making things good. So, it is here in particular that we should expect Aristotle to substantiate his claim in Book I.7 that Plato's theory of forms fails to provide final causes, given that this claim was based, as we have just seen, on a mathematical understanding of the forms.

Aristotle starts by arbitrating a discussion about the relationship of the good to the principles of the cosmos. Some, including Plato, Empedocles and Anaxagoras, say that first principle itself is good. Others object that the good and the beautiful only emerge at the end of natural processes, and therefore that the principle, which comes first in time, cannot itself be good. Aristotle accepts both that the principle is good and that it pre-exists the processes it brings about. However, he also sees the force of the objection, for it shows that the principle cannot be present in natural beings *as an element.* Taking the principle to be present from the beginning as an element is a mistake made by those who make the One their first principle. They take the One to be present as an element, namely as a factor in the other numbers, which are generated out of it. It is not entirely clear whether this point can be consistently made against Plato, as a point about natural processes, since he made the mathematical forms separate from the natural things and therefore presumably not an element in them, or whether it is not rather targeted against the Pythagoreans, who, as Aristotle said in I.6, made the numbers constituents of natural things. In any case, the objection serves to clarify that the way in which the good works as a cause by being an end has to be distinguished from the way in which the material cause works. The first principle while good does not make things good by being mixed in with them. This would be to confuse the role of the principle as final cause with the material cause.

But Aristotle has other arguments against the idea that the first principle can be both good and the One, arguments which do not hinge on the presence of the principle as an element. The first objection is that "all units become sorts of good, so that there is rather a plethora of goods" (1091b25–26).[15] The

---

15   All translations here of *Metaphysics* XIII and XIV are from or based on Julia Annas, trans., *Aristotle's* Metaphysics M and N (Oxford: Oxford University Press, 1976).

idea seems to be that anything, insofar as it is a unit, will be good since by being a unit it instantiates the One and the One is good. The objection applies also to the other Forms, which, as numbers, will participate in the One and also thereby be good. That in turn implies that anything that participates in these Forms, will be good. But this is clearly too generous. So participation in the One will not as such make something good. And since Aristotle agrees, as we saw, that the first principle is essentially good, the One cannot be the first principle.

Julia Annas notes a weakness in the argument: "An obvious rejoinder would be that a predicate true of the Form does not necessarily hold of what participates in that form; an individual man could participate in the Form of Man, which is a type of good, without therefore participating in a type of good and so being good."[16] However, I take it that the reason why Aristotle does not consider this reply is that he takes Plato's thesis to be that there is an essential connection between the One insofar as it is one and being good. It was after all the basis of his agreement with Plato back in XIV.4 that the principle had the very attributes that qualified it as a principle, namely, indestructibility and self-sufficiency, because it was good. And Aristotle also noted here that Plato's view was that the One itself was the Good itself even if he gave priority to its Oneness (*Metaphysics* 1091b13–14). So Aristotle must think that also for Plato the goodness of the principle is in some way part of its essence. Since Aristotle thinks Plato's view is that goodness is essential to his principle, the One, it seems reasonable for him also to think that whatever participates in the One also, to that extent, comes to be good. The force of the objection is, then, that because we are entitled on Plato's theory to think that whatever participates in the One becomes good, far too many things end being good, namely, as many things as are one.

This objection is an instance of a general pattern of argument, which one might call the "failure of determination argument": the argument seeks to show ways in which mathematical structure fails to determine goodness and therefore how goodness cannot, *pace* Plato, be an essential feature of mathematical structure. In the argument at which we just looked, it emerges that being one fails to make something good, in the sense that there are many things that are one that we would not think were thereby good.

It might still be thought that mathematical structure is a necessary, if not a sufficient, condition of goodness. But XIV.6 provides instances of the failure of determination argument which show that mathematical structure is not a necessary condition either of goodness:

---

16 Annas, p. 217.

T6 "One might also raise the question what the good is that things get from numbers because their composition is expressible by a number, either by one which is easily calculable or by an odd number. For in fact honey-water is no more wholesome if it is mixed in the proportion of three times three, but it would do more good if it were in no particular ratio but well diluted than if it were numerically expressible but strong." (*Metaphysics* XIV.6 1092b26–30)[17]

Having any mathematical arrangement is not required to make something good. The goodness of honey-water lies in its benefit to those who drink it, but no particular proportion of the mixture is required for this effect. What matters is just that there is a lot of water in relation to the honey. It may of course be that there is a certain beauty in a particular mathematical order itself, as Aristotle seems to grant in XIII.3 (1078a32–b6). But that is not the same as saying that the presence of that order in another thing will make it beautiful or a good thing of that kind. A proportion of 3 times 3, say, may be beautiful but its presence won't ensure that the honey-water is good honey-water. A certain proportion of mixture may be good to calculate (*eulogiston*), but does not make something else a good thing of its kind.[18] So mathematical structure fails to determine goodness, in this case even as a necessary condition.[19]

The failure of determination argument is related to Aristotle's critique of the Form of the Good in *Nicomachean Ethics* I, 6:

T7 "Furthermore, since things are said to be good in as many ways as they are said to be . . . clearly the good cannot be something universally present in all cases and single; for then it would not have been predicated in all the categories but in one only." (1096a23–29)

---

17 Ἀπορήσειε δ' ἄν τις καὶ τί τὸ εὖ ἐστὶ τὸ ἀπὸ τῶν ἀριθμῶν τῷ ἐν ἀριθμῷ εἶναι τὴν μῖξιν, ἢ ἐν εὐλογίστῳ ἢ ἐν περιττῷ. νυνὶ γὰρ οὐθὲν ὑγιεινότερον τρὶς τρία ἂν ᾖ τὸ μελίκρατον κεκραμένον, ἀλλὰ μᾶλλον ὠφελήσειεν ἂν ἐν οὐθενὶ λόγῳ ὂν ὑδαρὲς δὲ ἢ ἐν ἀριθμῷ ἄκρατον ὄν.

18 My phrasing seeks to capture Aristotle's play on τὸ εὖ and εὐλογίστῳ.

19 Note that the argument against the mathematical forms as final causes in XIV.6 is analogous to the argument against them as formal causes: just as the mathematical structure won't make the honey-water good, so it won't make it honey-water, since other things may have the same mathematical structure: "it was also possible for different things to fall under the same number; so that if things happened to have the same number, they would be the same as one another, having the same kind of number. The sun and moon, for example, would be the same" (1093a9–12). That formal and final failure of determination should follow each other is of course no accident if, as Aristotle, thinks formal and final cause often coincides.

Since 'good' is predicated in all the categories, good cannot be understood in a way that makes it a single thing, belonging to one category. What *Metaphysics* XIV.6 adds more specifically to the critique in the *Nicomachean Ethics* is the point that the single conception of goodness is a mathematical one which, being appropriate only to mathematics, will fail to apply to non-mathematical kinds of goodness. A mathematical conception of goodness will fail to determine goodness in its different expressions across the categories.[20] Mathematical structure fails to determine goodness in general. But if so there cannot be an essential connection between the two, between mathematical structure as such and goodness as such.

Consider now Aristotle's final objection to the mathematical conception of value in XIV.6:

> **T8** "The way they proceed does, however, make it clear that the good has application, and that we do find the odd, straight, equal-by-equal, and the powers of some numbers in the column of the beautiful. The seasons and a certain sort of number go together; and this is the force of all the other examples they collect from mathematical theorems. Hence they are like coincidences; they are accidental (though all appropriate to one another) but one by analogy. For there is an analogous item in each category of being; straight in length is as level in surface, and perhaps as odd in number and white in color." (1093b11–21)[21]

Aristotle agrees that there may be various mathematical structures corresponding to what is beautiful in different categories of being. But to say that there is a mathematical structure or a number that corresponds with beauty in each of the various categories of thing is of course not to say that the same mathematical structure is present in beautiful things of all categories, let alone that it is this structure that makes them all beautiful. Rather as Aristotle puts it, there is an analogy, for example "straight in length is as

---

20 It may of course also fail to determine goodness even within a single category, such as quantity, since it does not make allowance for the variety of goodness that obtains in different kinds of quantities (a beautiful triangle may not exhibit the same proportion as a beautiful quadrangle, say). But that is a different point.

21 ἔστιν ὡς μέντοι ποιοῦσι φανερὸν ὅτι τὸ εὖ ὑπάρχει καὶ τῆς συστοιχίας ἐστὶ τῆς τοῦ καλοῦ τὸ περιττόν, τὸ εὐθύ, τὸ ἰσάκις ἴσον, αἱ δυνάμεις ἐνίων ἀριθμῶν· ἅμα γὰρ ὧραι καὶ ἀριθμὸς τοιοσδί· καὶ τὰ ἄλλα δὴ ὅσα συνάγουσιν ἐκ τῶν μαθηματικῶν θεωρημάτων πάντα ταύτην ἔχει τὴν δύναμιν. διὸ καὶ ἔοικε συμπτώμασιν· ἔστι γὰρ συμβεβηκότα μέν, ἀλλ' οἰκεῖα ἀλλήλοις πάντα, ἐν δὲ τῷ ἀνάλογον· ἐν ἑκάστῃ γὰρ τοῦ ὄντος κατηγορίᾳ ἐστὶ τὸ ἀνάλογον, ὡς εὐθὺ ἐν μήκει οὕτως ἐν πλάτει τὸ ὁμαλόν, ἴσως ἐν ἀριθμῷ τὸ περιττόν, ἐν δὲ χροιᾷ τὸ λευκόν.

level in surface, and perhaps as odd in number and white in color."[22] Being one by analogy is the weakest form of unity for Aristotle in that it applies to cases where there is no single unifying genus.[23] So his claim that there is an analogy between the expressions of beauty in the various categories highlights the point there is no single structure that they all share. In particular, there is no single mathematical structure they all share in respect of which they are all beautiful. In this way, **T8** combines the critique of the mathematical forms earlier in the chapter with the sort of point made in **T7**: as transcategorical beauty, like goodness, cannot be represented by a single mathematical structure. The failure of determination arguments can be seen as grounded in the transcategorical nature of beauty and goodness.

This analysis brings us back to **T1**. Aristotle's complaint was that Plato said that the One was good and he said that it was a cause of good, but he did not show how as good the One worked so as to bring about good things. We can now see better that Aristotle thinks that the One didn't play this role simply because it couldn't. Neither the One nor any other specific mathematical structures could work in the manner of a principle of goodness. For as the failure of determination arguments show, being one or having a particular mathematical structure is neither a necessary nor a sufficient condition for something to be good or beautiful. There is no essential connection, then, between having a particular mathematical structure and being good, rather being good stands in general in an accidental relationship to having a certain mathematical structure. Neither the One nor other mathematical forms are therefore *per se* causes of goodness, even if this or that mathematical structure happens to be beautiful. Plato may *say* that the first principle is the One and that it is good or rather goodness itself, but he does not say how the One *as good* is a cause of goodness in things because the causal connection between its being One and its being able to bring about good things is missing. Similarly, nobody could show how the musician is a cause of buildings, other than *per accidens*, since there is no essential connection between being a musician and having the ability to construct houses. As the mathematical Forms are not *per se* such as to bring about good things, they fail as Aristotelian final causes, for these are essentially such as to bring about the good.[24]

---

22 Recall that the colors are composed according to mathematical proportion, cf. *On Sense and the Sensible* 3.
23 *Metaphysics* V.6 1016b31–1017a3.
24 I stress "in general" here, because Aristotle wants to allow that within mathematics as such, beauty may be just a certain proportionate arrangement.

Aristotle's Critique as Applied to the Timaeus

I have already emphasised that Aristotle's criticism of Plato in the *Metaphysics* does not appear to be based on the *Timaeus*, but I also insisted that to be effective it should be able to withstand reference to the *Timaeus*. So how does this criticism, as I have reconstructed it, fair if we apply it to the *Timaeus*? I want to suggest that it has considerable bite.

Timaeus makes it clear from the beginning of his account that beauty and goodness (these are not clearly distinguished in his account) are the aim of god's creation. The goodness of the demiurge prescribed that he would make a cosmos that was as good and beautiful as possible. To this end, he chose an eternal paradigm, specifically, an eternal living being. Given the excellence of the paradigm, he then proceeds to maximise the likeness of the creation to the paradigm. This is done by imbuing the cosmos with mathematical order. Mathematical proportion is the prime mode of representing goodness and beauty in the sensible world.

This point is clearly brought out both by the composition of the world body and by that of the world soul. Consider first the world body.[25] As perceptible, the cosmos has a body (cf. 28b8). To be perceptible by both sight and touch the body must be composed of both fire and earth. But how do you establish unity between these parts? Two elements do not suffice to make the body a unity. So the demiurge introduces a third:

> **T9** "But it is not possible to combine two things properly without a third; for there has to be some bond in the middle to hold them together. And the finest bond is one that effects the closest unity between itself and the terms it is combining; and this is best done by a proportion."(31b9–c4)

However, as the world body were to be a solid, not a two-dimensional plane, a second middle term was required:

---

25 The world is made after its model. So if there is more than one cosmos there must be more than one model. But if there is more than one model, these models must themselves be part of a bigger whole. But if so, that whole model will be the better paradigm for the world (remember the previous argument at 30c–31a to the effect that the world would not be modeled according to what is a mere part). So there will only be one. The argument does not seem to rule out that there could many cosmoses that were qualitatively the same, but then as Burnyeat has argued ("EIKÔS MYTHOS," *Rhizai* II:2 [2005], 160–162) we should not take this to have the status of an apodictic argument. However, it crucially turns on the idea that the uniqueness as the unity of the cosmos reflects the beauty or goodness of its model, for the singularity of model follows from its being the best model.

> **T10** "So for these reasons and from these four constituents the
> body of the world was created to be at unity through proportion;
> and from these the body acquired friendship, so that having once
> come together in unity with itself, it is indissoluble by any but
> him who bound it together." (32b–c)

The demiurge thus creates the world body out of four bodies to ensure that
it has the right proportions. For that is how it will have the strongest kind of
unity.[26] The passage thus promotes proportionality as *the* way to ensure the
unity of the world body.[27]

The principle of proportionality applies not only to the relationship between
the four simple bodies but also to the constructions of the four bodies themselves.
Mathematical proportion ensures the beauty of the constructions:

> **T11** "Such being their nature when god set about ordering the
> universe, his first step was to shape them completely according
> to forms and numbers. We must thus assume as a principle in all
> we say that god brought them to a state of the greatest possible
> beauty and goodness, in which they were not before." (53b)

The demiurge constructs the simple bodies of two simple geometrical triangles
so as to form the cube (earth), the pyramid (fire), the octahedron (air), and the
icosahedron (water). The geometrical proportionality of the bodies ensures both
their combinability in ordered wholes and their interchangeability.[28] Timaeus
concludes the construction of the bodies by stressing their proportionality:

> **T12** ". . . we must assume that when the bodies had been completed
> with total precision, god fitted together their numbers, movements
> and other capacities in due proportion, in whatever way the nature
> of necessity had been persuaded willingly to yield." (56c)

In every aspect of the construction of the simple bodies the demiurge is concerned to establish proportionality, where proportionality, as we saw in the
construction of the world body, is the privileged way of maintaining unity
and order in something that has many parts. From the simple bodies to the
world body as a whole mathematical proportionality is the guiding principle

---

26 Cf. 53e4.
27 On the passage, see Verity Harte, *Plato on Parts and Wholes* (Oxford: Oxford University
Press, 2002), pp. 228–235.
28 With the exception of earth, though parts of earth are still interchangeable with each
other, being composed of the same triangles.

of composition.[29] The proportion within and between the simple bodies serves to establish a single, complete universe:

> **T13** "The things we see were in a condition of disorderliness when the god introduced as much proportionality *(summetrias)* into them and in as many ways—making each thing proportional both to itself and to other things—as was possible for making them be commensurable *(analoga)* and proportionate *(summetra)*. For at the time they had no proportionality at all, except by chance, nor did any of them qualify at all for the names we now use to name them, names like fire, water, and so on. All these things, rather, the god first gave order to, and then out of them he proceeded to construct this universe, a single living thing that contains within itself all living things *(zôion hen zôia ekhon ta panta in heautôi)*, mortal or immortal." (69b–c)

Proportionality is no less the dominant principle of composition for the world soul than for its body. As in the case of the world body, the world soul is a composite of parts. As in the case of the world body, the question arises as to how the demiurge can promote unity and completeness within the world soul (35a1–36d7). The demiurge first mixes being, sameness and difference into one form (35a7). He then divides the mixture according to numerical values, filling the intervals by means of proportions representing the harmonic and numerical middles. He makes two circles out of the resultant stuff, subdividing the inner one, the circle of the different. The circles move at different speeds and in different directions but their motions are all proportionate *(en logôi)* to each other (36d6–7). In sum, the world soul is, as Timaeus puts it, "mixed together from three parts, divided, and combined according to proportion *(ana logon)*" (37a3–4).[30] The mathematical order of the world soul is expressed in its orderly, proportionate motions. Its orderliness makes the soul good—indeed,

---

29 See the helpful discussion in Harte, *Plato*, pp. 212–247. She concludes: "there is a parallel between the macro- and micro-structure of the body of the cosmos, such that the same geometrical structure is found between the elements of the body of the cosmos—instantiated in the relations between earth, air, fire, and water—and the elements of the regular solids—instantiated in the relations between the elementary triangles and the faces of the solids, or sides there of . . . . It is in this way that structure may be said to go all the way down, and the same kind of structure at that." (p. 247).

30 For details, see F. M. Cornford, *Plato's Cosmology* (London: Routledge, 1937), pp. 59–93.

it is the best of created things[31]—and presents a model for how we can become good ourselves.[32]

Geometrical proportion underlies the construction of both the world body and the world soul, indeed the same notion of geometrical proportion can be seen to be at work in both.[33] The reason for the choice seems clear: it is through geometrical proportion that the world achieves the greatest possible unity of parts. The demiurge thereby makes the universe a *kosmos* in its true sense, a beautiful ordered whole.

The *Timaeus* relies on an assumption that the presence in the cosmos of a certain mathematical structure, a certain notion of geometrical proportion in particular, is such as to show its beauty and goodness.[34] But this is exactly the point on which Aristotle disagrees. The failure of determination arguments showed that there is no essential connection between having a certain mathematical structure and being good or beautiful. Therefore the goodness or beauty of something cannot be demonstrated through its mathematical structure. As we saw in the case of the honey-water example in **T6**, there is no *particular* mathematical structure that ensures that something is a good thing of its kind. And as we saw in the 'columns' argument in **T8**, there is no *common* mathematical structure shared by beautiful or good things in different categories. It seems, therefore, that the *Timaeus* is an appropriate target for this kind of criticism. If so, it also seems that the claim that Plato failed to recognize final causes, even as a claim about the *Timaeus*, can be justified. It is, of course, another matter whether Aristotle's criticism in **T1** is conclusive: it may well be that Plato has good answers to the criticism.

My account of why Aristotle thinks Plato fails to offer final causes works better than the first account we considered on two counts, as a reading of Aristotle and as a reading of Aristotle's reading of Plato. First of all, the first account took Aristotle's point to be that Plato reduced the goodness to an aspect of the efficient cause. This seemed difficult primarily because Aristotle presents Plato as not recognizing efficient causes, only formal and material causes. The account I have offered, meanwhile, takes Plato's failure to be one of using formal causes as causes of goodness, specifically mathematical forms,

---

31   *Timaeus* 36e6–37a3: ". . . the soul is invisible and participating in reasoning and harmony, having, by the best of the intelligible and eternal beings, come into being as the best of all generated things."

32   See *Timaeus* 47c–d.

33   For the details see Cornford, *Plato's Cosmology*, p. 49, and Andrew Barker, *Greek Musical Writings*, II (Cambridge: Cambridge University Press, 1989), pp. 59–61.

34   As Myles Burnyeat says, "Mathematical proportion is the chief expression of the Divine Craftsman's beneficent design." "Plato on Why Mathematics is Good for the Soul," in Timothy J. Smiley, ed., *Mathematics and Necessity: Essays in the History of Philosophy* (Oxford: Oxford University Press, 2000), pp. 66–67.

but without being able to show what is good about them. Note, however, that even if we were to acknowledge an efficient cause in the *Timaeus*, such as god's intelligence, Aristotle's objection, as I have presented it, would still apply, since god would be aiming to realise mathematical features that fail properly to represent goodness. Secondly, on my account Aristotle's treatment of Plato can be justified, also in the face of the *Timaeus*. Plato in the *Timaeus* does try to represent the goodness of the cosmos in mathematical terms, particularly in terms of the unity and proportionality of its parts. Moreover, it seeks to represent this goodness by a specific notion of geometrical proportionality across a range of phenomena. Aristotle would think the *Timaeus* justified his claim that Plato's mathematical causes failed to work for the good.

Objections to the Relevance of the Timaeus

My thesis is not, to repeat, that Aristotle's criticism of Plato in **T1** was based on or particularly referred to the *Timaeus*. Rather, I have argued that Aristotle could reasonably have made the criticism also of this work, and therefore did not need to mention the *Timaeus* as an exception. That is why we should resist Cherniss' condemnation of Aristotle as a reader of the *Timaeus*.

However, there are several possible objections also to my relatively weak claim that the *Timaeus* is relevant to Aristotle's criticism of Plato in **T1**. I shall consider just one here. There is no mention in the *Timaeus* of the One or of any intermediary mathematical forms. So if Aristotle's objection in **T1** is based on the claim that the One fails to work as a final cause, and more specifically through the intermediary mathematical forms, then the *Timaeus* seems irrelevant to this objection.

In response, I want to make two points. The first is that the criticism in **T1** is not limited to a theory of mathematical forms: it is equally meant to apply to Pythagoreanism and, I take it, any notion of mathematical structure as a *per se* cause of goodness. Similarly, the objections in *Metaphysics* XIV.4 and 6 were not exclusively directed against the theory of mathematical forms but against any general mathematical representation of goodness and beauty. So it is unlikely that Aristotle means to limit his critique to a theory of mathematical *forms*, thought of course it also applies to it. The absence of mathematical forms from the *Timaeus* does not, therefore, make this work irrelevant to the criticism in **T1**.

My other point is this: where we might expect a reference to entities like mathematical forms there is a deliberate gap in the *Timaeus'* account. The gap is advertised in the account of the geometrical construction of the simple bodies. Timaeus starts by criticizing his predecessors' failure to identify the proper nature of the four bodies.[35] His predecessors thought that the four were basic elements (or 'letters', *stoikheia*) when they in fact are not even to be likened to *syllables;* that is to say, they thought that the four bodies themselves were principles when they are not even the immediate derivatives of the first principles. Timaeus will try to do better; he will try to lay out more basic principles for the construction of the four bodies than his predecessors. But he also recognizes that he cannot within the context of cosmology identify the highest principle of their construction. Later he returns to the point:

> **T14** "All triangles derive from two triangles, each having one right angle and two acute angles: in one of them these two angles are both half right angles, being subtended by equal sides, in the other they are unequal, being subtended by unequal sides. This we postulate *(hupotithemetha)* as the principle of fire and the other bodies, proceeding in accordance with the account that combines likelihood and necessity; the principles that are even higher than these are known to god and to men whom god loves." (53c–d)

The language is reminiscent of the account of the mathematicians' practice in *Republic* VI. The mathematicians make certain assumptions, hypotheses, which are not themselves subjected to further inquiry. The *Timaeus* is not a work of dialectic; nor is it a treatise in abstract mathematics of the sort envisaged in *Republic* VII as an aid to the trainee philosopher in ascending to the study of the Forms. Rather it offers an account of the visible world to the extent that it is an image of the Form of living being. In terms of the *Republic*'s image of the Line, the *Timaeus* considers those features of mathematics that are relevant to making the visible world an image of this Form. There is no account of the Form of living being as such, nor of any other Forms. All we have is an assurance that the world was made in the image of

---

35 *Timaeus* 48b–e: "We must, that is, consider what was the nature of fire, water, earth, and air before the coming into being of the world and what were their attributes before then. For no one has yet indicated their coming into being, but we talk to people as if they knew what fire and each of the others are, and treat them as the letters of the universe, whereas they ought not properly to be likened even to syllables by anyone with the least sense. Our own position may therefore be described as follows. It is not for us to state the principle or principles of all things or whatever seems to be true of them, if for no other reason because it is difficult to set forth one's views according to the present manner of exposition. You must not therefore expect such an account from me, nor could I persuade myself that I would be right to undertake a task of such magnitude. I shall stick to the value of the likely accounts which I laid down at the start, and try to give an account of everything in detail from the beginning that will be no less likely than another man's, but rather more so. So let us begin again, calling also now at the beginning of our speech on a saviour god to see us safely through a strange and unusual argument to a likely conclusion."

the Form, and a demonstration of how that Form might best be mathematically represented in the perceptible world. In terms of the Line we're moving down from intelligible, mathematical assumptions to the sensible world, not up from the sensible world to the Forms. We are not in the realm of dialectic or even abstract mathematics, but rather at the interface between mathematical reasoning *(dianoia)* and opinions of perceptible matters *(pistis)*. The omission of a discussion of mathematical Forms from the *Timaeus* may thus be methodologically grounded. They are not an aspect of Plato's theory that needs or can be articulated in the context of a likely account or myth of the sensible world; rather the mathematical Forms might be a background assumption that could be brought in if it had to be further justified why appeal to particular mathematical principles was the best way to represent the paradigm; but that is not a task that Plato thinks falls within the proper purview of cosmology; it is a job for higher studies.

Conclusion

As is often the case when assessing Aristotle's response to Plato, we are left with the impression, to borrow a saying of Myles Burnyeat, that Aristotle is using a point *of* Plato's *against* Plato. Plato's insistence that the same mathematical order conveys goodness all over the cosmos, understood politically, ethically, naturally, becomes the target for Aristotle's criticism that no single mathematical conception of goodness can work across a range of categorically different things.[36] But we may suspect that Plato's answer to this criticism would just be that it shows our failure as yet to understand the deeper objective unity of goodness beyond its multifarious manifestations. For Aristotle the failure of mathematics to determine ethics would read for Plato as a sign of our failure to understand goodness at its most basic level.

In *Eudemian Ethics* I.8 Aristotle criticizes Plato's conception of the good as being out of touch with common opinion:

---

36 I am here relying on Burnyeat's interpretation according to which Plato's emphasis in the *Timaeus* (as in the *Republic*) on unity and order is evidence of fundamentally mathematical conception of goodness. Christopher Gill suggests that the emphasis "may more plausibly be taken as conveying the broader idea that goodness, as unity and order, is a transcategorical norm that can be realised, in different forms and degrees, in mathematics, in the natural universe and in human life and society." ("The Good and Mathematics," in Douglas Cairns, Fritz-Gregor Herrmann and Terry Penner, eds., *Pursuing the Good: Ethics and Metaphysics in Plato's* Republic [Edinburgh: Edinburgh University Press, 2008], p. 268). But whatever Plato's actual view, I take it that Burnyeat's reading is not implausible and, importantly for my purposes, that it is closer to the way Aristotle reads Plato.

T15 "But we should show the nature of the good *per se* in the opposite way to that now used. For now from what is not agreed to possess the good they demonstrate the things admitted to be good, e.g., from numbers they demonstrate that justice and health are goods, for they are arrangements and numbers, and it is assumed that goodness is a property of numbers and units because unity is the good itself." (*Eudemian Ethics* 1218b16–20, revised Oxford translation)

From Plato's point of view, one suspects, this objection just shows how limited the scope of people's understanding of goodness is: the mathematical structures whose goodness they dispute is in fact the ground of the goodness of those goods whose value they think obvious. And so with the One, Plato's comeback to Aristotle might well be that its essential connection with goodness will only become apparent once we look beyond categorically different goods and come to understand at the most fundamental level what they have in common. At that point, Plato may well have thought that his mathematical forms could be redeemed as final causes.*

*An early version of this paper was given at a conference in Lille on 'Le Platonisme d'Aristote'.

13

Aristotle on Plato on Weight

Alan Code

The purpose of this paper is to examine a definition of weight that Aristotle attributes to the *Timaeus*, as well as one of his criticisms of this definition. Some considerations will be adduced to show that this definition (allegedly from the *Timaeus*) is not intended by Plato as a general definition of weight, and I will indicate briefly some alternative ways of understanding the remark in that dialogue on which it appears to be based. Additionally, it will be urged that the *Timaeus* is not subject to the Aristotelian objection that I will consider. My aim is not to present or evaluate an alternative general definition of weight on Plato's behalf, but rather to indicate some problems in Aristotle's treatment of this topic. Some points of interpretation seem to me to be underdetermined by the text, but I think that in such cases my assessment of the soundness of Aristotle's criticism would be the same on a number of plausible views about the relevant passages in the *Timaeus*.

Let us start by identifying a definition of weight that Aristotle attributes to Plato in *On the Heavens* III.1 (299b31–300a1). Here Aristotle considers two alternative accounts that define weight in terms of certain plane figures. He attributes the first of a pair of definitions of weight to the *Timaeus* as follows:

> "Again, if it is the number of planes in a body that makes one heavier than another, as the *Timaeus* explains, clearly the line and the point will have weight. For the cases are, as we said before, analogous. But if the reason of differences of weight is not this, but rather the heaviness of earth and the lightness of fire, then some of the planes will be light and others heavy (which involves a similar distinction in the lines and the points); the earth-plane,

I mean, will be heavier than the fire-plane." (*On the Heavens,* III.1, 299b31-300a7)[1]

The concept that these definitions attempt to capture is comparative, not absolute. It is the relational concept of one physical body being heavier than another, and not a concept of weight as an intrinsic, absolute property that a body possesses on its own. On this account something is heavy or light only in relation to something else. Just as in Plato's *Phaedo,* Simmias is said to be both large and small because he is larger than Socrates and smaller than Phaedo, so too here a physical body is both heavy and light (in comparative senses).

According to the first of the two accounts, the one that he attributes to the *Timaeus,* what makes one body heavier than another is the *number* of planes in that body. I will refer to this strictly quantitative account as the definition of weight in terms of number. This is a reductive account in that it reduces statements of comparative weight to statements simply about the number of plane figures that a body contains. By way of contrast, the second account attributes differences in weight to qualitative differences in different plane figures. On this conception, the weight of a physical body is due not simply to the sheer quantity of plane figures it contains, but is at least in part due to qualitative differences of those constituent figures.

Aristotle's attribution to the *Timaeus* of the definition of weight in terms of number is based on a fairly brief mention of the topic at 56a6 ff., and seems not to take into consideration the considerably fuller discussion of weight later at 62c3–63e8. The first of these two passages occurs in the context of an account of the geometrical structures assigned to the four elemental bodies (fire, earth, water, and air). Speaking specifically of fire, the smallest of the elemental bodies, and the one that is assigned the structure of a tetrahedron, Plato writes:

> "Now in all these cases the body that has the fewest faces is of necessity the most mobile, in that it, more than any other, has edges that are the sharpest and best fit for cutting in every direction. It is also the lightest, in that it is made up of the least number of the same kind of parts *[tôn autôn merôn]*." (56a6–b2)[2]

Here the term translated as "lightest" is "*elaphrotaton.*" Although the term could also be translated as "fastest," this is not how he is using the term here. In the latter passage the term "*elaphron*" is again associated with smallness in

---

1 Translations of Aristotle are taken from Jonathan Barnes, ed., *The Complete Works of Aristotle: The Revised Oxford Translation* (Princeton: Princeton University Press, 1984).
2 Translations of Plato are taken from Donald J. Zeyl, translator, *Timaeus* (Indianapolis: Hackett Publishing Company, 2000).

quantity, and explicitly contrasted with that which is larger in quantity and heavy (63c4–5).

The latter passage is part of a more extended discussion of human sense perception and the nature of sensible properties, and associates differences of weight with differences in direction, or differences in motion up and motion down. For shorthand, I will refer to this as the analysis of weight in terms of direction.

One of Aristotle's main criticisms in Book IV of *On the Heavens* of the definition of weight in terms of number is that it cannot explain the phenomena associated with the directionality of motion for light and heavy things. As we shall see, this criticism there not only fails to take into consideration the second passage in the *Timaeus*, but also presupposes a theoretical interpretation of the alleged observed facts that this passage is meant to challenge explicitly.

Some scholars—most notably Harold Cherniss—think that the earlier passage in the Timaeus is no more than a 'passing remark' and that it is a mistake for Aristotle to base a definition of weight on it. Cherniss thinks that the definition of weight in terms of number is contradicted by the later passage in the *Timaeus* and should not be attributed to Plato at all.[3]

Whether or not Plato intended to suggest some kind of definition of weight in this later passage, this earlier passage is not intended as a *general* discussion of weight. His remark about the lightness of fire compares fire to two other elemental bodies (water and air) and judges it to be the lightest of those three due to the fact that it contains the least number of identical or like parts. Within the context of this limited comparison Plato is not comparing fire to the fourth element, earth, nor is he offering an account of weight that would apply to non-elemental bodies such as bronze, lead or wood—or in general, physical bodies that are constituted out of primary, elemental bodies.

Additionally, the later passage in the *Timaeus* requires—in a manner that I will examine later—that the motion of fire towards the periphery of the cosmos, and away from the center, is at least in some contexts downward motion due to heaviness. Cherniss and others have seen in this a reason for declaring that the definition of weight in terms of number is contradicted by the later passage. The reasoning seems to be that in the later passage fire, when located in the vicinity of the periphery, is actually *heavier* than the other three elements, despite the fact that it contains the fewest parts in its structural composition. If so, the definition of weight by number conflicts with Plato's description of a situation in which the element with the fewest parts is also the heaviest.

I will return later to the question of the consistency of the definition of weight by number with the analysis of weight in terms of direction. However,

---

3 Harold Cherniss, *Aristotle's Criticism of Plato and the Academy* (Baltimore: The Johns Hopkins Press, 1944). See pp. 136–139 and 161–165.

before examining this alleged conflict we need to get clearer on the nature of the limited comparison in the earlier passage at 56a ff. I pointed out that the statement that fire is the lightest body is meant to compare fire to water and air, but not to other bodies quite generally. To appreciate the significance of this one should take into consideration certain features of Plato's geometry of the elements, and in particular his use of different kinds of triangle. The 'parts' to which he refers when he says that fire has the least number of like or 'identical parts' are triangles, and triangles come in different sizes and shapes.

Earth is assigned the structure of a cube. Since each side of a cube is a square, he constructs the sides out of half squares, or right angle isosceles triangles only. Each side of the cube could be constructed from just a pair of such identical triangles, and since the cube has six sides, a cube could be generated out of a total of twelve right angle isosceles triangles. However, for the purpose of the initial construction at 55b Plato employs four triangles for each side, and hence twenty-four triangles for the entire cube.

Of the elemental bodies, only earth is constructed out of right angle isosceles triangles. The other elements are constructed out of right angle scalene triangles with 30° and 60° angles. Water is given the structure of an icosahedron, air that of an octahedron, and fire that of a tetrahedron. Consider, for instance, air. Its structure has eight sides, and each of these is an *equilateral* triangle. These equilateral triangles are in turn constructed out of the more basic half equilateral triangle—the right angle, scalene 30/60 triangle. One could construct each of the equilateral triangles out of just a pair of the 30/60 triangles, but in the initial constructions of elements at 54d–e Timaeus instead uses a total of six for the construction of the equilateral triangles of which water, air, and fire are composed. Thus each side has 6 of these 30/60 triangles, and since the entire figure has eight sides, this yields a total of 6 times 8, or forty-eight of the more basic 30/60 triangles for one unit of water.

If we think of the triangles solely in terms their geometrical construction, as opposed to their being physical constituents of physical bodies, there would of course be no determinate answer to the question as to how many triangles a Platonic solid is composed of. Both isosceles right triangles and 30/60 right triangles can be divided without limit into smaller, and still smaller triangles of the same kind. Accordingly, it would make no sense to account for weight by counting up the number of constituent triangles in the constitution of an elementary body unless we suppose there are triangles of some minimal, uniform size.

When Plato says that fire is the lightest due to being made up of the smallest number of like parts he is comparing it only to the two other elements constructed out of equilateral triangles—air and water. The parts of earth are its faces (the squares) and the isosceles right angles of which squares are composed. Hence earth does not have the same kind of parts as the other three elements. It is for this reason that earth cannot be transformed into one of the other elements, whereas each of the others can be broken down into constituent equilateral triangles, and even further into their component half equilaterals, and re-arranged into the geometrical configuration of one of the others.

There are many details lacking in his account of the lightness of fire in terms of the number of like parts. For one thing, we are not told what counts as a part. Earlier in the passage the fact that fire is the most mobile of these three elements was attributed to the smallness of the number of faces, and it is possible that in the account of the relative weight of fire in terms of number of like parts it is these parts, the faces, that he has in mind. However, in Plato's later discussion of the different varieties of the four elements at 57c–d we learn that the faces themselves are not all of the same size. In light of this one could not get a plausible account of weight simply in terms of counting the number of sides, or the number of equilateral triangles. However, the faces are themselves constructed out of still more basic triangles, the half equilaterals, and in the definition of weight in terms of number he might instead be attributing differences in weight to differences in the number of these more basic 30/60 triangles. Cornford has pointed out that given a set of basic 30/60 triangles of the same size one could go on to construct equilateral faces of varying sizes by increasing or decreasing the number of constituent 30/60 triangles used to construct the equilateral triangles.[4] In the same way, on the assumption that there are basic isosceles triangles, one could use these to construct squares of varying sizes.

A good example is Plato's distinction between liquid and fusible water at 58d. When water, or bodies containing water, are in a liquid state this is due to the fact that the units of water are small, and of varying sizes. Water that is made up of small bits that are not uniform in size is very mobile and flows easily. However, if the units of water are large, and all are of the same uniform size, then the body of water is much harder to move, and is heavy compared to liquid water. This heaviness is not due to the sheer number of faces, or equilateral triangles, contained in it. Such a large unit of water has the same number of faces as a small one, but it is heavier. It is heavier because of the greater number of basic, or elementary, 30/60 triangles of which its equilateral sides are composed. This by itself should make us doubt Aristotle's report in *On the Heavens*.

So far I have been urging that in the *Timaeus* the relative heaviness or lightness of water, air, and fire results from the total quantity of basic 30/60 triangles. Additionally, there are (let us call them) 'atomic' isosceles triangles, and different bodies of earth can be compared quantitatively in terms of the number of basic isosceles triangles they compose. It is a simple and obvious

---

4   F. M. Cornford, *Plato's Cosmology* (London: Routledge: 1937), p. 231 ff.

step to correlate the relative heaviness or lightness of bodies of earth with the quantities of these atomic isosceles triangles. However, this does not give us a way to account for the fact that earth is the heaviest of the elements, or other comparisons in weight of various quantities of earth with various quantities of the other three elements.

In the later analysis of weight in terms of direction Plato makes use of the idea of a measuring device, a balance that could be used to determine when one body weighs the same as another (63b-c). Put body A on one side of the balance and body B on the other. If the two sides are perfectly level, then A and B weigh the same. If A is higher than B, then B is heavier than A; if B is higher than A, then A is the heavier of the two.

This procedure gives us a way of telling what weighs the same as what, what is heavier, and what is lighter. However, it does not tell us what it is about the two bodies that makes one heavier, or that makes them the same in weight. If we were to define weight in terms of the number of atomic figures the bodies contain we would need a common metric for the atomic plane figures involved. As we have seen, in the case of water, air, and fire the atomic triangles are all of the same kind, and so for them, a common metric could be provided simply by counting the number of parts.[5] To extend this method to account for comparisons of weight with bodies containing earth, one would need a common numerical metric for basic isosceles and basic 30/60 triangles. None is given in the *Timaeus*, but the most obvious way to do this would be in terms of the surface area of a plane figure. A unit of earth, of whatever grade, would then be heavier than a unit of water, of whatever grade, in virtue of the fact that the sum total of the surface areas of its faces is greater than the sum total of the surface areas of the water's faces. However, on this approach one has abandoned the attempt to define weight in terms of the number of parts involved in the construction of the items being compared.

This is not a point against Plato, but rather tells against Aristotle's attribution to him of a general definition of weight in terms of number. As I have indicated, the passage in the *Timaeus* that invokes the number of parts to account for lightness is not concerned with the problem of comparing the weight of fire with that of earth, and does not suggest that the comparison should be accounted for in terms of the number of like parts. That is an Aristotelian addition to what is actually said in the *Timaeus*.

The situation seems rather to be this. When considering comparisons of weight between two quantities of pure elementary bodies of the same kind, the larger quantity is the heavier of the two bodies. Take two quantities of water. The larger quantity of water is the one having more parts (more atomic triangles),

---

5   Of course, this would involve the assumption that the atomic triangles were all of the same weight. One would still need some account as to why this assumption is correct.

and in having more parts is the heavier. However, when comparing elementary bodies of different kinds, more than just the sheer number of parts must come into play. To see this, consider an *individual* fire particle and an *individual* particle of air, where each is made of the smallest number of elementary triangles possible for an element of its sort. The *individual* fire particle is lighter than the individual particle of air in that it has fewer parts, but there is more to its being lighter than its simply having fewer parts. Its having fewer parts in turn entails its having a different shape, and differences in shapes give rise to the differences in mobility. For now let us note provisionally that the differences in mobility lead to motion to different regions. Before considering how and why this might be so, let us turn to the analysis of weight in terms of direction.

Aristotle's criticism of the definition of weight in terms of number brings us directly to this topic because although Aristotle criticizes the definition of weight in terms of number on a variety of grounds, one of his chief attacks makes use of a premise that Plato actually attempts to refute in his account of directionality.

Aristotle puts the criticism as follows:

> "But this analysis says nothing of the absolutely heavy and light. The facts are that fire is always light and moves upward, while earth and all earthy things move downwards or towards the centre. It cannot then be the fewness of the triangles (of which, in their view, all these bodies are composed) which disposes fire to move upward. If it were, the greater the quantity of fire the slower it would move, owing to the increase of weight due to the increased number of triangles. But the palpable fact, on the contrary, is that the greater the quantity, the lighter the mass is and the quicker its upward movement; and, similarly, in the reverse movement from above downward, the small mass will move quicker and the large slower." (*On the Heavens*, IV.2, 308b12–21)

In this criticism of the *Timaeus* he claims that there are facts that refute the definition of weight in terms of number:

(i)   Fire is always light and moves upward.
(ii) Earth and all earthy things move downward.

He objects that it cannot be the case that fire by nature moves upward because of the smallness of the number of constituent triangles. He here assumes that a light body will travel upward more quickly than a heavy body, and a heavy body will travel downward more quickly than a light. Hence if the body with fewer triangles is lighter, it will move more quickly. However, he claims that the greater quantity of fire actually moves up more quickly than a smaller quantity of fire. Nonetheless, on Plato's theory a larger quantity of fire contains more triangles than a smaller quantity of fire, and hence the alleged facts are supposed to refute the Platonic theory.

Unfortunately, this attempted refutation of Plato does not acknowledge the account of the connection of weight to directionality in the second and later passage dealing with weight in the *Timaeus*. Although Plato's discussion of relations between the pair up/down and the pair heavy/light is fairly complex, it is not hard to see that Plato would interpret these alleged facts quite differently. In particular, he presents an account of weight and directionality according to which propositions (i) and (ii) are true only in situations in which the elements in questions are at or near the surface of the earth, and would be false for an observer near the circumference of the universe. He asks us to consider the thought experiment in which somebody is standing in the vicinity of the periphery of the cosmos and places a larger quantity of fire on one side of a balance, and a smaller quantity on the other. If the balance is then pushed away from the circumference of the cosmos and towards the center, the side with the greater quantity of fire will be closer to the circumference and the side with the lesser quantity will be further from it.

According to the Platonic account *in that situation* the larger quantity of fire is *heavier* than the smaller, and *in that situation* its motion towards the circumference is *downward*. Plato would agree with Aristotle that it is a fact that the large quantity moves more quickly away from the center and towards the periphery. Nonetheless, he rejects the idea of an absolute up and an absolute down, and would refuse to accept the identification of the motion towards the center as in an absolute sense downward, or the motion towards the periphery as in an absolute sense upward.

Aristotle thinks that Plato is committed to saying that the larger quantity of fire is heavier than the smaller, and this is right. However, on the Platonic theory this does not commit him to saying that it would move more slowly towards the circumference. Rather, precisely because it has more triangles than a smaller quantity of fire and thus is heavier it would move more quickly towards the circumference and away from the center. In the situation envisaged (that of comparing the motions of the two quantities of fire from the perspective of an observer in the vicinity of the periphery) Plato claims that this motion towards the circumference is motion in a downward direction. In his objection Aristotle, with his conception of absolute up and down, describes such a motion as upward.

The concluding section of the second passage about weight in the *Timaeus* contains the ideas that there is a place for each of the four elements, and that each element's motion to its place is also the motion towards more of the same kind of element. It is when a quantity of fire, for instance, is in its own region, that the larger quantity is the heavier, and then and in that situation its motion towards the center of the cosmos is upward motion:

> "The path towards its own kind is what makes a thing moving along it 'heavy' and the region into which it moves, 'below', whereas the other set of terms ['light' and 'above'] are for things behaving the other way." (63e4–7)

The motion of the fire that he describes as downward and to the periphery is the movement to its own kind, and the larger the quantity, the harder it is to move it away from its own kind. However, once it is removed from its own kind, the larger the fire is, the more quickly it moves in the direction of the kindred quantity of fire in its 'downward' region at the periphery.

One might think that this contradicts the claim in the earlier passage that of the three elements composed of 30/60 triangles fire is the lightest. However, this claim was made before the explanation of the relative nature of the pairs up/down and heavy/light that we have just been discussing. It can easily be made consistent with it by construing the earlier comparison of the three elements in terms of lightness as being relative to the ordinary circumstances of observers such as us. We are not located in or near the circumference of the cosmos, and given where we in fact are located we do indeed experience fire as being the lightest. Although a larger quantity of fire is heavier than a smaller, both are light in comparison with the other elements, and both a large and a small quantity of fire on the surface of the earth would move towards the periphery. Although both would be light, the larger quantity of fire would move more quickly to its own kind and its own place. This does not, however, mean that the one with more triangles would *in that situation* be the heavier of the two. Even though if the two parcels were instead observed near the circumference the larger would be the heavier, when observed from the surface of the earth, the larger, faster moving body of fire is lighter than the smaller.

There would, though, be an irresoluble problem if Plato were defining weight in terms of the number of constituent triangles. For if he were, then a large quantity of fire would be heavier than a smaller quantity regardless of where it was located when observed. Furthermore, a huge fire would be heavier than a small pebble, and the small pebble would be lighter than a large quantity of fire. In that case, the pebble should (contrary to fact) move towards the periphery faster than the enormous fire. Nonetheless, Plato should not be saddled with this view since the earlier passage did not define weight in terms of number. That passage did, though, commit him to the claim that an element having fewer like parts is lighter than one having more of the same kind of part. If we do not read the passage as giving us a general definition of weight in terms of number, then we also should not read it as answering the question as to why having fewer like parts makes fire lighter than water or air.

This completes my evaluation of Aristotle's critique of Plato's treatment of weight in the *Timaeus*. I have argued that Aristotle is wrong to attribute to Plato a definition of weight in terms of number, and that the attack on this account in *On the Heavens* IV.2 makes use of an absolute notion of up and down that is at odds with the treatment of weight put forward in the *Timaeus*.[6] However, if the *Timaeus* does not define weight in terms of number then there should be some alternative story as to how the fact that individual bits of fire (presumably the smallest individual bits) have fewer parts than individual bits of water or air has an explanatory connection to its being the lightest of the three. Though neither of the two passages on weight in the *Timaeus* explicitly addresses this issue, what he says certainly does not preclude there being an answer, and what it says elsewhere (both before and after this passage) provides information that indicates why having the fewest parts makes fire the lightest of elements. Although the aim of this paper was simply to examine Aristotle's assessment, I conclude with a brief sketch of one plausible answer.[7]

Prior to the creative activity of the demiurge there were already 'traces' of the four elements, and due to the shaking of the receptacle they separated out into four regions.[8] Using the Democritean image of a winnowing basket, Plato describes a process in which like joins like, and different kinds come to occupy different regions. Even at this primitive stage there were distinctions between heavy and light. Heavy particles accumulated in the center, the lightest towards the circumference, and particles of intermediate weights in intermediate regions.

The demiurge improves on this situation by imposing determinate order, and to the extent possible making the elements proportionate and commensurable:

> "The god fashioned these four kinds to be as perfect and excellent
> as possible when they were not so before." (53b5–6)

What we learn from the passage that Aristotle thinks contains a definition of weight in terms of number is that the geometrical shapes of the elements facilitate their motions to their respective regions. It is these shapes that give rise to degrees of mobility, with earth being the least and fire the most mobile.

---

6 For a comprehensive examination of a variety of issues concerning Aristotle's criticism and the extent to which it engages (or fails to engage) Plato, see D. O'Brien, *Four Essays on Democritus, Plato and Aristotle: A Study in the Development of Ideas*, Vol. 2: *Plato, Weight and Sensation: The Two Theories of the* Timaeus (Leiden: Brill, 1984).

7 A fuller account along similar lines may be found in chapter 6 (especially pp.141–144) of Richard Mohr, *God and Forms in Plato* (Las Vegas: Parmenides Publishing, 2005).

8 52e5–53b5.

When combined with the earlier 'winnowing analogy', this in turn would explain why the piercing shape of fire accounts for the motion of fire towards the outermost region. The weight of fire is, on such an account, a direct result of the way it is put together out of basic, atomic triangles.[9]

Of course, even if this shows how the lightness of fire is connected to its having the fewest parts, a general account of weight would also have to apply to compound physical bodies and show how their weight results from the ratios and positions of the pure elements within them. Nonetheless, the basics of an account of weight are in place. The universe is spherical, with an absolute center, and a circumference, every part of which is equidistant to the center. Space itself is subject to a kind of movement or shaking that has separated particles of matter into four regions, drawing like to like. In a creative act, precise geometrical structures have been imposed upon matter, and these geometrical structures themselves are constructed out of primitive or atomic triangles. The shapes can be classified in terms of the number and types of primitive parts, and this in turn gives rise to degrees of mobility. As a result, like bits of matter are attracted to their own kind, and this is at the heart of the nature of the phenomena we perceive as heaviness and lightness.

9   As Mohr puts it weight in an objective sense is treated "as being an inherent property that the primary particles have as a direct result of their geometrical construction (56b2)" (*God*, p. 141).

14

What Makes a Myth eikôs?
Remarks Inspired by Myles Burnyeat's
'EIKÔS MYTHOS'

Gábor Betegh

1.

There is every chance that Myles Burnyeat's paper on εἰκὼς μῦθος will very soon become a classic that initiates fruitful discussions by challenging traditional interpretations and by drawing attention to hitherto underappreciated aspects of well-known texts. The paper was first published in 2005 in a thematic issue of the young journal *Rhizai* and was republished in 2009 in *Plato's Myths,* a collection of papers edited by Catalin Partenie at Cambridge University Press. And I am happy to announce that the paper is already available in Hungarian translation.[1] The fact that the organizers of the Urbana conference on the *Timaeus* selected it to be the topic of a special session is further testimony for the importance of the paper.

In what follows, I shall offer a series of remarks, the general tendency of which will not be polemical, simply because I find the gist of the paper compelling. What I shall try to do, instead of raising objections, is to explore and develop certain points coming up in Burnyeat's discussion, to call attention to certain passages in both the *Timaeus* and other Platonic texts that may give further nuances to the picture, and in some cases to suggest some shift of emphasis.

---

1 M. F. Burnyeat, "EIKÔS MYTHOS," *Rhizai* II:2 (2005), 143–165; Catalin Partenie, *Plato's Myths* (Cambridge: Cambridge University Press, 2009); Hungarian translation by Tamás Böröczki in Gábor Betegh and Tamás Böröczki, eds., *A formák és a tudás. Tanulmányok Platón metafizikájáról és ismeretelméletéről* (Budapest: Gondolat, 2007).

2.

Let me start by stating that I fully accept what I take to be Burnyeat's central claim, i.e., that the term εἰκώς in the phrases εἰκὼς λόγος and εἰκὼς μῦθος designates a positive norm or standard which the relevant discourses ought to aspire to satisfy. What I would nevertheless stress is that this contention is not incompatible with the claim—which is the core of the traditional interpretation—that the term εἰκώς is limitative and restrictive. The two are not exclusive alternatives, because the same term can express a positive standard *and* a limitation in the relevant contexts.[2] Take for example the term "graduate level" as in expressions like "graduate level work." On the one hand it states a positive requirement, standard, or norm. The fact that a paper was written by a graduate student will not in itself guarantee that this norm is satisfied; it is something the graduate student ought to aspire to in writing the paper, and if the expression can justifiably be applied to the result, it is an indication that the effort was successful. This corresponds, I think, fairly well to what Burnyeat says about the term εἰκώς: an account about a generated thing will not automatically be εἰκώς, but ought to aspire to live up to that standard.

Consider now the following sentence: "Professional scholars are expected to produce professional, publishable pieces, whereas graduate students are expected to produce graduate level work." In this sentence, which is meant to be roughly analogous to the way Burnyeat suggests to read the crucial sentence at 29b3–c3, the same term "graduate level" can express both a positive norm (with respect to graduate students) and a comparative limitation (with respect to the work expected from established scholars). In such a sentence there is no pressure to choose between normativity and comparative restriction.

It remains nonetheless true that if we insert a "but" and an "only" in the sentence and say that "*but* graduate students are expected to produce *only* graduate level work" we emphasize the limitative aspect; so Burnyeat's complaints about translations like Cornford's—which introduce a "but" and an "only" absent from the Greek—and the corresponding interpretations, remain fully justified.

---

2 I am not thereby implying that Burnyeat would deny this point; indeed when he turns to discuss the "permissibility . . . of translating εἰκώς as 'probable' or 'likely'," he makes a move in this direction. But the point I am making is different in so far as it has nothing to do with the semantic richness of the word εἰκώς, but is based simply on the structural features of the relevant sentences. Moreover, it has become manifest in discussions of the paper that Burnyeat's greater emphasis on the normative aspect of the term—surely, an effect of the polemical context of his paper—may create the impression that the restrictive aspect of the term is now in need of a defense.

3.

This is how Burnyeat introduces the discussion of that part of the text where Timaeus turns to describe discourses about likenesses (section D in Burnyeat's apportioning of the text): "Please note that the subject of the sentence is not any old statement about a likeness, still less any old statement about the sensible world, but accounts exegetic of a certain type of likeness, namely, one fashioned after an eternal unchanging model. These accounts will be akin to their subject matter in the sense of being εἰκότες accounts of that subject matter" (pp. 151–152). I am not entirely sure whether Burnyeat wants to suggest here that we should restrict the class of εἰκότες accounts to successful accounts about copies made after an eternal model, excluding thus accounts about such copies which have generated things as their models—but in any case his reminder calls attention to a problem that seems to be in need of some further discussion and clarification.

The problem is that the binary distinction of the sentence about discourse types at 29b3–c3 does not map onto the original binary ontological and epistemological distinction announced at 27d6–28c4. The original division distinguished between everlasting beings (let's call them A's) on the one hand, and becoming things (let's call them B's) on the other. In the next step we learn from Timaeus that B things fall into two major classes: those that were fashioned after an A (let's call these B^A things), and those which were created after another B (let's call these B^B things). Timaeus then applies a special argument to show that the cosmos is a B^A thing (28c5–29a5). When Timaeus turns next to discourse types at 29b2, he first speaks about discourses that are exegetical of, and akin to, A things in general, and specifies the characteristics and norms of such discourses. Then, as Burnyeat reminds us, Timaeus refers not to discourses about B things in general, but only to successful discourses about B^A things, characterizing *these* discourses as εἰκότες. But does this mean that Timaeus wants to say that *only* such discourses can be εἰκώς? Or is there some other reason for the restricted scope of this sentence?

Prima facie, the text suggests that discourses about B^B things are not excluded from εἰκότες accounts—Timaeus just does not mention them. First, the explanatory clause ὄντος δὲ εἰκόνος is general enough to accommodate both B^A and B^B things in so far as both are copies. Second, when Timaeus specifies the terms of the proportion, he compares οὐσία (being) to γένεσις (becoming). So, once again, he uses the more general term, γένεσις, which corresponds to the term used in the original ontological division prior to the introduction of the more fine-grained distinction between B^A and B^B things: γένεσις encompasses both B^A and B^B things. These considerations seem to suggest that a successful account about a B^B, in so far as B^B is a copy and is characterized by γένεσις, will be an εἰκώς account.

However, the ἐξηγηταί language that Burnyeat emphasizes may become crucial at this point. For Timaeus' major premise in the argument about discourse types seems to tie the kinship relation between discourses and their objects to the discourses' being 'exegetical' of their objects: "accounts are akin to those things which they are *exegetai*" (29b4–d5, ὡς ἄρα τοὺς λόγους, ὧνπέρ εἰσιν ἐξηγηταί, τούτων αὐτῶν καὶ συγγενεῖς ὄντας). The account thus needs to be 'exegetic' of its object to be akin to it; using this assumption one may suggest at this point that an account about a B^B thing cannot be εἰκώς because it cannot be 'exegetic' of its subject. For Burnyeat stresses the strong religious connotation of the word ἐξηγητής, i.e., that an *exegete* is someone who explains something that is divine or comes from a divine source. Now if this connotation is strong enough to guarantee that an account can only be an ἐξηγητής if it successfully explains something divine or issuing from the divine, the restriction to discourses about B^A things, as opposed to B things in general, may perhaps be explained in this way. For a successful, 'exegetic' account of a B^A thing will explain the object's essential connection to the divine, either by explaining that it came into being by the agency of a god or by referring to its divine model, or indeed by saying that the generated thing itself is a god (as in the case of the cosmos). An account of a B^B thing, by contrast, will, for the most part, remain in the sphere of B things without mentioning anything divine: both the copy and the model is a B thing, and, a god will rarely make a copy after a B thing (I shall return to this point in a moment). The divine does not enter such an account; consequently the account will not be an ἐξηγητής, and if it is not ἐξηγητής, it will not be akin to its object, and therefore even though the object is an εἰκών, the account, even if successful in presenting its object as far as possible, will not be εἰκώς.

The force of this line of thought ultimately depends on the question whether the connection between the word ἐξηγητής and the divine is strong enough—strong enough to bear the weight of this argument. And this, I think, is open to debate. It is of course true that the religious connotation of the word generally speaking is very strong; the question is whether the word necessarily implies a reference to the sphere of the divine or it can be used also in a more general, 'secularized' way.

It turns out that the latter is the case. Surely, an ἐξηγητής in the strict sense offers advice on religious matters, explaining what the relevant sacred law is, and how it applies to the particular case. But we see very soon that the word can figure in a looser sense where the ἐξηγητής becomes someone who offers advice on *any* practical matter, without any reference to the sphere of the divine. Thus the author of a shrewd political plan can be called an ἐξηγητής (Herodotus, 5.31; ἐξηγητής is the reading of all the manuscripts, but was emended into ἐσηγητής by Herwerden and Madvig). The word can be used even in clearly negative contexts to refer to someone who masterminded a series of frauds (Demosthenes, *Against Lacritus*, 17.6). If we take the other aspect of the function of a religious ἐξηγητής, i.e., to explain something the meaning of which is obscure, we can observe a similar, secularizing semantic development. For example Aeschines can call his traveling companion an ἐξηγητής τῆς ἀπάσης κακοηθείας, "the expounder of all mischief," because he learnt from him the apparently improper and naughty meanings of such words as κέρκωψ, παιπάλημα and παλίμβολον (Aeschines, *On the Embassy*, 40.5). It seems clear that the religious overtone is gone or has turned into very strong irony. These occurrences show, I think, that the reference to the divine is not a *necessary* feature of the word. This means in turn that the religious, theological connotation of the word ἐξηγητής may not be strong enough to restrict the group of 'exegetical' discourses to such discourses which necessarily have a reference to the divine, i.e., discourses about A and B^A things; it may be sufficient if the accounts successfully explain something.

If so, the easiest way to explain the fact that Timaeus in our sentence refers only to discourses about B^A things is that he has already established that the object of his discourse is a B^A thing, so he can now focus only on the relevant class—without thereby excluding that a discourse about a B^B thing, if certain requirements are met, can also be εἰκώς.

Incidentally, it appears that Timaeus also speaks about B^B things, and Burnyeat explicitly calls attention to this fact in a different context. Take for example the way the younger gods created the head after the shape of the cosmos (44d3–4: τὸ τοῦ παντὸς σχῆμα ἀπομιμησάμενοι, with Burnyeat's analysis on pp. 157–158). This is thus an account of a B^B thing, but should, I assume, be considered an εἰκὼς λόγος nonetheless. What, of course, complicates the picture here is that the head is a divine creation as well, even though it is created by the younger gods. But it could hardly be otherwise, since the *Timaeus* speaks only about divine creations. Yet, this is a good reminder that divine agents can also create B^B things in the appropriate circumstances, and that teleological reasoning can also enter the creation of B^B things, even if, as we have learned in the proem, such things can never be καλός (beautiful, good, cf. 28b1–2).

Yet, there may be a further twist: For in their works of creation the younger gods are doing what the demiurge told them to do. Now in his speech to the gods, the demiurge instructed them "to turn according to your own nature to the making of living creatures, *imitating my power in generating you*" (τρέπεσθε κατὰ φύσιν ὑμεῖς ἐπὶ τὴν τῶν ζῴων δημιουργίαν, μιμούμενοι τὴν ἐμὴν δύναμιν περὶ τὴν ὑμετέραν γένεσιν, 41c4–6). So when the younger gods create the heads of mortal beings they model it after a B thing—yet in doing that they are at the same time imitating something that is an A thing, i.e., the demiurge.[3] What they are imitating is, most importantly, the teleological nature of demiurgic creation; their creative activity becomes a likeness of the demiurge's action. Now, is that part of Timaeus' discourse 'exegetic' of the human head, a B^B thing, or the demiurgic activity of the younger gods, a B^A, or at least a quasi-B^A, thing? This consideration, I believe, introduces an important novel dimension into what initially appeared to be a clear-cut distinction between discourses about B^A and B^B things.

To sum up, the qualification εἰκώς applied to a discourse could mean in a more general sense that the discourse in question successfully reveals a B thing *as* a copy as opposed to merely exposing it as a thing that has come to be. This is also what Timaeus' parallel between the two types of discourse ultimately suggests. When discourses are successful, they effectively reveal the most salient ontological fact about their objects. A successful discourse about an εἰκών will be εἰκώς precisely in so far as it presents its subject *as* an εἰκών, explaining what its model is, why it was created after that particular model, by whom, etc.

Now assuming that εἰκὼς λόγος is the more general term, εἰκὼς μῦθος being a subset of it (on this see below), I find it tempting to think that, in the case of a B^A thing, an account which reveals only the connection between the B^A thing in question and its model is already a *bona fide*, albeit not complete, εἰκὼς λόγος; in this sense an explanation in terms of the relevant Form or Forms is already an εἰκὼς λόγος. What makes an account an εἰκὼς μῦθος is that we also get a narrative in which we hear about the maker and the maker's reasons for creating the thing in question.

4.

The last sentence of Timaeus' proem contains further notable features relevant to Burnyeat's discussion. It will be useful to have the sentence in front of our eyes:

> (i) If, therefore, Socrates, in many respects concerning many things, regarding gods and the generation of the universe, (ii) we find ourselves unable to furnish accounts which are entirely and in every way in agreement with each other and made completely precise, do not be surprised; (iii) but if we can offer accounts no less likely than anyone else's, we must be content, (iv) remembering that I the speaker and you the judges have human nature, (v) and consequently it is fitting that we should accept the likely narrative about these matters (vi) and seek nothing further. (translation by Burnyeat, slightly modified, my numbering)

---

3   For the point that the demiurge is an A thing, see, e.g., 37a1, where the demiurge is characterized as "the best of the intelligible and eternal beings."

The sentence immediately follows the sentence which states the analogy between discourse types and their respective objects. The οὖν, "therefore," in the first part of our sentence indicates that Timaeus is now drawing the lesson from his previous claims. Section (i) then designates the scope of the ensuing claim, first more loosely ("in many respects concerning many things") and then adding some precision ("regarding gods and the generation of the universe"). It may be asked at this point what the force of this addition is. First, is it meant to be exhaustive of the "many things" or is it simply calling attention to some salient examples, especially relevant to Timaeus' current project? Second, how exactly is it supposed to connect to the claims about discourses and their objects in the previous sentence? For we have learned from Timaeus' previous arguments that the universe is a copy (a B thing), and that it is a copy made after an eternal model (B^A thing); a successful discourse about it will be εἰκώς. But what about the gods? As it will become clear in Timaeus' speech, a god can be an A thing (the demiurge) or a B^A thing (the cosmos, the younger gods). However, it seems fairly clear to me that the gods are not mentioned here merely because they fall into one of the ontological categories discussed in the previous sentence. The important point about them is not only that they themselves may be εἰκόνες, and therefore the discourse about them may be an εἰκώς account, but also, or even primarily, that they are the *makers* of the εἰκόνες which are the objects of the εἰκώς accounts.[4]

This point provides, I think, immediate support to Burnyeat's claim that a successful, full account about a likeness will reveal not only the likeness' relation to its model, but will also make reference to the maker, his or her motivations for creating the likeness and the practical reasoning governing his or her creative activity. And if this is so, it gives good justification to Timaeus' disclaimer: speaking about the makers' motivations and reasoning may be particularly difficult when the makers are gods. After all, Timaeus has just reminded his audience how difficult it is to find and speak about the father and maker of this universe (28c3–5). The οὖν refers back not only to the previous sentence, but also to what we learned in the earlier parts of the proem.

The upshot is that the difficulty we may face in formulating an account of a likeness depends not merely on the ontological status of the likeness, but also on our cognitive access to the maker, to his or her motivations and reasoning, and the process of the creation of the likeness. The maker, and the creation of the copy are all-important elements of an εἰκώς account—and this is a marked

---

4   *Contra* A. E. Taylor, *A Commentary on Plato's* Timaeus (Oxford: Clarendon Press, 1928), p. 74 ad loc. and translation in A. E. Taylor, *Plato:* Timaeus *and* Critias (London: Methuen, London, 1929), who takes the genitive of θεῶν to be dependent on γενέσεως. Other translations, like F. M. Cornford, *Plato's Cosmology* (London: Routledge, 1952), and Donald J. Zeyl, *Plato:* Timaeus (Indianapolis: Hackett, 2000), and Luc Brisson, *Platon:* Timée / Critias (Paris: Garnier-Flammarion, 1992), make it coordinate with the genitive of γενέσεως.

difference as compared to the Divided Line, and its possible echoes in the first part of the proem, where the cognitive state is made correlative merely to the ontological status of the object.

Sections (iii)–(vi) of the same sentence provide strong confirmation to this contention. The crucial point comes with Timaeus' emphatic reference to our human nature in (iv). Both the claim in (iii) that we must be content if we are able to produce a likely account which is not less likely than anyone else's,[5] and the claim in (v) that it is fitting (πρέπει) to accept the resulting εἰκὼς μῦθος, are made dependent on the fact that both the speaker and the listeners are human beings. If there would be a simple strict correlation between the status of the subject matter of the discourse, i.e., that it is a likeness, and the status of the ensuing discourse, then the heavy stress on the human nature of the speaker and the audience would not make much sense.[6]

What is meant, I assume, must be that in so far as the relevant accounts need to include claims about the motivations and reasoning of the demiurgic god or gods, no human being is in a position to say anything certain about these matters. If it is the case that the cosmos was created (in some sense or other) by one or more divine beings—and Timaeus is certainly committed to this much—then there are facts of the matter that are naturally accessible to these divine beings, but are not available to us humans. If those gods wanted to give an account of the way they created the cosmos, its structural parts and inhabitants, that would be an εἰκώς account as well in so far as it would be an account about an εἰκών—yet that account would be at another level of certainty, one that humans cannot even aspire to. The μηδενός at 29c7 must refer to our fellow human beings. There is thus an element of certainty or

---

5   I find Burnyeat's arguments for taking μηδενός at 29c7 as referring to other people who produce alternative accounts attractive. Two small remarks, however. It is notable that Taylor who, following Chalcidius, took μηδενός to refer to people, translate the parallel phrase at 48d3 μηδενὸς ἧττον εἰκότα differently: "Mindful of what I said at first of the character of probable discourse, I shall endeavour to make a statement in each point and all not less but more probable than what has been said from the beginning of our discourse until now" (Taylor, Timaeus and Critias; cf. Taylor, Commentary, pp. 310–311, ad loc.). This is especially remarkable since the sentence at 48d explicitly refers back to the sentence at 29c. The case is of course complicated by the notorious textual problem posed by the following ἔμπροσθεν at 48d3. But if one decides to construe μηδενός as a neuter at 48d3, it becomes considerably more difficult to keep it masculine at 29c7. Incidentally, Burnyeat mistakenly groups with the majority view T. K. Johansen's Plato's Natural Philosophy: A Study of the Timaeus-Critias (Cambridge: Cambridge University Press, 2004), p. 49.

6   Cf. Taylor, Commentary, p. 75, ad loc.: "As Timaeus holds that 'from the nature of the subject' there can be no exact knowledge in cosmology, he probably does not mean to suggest that the exactitude he is denying to man is enjoyed by God." Fair enough—but then Taylor does not offer an alternative explanation of Timaeus' insistence on his and his listeners' human nature.

uncertainty in such discourses that is quite independent of the epistemological limitation stemming from the fact that the object of the account is a generated physical object. This second limitation is absolute, one that human and divine beings share; but in respect of the first one, humans have a handicap that they can never compensate. What we must accept and be content with is the εἰκώς account available to us humans,[7] in so far as we can try to attribute reasons to the divine artificers with some probability.

To sum up, due attention paid to sections (i) and (iv) of the closing sentence of the proem may offer significant support to Burnyeat's contention that the qualification εἰκώς goes beyond the epistemological limitations set by the ontological status of the likeness and incorporates reference to the practical reasoning of the maker.

5.

Thus far, I have concentrated on the adjective εἰκώς saying very little about the words μῦθος and λόγος that it qualifies. In this respect, Burnyeat argues, first, that μῦθος should not be rendered by some innocuous word like "story" or "narrative," but should be translated by the more marked term "myth." This is so, on Burnyeat's argument, not merely because Timaeus relates the deeds of divine beings, but because what he tells us is also a *theogony*. The variation between εἰκὼς μῦθος and εἰκὼς λόγος should then be viewed, on Burnyeat's account, against the backdrop of the opposition between Hesiod's *Theogony* and Presocratic cosmogonies, corresponding to the more general μῦθος/λόγος opposition (pp. 144–145). The variation between εἰκὼς μῦθος and εἰκὼς λόγος indicates that Timaeus' discourse transcends this opposition (pp. 145 and 156).

First, I would have a brief remark about the relationship between μῦθος and λόγος. This is obviously not the place to try to tackle the dauntingly complex issue of the relationship between this pair of concepts more generally. But if we concentrate on the way Timaeus uses these terms in his speech, and more specifically in its proem, it appears that there is no real opposition between the two at all. So it is not so much the case that there is an initial assumed opposition which the εἰκὼς μῦθος, being rational and reasoned, overcomes or transcends. It seems to me rather that Timaeus already starts with a sufficiently general and generous concept of λόγος that can encompass mythical accounts or, indeed, which in the relevant cases invites such accounts.

Note first of all that λόγος is used as the most general term for accounts or discourses in the sentence on discourse types at 29b3–c3: λόγοι can have as their objects entities from either ontological realm, so λόγοι can express

---

7   Note also the definite article in front of εἰκὼς μῦθος at 29d2: If we can produce an account that is no less εἰκώς than those given by other humans, then we have to accept *that* one.

both νόησις (knowledge) and δόξα (opinion) from the original epistemological distinction. Note also that when Timaeus refers for the first time to the speech that he is about to deliver about the universe, he calls it a λόγος, before he settled the question whether it was born or is without birth (ἡμᾶς δὲ τοὺς περὶ τοῦ παντὸς λόγους ποιεῖσθαί πῃ μέλλοντας, ᾗ[8] γέγονεν ἢ καὶ ἀγενές ἐστιν κτλ., 27c4–5).

As commentators have often pointed out, it is remarkable that as soon as Timaeus has established that everything that has come to be has a cause, he immediately translates the cause into a personal agent; he then applies this point to the case of the cosmos as well. This personalizing move strongly suggests that, for Timaeus, a λόγος about anything that has come to be can naturally take the form of a narrative, and in those cases where the personal agent responsible for the coming into being of the object in question is not a human being, this narrative will be a myth in the narrower sense. In view of this, it becomes relatively unsurprising that Timaeus can switch to the μῦθος language at 29d without any further preparation or explanation; after what we were told in the earlier parts of the proem, it is natural that these λόγοι will take the form of myths.

This consideration also suggests, I would maintain, that the appropriate context to understand Timaeus' use of μῦθος here is what we would call aetiological myths, i.e., narratives that seek to account for the origin of a certain phenomenon, state of affairs, institution, plant or animal species by reference to divine actions in some unspecified moment in the past. So without denying the relevance of Hesiod's *Theogony* (and other, non-Hesiodic theogonies for that matter), what I would emphasize is the relevance of the broader stock of such mythical narratives. More specifically, I would suggest that Plato's use of aetiological myths in other dialogues may bring us closer to understanding what makes a myth εἰκώς for Timaeus.

Consider for example the little myth Socrates relates in his very first sentences in the *Phaedo* as one that Aesop would have told had he noticed a salient fact about pleasure and pain.[9] Socrates first speaks in his own voice:

> What a curious thing, my friends, he said, what people call pleasant seems to be; what an amazing relationship it has to what is considered its opposite, pain. They are unwilling both to come to us at the same time, but if we pursue one of them and catch

---

8 Accepting the reading of F and Y.
9 Here I am building on the analysis of the Aesop myth I develop in Gábor Betegh "Tale, Theology and Teleology in the *Phaedo*," in Catalin Partenie, ed., *Plato's Myths* (Cambridge: Cambridge University Press, 2009); by a happy chance the paper appeared in the same volume in which Burnyeat's paper got republished.

it, we are pretty much compelled to catch the other as well, as if these two were joined at a single tip. (60b3–c1)

So Socrates notices a phenomenon—the relationship between pleasure and pain—and he finds that this phenomenon is strange. He calls pleasant curious (ἄτοπον), and its relationship to pain amazing (θαυμασίως πέφυκε). But then he adds the following:

> And it seems to me, he said, that if Aesop had thought of it, he would have composed a myth that the god wanted to reconcile them as they were fighting against each other, but when he could not, he attached the tip of their heads together, and this is why if one of them comes to someone, the other as well will later visit the same person. (60c1–5)

This apparently insignificant little fable connects at important points to Timaeus' cosmological myth and, moreover, gives excellent support to Burnyeat's central thesis. Note, first of all, that Socrates says that this is a myth Aesop would have told. Now Aesop's name turns up again a page later, where Socrates says that when he recently felt that the god might expect some poetic work from him, he put into verse Aesop's myths that he knew by heart. It is a clear indication that Socrates considers Aesop a good composer of myths, and, moreover, one who composes such myths that would please the god. Remember that this was after all what Timaeus also asked in his invocation and prayer to the gods: that everything he says should please the gods or should be according to the *nous* of the gods (θεούς τε καὶ θεὰς ἐπικαλουμένους εὔχεσθαι πάντα κατὰ νοῦν ἐκείνοις . . . εἰπεῖν, 27c7–d1[10]). And it is easy to see that Aesop's myth about pleasure and pain, had he written it, would have pleased the god, because, as far as we can get a glimpse of it from the preview Socrates relates to his friends, it is an expression of the correct views about the god and the relationship between god and the world.

Let's take a look at the structure of this little myth. The narrative starts with a negative state of affairs: there is a warfare between pleasure and pain. This situation, at the same time, is the privation of the phenomenon Socrates has noticed: pleasure and pain are not yet tied together. Then the god enters the scene and wants to mend the situation by creating order in the relation

---

10 I cannot develop the point here, but it is rarely remarked how rich in meaning this prayer becomes when we read it from the perspective of the later developments of Timaeus' speech. For Timaeus' speech will also specify who the addressees of his prayer really are—most importantly the maker of the cosmos and the makers of its inhabitants. And if he could manage to speak according to their νοῦς (reason), he would indeed accomplish his task to full success.

between pleasure and pain. What he first intends to achieve would certainly be the best solution: "the god wanted to reconcile them." But even the god does not have the power to do anything he would wish, but has to count with certain limiting conditions; for, surely, pleasure and pain are by their very natures opposites, so even a god cannot attain a total reconciliation between them. This is why the god has to find a second best solution, which is at the same time the best available, practicable solution. This course of action then leads to the emergence of the current situation, to the conjunction of pleasure and pain, the phenomenon noticed by Socrates. The myth is supposed to have explanatory power with respect to the phenomenon as the phrase "and this is why" (καὶ διὰ ταῦτα, 60c4) indicates.

The structural parallel with Timaeus' myth, I think, is obvious. The crucial elements are all there: the disorderly negative initial situation, which is a privation of the explanandum, the divine intention to install the best possible state of affairs, the limiting conditions set by the nature of the material. And the overall effect and explanatory force of the two myths may also be comparable. For remember that Socrates found the phenomenon curious. The force of Aesop's myth is that it integrates the phenomenon into the order of the world by explaining it as the result of a purposeful action of a god who wants order in the world and aims at the best. If Aesop had composed a myth along these lines, filling in all the details that are missing from Socrates' skeletal formulation—explaining for example why the god went for exactly this solution, whether he considered it a form of punishment, or a reconciliation as far as possible, or a mixture of the two—the outcome would have been a good, appropriate, reasonable myth—an εἰκώς myth, if you wish, at least in the non-technical sense—because it would have revealed why it is good and reasonable that pleasure and pain are so related.

But Aesop would still not be either a philosopher or an expert scientist. He would not have the scientific resources to integrate into his myth the relevant facts about the physiology of pleasure and pain, nor would he have the correct general metaphysical framework about the ontology of things that have come to be. Most importantly, he would not know that they are likenesses. His myth would be appropriate and reasonable in so far as it would be based on the correct theological assumption, that the god is good and wants everything to be as good as possible, and would use the corresponding teleological explanatory scheme for the explanation of a given phenomenon; this much he shares with Timaeus. But Timaeus may remain content because his version would be still more εἰκώς due to his expertise in philosophy, mathematics, and natural science.

15

The Epistemological Section (29b–d) of the Proem in Timaeus' Speech: M. F. Burnyeat on eikôs mythos, and Comparison with Xenophanes B34 and B35

Alexander P. D. Mourelatos

The long speech by Timaeus that constitutes the main body of the homonymous Platonic dialogue famously starts with a *prooimion*, "proem" or "prelude" (27d–29d). This proem has its conclusion in an epistemological or methodological section (29b–d). Of salient importance in this particular section is the introduction and initial deployment of the *eikôs mythos* concept (often translated "likely story," but see immediately below). Plato formulates the concept for the purpose of characterizing the tenor of such claims as may be made in contexts of theogony, cosmogony, cosmology, and natural philosophy. Myles Burnyeat's masterly study of this Platonic concept and of the relevant section of the proem of Timaeus' speech[1] has already made, and merits continuing to make, a strong impression on the community of scholars in ancient philosophy. First published in 2005, the study has recently been reprinted in a collection that is likely to attract a large readership.[2] But even before its first publication, Burnyeat's "EIKÔS MYTHOS" paper had engaged, in lecture-form versions, and over more than ten years, the interest and appreciation of numerous academic audiences, both in Europe and in the USA. It was a happy thought on the part of the conveners of the 2007 conference on the *Timaeus*, held at the University of Illinois, Urbana-Champaign, that one entire session of the conference be devoted to discussion of Burnyeat's important paper. For the honor of my

---

1 M. F. Burnyeat, "EIKÔS MYTHOS," *Rhizai* II:2 (2005), 143–165.
2 Catalin Partenie, ed., *Plato's Myths* (Cambridge: Cambridge University Press, 2009), pp. 167–186.

having been assigned, along with Gábor Betegh, the role of discussant in that conference panel, I felt—and continue to feel—not only grateful and pleased but also keenly challenged. My essay here is a fuller and revised version of what I presented at the University of Illinois event in September of 2007. My references to Burnyeat are to the paper in its 2005 version, in *Rhizai*.

Major Themes and Claims of Burnyeat's Paper

Central in Burnyeat's overall argument is the thesis that the mode of reasoning represented by the phrase *eikôs mythos* is not theoretical but practical: what any competent craftsman, let alone the Divine Craftsman, would have recourse to in determining how to produce the best product from materials that are given. Such "practical" reasoning operates under two sorts of constraints. The first of these is familiar enough: the constraints imposed by the nature (whether propitious or recalcitrant) of the materials. The second has often been overlooked, or its role has been underestimated, but Burnyeat gives it emphasis: after the start of the productive process, and throughout its course, there are also *choices* to be made; and each such choice progressively further limits subsequent choices (pp. 157–158). Plato's cosmological "myth," accordingly, "is not trying to disclose what is true about the physical world so much as to disclose why this is the best of all possible worlds that the materials allow the Maker(s) [the *dêmiourgos* and the Lesser Gods who assist him] to make" (p. 157). In sum—using my own words here, not Burnyeat's—the *Timaeus* is more a venture in theodicy than it is a project in speculative physics.

Burnyeat's approach has the virtue of disposing of some egregious issues in the interpretation of the dialogue: Plato's Divine Craftsman is not "mad" (as David Keyt once charged); for Plato does not seek to "infer" that the copy must be unique if the model is unique (pp. 160–161). Nor does Plato indulge in "preposterous inferences" (as Gregory Vlastos charged) of "what is, or is not, the case" from premises that posit "what would be good and beautiful . . . if it were the case" (p. 62).[3] Moreover, in the course of his argument, Burnyeat adopts or supports a number of claims that I find both attractive and convincing:

- *eikôs* does not mean "probable" tout court, but rather "appropriate, reasonable, rational" (pp. 146–147).
- *mythos* should not be simply equated with *logos*, and thus be weakened into "account." An *eikôs mythos* is a special kind of *logos* and a special kind of myth; the collocation envisages a blending of the two genres (p. 145).

---

3 Burnyeat quotes from Vlastos' *Plato's Universe* (Seattle: Washington University Press, 1975). Reprint Las Vegas: Parmenides Publishing, 2006), p. 62.

- The term *exêgêtês*, which plays a distinct and important role in the target text (29b–d), has a rich but overlooked history of associations that are highly relevant to Plato's use of the term. A *logos exêgêtês* serves to "expound or explain the unobvious significance of an object" (p. 149).
- In the target text, *logoi* are not simply "about" their subject matter. Whether in reference to the permanent exemplar or to the changeable copy, they are "accounts which *succeed* in providing an exegesis of their subject matter" (p. 152).
- Plato's cosmological "myth" involves a mode of reasoning which, if "lacking the rigour of mathematical proof," envisages and observes "standards of its own by which it can be judged to succeed or fail" (p. 154).

I also think that Burnyeat is right on yet another important detail in Plato's wording. In this case a longer comment and a qualification are immediately in order. If we go along with the majority of translators, the pronoun *mêdenos* in the key phrase *mêdenos hêtton* should be construed as referring distributively to *logoi*, not to the speaker of any such *logos*. Accordingly, the translation at 29c would be: "accounts that are no less *eikotes* than any other such." Burnyeat, however, opts for taking the pronoun *mêdenos* as referring to persons (I shall henceforth refer to it as the "personal construe"), both at 29c and in a later passage in which the "no less" phrase is paired with *eikota*, 48d.[4] For the earlier passage this yields the translation: "accounts no less *eikotes* than anyone else's." For the later passage we have two possible translations: "arguing (*legein*) things that are no less *eikota* than anyone else's"; or "putting forward a *logos* (or a *mythos*) that is no less *eikôs*, than anyone else's."[5] The translations Burnyeat himself gives are, in fact, slightly different from the ones just offered here. Presumably seeking to avoid wordiness, he writes: "no less than another's." While this makes for smoother English, it also has the potential of misleading. The Greek pronoun definitely imports universal quantification: it conveys the sense "than *any* other's." The looser "than another's" might be wrongly understood as "than some other's," or "than of many others," which would make for much too weak a claim, and certainly does not represent what Burnyeat wants.

---

4 In adopting "the minority's choice," as he calls it, Burnyeat can claim more support (besides mine) than he does. At 148 n. 13 he lists Johansen as supporting the non-personal construe of *mêdenos*. In fact, Johansen too prefers the personal construe in his translation of 29c7–8. Cf. Thomas K. Johansen, *Plato's Natural Philosophy: A Study of the* Timaeus-Critias (Cambridge: Cambridge University Press, 2004): "If we can furnish accounts no less likely [*eikotas*] than *anyone else's* [my emphasis], we must be content" (p. 49; cf. 49 n. 2).

5 For the grammatical ambiguity of *eikota* at 48d, see further below, pp. 241–244.

While appropriating Burnyeat's construe of the pronoun as personal, I shall use the more precise rendering, "than anyone else's."

In addition to the considerations Burnyeat himself puts forward in support of the personal construe (p. 148 n. 13), what strikes me as compelling is that Timaeus' language evokes forensic structures and contexts, such as those of a court trial or of an oratorical or thespian or sophistic contest: "I the speaker and you the judges" (*kritai*, 29c8–d1).[6] I shall have more to say, and with more examples, in later sections of this essay, about the importance of the forensic theme in the whole of our target passage.

Revisiting Burnyeat's Analysis of the Passage

I now turn to issues with respect to which I find myself less convinced by, or less sympathetic to, Burnyeat's argument. In propounding and supporting his central thesis—viz., that the tenor of reasoning in the *Timaeus* is essentially practical rather than theoretical—Burnyeat sees himself refuting two alternatives. On one front, he counters the traditional reading, which interprets *eikôs mythos* as reflecting an overarching Platonic assumption that "no statement about the world of becoming can be certain" (p. 143). On another front, he counters various readings he considers "anachronistically" inspired by "modern empiricist philosophy of science." These modernist readings find Plato's cosmological myth operating under limitations that are roughly and broadly similar to those that apply to scientific theories generally, inasmuch as the latter are "subject to revision as we learn more and more about the physical world" (p. 143, cf. pp. 144 and 163).

My instances of reserve, my doubts, or criticisms are directed mainly against Burnyeat's disputing of the two alternatives just listed. With respect to the first alternative (taken up by Burnyeat as second at the start of his article), I intend to argue that—quite apart from its carrying the authority of tradition—this alternative has more support from the text of the *Timaeus* than is recognized in Burnyeat's analysis. With respect to the second (the "modernist") alternative, it is very much worth noting that Burnyeat at one point does seem to allow for co-existence of practical and scientific-theoretical reasoning in the *Timaeus*. In the remark I just quoted from p. 157, to the effect that Plato aims not at truth but at disclosing "why this is the best of all possible worlds," the guarded phrasing implies apportionment between alternatives: "not so much X as Y." This, however, may simply be a case of rhetorical litotes for the stronger claim: "not really X but rather Y." For in contexts outside that of p. 157, Burnyeat seems intent on eliminating this modernist alternative. I think the more literal—tempered and apportioned—reading of the phrase (viz., "less of

---

6   This has been emphasized by Johansen, *Plato's Natural Philosophy*, pp. 52 and 55.

X, more of Y") is the one that would do justice to the project of the *Timaeus*. If properly formulated, the traditional and the modernist alternatives, whether judged separately or in combination, can be found no less fair and plausible (no less *eikotes* or *eikuiai*) as interpretations of the *Timaeus* than the one which puts all the emphasis on the project of practical reasoning.

Much of the strength in Burnyeat's argument derives from his exquisitely close analysis and translation of 29b–d. This fine-grained and incisive analysis deserves—at the very least—a comparably careful essay. My critical comments will emerge in the course of this essay. Within the longer proem, the target text has two main parts.[7] In the first, 29b2–c3, we have an argument intended to establish a pattern of coordination between (i) certain *logoi* and (ii) the objects or circumstances with respect to which the *logoi* at issue serve as *exêgêtai*, "explainers." The second part, 29c8–d3, the "dénouement" as I shall call it, describes the methodological and epistemological stance that is motivated and justified by the immediately preceding argument. In the sections that follow, here I lay out schematically, in Tables I and II, and then I canvass in detail, the structure of the Greek text in each of the two main parts. My aim is to highlight correspondences between the relevant logical, syntactical, and rhetorical components of the passage in each of the two main parts.

The Syntactic-Rhetorical Structure of 29b2–c3

The overall contrast in the first part, between *logoi* concerning the *paradeigma* and *logoi* concerning an *eikôn* of it, is displayed in Table I (p. 230), above the continuous double line, in a scheme of two columns with corresponding rows. The text that is shown at the top with underlining, straddling the vertical divide, applies equally to the two sides in the contrast. The four lines of text shown in continuous shading, on the left side, below the single line, are syntactically a parenthetical comment, as they interrupt in asyndeton the long *men/de* ("on the one hand, . . . on the other") construction. All editors who do not opt for emending the text (so as to eliminate the asyndeton)[8] punctuate the shaded text as a parenthesis; so, I shall refer to it as "the parenthesis" in what follows. In using this term, I do not at all wish to suggest that the passage is subordinate, or of lesser or incidental significance. Quite the contrary: I believe the parenthesis provides the key for our understanding of the entire section on the epistemological standing of an *eikôs logos* and ultimately an *eikôs mythos*. (In his translation Burnyeat sets the parenthesis off from what precedes by a colon

---

7 Burnyeat marks the second part as "E" after distinguishing four shorter sub-parts, "A" to "D," in what precedes (pp. 147–148, and again 148–154).
8 Emendation (deleting οἶον) is the solution adopted by R. D. Archer-Hind, *The* Timaeus *of Plato* (London: Macmillan and Co., 1888), pp. 88–89.

Table I: Plato, *Timaeus* 29b–c

καὶ περὶ τοῦ παραδείγματος	περί τε εἰκόνος	
διοριστέον ὡς ἄρα		
τοὺς λόγους, ὧνπέρ εἰσιν ἐξηγηταί, τούτων αὐτῶν καὶ συγγενεῖς ὄντας		
τοῦ μὲν	τοὺς δὲ	
μονίμου καὶ βεβαίου	τοῦ ἀπεικασθέντος μὲν	
καὶ μετὰ νοῦ καταφανοῦς	ὄντος δὲ εἰκόνος	πρὸς ἐκεῖνο
μονίμους καὶ ἀμεταπτώτους	εἰκότας ὄντας	
καθ᾽ ὅσον οἷόν τε καὶ προσήκει		
λόγους	(λόγους)	
ἀνελέγκτοις εἶναι καὶ ἀνικήτους	(εἰκότας)	
τούτου [τοῦ μὴ ἐλέγχεσθαι & μὴ νικᾶσθαι δεῖ μηδὲν ἐλλείπειν]	ὅπερ πρὸς γένεσιν οὐσία, τοῦτο πρὸς πίστιν ἀλήθεια	ἀνὰ λόγον τε ἐκείνων [= τῶν μονίμων & ἀμεταπτώτων λόγων]

A. *ousia*, "being, reality"	to	B. *genesis*, "becoming"
C. *alētheia*, "truth,"	to	D. *pistis*, "belief, persuasion"
E. the *paradeigma*	to	F. the *eikōn*
G. *logoi* exegetic of the *paradeigma*	to	H. *eikotes logoi* exegetic of the *eikōn*

"We ought to distinguish things in the following way with respect to an image and with respect to its exemplar: in providing an *exēgēsis*, accounts are also [note καί] cognate to the things at issue. Accounts of what is permanent, stable, and evident to the intellect are permanent and not subject to overthrow—to the extent that it is possible and proper for accounts to stand unrefuted and undefeated, they ought not to fall short of that [standard of non-refutation, non-defeat]. On the other hand, accounts of what has been fashioned as an image of that other [the stable, etc.], and insofar as it is an image, are *eikotes*, and [are so] in proportion to [the accounts] of that other: the relation that Being has to Becoming is precisely the one (ὅπερ . . . , τοῦτο) that truth has to belief." (A. P. D. M. translation) and then closes it off with a period, punctuation that is quite reasonable and apt in translation, inasmuch as English cannot sustain the long periodic style of Greek.) It is important to note that the parenthesis belongs to, and directly bears on, only the left side in the contrast. Everything that appears above each of the two single lines—i.e., both sides in the *men/de* construction—is governed by *dioristeon hôs* (+ participle *ontas*): "We ought to distinguish things as follows: the *logoi* of the *paradeigma* are M; those of the *eikôn* are E" (to highlight structure I represent the predicate complements by open variables). Except for the modality that is inherent in the "*-teos*" adjective, *dioristeon* ("we ought to distinguish"), the main syntax on both sides is purely assertoric.

I am calling attention to the assertoric force of the main syntax because Burnyeat, at one point, referring to the *dei*, "ought," in the parenthesis, makes this comment: "Expect a parallel message in the other half . . . . Being *eikôs* will not be an automatic consequence of undertaking the exegesis of a likeness . . . . Rather it will be an *aspiration* . . . a standard to judge it by" (p. 150). I think Burnyeat is right that there is a parallel message on the right-hand side; but we must be careful not to transpose the parenthesis, simply reapplying it to the other side. It is not Timaeus' message that the *logoi* of the *eikôn* "ought not fall to any extent short of" the standard of the *eikôs*. The remarks which introduce the *eikôs* concept, or which make use of it, have the softer tone of contentment and tolerance—not those of exigent observance of a standard. In fact, the characterization of *logoi* of the *eikôn*, on the right-hand side, as *eikotes* is shown by the structure of the passage to be precisely what Burnyeat says it is not: a simple consequence, one derived from the principle of *syngeneia*. The obvious context in which we should look for that "parallel message in the other half" is the remark which, as shown in Table I, occupies structurally a position exactly opposite the parenthesis, viz., the remark about proportionality *(logous . . . eikotas . . . ana logon te)*. But identifying and spelling out that parallel message on the right-hand side can be done best after we have canvassed details of the two texts that appear, respectively, below the two single lines.

One other feature of the overall structure of the passage (both sides of the contrast) needs our attention. The text that straddles the two sides, the underlined text in Table I, is a completely general premise, and it is the only premise that supports everything in the immediate sequel. I agree with Burnyeat that Plato's interest lies ultimately in supporting the claim that a special sort of *logoi*, those that offer an explanatory account *(exêgêsis)* are the ones that are said to be "also" (note the *kai*) *syngeneis*, "cognate, akin to, having family-affinity with," the object or objects at issue. And yet the claim, albeit more narrowly thus defined, remains controversial. We can well imagine that someone should argue the opposite: that exegetic *logoi* are not necessarily, or should in no way be, affected or contaminated by features of the object they explain. The explanandum may be dark and hard to detect, but the *exêgêsis* can be and ought to be clear; the explanandum fuzzy and characterized by randomness, the *exêgêsis* precise and well-structured; the explanandum enormous in compass, the *exêgêsis* succinct; and so on with like antitheses. What gives Timaeus the license to proclaim this premise with utter confidence that it will not be disputed?

I am well aware that Burnyeat eschews recourse to the *Republic*.[9] But I cannot follow him in this. In the long metaphysical-theological passage that precedes the epistemological-methodological section of the proem, the opening lines, 27d5 to 28a4, track closely the Being–Becoming division of *Republic* V, 476e–479d, and the doctrine of degrees of reality that complements the division. So, I can see only one plausible answer to my question concerning Timaeus' unhesitating avowal of *syngeneia* between exegetic *logos* and explanandum. Timaeus views this as a special case of a principle of wider scope, which (in the dramatic context of the dialogue) he assumes is known to his interlocutors—perhaps from the discussions represented in the *Republic*, perhaps from a like context or occasion.[10] At its widest scope, this is the principle that there is correspondence between the epistemic grade of *logoi* generally and the ontological grade of their appropriate object or objects. To be sure, this principle must be stated with care, so as not to imply that the mere fact that a *logos* is "about" eternal verities makes it true (cf. Burnyeat, p. 150). Even at the widest scope of the principle, *logos* must be understood as "*logos* at its best," as "successful *logos* by the standard implied by the context of the statement." At a narrower scope, but still wide enough to cover the *exêgêsis* that is at issue in the *Timaeus*, the principle is that the *logoi* of an exemplar and the *logoi* of an image or copy of that exemplar are *syngeneis*, respectively, to the exemplar itself and to its image as such: the higher epistemic grade of *logoi* of the original reflects the high ontological grade of the original qua original; the lower epistemic grade of *logoi* of the image reflects the lower ontological grade of the image qua image. In either version, the principle is the one invoked by the traditional interpretation of the *Timaeus*—which is the alternative directly rejected by Burnyeat (p. 143, cf. pp. 149 and 151–152).

More evidence in support of the traditional reading will be forthcoming when we look at details of the text on the right-hand side of Table I. But one simple observation is relevant immediately. Note that in the opening words of

---

9   He insists that in *Timaeus* 29c we are "far from the atmosphere engendered by the metaphysical downgrading of the sensible world in the central Books of the *Republic*" (p. 150). But quite apart from the downgrading of various components of the sensible world in later passages in the *Timaeus*, we are told at 28a8–b2, less than a page before 29b, that the copy of a *gennêton paradeigma* (and governance by *ex anankês* and *pan* from the preceding sentence are very strongly implied) is *ou kalon*.

10   Cf. Johansen, *Plato's Natural Philosophy*, p. 51.

our text, ὧδε οὖν περί τε εἰκόνος καὶ περὶ τοῦ παραδείγματος αὐτῆς, there is no article before εἰκόνος. Burnyeat correctly translates "*a* likeness" (my emphasis, p. 149). There is little doubt that in speaking of the *paradeigma* Plato has in mind the single total domain of "what always is, subject to no coming-to-be, . . . graspable by reason (or 'by intelligence'), always being the same, in the same way . . . eternal" (*Timaeus* 27d6–29a7).[11] But in speaking of an *eikôn*, he need not be focusing either on a specific single global image of the exemplar or on a specific single image of some part or aspect of the exemplar. For when Timaeus says at 29b1–2 (one line before the passage displayed on Table I) that "there is every necessity that this cosmos is an image of something *(eikona tinos einai),*" what is striking is the generic scope in the use of the term *eikôn*. In the text shown in Table I (i.e., the entirety of the text from 29b3 to 29c3), there is nothing—not even the term *exêgêtai*, when that term is endowed with the rich sense Burnyeat assigns to it—which precludes that the terms *logoi* and *eikôn* should simply be assigned a broadly general sense. Timaeus' call at 29b2–3 for "making a natural start" *(arxasthai kata physin archên)* promotes the expectation that what comes next is something at the highest level of generality. It is only at 29c4 (immediately beyond the text laid out in Table I) that a specific application of the preceding remarks is made to the theogony-cosmogony-cosmology context ("about gods and about the coming-into-being of the All"). And—here again I agree with Burnyeat—the connecting particle *oun* "draws the consequence" (p. 154).

Modal Terms in the Parenthesis

After this overall survey of the structure of 29b–c, let us next examine the wording of the parenthesis (29b7–c1; see the lower left half in Table I). Burnyeat translates as follows: "to the extent that it is possible and fitting for accounts to be irrefutable and invincible, there ought to be no falling short of this" (p. 150); other translators have given essentially similar renderings. I have no quarrel with the translation; but, on a first reading, the Greek appears to be marred by jarring wordiness, and this calls for some closer probing. The parenthesis appears overloaded with modal terms. Unless we put some diminutive connotation into *logois* (e.g., "for accounts offered by mere humans"), the phrase *kath' hoson hoion* makes no sense. For if something is "irrefut*able*" and "invin*cible*" (strong sense of the *-tos* adjectives), what is the point of the qualification "to the extent possible"? Besides, in the first

---

11   There is extraordinary emphasis through repetition in the course of just one and a half Stephanus pages: τὸ ὂν ἀεί, γένεσιν δὲ οὐκ ἔχον, 27d6; νοήσει μετὰ λόγου περιληπτόν, ἀεὶ κατὰ ταὐτὰ ὄν, 28a1–2; τὸ κατὰ ταὐτὰ ἔχον, 28a6–7; τὸ κατὰ ταὐτὰ καὶ ὡσαύτως ἔχον, 29a1; τὸ ἀίδιον, 29a5; τὸ λόγῳ καὶ φρονήσει περιληπτὸν καὶ κατὰ ταὐτὰ ἔχον, 29a6–7.

of the two sentences that comprise the parenthesis, we have both *kath' hoson hoion* and *prosêkei*, "is fitting, is right." What is being contributed by the second modal? As though two modals were not enough, we get reinforcement with *dei*, "ought, must," in the second sentence, the main clause in the parenthesis. And why, for that matter, is the second sentence in the parenthesis (*toutou dei . . .*, "there ought to be . . .") needed at all? If we give full modal force to the *-tos* adjectives, and thus to the "-ble" translations, i.e., if the sense is that of "*in principle* irrefutable and invincible," the first sentence all by itself could be attached to the two adjectives that precede in the text, thus making the parenthetical syntax unnecessary. Finally, what exactly is the difference between "irrefutable and invincible" when these adjectives are both being applied to *logoi*?

Since more than one of these effects of pleonasm arise from assuming that the *-tos* adjectives bear strong modal sense, the obvious remedy is to give these adjectives the factual sense, "unrefuted and undefeated." The sense would then be: "To the extent that it is possible and fitting for accounts to be unrefuted and undefeated . . . ." As Burnyeat rightly emphasizes, the fact that an exegetic *logos* is about entities that are "permanent, and stable and manifest to reason" does not guarantee that the *logos* will be true (cf. p. 150). It is possible for a false *logos* in mathematics, for example, to escape refutation and defeat for a long time.[12] It would not, however, be fitting or right that such an account had escaped refutation. With this adjustment, we get rid of two pleonasms. We do not have the modality of "in principle" possibility both in the *-tos* adjectives and then again in the second sentence. Moreover, use of the two modal verbs imports a significant distinction: possibly not being refuted is not the same as rightly not being refuted.

But, still, what is the point of the second sentence in the parenthesis? Let us, at least provisionally, accept the non-modal translations of *anelenktois* and *anikêtois*. What might be the point of characterizing *logoi* as "unrefuted" and "undefeated"? I remarked earlier that the entire passage is framed by a forensic (in the broad sense of the term) metaphor. The two adjectives just cited are perfectly suited to the context of a debate: as though in a court of law, or in the assembly, or in an oratorical competition between speakers. The first of the two adjectives back at 29b, "unrefuted," could be used to mark the standing of a given *logos* while the deliberation or competition is still in progress—say, after the first or second round. The second adjective, however, marks the outcome: one *logos* stands undefeated; or several *logoi* are in a tie. Now this outcome, as well as the intermediate outcome of escaping refutation,

---

12   The early Pythagoreans assumed that all quantities were commensurable; generations of Greek mathematicians were sure that squaring the circle was possible; the belief that there were only five regular solids was firmly held till Johannes Kepler constructed non-convex regular solids.

would certainly be "fitting and right" if the *logos* or *logoi* at issue intrinsically merits, or they intrinsically merit, this rating. But, of course, in any sort of forensic context, a *logos* can also be judged unrefuted, or be declared either a winner or co-winner in a tie, and rightly so, merely because the opposing side performed poorly. With this fleshing out of the forensic metaphor, the rationale of the second sentence in the parenthesis becomes immediately clear. When it comes to the standard of non-refutation and victory for *logoi* that are exegetic of the *paradeigma*, the standard is not relative, it is absolute: "there ought to be no falling short of it"; it should not even be *logically conceivable* that there are candidates that could have been judged of equal rank, let alone superior. In effect, what the second sentence in the parenthesis accomplishes is to transform "unrefuted" and "undefeated," respectively, into "in principle irrefutable" and "in principle invincible."

So, then, Burnyeat's modal translation is not wrong; but the Greek involves subtle semantic shifts that are not easy to reproduce in translation. The ambiguity of *-tos* adjectives allows the modal sense to remain in the background till it can emerge—without second use of the adjectives, and yet with the strongest possible force—at the end of a carefully crafted statement. What on a first reading may appear as needless wordiness and pleonasm is a well-motivated rhetorical crescendo that builds to a climax:

1. It is possible *(hoion)* for *logoi* that are exegetic of the *paradeigma* to be unrefuted and undefeated (factual sense of *-tos* adjective).
2. Moreover, such *logoi* should be fittingly or rightly *(prosêkei)* unrefuted and undefeated.
3. Indeed, they ought *(dei)* not fall at all short *(mêden elleipein)* of the standard of non-refutation and non-defeat.
4. Accordingly, the standard they are to be judged by is that they are in principle irrefutable and invincible (modal sense of *-tos* adjective).

eikotes *vs. "Irrefutable"* logoi: *The Play of Ratios*

Let us now turn to the other side, that of the *eikôn*. An eloquently telling feature here is the heavy alliteration. (On Table I, shading of syllables is used to highlight it.) The alliterative play in *eikonos eikotas* at 29c2 is unmistakable and it has often been pointed to by commentators. The play is actually more extended. I list five words here in the chiastic order (XYYX) in which they occur in the text: *EKEINo; apEIKasthentos/ EIKOnos; EIKOtas; EKEINôn.* One might again think that there is pleonasm, and even rhetorical excess to boot. Closer examination shows that there is excellent motivation for the effect. This is made clear in the following scheme (which dismantles the chiasmus in order to highlight the logical connections):

EKEINo (the exemplar)   *apEIKasthentos/ EIKOnos*
                                                    (the copy)
EKEINôn (the accounts of   *EIKOtas* (the accounts of
   the exemplar)   the copy)

The rhetorical effect is extraordinary. In the vertical pairings, Plato has actually modeled in sounds and in letters the *syngeneia*: the kinship that binds the exemplar with its cognate accounts, and likewise the copy with its own cognate accounts.

The text also tells us that there is a certain ratio or proportion *(ana logon)* between the accounts of the exemplar and those of the copy. Explicitly what that ratio is we learn in the next sentence. But the sound-and-letter-modeling has already suggested the ratio implicitly by displaying it in the modeling: accounts of the copy are epistemically related to the accounts of the exemplar in the ratio in which the copy as such is ontologically related to the exemplar. At 29c3, the ratio is fixed by referring to another four-term analogy, which may be represented schematically as follows (cf. Table I, immediately below the continuous double line):

A. *ousia*, "being, reality"   is related to   B. *genesis*, "becoming"
                           IN THE RATIO IN WHICH
C. *alêtheia*, "truth"   is related to   D. *pistis*, "belief, persuasion."

It is clear, then, that we are to apply this same ratio to the two other pairs that were suggestively introduced by the figures of alliteration and chiasmus:

E. the *paradeigma*   is related to   F. the *eikôn*
                           IN THE RATIO IN WHICH
G. *logoi* exegetic of the   are related to   H. *eikotes logoi* exegetic of
      paradeigma   the *eikôn*.

Burnyeat mentions only three pairs in the analogy. In fact, four pairs are at play. And Plato has given enough in mathematical hints to permit us, and even to encourage us, to explore specificity in the parameters of the ratio. Let us focus first on the left side in the four-pair scheme above, and let us ask what the ratio is between A and C, and again between E and G. Unmistakably, the ratio of *ousia* to *alêtheia* is 1, or, as we would say, 100%. Moreover, the ratio of *paradeigma* to its proper accounts is likewise 1 or 100%. We know this from the second sentence of the parenthesis in 29b–c, "not to fall at all short of." We can likewise make inferences about the ratios implied for paired terms on the right-hand side, B to D, and F to H. Necessarily, the same ratio of 1 or 100% holds in the relation of *genesis* to *pistis* and that of *eikôn* to *eikotes*. All this does nothing more than spell out in quasi-mathematical terms the principle of *syngeneia* posited at 29b.

There is little doubt that the degrees-of-reality doctrine assigns a higher value to A in comparison to B and again to E in comparison to F. Accordingly, we now have it as a further consequence that the ratio in the horizontal pairing of terms, taken from right to left (B to A; D to C; F to E; H to G) must be either of the following: (i) some specific fraction smaller than 1, or specific percentage less than 100%; (ii) a range of such fractions or percentages, depending on the explananda at issue, and assuming, of course, that a specific such fraction or percentage applies to all cases of explananda of the same type. Almost certainly we ought to opt for (ii). The range (of fractions or percentages) need not have precise boundaries; it could have fuzzy edges. But whether precise or open-textured, the four-pair analogy prescribes that the relevant parameters for that range must be the same from top to bottom on the right-hand column. For we know from within the *Timaeus*—let alone from the doctrine of degrees of reality in the *Republic*—that such members of the realm of becoming as souls or stars have a much higher ontological rank than, say, a biological organ, or a gold nugget. If then the standard of non-refutation posited by the parenthesis in 29b–c is 100%, the standard of non-refutation for *eikotes logoi* will certainly be below 100% but will vary widely and appropriately, depending on the phenomena at issue. In the case, for example, of a mathematical construction of the annual movement of the sun through the band of the zodiac, that standard could be very high—say, 90%. What it could not be is 100%, which is the absolute standard reserved for *logoi* exegetic of the *paradeigma*. By the same logic, the standard of non-refutation for a theory concerning the physiology of respiration or digestion, or the physical and chemical properties of metals, might be fairly low, say, 35%.

This examination of the same text Burnyeat analyzed has produced results which, on many details, are in accordance with his. I note his comment at p. 153: "the contrast Timaeus' proportion illustrates is a contrast in degrees of argumentative rigour." But I believe my analysis has also provided further support for the first of the alternatives Burnyeat seeks to eliminate, the traditional reading. The eight-term analogy, with its emphatic recourse to the principle of correspondence of ontological and epistemic grades (A to B as C to D), so strongly reminiscent of themes and contexts of the *Republic*, does seem to me to justify the comment that "physics precludes anything better than probability, because physics deals with the changeable realm of becoming, not the fixed realm of being"—which is precisely the formulation of the traditional reading Burnyeat disputes (p. 143).[13]

---

13 And if the standard for *eikotes mythoi* must always be below 100%, it would seem that Burnyeat is being unduly polemical when he criticizes Cornford (and indirectly Taylor) on just this point (p. 143 n. 2). F. M. Cornford, exploiting the word-play *eikonos eikotas*, gave this translation in *Plato's Cosmology* (London: Routledge & Kegan Paul, 1937. Reprint New York:

Why Not "Better *Than Anyone Else's*"? The Bearing of Parmenides B8.60–61

Let me now turn to the dénouement of Timaeus' "natural start," 29c–d, the passage in which the principle of   and the four-pair analogy are finally applied to the project of theogony-cosmogony-cosmology. Table II (p. 239) quotes the text in full, with the word-order unaltered, except for dividing it into semantically distinct cola or lemmata—the division intended to facilitate certain comparisons I shall pursue presently. I ask the reader to ignore, for the moment, the lines excerpted from Xenophanes and from Aristotle. I think it is highly significant that the collocation *eikota mython* occurs for the first time only at the end of this dénouement, at 29d2. In this effect of delayed entry of the famous expression, we have yet one more indication that the preceding remarks, in which the collocation was not *eikôs mythos* but *eikôs logos*, were more general in scope. Now that the subject has been suitably narrowed, we get a fuller statement of the standard of *to eikos*.

Whenever I have read or taught the *Timaeus*, I have found myself puzzled by, and even amazed with, the restrained, modest, negative, and deflationary character of the statement, "if we can offer accounts that are no less *eikotes* than anyone else's . . . we ought to be content; . . . [inasmuch as] about these things it is fitting to accept the *eikôs mythos* and seek nothing further" (Burnyeat's translation, pp. 148 and 154, but with "anyone else's" substituted for "another's"; cf. Table II, lines 4–10). Why does Plato so studiously avoid setting the standard just slightly higher, "at least as good as anyone else's," or, for that matter, "better than that of anyone else"? To be sure, either in English or in its equivalent in Greek or in any other language, "no less than" is correctly interpretable as "either equal to or more than." But while logic may allow the *possibility* that "no less *eikôs* than anyone else's" could be understood as "more *eikôs* than anyone else's" (or, if we should opt for the non-personal translation of *mêdenos*, "more *eikôs* than any other such"), the rhetoric and the pragmatics of the negative and deflationary formulation emphatically point lower: our account could well be judged better than many; but not better than all possible alternatives. A *tie* constitutes the ceiling for best foreseeable outcomes.[14] This is evident from the tone of resigned humility, even of pessimism, in the main and concluding

---

The Liberal Arts Press, 1957; and other subsequent reprints), p. 23: "an account of what is . . . *only* a likeness will itself be *but* likely" (the italics added, as in Burnyeat, to flag words that are missing in the Greek).

14   This has been emphasized by Johansen: "amongst the different possible likely accounts we should be content with one that is as likely as anybody else's account" (*Plato's Natural Philosophy*, p. 61, cf. p. 61 n. 17).

Table II: Plato, *Timaeus* 29c–d and Some Comparable Texts

Timaeus 29c–d

(c3) ἐὰν οὖν, ὦ Σώκρατες
(1) πολλὰ πολλῶν πέρι, θεῶν καὶ τῆς τοῦ παντὸς γενέσεως
(2) μὴ δυνατοὶ γιγνώμεθα πάντῃ πάντως ἀποδοῦναι
(3) αὐτοὺς ἑαυτοῖς ὁμολογουμένους λόγους καὶ ἀπηκριβωμένους μὴ θαυμάσῃς
(4) ἀλλ' ἐὰν ἄρα μηδενὸς ἧττον
(5) παρεχώμεθα εἰκότας
(6) ἀγαπᾶν χρή

μεμνημένους
(7) ὡς ὁ λέγων ἐγὼ (d1) ὑμεῖς τε οἱ κριταὶ φύσιν ἀνθρωπίνην ἔχομεν,

(8) ὥστε περὶ τούτων
(9) τὸν εἰκότα μῦθον ἀποδεχομένους
(10) πρέπει τούτου μηδὲν ἔτι πέρα ζητεῖν.

Aristotle, *Meteorologica* I.7.344a5–7
περὶ τῶν ἀφανῶν τῇ αἰσθήσει νομίζομεν ἱκανῶς ἀποδεδεῖχθαι κατὰ τὸν λόγον, ἐὰν εἰς τὸ δυνατὸν ἀναγάγωμεν.

Xenophanes B34

ἀμφὶ θεὸν τε καὶ ὅσσα λέγω περὶ πάντων
οὔ τις ἀνὴρ ἴδεν οὐδὲ τις ἔσται εἰδὼς
τὸ σαφές
εἰ γὰρ καὶ τὰ μάλιστα
τύχοι τετελεσμένον εἰπών
αὐτὸς ὅμως οὐκ οἶδε

δόκος δ' ἐπὶ πᾶσι τέτυκται.

Xenophanes B35
ταῦτα
δεδοξάσθω μὲν ἐοικότα τοῖς ἐτύμοισι.
cf. δεδοξάσθω]

sentence: *agapan chrê*, "we ought to be content," *apodechomenous*, "accepting,"[15] and, most discouragingly, *toutou mêden eti pera zêtein*, "to seek nothing further." Granted, Timaeus is not reaching for accounts that are absolutely true—that standard is for accounts of the exemplar. But why could he not expressly strive or hope to produce accounts that might be judged "*better* than anyone else's"?[16]

In this connection, there is some ambivalence in Burnyeat's presentation. Generally his paraphrasing adheres to the guarded formulation in Plato's text. But an exception occurs when Burnyeat cites a potentially significant parallel, viz., the characterization by "the goddess" in Parmenides' didactic poem of the epistemic authority of "Doxa," the cosmological and cosmogonical second part of the poem. "Like Parmenides," writes Burnyeat, "Timaeus . . . [offers] an appropriately ordered account of the sensible world, which he—again like Parmenides (fr. 8, 60–61)—hopes will *surpass* [emphasis by A. P. D. M.] any given by other mortal minds" (p. 153). In fact, by a strict criterion of literalness, Parmenides does not say "it will surpass." The formulation in Parmenides is equally restrained: "so that no mortal may ever outstrip you in judgment (*gnômêi*)" (B8.61). And the restraint is reinforced by the stance of distance and irony Parmenides' goddess maintains as she expounds the views of "mortals."[17]

There is also, however, much of chariot imagery in Parmenides' poem; the main verb at B8.61 could easily bring to the mind of readers or hearers of Parmenides' poem (as it has done so for modern scholars) the language of chariot racing;[18] and given that Parmenides appropriates the language of Homer and exploits Homeric motifs and themes, another associative link is likewise within easy mental reach, viz., the famous formulaic challenge to success that is addressed to Homeric heroes: αἰὲν ἀριστεύειν καὶ ὑπείροχον ἔμμεναι ἄλλων, "always excel and be superior to others" (*Iliad* 6.208 and 11.784). It is understandable, therefore, that in an allusion, as in Parmenides B8.61, to the

---

15   Using this very term in phrasing my comment here, I find it hard to *apodechesthai* (accept, be content with, consent to, countenance) Burnyeat's proposal (pp. 154–155) that *apodechomenous* could in this context of the *Timaeus* be understood as conveying an "aspiration."

16   Selecting the roots LOG- and either BELT- (for forms of *beltiôn, -on*) or KREITT- (for forms of *kreittôn, -on*), I have searched the Thesaurus Linguae Graecae text of the *Timaeus* for contexts in which comparatives (either in various adjectival forms or as adverbs) might have been used to express claims such as "[some *logos* at issue] is better than any other." The only "hit" was 75b6–c3, in which *analogizomenois* and *beltion* occur in the following context: the gods were "calculating" whether it would be "better" to give human beings longevity but with a poorer quality of life or vice versa.

17   Burnyeat (p. 148 n. 13) rightly adopts the slight emendation *gnômêi* (dative), in place of the nominative *gnômê* of the MSS. For irony in Parmenides, see my discussion in *The Route of Parmenides* (New Haven: Yale University Press, 1970. Reprint Las Vegas: Parmenides Publishing, 2008), ch. 9.

18   See Mourelatos, *Route*, p. 13 and n. 15, but also p. 226 n. 15.

aggressively competitive situation of a chariot race, "let no one get ahead of you" might be perceived as pragmatically upgradeable to "get ahead of everyone."

I have already observed that a forensic metaphor frames and articulates the whole of *Timaeus* 29b–d. But à propos the Parmenides parallel, it needs to be said that there is a huge difference in the ways in which Parmenides and Timaeus envisage the *agôn*. The remark in Parmenides B8.61 comes as the climax in an extended polemic in which rival views are excoriated in tones of extreme disparagement. Timaeus' speech, by contrast, is remarkably free of polemicizing. The *agôn* between competing *logoi* takes place in a genial arena of argument and persuasion. If we should bring Parmenides B8.61 to bear on Plato's "no less *eikotes* than anyone else's," it is best we do so by attending not to the polemics in which the Parmenidean line is embedded but rather to the prima facie import of restraint in the literal reading of the clause, "so that no mortal may ever outstrip you in judgment."

Is the Standard Upgraded at Timaeus 48d?

I alluded earlier to 48d, the passage which unmistakably recalls what was said at 29c–d. Might this later passage be read as providing support for the "upgrade-able" reading of "no less *eikotes*"? It is important to note and to emphasize that, out of a total of 35 occurrences of the comparative adverb *mallon* ("more, more so" or "more than") in the dialogue, the one at 48d constitutes the only case in which the adverb has the potential of being syntactically associated with allusions to the theme of the *eikôs logos* or *eikôs mythos*.[19] Isolated though this case is, it might nonetheless encourage—and has encouraged—projecting the sense of *mallon eikotes* back on to the earlier passage. I quote the lines at issue in their received form, but I omit a crucial comma, the placement of which is at the center of philological disputes concerning this text.

> τὸ δὲ κατ' ἀρχὰς ῥηθὲν διαφυλάττων, τὴν τῶν εἰκότων λόγων δύναμιν, πειράσομαι μηδενὸς ἧττον εἰκότα, μᾶλλον δὲ καὶ ἔμπροσθεν ἀπ' ἀρχῆς περὶ ἑκάστων καὶ συμπάντων λέγειν. (48d1–4)

If we were to place a comma both before and after *mallon de*, the main clause could be translated in either of two ways:

---

19 At 55d *mallon* does occur in the vicinity both of *eikotôs* and *eikota logon*. But the syntax directly connects the adverb with the aorist participle *stas*: cf. Zeyl's translation, "it would be better to stop with the question . . ." (p. 47). On this passage, see further below, p. 244 n. 24.

> (i) I shall try to offer a *logos* that is not [merely] less *eikôs* than anyone else's (alternately, "than any other such"), but more so (i.e., "more *eikôs* than . . .").
>
> (ii) I shall try to propose (literally "to speak") things that are *eikota* no less so than anyone else's (alternately, "than any other such"), but more so (i.e., "more *eikota* than . . .").[20]

In these translations I have retained preference for Burnyeat's construe of *mêdenos* as personal; but I have allowed for construing *eikota* either as masculine, in (i), or as neuter plural, in (ii). For the present discussion, what matters is neither the preference for the personal construe of *mêdenos* nor the masculine-neuter ambiguity of *eikota*. At issue rather is taking *mallon de* as connected with *eikota* and thus permitting the *mallon* to supersede and enhance the standard of *mêdenos hêtton*. If this were the right construe, we would have to assume a drastic volte-face on Plato's part. With a peremptory and merely parenthetical, "nay, more so,"[21] Timaeus would be setting aside the more deliberately phrased and carefully argued statement of 29c–d, which had given a pointedly more restrained characterization of the purview of *eikotes logoi*.

It is hardly credible that we have this sort of volte-face. Understandably, the majority among the scholars who have grappled with the textual difficulties of this passage have concluded, on strictly philological grounds, that the *mallon de* should be connected not with what precedes but with what follows.[22] A. E. Taylor remarked, "[T]he traditional text seems quite incapable of translation . . . . The difficulty is to make sense of the *emprosthen*."[23] Almost certainly,

---

20 Translations conforming to either of these patterns have been offered—among others—by Jowett, Archer-Hind, Cornford, and Bury. See Edith Hamilton and Huntington Cairns, *The Collected Dialogues of Plato, Including the Letters* (Princeton: Princeton University Press, 1961), Benjamin Jowett's translation of the *Timaeus*, p. 1176; Archer-Hind, *The* Timaeus *of Plato*, p. 169; Cornford, *Plato's Cosmology*, p. 161; R. G. Bury, translator, *Plato:* Timaeus, Critias, Cleitophon, Menexenus, Epistles [*Plato, With an English Translation*, 12 vols., vol. 7], Loeb Classical Library (Cambridge: Harvard University Press, 1952), pp. 110–111.

21 This is exactly Bury's translation in the Loeb Plato (see above), p. 111.

22 See Th. Henri Martin, *Études sur le* Timée *de Platon*, 2 vols. (Paris: Ladrange, 1841. Reprint New York: Arno Press, 1976), vol. 1, pp. 130–131; cf. vol. 2, n. 56; J. Cook Wilson, *On the Interpretation of Plato's* Timaeus: *Critical Studies with Special Reference to a Recent Edition* (London: David Nutt, 1889), p. 89 [the "recent edition" referred to in the title is Archer-Hind's]; A. E. Taylor, *A Commentary on Plato's* Timaeus (Oxford: Clarendon Press, 1928), p. 311; also his *Plato:* Timaeus *and* Critias (London: Methuen & Co., 1929), p. 47; Βασίλης Κάλφας [Vassílis Kálfas], *Πλάτων Τίμαιος: Εισαγωγή, μετάφραση, σχόλια* [*Plato,* Timaeus: *Introduction, Translation, Comments*, in Modern Greek] (Athens: Polis, 1995), pp. 236–237, and p. 418 n. 249; Donald J. Zeyl, *Plato:* Timaeus (Indianapolis: Hackett Publishing Co., 2000), p. 37 and n. 52.

23 *Commentary*, p. 310. Taylor's explication is somewhat misleading. He objects to the failure of 19th century editors to put a comma after *mallon de*, he stresses that "*mallon de* answers

something is missing in the text; and this makes the adverb seem syntactically superfluous or disjointed. Of the various insertions or emendations that have been proposed, two seem least invasive and most plausible: either <τῶν> καὶ ἔμπροσθεν, "of what has also been said earlier," or <ἢ> καὶ ἔμπροσθεν, "than what has also been said earlier." Accordingly, the translation of the full text ought to yield this sense (my translation):

> Keeping to what was stated at the start, about the purview of *eikotes logoi*, I shall endeavor, making a fresh start concerning things both individually and collectively, to offer a *logos* that is not less *eikôs* than anyone else's (alternately, "than any other such"), yet more *eikôs* than what I also offered earlier.

So, then, the modest standard for *eikotes logoi* has not been abandoned, after all. The comparison envisaged is purely intra-mural. Timaeus is still in the process of formulating his own best proposals, the ones which—in the extra-mural competition—will stand a good chance to be judged "no less *eikotes* than anyone else's" or "no less *eikotes* than any other such."

In the absence of the sort of considerations (irony, imagery of chariot-racing) which, in the Parmenides context, might permit the more ambitious message ("no one will surpass you"), and given the tone of humility and pessimism in the concluding sentence in 29d, we must assume that Timaeus' "no less *eikotes* than another's" is intended seriously, precisely, and literally—with its normal pragmatic force. One more consideration serves to clinch the case in favor of the non-upgradeable reading. The negative phrasing *mêdenos hêtton*, "no less than anyone else's," is manifestly designed to evoke, and to contrast with, the likewise negative phrasing for the absolute superlative standard that is applicable to accounts of the exemplar: *mêden elleipein*, "not at all falling short of" (compare line 4, left column of Table II with the last two lines of Greek on the left column in Table I). The *absolute* mathematical equality in the relation of exemplar with its cognate *logoi* is implicitly being compared to, and contrasted with, the *relativized* equality of a select set of *logoi*, each of which, while superior to many *logoi* outside the set, is still "no less *eikôs*" than any other within the select set.

---

to the preceding *hêtton*," and he argues that the four words, *mêdenos hêtton mallon de* "go together" (p. 310). Nonetheless, his solution is to insert <tôn> before *kai emprosthen*, and thus connect the whole of the "not less but more" phrase to what follows: "a statement which is not less but more probable than anything which has been said before since we began" (p. 311). It is, therefore, correct to place him, as is done in the preceding note, in the "majority" vis-à-vis the dispute over translating 48d.

It remains, then, for us to search for the philosophical reasons that led Plato to eschew setting the standard to the next higher rung, that of "better than anyone else's." I turn to this issue in the next section.

The Forensic Metaphor and Equipollence of Theories

Some important clues can be found in the details of the structure of the parenthesis at 29b–c. Recall Plato's emphasis that for *logoi* of what is "permanent, stable, and utterly evident to the intellect" there is both the possibility *(hoion)* and the right necessity *(dei)* of *absolute* non-refutation and victory: no *agônes*, no competition; we have advanced beyond the possibility of refutation and defeat. The relative standard, by contrast, either awards the victory to the single *logos* which currently stands undefeated or declares a tie among the contenders. After the prizes have been awarded, the first-place winners are left with the poignant awareness that on some future competition they may be among the losers. In terms of that four-step crescendo (see above, p. 235) of modal expressions in the parenthesis (*hoion, prosêkei, dei*, in principle *anelenktos*, and in principle *anikêtos*), the *eikôs logos* (and a fortiori the *eikôs mythos*) cannot advance beyond step 2. Yes, the *logos* should be undefeated in all rounds; but not just because all the other contenders were shabby; the victory should be merited (cf. *prosêkei*); so, there must be many other contenders of equal stature in performance. And yet, none of these equally successful contenders can arrogate to itself the title of "irrefut*able*" and "invinc*ible*." Each faces the risk of overthrow by a worthier contender in the future; and when this comes about, it merely establishes a new possibility either for overthrow or for a tie.[24]

Once the forensic metaphor has provided us with the relevant clues, we may also use more technical language and speak of the epistemic status of *eikotes logoi* as one of explanatory "equipollence." Using this terminology, we are in a position to formulate the question, "Why not aim for 'better'?" with greater precision. What are the epistemological concerns or principles that dictate to Plato that exegetic *logoi* in the field of theogony-cosmogony-cosmology will always and ultimately turn out equipollent?

I can think of only one such principle: that of multiplicity-in-explanation. I could perhaps indulge here—*pace* Burnyeat—in some modernist anachronism to invoke the Duhem-Quine principle of the indeterminacy of theories:

---

24 Cf. Johansen, p. 61: "Timaeus . . . is . . . making the further point that amongst the different likely accounts we should be content with one that is *as likely* [my emphasis] as anybody else's account." Cf. n. 17 on the same page: "Timaeus seems again to hint at the idea that there may be several more or less likely accounts for the same explanandum at 55d4–6." Since Johansen cites this other passage in support of the "as likely" reading, he clearly expects his reader to understand the phrase "more or less likely" as equivalent to "roughly" or "approximately"—not in the sense of "more likely in the best case; less or equally likely so in the case of others."

any number of theories can "cover" the same finite set of data. But there is no need for us to look for parallels beyond the horizon of ancient thought. Students of the Epicureans are familiar with the heavy use philosophers of that school make of the principle of multiplicity-in-explanation in contexts of natural philosophy. And there is good evidence that Epicurus' precursor and philosophical master, Democritus, had proclaimed the principle and made use of it.[25] Less familiar is the fact that the classical philosopher who is least prone to skepticism, Aristotle, allows that within the domain of meteorology (one in which we deal largely with *adêla*, i.e., with processes that lie beyond the limits of observation) the best explanatory outcome is epistemically limited. The relevant text is quoted in Table II:

> In the case of things not evident to the senses, we judge that there has been sufficiently rational proof if we succeed [note aorist, *anagagômen*] in delimiting what is possible. (*Meteorologica* I.7.344a5–7)

Aristotle may not have wanted to go so far as to embrace either equipollence or multiplicity-in-explanation. For, in the passages and chapters of the *Meteorologica* that come after this remark, his project is focused on eliminating explanations, ruling them *im*possible. Yet this essentially elenctic approach courts the positing of unrefuted, equipollent, alternatives. In any event, Aristotle's pupil, Theophrastus, did embrace multiplicity-in-explanation, proclaiming it as the standard, in his own *Meteorology* or *Metarsiology*. The authority thus conferred upon the principle reinforced its sway in natural philosophy generally. The pattern of wide adherence, after Theophrastus, to the principle of multiplicity-in-explanation is beautifully narrated in Liba Taub's, *Ancient Meteorology*.[26]

A Pre-Platonic Parallel for Multiplicity-In-Explanation: Xenophanes B34 and B35

Indeed, something recognizably close to multiplicity-in-explanation is already playing a role in Presocratic philosophy before Democritus. Burnyeat cited Parmenides B8.60–61. For the reasons I gave earlier, I find that text rather ambiguous and oblique in its bearing on the theme of equipollence. The much better text is Xenophanes B34. This has often been interpreted as the earliest statement of skepticism in the Greek philosophical tradition. But, from what we can learn from both the fragments and the testimonia for Xenophanes, there is much that is not only boldly speculative but also quite positive and dogmatic

---

25 See Liba Taub, *Ancient Meteorology* (London and New York: Routledge, 2003), p. 151.
26 See pp. 78–79, 117–124, 130–139, 180–184.

in this philosopher's thought. The label "skeptic" fits him poorly. I would not argue that multiplicity-in-explanation is exactly what is being voiced in B34. What I hear in it, rather, is a guarded statement of *indeterminacy* in explanation—reflecting a theme of "non-boundedness" *(apeiron)* that runs through much of Xenophanes' natural philosophy.[27] Be that as it may, placing B34 and its obvious companion B35 next to Timaeus' deflationary statement, we see parallels in phrasing which, if not perfect, are nonetheless worth notice. The structural parallelism is impressively close; and a brief characterization of the corresponding lemmata, which in Table II are marked by numbers, will suffice to bring this out:

    (1)   Scope of the investigation; subject matter.
    (2)   Citing and decrying limitations.
    (3)   Higher aim that must be forgone.
    (4)   Testing through competition: "no less than"; "at most."
    (5)   Outcome in the competition.
    (6)   Concessive remark.
    (7)   Anthropological remark.
    (8)   Recurring to the subject matter.
    (9)   Acceptance of the appropriate, more modest, standard.
    (10) Jussive remark promoting this appropriate standard.

Without dwelling here on details of Xenophanes B34 and B35, let me simply observe that the affinity of the corresponding lemmata at (4), above and in Table II, is stronger than is generally realized, because Xenophanes' words have often been mistranslated. The phrase *tetelesmenon eipôn* refers not to "an absolutely perfect statement" but rather to "a prediction that comes to be fulfilled" (e.g., of Thales' successful prediction of a solar eclipse). And *ta malista tychoi eipôn* does not mean "should have the best luck to state" but "should to the highest degree [or 'most exactly'] succeed in stating." Xenophanes was well aware that many predictions are fulfilled, and a smaller number are fulfilled exactly as stated. He is not speaking of a single super-scientist but of the whole crowd of prophets, soothsayers, astrometeorologists, scientifically minded forecasters, and cosmologists—himself included. Though Plato uses a comparative term and Xenophanes a superlative, the sense is the same: no one is epistemically ahead of the others; the competitive outcome is, in Xenophanes too, a tie.

---

27 See my studies: "La Terre et les étoiles dans la cosmologie de Xénophane" [Earth and Stars in the Cosmology of Xenophanes; translation by C. Louguet], in A. Laks and C. Louguet, eds., *Qu'est ce que la philosophie présocratique?* (Lille: Presses Universitaires du Septentrion, 2002), pp. 332–337; "The Cloud-Astrophysics of Xenophanes and Ionian Material Monism," in *The Oxford Handbook of Presocratic Philosophy*, Patricia Curd and Daniel W. Graham, eds., (New York: Oxford University Press, 2008), pp. 138–139.

My review of the ancient meteorological tradition and the comparison with the two Xenophanes fragments are admittedly cursory. But perhaps they suffice for the purpose of mitigating Burnyeat's opposition to the "modernist" reading. Ancient meteorology and its various congeners in natural history do not, of course, demand the degree of sophistication in gathering and controlling empirical data that we associate with modern science. But the attitude of treating theories as "always 'provisional', because held subject to revision as we learn more and more about the physical world" (p. 143) is no modern invention or breakthrough; it is an attitude we share with the scientists or natural philosophers of Graeco-Roman antiquity. So, I don't see "anachronism" in entertaining the possibility that this attitude—call it provisionalism or fallibilism—might be germane to our understanding and appreciation of Plato's doctrine of the *eikôs mythos*. Moreover, it is highly significant that, unlike the *Timaeus*, ancient Greek enterprises of *physiologia* and *meteôrologia* do not involve a creation story. We can, after all, have explanatory equipollence and an *eikôs mythos* even in the absence of the sort of practical reasoning that goes with world-making and with theodicy.

That in the *Timaeus* we do have practical reasoning and theodicy is certainly true. Burnyeat is right on this. And yet the practical reasoning in this work of Plato's has a big component of purely theoretical motivation. Coming up with stories, conjectures, hypotheses, theories to explain the phenomena, especially at the highest levels of explanatory success, leaves big "Why?" questions hanging. Actual multiplicity of explanations is bound to be unsettling. Some a priori theoretical criteria will serve to limit further the field of explanatory options. And should it happen that one single option is left standing, this still poses the haunting challenge of virtual equipollence: why this state of things and not some logically conceivable alternative? To make for theoretical closure, heavier recourse to a priori criteria is needed. As the *Timaeus* explores and rehearses the practical reasoning that justifies our viewing the cosmos as "the best of what is possible," it also seeks to elicit from Reason answers to theoretical "Why?"s that are paramount and ultimate.[28]

---

28   The idea that the *eikôs-mythos*-stance should be interpreted in the light of the Epicurean doctrine of multiplicity in explanation was suggested to me decades ago by Edward N. Lee. I am also grateful to Ed Lee for very thoughtful and detailed comments on an early version of this paper. The same version received the benefit of critical discussion by the "Euthyphrones," the students-and-faculty discussion group in ancient philosophy at The University of Texas at Austin, in July of 2007 and again at a follow-up session in September 2008. For assistance with proofreading, my thanks to Olive Forbes and to Mina Fei-Ting Chen. My sincere thanks also to Karen Succi of Parmenides Publishing for thoughtful, attentive, and efficient handling of matters of copy-editing and corrections.

16

A Time for Learning and for Counting: Egyptians, Greeks, and Empirical Processes in Plato's Timaeus

Barbara M. Sattler

In the *Republic*, the motions of the heavenly bodies are understood to serve only as an insufficient example for "real astronomy" which is independent of all the irregularities observable in the sky:

> Then don't you think that a real astronomer will feel the same when he looks at the motions of the stars? He'll believe that the craftsman of the heavens arranged them and all that's in them in the finest way possible for such things. But as for the ratio of night to day, of days to a month, of a month to a year, or of the motions of the stars to any of them or to each other, don't you think that he'll consider it strange to believe they're always the same and never deviate anywhere at all or to try to in any sort of way grasp the truth about them, since they're connected to body and visible? . . . Then if, by really taking part in astronomy, we're to make the naturally intelligent part of the soul useful instead of useless, let's study astronomy by means of problems, as we do geometry, and leave the things in the sky alone. (530a–c, Grube's translation, revised by Reeve)

While the motions of the planets are considered to be irregular and thus not rational in the *Republic*, so that learning requires abstracting from these motions, the *Timaeus* seems to paint quite a different picture of the heavenly revolutions:

> The motions akin to the divine part in us are the thoughts and revolutions of the universe; these, therefore, every man should

> follow . . . and thereby win the fulfilment of the best life set by
> the gods before mankind both for this present time and for the
> time to come. (90c–d Cornford's translation)[1]

Rather than abstracting from the motions of the universe in order to be able to retreat to the realm of reason, our thoughts should now imitate the motions of the universe so as to achieve the most excellent life.[2] Moreover, in the *Timaeus,* Socrates wants to see the ideal state, summarized at the beginning of the book, *in motion* (*kinoumena*, 19b–c), a wish that Critias' recounting of the Egyptian tale of Ancient Athens is meant to fulfil.

These quotes and citations already indicate that in the natural as well as in the human realm the status of at least certain kinds of empirical motions has changed significantly between Plato's middle and his late period.[3] But before we investigate how Plato can conceive of empirical processes as being indeed in accord with reason in the *Timaeus*, we should first have a closer look at his understanding of rationality.

In the middle Plato, empirical processes seem to be irrational since rationality is a feature of the realm of being and thus of the purely intelligible world. Empirical things are seen to possess a fairly limited rationality: they are rational in so far as they participate in the Forms and thus in the realm of being, but irrational precisely in so far as they undergo change and thus belong to the realm of becoming. Consequently, the quote from the *Republic* takes the motions of the planets—processes of empirical things—as belonging to the realm of becoming, and thus as neither rational themselves nor available for rational understanding.

But what does Plato understand by rationality in the *Republic* and in his other works of the middle period? According to the Divided Line passage, the

---

1   Francis M. Cornford, *Plato's Cosmology: The* Timaeus *of Plato* (1937; Indianapolis: Hackett, 1997). Cf. also *Laws* VII, 820e–822d, where the Athenian Stranger points out that the moon, the sun and the other heavenly bodies only *seem* to wander while really they always move in a circle along one and the same path. Cf. also Elena Cavagnaro, "The *Timaeus* of Plato and the erratic Motions of the Planets" in Tomás Calvo and Luc Brisson, eds., *Interpreting the* Timaeus-Critias (Sankt Augustin: Academia Verlag, 1997), pp. 351–362.

2   The account of birds as coming to be from men studying the heavens in 91d–e is not speaking against this as it a) rather vaguely refers to the object of study as the "high up things" (*meteôrologikôn*) and b) points out that birds descend from those men "who studied the heavens *but* imagined in their simplicity that the *surest* evidence in these matters comes through the eye" (Cornford's translation, my italics). Even if this passage is indeed referring to men dealing with the heavenly bodies, we do not have to assume that the surest evidence comes through the eye, only that the visible motions are indeed exhibiting *rationality*, which is not at all denied by this passage; cf. also *Timaeus* 47a–c.

3   That this does not encompass all empirical motions can be seen from the discussion of necessity in the *Timaeus*, which deals with the undetermined errant cause and chaotic motions "before" creation (48a ff).

objects of knowledge, and thus what can be rationally grasped, are Forms and, in principle, mathematical objects (*Republic* 509d ff.).[4] Forms, as can be best seen from the *Phaedo*, are uniform *(monoeides)*, and always remain the same and in the same way *(aei kata tauta kai hôsautôs echei)*. They are thus also unchanging, as that which always is in the same condition is not compound, and it is only compounds that are subject of change; for what is compound dissolves into its constituents again (so, for example, *Phaedo* 78c–e and 80b).[5] Complete uniformity is the basis for stability. Only that which is always the same, which is without any differences, completely simple and thus stable is considered as conformable to reason. This obviously has to lead not only to the exclusion of the necessarily complex empirical things from the realm of what can be rationally understood, but, of course, also to the exclusion of empirical processes.

The attempt to rationalize empirical processes in the *Timaeus* thus already presupposes a certain change of Plato's notion of rationality. The *Sophist* shows that even the most basic Forms are necessarily complex; identity essentially includes difference (254c–259d).[6] The paradigm of rationality is sketched as the systematic relation of different Forms. This understanding of what is rational provides a necessary basis for giving an account of empirical things and processes.[7] However, while the complexity of Forms can account for complex empirical things, it does not seem to be sufficient to explain the complexity of processes. As we will see, a mediator is required to transfer the unity and thus the rationality of the complex but unchanging Forms to

---

4 Though geometry and other mathematical disciplines do not go back to the real beginnings, in contrast to dialectic, i.e., Plato's philosophy of the Forms, Glaucon and Socrates agree that in principle mathematical objects could be objects of mere reason: ". . . because they [those who study the so-called sciences] do not go back to a genuine principle, but proceed from hypotheses, you don't think that they understand them [the objects of these sciences, i.e. mathematical objects], even though, given such a principle, they are intelligible" (511c–d, Grube's translation, revised by Reeve).

5 The same thought is expressed by the demiurge when he tells the minor gods that "anything that is bound together is liable to being undone . . . . This is the reason why you, as creatures that have come to be, are neither completely immortal nor exempt from being undone." However, he promises them that "you will not be undone nor will death be your portion, since you have received the guarantee of my will—a greater, more sovereign bond than those with which you were bound when you came to be" (41b, Zeyl's translation with alterations), and a similar guarantee seems to hold for the world as a whole.

6 Even if one does not share the assumption that the *Sophist* was written before the *Timaeus*, as I do following Cornford, Ledger and others, both dialogues clearly belong to Plato's late phase, as, among other things, stylometric results have shown. Thus the thoughts of the *Sophist* can in any way be seen to be in the background of the *Timaeus,* as the employment of the prominent three concepts from the *Sophist*, Being, Sameness, and Difference, for the construction of the World Soul in the *Timaeus* demonstrates.

7 Processes always require a prior and a later stage, location, etc., and are thus necessarily complex.

empirical processes. The mediator needed to confer rationality on empirical processes has to be created itself—if it were uncreated it could only belong to the realm of unchanging Forms or to the chaotically and thus irrationally moved receptacle within the picture of the *Timaeus*; yet at the same time this mediator has to be as similar to reason as possible, otherwise it could, according to Plato's isomorphic background assumption, not bestow rationality. The mediator Plato entrusts with this task in the *Timaeus* is time, or so I want to argue in the following. Let us thus first look at the explicit introduction of time in the *Timaeus*:

Ὡς δὲ κινηθὲν αὐτὸ καὶ ζῶν ἐνόησεν τῶν ἀιδίων θεῶν γεγονὸς ἄγαλμα ὁ γεννήσας πατήρ, ἠγάσθη τε καὶ εὐφρανθεὶς ἔτι δὴ μᾶλλον ὅμοιον πρὸς τὸ παράδειγμα ἐπενόησεν ἀπεργάσασθαι. καθάπερ οὖν αὐτὸ τυγχάνει ζῷον ἀίδιον ὄν, καὶ τόδε τὸ πᾶν οὕτως εἰς δύναμιν ἐπεχείρησε τοιοῦτον ἀποτελεῖν. ἡ μὲν οὖν τοῦ ζῴου φύσις ἐτύγχανεν οὖσα αἰώνιος, καὶ τοῦτο μὲν δὴ τῷ γεννητῷ παντελῶς προσάπτειν οὐκ ἦν δυνατόν· εἰκὼ δ᾽ ἐπενόει κινητόν τινα αἰῶνος ποιῆσαι, καὶ διακοσμῶν ἅμα οὐρανὸν ποιεῖ μένοντος αἰῶνος ἐν ἑνὶ κατ᾽ ἀριθμὸν ἰοῦσαν αἰώνιον εἰκόνα, τοῦτον ὃν δὴ χρόνον ὠνομάκαμεν. ἡμέρας γὰρ καὶ νύκτας καὶ μῆνας καὶ ἐνιαυτούς, οὐκ ὄντας πρὶν οὐρανὸν γενέσθαι, τότε ἅμα ἐκείνῳ συνισταμένῳ τὴν γένεσιν αὐτῶν μηχανᾶται· ταῦτα δὲ πάντα μέρη χρόνου, καὶ τό τ᾽ ἦν τό τ᾽ ἔσται χρόνου γεγονότα εἴδη.

Now when the father who had begotten the universe observed it set in motion and alive, a thing that had come to be as a shrine for the everlasting gods, he was well pleased, and in his delight he thought of making it more like its model still. So, as the model was itself an everlasting Living Thing, he set himself to bringing this universe to completion in such a way that it, too, would have the character to the extent that was possible. Now it was the Living Thing's nature to be eternal, but it isn't possible to bestow eternity fully upon anything that is begotten. And so he began to think of making a moving image of eternity: by bringing order to the heavens, he makes an everlasting image of eternity remaining in unity, (an image) moving according to number; this is, of course, what we have named 'time'. For before the heavens came to be, there were no days or nights, no months or years. But now, at the same time as he framed the heavens, he devised their coming to be. These all are parts of time and *was* and *will be* are forms of time that have come to be. (37c6–e5, Zeyl's translation with alterations)

Time is introduced, according to our quotation, in order to make the universe even more similar to the model. Since what is contemplated by the demiurge is an *increase* of similarity *(mallon homoion),* there are obviously other features of the world that ensured a certain amount of similarity already, for instance, the oneness of the world is the adequate expression of the uniqueness of the model (31a–b). But it is only the similarity brought about by the introduction of time that will turn out to be relevant for the assessment of the rationality of processes in the created world. So to what extent is the similarity between the model and the world heightened by time?

The world becomes more similar to the model by having the model's eternity conveyed to it by time. But since eternity cannot be fully bestowed on something created, all that can be accomplished is the creation of time as an *image* of eternity. This image is brought about as the order of the heavens. What kind of order time is meant to be becomes clear when we look at what exactly time confers on the world by imitating eternity. Eternity is "remaining in unity," which is taken up by the image "moving according to number." The image is moved since it is an image in the realm of becoming; so remaining or abiding in the model corresponds to moving in the world of becoming. And the way to imitate the unity of eternity in the realm of becoming is by having this motion proceed according to numbers. The simple unity of the model is transformed into the complex unity of a process, which is granted by a rule, a rule that is numerically graspable.

Thus, time is to be understood as an order that works according to numbers. It is the numerically ordered motions of the heavens. This connection between motions and numbers called time shows that nature and its changes are compatible with certain intelligible structures, namely with numerical structures; it is thus established that these processes are in accord with reason. The immediate expression of this rationality of processes is their regularity, a feature that stands in contrast to the random motions and changes in the receptacle "before" creation[8] and that we saw clearly missing in the account of empirical processes given by the middle Plato.

Time is not only the numerical order of the motions of the heavens, it also allows us to understand other processes as being ordered and thus as rationally graspable. Now, which are the processes in the world that the late Plato assumes to be and is able to show as rationally understandable? The processes the *Timaeus* puts forward as being in accord with reason are on the one hand those in the realm of cosmology, and on the other hand cultural developments, hence processes in the human as well as in the natural realm.

We saw above that processes in the domain of becoming (though we did not determine whether they are human or natural) can be understood as rational

---

8 Where we can neither identify *what* is moving (cf. 49d–50a) nor the course of a motion, e.g., as distinct from another motion.

thanks to time mediating between the rational structures of the model and the world. Now if there can only be one such mediator, then it has to be effective in both realms that Plato puts forth as allowing for rational processes, human and natural. In this case it will also be a unifying basis for the two main realms of becoming under investigation.

The only mediator we have looked at so far was time. But we do indeed find two other functions of ordering in the *Timaeus*, geometrical and arithmetical functions. However, the former is exclusively used as a principle for the *ordering of matter* (cf. 53b–57d), while the latter is employed for two different tasks: first, numerical proportions forge the connections between the four elements in such a way that they hold together in one World Body without dissolution (31b–32c). The second task of arithmetical proportions is the composition of the World Soul—Being, Sameness, and Difference as the ingredients of the World Soul are mixed, and this mixture is divided in a proportion following the powers of two and three (35a–36b). Like the geometrical function of ordering, these two arithmetical functions are certainly responsible for the rationality of some features of the world of becoming, but they have nothing to do with the ordering of *processes*. For processes, no other mediator for rationality can be found in the *Timaeus* apart from time. Hence, it seems to be clear that at least in the Platonic picture time has to account for the regularities of changes in nature as well as in culture, showing thus that both realms can be understood as being conformable to reason.

But can time indeed grant regularity in both cases? And if so, how? Let us start with examining time's role in nature first as it can be derived immediately from the quote above. The "instruments of time" (41e6), i.e., the revolutions of the stars and planets, equip the universe with motions that are standards in so far as they are regular and accessible from everywhere—one of the orbits is even furnished with light, which can not only serve as a "conspicuous measure of their [the planets'] slowness and quickness" (39b), but also enhances the accessibility of the regular motions by being everywhere visible. This accessibility of the standard motions allows us observers to compare all other regular processes with them.

Furthermore, as a result of the regularity and circularity of the heavenly motions, we gain what Plato calls "parts of time," temporal measurement units like days, nights, months and years. Thus, we can connect the regular circular motions with the number series and assign it to a linear succession. This in turn allows us not only to compare all natural processes to the standard motions, but also to use these heavenly motions to *measure* other natural motions, i.e., to connect the natural motions with numbers in a systematic way. The numerically ordered motions of the heavens thus pass on their regularity to other motions. Time as an image "moving according to number" thus shows that the demiurge has bestowed one and the same kind of rationality on all of nature since all processes in the natural world can be brought under one measure—expressed as days, nights and so on.

While the circularity of the heavenly motions allows us to gain units of measurement from a continuous process—the return of the planets to their starting point of motion allows us to mark off a unit—the regularity of the motions secures that we will always gain the same unit and thus can measure and hence compare different motions that take place at different times.[9] Thus the instruments of time grant universal comparability of processes and allow us humans to understand the changes of the whole natural world as ordered—its order is bestowed by the demiurge with the help of time. We can, for instance, determine how long a flood lasted (e.g., 40 days), whether it is as long as, shorter or longer than another process (e.g., the flood described in *Genesis*), and whether it happened before, after or simultaneously with some other event (e.g., whether Noah or the ancient Athenians had to fight with the waters first). Even more, time not only allows us to connect numbers and motions (and thus to understand motions as ordered), one of its tools, the sun in its motion, first of all allows us humans also to learn how to count (cf. 39b). So it is clear that in the picture of the *Timaeus*, the rationality of the natural processes is not something that we as observers are projecting onto the world. Rather it is time that mediates number to the world, thus establishing the rationality of the regular processes in the world, as well as enabling us to develop our rational ability further by bestowing us with "a share in number."

Looking at the realm of nature, we saw how time establishes the order of the natural processes as an order of before and after, which we can further determine with the help of the parts of time.[10] This temporal structure is the basis for an ordered linear succession.[11] But what about the rationality of

---

9 Phenomenologically, days, nights, months, and years are actually not straightforwardly regular units, since, e.g., the length of day and night is not equal during the year, as Plato complains about in the quote from the *Republic* given at the beginning. The way to understand them as fully regular would require conceiving of a regular change of a change, which neither Plato nor Aristotle can do. Nevertheless, Plato posits their regularity as the basis for rationalizing empirical processes. Cf. 39b–d, where we are told for example that "νὺξ μὲν οὖν ἡμέρα τε γέγονεν οὕτως καὶ διὰ ταῦτα, ἡ τῆς μιᾶς καὶ φρονιμωτάτης κυκλήσεως περίοδος" ("thus night and day came into being as the period of the single and most intelligent revolution").

10 We can compare this order established by time in the realm of nature with the help of the regular and visible motions of the planets to what McTaggart calls the order of the B-series, the order of before and after, adequate for the understanding of a mere succession.

11 It is also one condition for what we can call, using Aristotelian terminology, the causality afforded by efficient causes—the notion of a necessary succession such that because of what has happened before, what happens afterwards takes place. However, it is only a condition if cause and effect are not taken to be temporally simultaneous, but rather the first is seen as temporally preceding the second.

processes in the human realm? Is the order of before and after and the notion of a linear succession enough to establish that also this realm is conformable to reason?

As was mentioned in the beginning, Plato's notion of rationality changed from the middle to the late works, in such a way that what counts as being rationally understandable need no longer be thought of as being absolutely simple but might involve complexity. The feature of rationality that stayed the same, though, is stability; nothing can be rationally understandable without the basic structure staying the same in one way or other. Stability is given in nature due to the regularity of the motions of the heavens, since the rule of their motions is stable and unchanging. So, for example, the motion of a particular planet will always cover a certain section x on its revolution before the next section y. However, this feature seems to rule out the realm of human action from being considered as rational since the sequence of human events is not stable in this way: from a certain event x we cannot always infer what will come after it, the next event that will take place could be y or z, or yet something else. But does this mean that time cannot operate as a mediator between the model and the world of human processes?

We saw above that time proved to be the only mediator for the rationality of processes in the *Timaeus*. So if time is not mediating, it seems that the realm of human actions cannot be understood as being rational at all. In order to find out whether Plato does indeed assume processes in the cultural realm to be rationally graspable and, if so, how time is involved in their being rational, let us first have a quick look at the human processes presented in the *Timaeus*.

The main human processes discussed are the sequences of historic events in the development of different societies contrived by Plato: of Atlantis, of Athens, and of Egypt. The development of the first one is dealt with in more detail in the *Critias*, so we will concentrate here on Plato's Egyptians and Athenians and their account of history. Plato's Solon, representing the attitude of the Greeks of his and Critias' time, reports Greek history as a succession of individual events, a succession of destruction and reconstruction:

καί ποτε προαγαγεῖν βουληθεὶς αὐτοὺς περὶ τῶν ἀρχαίων εἰς λόγους, τῶν τῇδε τὰ ἀρχαιότατα λέγειν ἐπιχειρεῖν, περὶ Φορωνέως τε τοῦ πρώτου λεχθέντος καὶ Νιόβης, καὶ μετὰ τὸν κατακλυσμὸν αὖ περὶ Δευκαλίωνος καὶ Πύρρας ὡς διεγένοντο μυθολογεῖν, καὶ τοὺς ἐξ αὐτῶν γενεαλογεῖν, καὶ τὰ τῶν ἐτῶν ὅσα ἦν οἷς ἔλεγεν πειρᾶσθαι διαμνημονεύων τοὺς χρόνους ἀριθμεῖν.

On one occasion, wanting to lead them [the Egyptians] on to talk about antiquity, he [Solon] broached the subject of our own *most ancient* history. He started talking about Phoroneus—the *first* human being, it is said—and about Niobe, and then he told the story of how Deucalion and Pyrrha survived the flood. He went on to trace the *pedigree of their descendants,* and tried to *compute* their *dates* by *calculating the numbers of years* that had elapsed since the events of which he spoke. (22a–b, Zeyl's translation with alterations, my italics)

Like a sequence of natural phenomena, Greek history, according to Solon's account, seems to be structured solely by before and after,[12] there is the first human being and his companion Niobe, and then there are the only survivors of the flood, Deucalion and Pyrrha,[13] who are in turn succeeded by their descendants. As the words in italics show, Solon's connection of the events of the Greek past is established by counting: by the calculation of years that have passed, and by the enumeration of the family tree of the descendants of the only survivors of the flood. So the rationality of this account is granted by the temporal structure of before and after, which forms the basis for an ordered succession, here the succession of parents bringing about their children.[14] Thus, along the lines of the Greek account, we should find in history the very same rationality as in the natural realm, also mediated by the same temporal structure; and the human share in number bestowed to us by the motions of the sun is what allows us to give an account of it.

However, in the reply of an old priest to Solon's account of Greek history we are shown how the Greek treatment of human history leads to severe problems:

›Ὦ Σόλων, Σόλων, ″Ελληνες ἀεὶ παῖδές ἐστε, γέρων δὲ ″Ελλην οὐκ ἔστιν.‹ . . . ›Νέοι ἐστέ,‹ εἰπεῖν, ›τὰς ψυχὰς πάντες· οὐδεμίαν γὰρ

---

12 However, in contrast to the recurring phenomena in nature, we are dealing with individual events in the human realm.

13 Solon does not clarify the relation between Phoroneus and Niobe on the one hand and Deucalion and Pyrrha on the other. Both couples are reported as the first human beings in different sources. Nevertheless, Phoroneus as the forefather of the Pelasgian race could be seen as living before Deucalion who is the ancestor of the more recent Hellenic race; cf. Brill's New Pauly and also Proclus, *Commentary on Plato's* Timaeus, translated with introduction and notes by Harold Tarrant (Cambridge: Cambridge University Press, 2007), p. 101. This vagueness in Solon's account might be an indication of Plato that the Greeks have some information about some of their ancestors that lived before one of the floods. However, as these pieces of information were not properly stored (see below), they do not know how to incorporate them exactly in their account of history, cf. also *Critias* 109d–110b where it is pointed out that the Greeks of Solon's and Critias' time have preserved the names of the ancient Athenians, but not their deeds, which would be what really matters.

14 An extreme version of this can of course be found with the register of lineage in the books of Moses.

ἐν αὐταῖς ἔχετε δι᾽ ἀρχαίαν ἀκοὴν παλαιὰν δόξαν οὐδὲ μάθημα
χρόνῳ πολιὸν οὐδέν . . . . τὰ γοῦν νυνδὴ γενεαλογηθέντα, ὦ
Σόλων, περὶ τῶν παρ᾽ ὑμῖν ἃ διῆλθες, παίδων βραχύ τι διαφέρει
μύθων, οἳ πρῶτον μὲν ἕνα γῆς κατακλυσμὸν μέμνησθε πολλῶν
ἔμπροσθεν γεγονότων, ἔτι δὲ τὸ κάλλιστον καὶ ἄριστον γένος
ἐπ᾽ ἀνθρώπους ἐν τῇ χώρᾳ παρ᾽ ὑμῖν οὐκ ἴστε γεγονός, ἐξ ὧν σύ
τε καὶ πᾶσα ἡ πόλις ἔστιν τὰ νῦν ὑμῶν.‹

'Oh, Solon, Solon, you Greeks are ever children; in Greece there
is no such thing as an old man . . . . You are all young in soul',
he said, 'your souls are devoid of beliefs about antiquity handed
down by ancient tradition. Your souls lack any learning made
hoary by time . . . . the account you just gave, Solon, of your
people's lineage is just like a nursery tale. To begin with, your
people remember only one flood, though there were many earlier;
and moreover, you do not know that the bravest and noblest race
in the world once lived in your country. From a small remnant of
their seed you and all your fellow-citizens are derived' (22b–23c,
Zeyl's translation with alterations).

The Greeks are missing *doxa* about the past, we are told, they have not learned
anything from ancient times; they lack *mathêma*, things learnt, *chronô polion*,
which have become hoary by time. Accordingly, they are like children. What
they give as a true account of the past, what Solon tells about the Greek history,
is really just a nursery tale children tell and think to be true.

From the Egyptian perspective, which in the *Timaeus* seems to be the
perspective of the wise grown-ups, the Greeks have not *learned* anything from
the past. So the Greeks' report of history, their counting of events, seems to miss
the specific human form of rationality—learning. But what is it exactly that
went wrong with the Greeks, why do they lack learning from the past? In order
to learn from history, we have to look back to the past with a view in mind of
what we want or do not want in the future. So we evaluate the past events in
history and then choose those appropriate as aims or basic structures for our
aims for the future. Looking back to evaluate the past and using the past to
plan for the future, however, requires certain temporal structures. Accordingly,
also this rationality of the human realm is dependent on the mediator time. But
the temporal structures on which learning is based are different from the ones
we reconstructed for the natural realm. Learning requires, first, the possibility
that human beings use their experience with past actions for shaping present
and future processes. This means that events of the past are understood only
as a *reservoir* of possibilities, which humans can use in order to achieve an aim
in the future—leaving open different possible futures that might ensue from a

specific past.[15] Second, not only events in the past can influence human actions in the present, but also aims envisaged for the future. I can choose different possible actions to pursue according to different results that I want to reach in the future. As my action in the present is directed towards a goal in the future, the direction of influence runs not only from what happens before to what happens afterwards, but to some extent also goes the other way round; for short, we can talk about a bidirectional temporal structure.[16]

That time can be gone through in different directions and itself leaves open the possibility of different events following a given event x is a necessary (though, of course, not sufficient) condition for learning. For only if an event x does not necessarily lead to one single event y, but allows for different continuations, is it possible for us humans to deliberate which event y or z has led to better results in the past. Accordingly, we can take y or z as an aim for our future and adapt our present actions to this aim.[17]

Learning from the past, on the individual and on the collective level, leads to a greater stability within the realm of humans, for human processes can thus be better planned and will become more regular. And it is this potential of establishing stability within the human realm, provided by the "bidirectional" temporal structure, that Plato's Greeks do not seem to take advantage of. Their mere counting of the past does nothing to make human actions more rational since, in contrast to learning, it does not affect human actions at all.[18]

That Plato, too, sees a different temporal structure as a basis for the rationality within the human realm can be seen from the fact that he introduces not only "parts" of time, which we saw at work in the natural realm, but also

---

15 That the human realm is not determined to the same degree as the natural realm in Plato seems to be clear, not only because it enables him to account for learning, but also because Plato, in contrast, e.g., to Hesiod, does not mention agriculture in his account of human history here. Agriculture, however, is probably the one area within the human realm most dependent on the cycles and changes of nature; so he couldn't leave it out if he conceived of nature as fully determining the realm of humans. Plato does not use agriculture as a bridge between nature and culture here, not because he wants to keep this indeterminacy in the human realm as something positive, but rather because he considers it as a serious problem for the rationality of our actions, which must be attended to and countered by learning. Cf. also Samuel Scolnicov, "Freedom and Education in Plato's *Timaeus*" in Calvo and Brisson, eds., *Interpreting the* Timaeus-Critias (Sankt Augustin: Academia Verlag, 1997), pp. 366–370.

16 We can compare this notion of time to McTaggart's A-series, though the emphasis here is not so much on the change of position of an event in a series—this is the crucial feature for McTaggart: what was future becomes present and will be past—but on the fact that there is no unidirectional influence from the past to the future.

17 This structure is necessary even if, following only reason, there is *only one right aim* to choose for the future.

18 This does not mean, of course, that counting and the order of before-and-after would not play a role at all within a bidirectional temporal structure and thus for the Egyptians; the problem is that the Greek's *merely* count the past.

"forms" of time, "*was* and *will be*" (cf. the quotation above, 37e5). "Was and will be," and thus past and future, are not simply reducible to the parts of time. In the passage following the introduction of the forms of time, Plato does not develop the notion of the forms of time any further since his primary concern there is not to examine one or the other temporal notion, but rather to keep the eternal model free from *any* notion of temporality. And so one could think *prima facie* that "was" and "will be" also establish only a single direction, very much as we find it with the unidirectional succession of natural events. However, Plato's remark about the model neither growing older nor younger in 38a2 indicates that in the realm of past, present and future both directions are possible in principle. Thus, Plato introduces the bidirectionality which we saw to be a crucial feature of the temporal structure enabling learning. And he develops this temporal structure further with the help of the example of the Egyptians at the beginning of the *Timaeus*.[19]

We have already seen a glance of this in the Egyptian priest's reply to Solon above. But Plato gives us a fuller account of the Egyptian way to use this temporal structure in order to learn and thus to make human history rational.[20] This does not mean that the Egyptians know in any way of the structure of time just sketched. It just means that the Egyptians act in a way that uses the potentiality of this structure. And this can be seen, for a start, from the fact that Plato's Egyptians select the best actions from the past: "Now of all the events reported to us, no matter where they've occurred—in your parts or in ours—if there are any that are *noble* or *great* or *distinguished* in some other way, they've all been *inscribed* here in our temples and preserved from antiquity on" (23a, Zeyl's translation, my italics). The Egyptians obviously evaluate the past—they look for those events that they judge to be noble, great or distinguished. And they make sure that these events are well kept by inscribing them in the temple.[21]

---

19   It would need a separate paper to sketch how these temporal structures are related to Plato's notion of history. For some thoughts on the later, see, e.g., Arthur Lovejoy and George Boas, *Primitivism and Related Ideas in Antiquity* (1980; Baltimore: The Johns Hopkins University Press, 1997) and Thomas Cole, *Democritus and the Sources of Greek Anthropology* (Cleveland: American Philological Association/Western Reserve University Press, 1967).

20   For the Egyptians of the *Timaeus* there is an additional incentive to learn from the past, since the laws from the very beginning of human history in Greece actually derive from the goddess Athena directly (24c–d). So to preserve the past in this case also allows the whole society to be in contact with the divine order, just as the individual human being in Timaeus' account is close to the gods before birth and can get back to this starting point through learning how to master what is irrational within himself (42b–42d).

21   Cornford translates *graphô* as "write down," Zeyl as "inscribe." Given the context, and the stress that is laid also in the following few pages on preservation, I favor Zeyl's translation and even think that *graphô* here may be understood as making an inscription in stone (for this usage of *graphô* cf. Liddell and Scott, entry II, 2 "*inscribe*, eis skula, eis stêlên") as the element that might preserve the inscription for the longest time possible; cf. also Proclus, *Commentary*

We've sketched above the temporal structure that allows for treating the past as a reservoir evaluated for possible plans in the future. This evaluation of the past is now presented as the incentive to build up a common memory of past happenings. For if the past is assessed for possible future applications and thus parts of it are understood as valuable for the present and future, the question how to preserve the past best will become important. A common memory provides the Egyptians with a considerable reservoir of possible actions, and its evaluation grants orientation not only for individual learning and actions, but also for learning on the collective level.

And the Egyptians do learn on the collective level on the basis provided by their common memory—by keeping records of what is best, the Egyptians know of the best race that has ever lived and its outstanding constitution: "The city that is Athens today not only excelled in war but also distinguished itself by the excellence of its laws *(eunomôtatê)* in every area. Its accomplishments and its social arrangements *(politeiai)* are said to have been the finest of all those under heaven of which we have received report" (23c–d, Zeyl's translation). The Egyptians take over these best institutions, they learn collectively by re-enacting these laws. Accordingly, Solon can find many *paradeigmata* of the institutions of ancient Athens in "today's" Egypt (24a). We can see how laws bring about stability and thus rationality in a society, if we understand them as rules that regulate the relations and actions between humans by promoting what a society considers as good, and by determining the boundaries of what is considered to be an acceptable action. For, thus understood, laws determine which kind of actions are permitted to occur, and which ones are promoted by society and are thus likely to occur; they establish a common frame for evaluating actions for society, and, accordingly, a certain degree of stability.

The stability established by the laws and political institutions which manifested themselves as best in human history and were taken over by the Egyptians are indeed also *objectively* rational to the highest degree. This Plato clearly indicates by having Socrates, through 'mere' acts of reason, come up with a very similar model—that's how the *Timaeus* is connected with the discussion

---

on Plato's Timaeus, p. 69, where an inscription on pillars is discussed. The good events are inscribed in the temples, we are told, and preserved *(sesôsmena)*. Susemihl translates the *kai* between *gegrammena* and *sesôsmena* as "von alters her in den Tempeln aufgezeichnet *und* bleibt *also* erhalten" (my italics), so his translation makes it explicit that because of the inscription the events get preserved. Having inscribed the noble past events in stone might also be a way the Greeks could have saved their history in spite of natural catastrophes. For there is at least a chance that the inscribed stones might survive a flood or fire, so that once the culture has regained the "necessaries of civilisation" (23a), the people might be able to connect to the achievements of their ancient culture via these inscriptions. *Laws* III, however, seems to give an account of the destruction of civilisations that would not allow for such a line of thought.

of an ideal state in the *Republic*, or some analogue of the *Republic*.[22] Moreover, these best laws also provide the Egyptians with the possibility of acquiring all the different sciences by fostering *phronesis* right from the very beginning:

> Again, as for wisdom *(phronesis)*, you see what great care the law has bestowed upon it here from the very beginning as concerns the order of the world, deriving from those divine things the discovery of all arts applied to human affairs, down to the practice of divination and medicine with a view to health, and acquiring all the other branches of learning connected therewith. (24b–c, Cornford's translation with alterations)

In Plato's account even the possibility of the sciences for humans rests on a certain temporal structure since it is the bidirectional structure that allows for the establishment of legislation promoting learning and the sciences. The latter seem to include also the sciences of the planets,[23] whose motions as natural processes are ordered merely according to a temporal before and after. Learning about their behaviour, however, is only possible for humans on the basis of the bidirectionality of time.[24]

The sciences thus established allow the Egyptians to give a rational account of natural catastrophes, for instance, that the great conflagration is caused by a recurring deviation of heavenly bodies. The Greeks, on the other hand, can only give one of their child-like versions of this event—they report it as Phaethon's unfortunate journey in his father's chariot (22c–d). Even an event that as such is only structured by temporal unidirectionality cannot be rationally accounted for by the Greeks, since learning and thus properly understanding this event is only possible on the basis of a different temporal structure. This will become yet clearer by looking in somewhat more detail at the failure of the Greeks; we will start with the points that they are missing in their account of history.

According to the old Egyptian priest, the Greeks do not remember the past before the last flood, they are not acquainted with the best people that have ever lived, and they are not aware that these best people were their own ancestors (cf. 22b–23c above). In contrast to the Egyptians, the Greeks are

---

22 I do not want to take a stand here in the debate whether the beginning of the *Timaeus* is meant to summarize the *Republic* or only some similar sketch of a *polis*, since I think my account works under both interpretations.

23 "Those divine things," cf. Cornford, *Plato's Cosmology*, p. 17 n. 2.

24 We might think of astronomy, the science of the motion of the stars and planets, as a sort of learning genuinely different from the kinds of learning dealt with so far, since the former does not seem to affect our actions and how we lead our lives. That this is, however, not Plato's understanding of astronomy can be seen from passages like 90c–d, quoted at the beginning of this paper.

missing a complete account of the succession of past events, which goes back far beyond the last flood to the founding of Athens and Sais some 9,000 and 8,000 years ago; they only grasp a short span. Moreover, the Greeks do not use the potentiality of bidirectional influences of past, present and future, since they have not developed anything from the past. They are thus foregoing the possibility of growing up mentally, "in soul." For the Egyptians, the Greeks are always children, since it is the process of learning that allows a culture to develop continuously without having to start anew with each generation—the Greeks are a culture kept in constant infancy.

Accordingly, the mere extension of the Greek account of the temporal succession of prior events does not help them to "grow up," if by accident this succession of events is completed again, as it is in the case of Solon learning about the Greek past happenings from the Egyptians. For, first, Plato shows that even from a complete account of a paradigmatic past the Greeks fail to learn anything. Critias knew about ancient Athens and Atlantis ever since he was a little boy without it having any influence on his life[25] or on the culture in which he lived. He simply takes the past events as a story, as a given piece of information of a historical succession. He is not looking back to these past events as a reservoir for future planning, evaluating some aspects of them as desirable (or exactly not desirable) future so that it would influence his present. Critias' mere re-counting as well as Solon's mere counting of past events misses the possibilities provided by a bidirectional structure and reduces their actions to such as could also be performed on the basis of a series of before-and-after. For mere counting and re-counting does not allow for assessing and re-enacting past events, which would have affected Critias' and Solon's present as a possible option for how to lead their lives; an effect that the sole counting of the past cannot have.

Second, the Greeks do not take care to preserve this past exactly because they do not take it as something from which to learn and thus as something of real importance for them. Solon fails to write it down.[26] And Critias only

---

25 As Sarah Broadie pointed out in her paper "Descent and Reminiscence in the *Timaeus-Critias*" given at the Chicago Ancient Philosophy Conference "Philosophy and Religion in Ancient Greece," organized by the University of Chicago, the University of Illinois at Chicago and Northwestern University in Chicago, November 3–4, 2006.

26 Solon's literary work gets qualified by two epithets in the context: one clansmen calls Solon the most noble *(eleutheriôtatos)* poet with regard to wisdom and poetry, and the old Critias himself is convinced that if Solon had written down this story neither Homer nor Hesiod would have been more distinguished *(eudokimôteros)*, cf. 21d. A. E. Taylor, *A Commentary on Plato's* Timaeus (Oxford: Oxford University Press, 1928), ad loc. deals only with the first characteristic pointing out that it must be a compliment to Solon's style not his matter since "the political sentiment expressed in Solon's verse would not have improved if Solon had made poetical composition the main business of his life." And he regards the idea of Solon being potentially a worthy rival of Homer as "an absurd one; Solon really had no considerable poetical

stores the Egyptian account of their past in his memory[27] as a story that he does not even bother to disseminate widely.[28] If Socrates had not come up with the sketch of a state similar to the one of the ancient Athenians, this account would probably have been lost with Critias' death (that's at least what the logic of the Critias character seems to suggest).[29]

Solon's and Critias' treatment of the Greek past also makes it clear that the failure of the Greeks to grow up is not just bad luck: it is not simply the case that the Greeks live in a region which undergoes natural disasters, where human culture is thus destroyed over and over again, while the Egyptians are blessed by living in a region that is safe from such catastrophes. Rather, it is also the attitude the Greeks have toward their history that prevents them from learning from their past on the collective as well as on the individual level.

While the Greeks of Critias' time serve as an example of failure in the *Timaeus*, the Egyptians are shown as a model for rationalizing processes in the

---

endowments." However, given the context of Critias' remark just sketched, it might actually be a judgement about content, not about any concrete political sentiment, as Taylor would have it, but rather about its *moral* value: If Solon had written down the account of ancient Athens, it would have allowed many more people to know about this morally excellent state, and perhaps some would have taken it seriously enough to let it influence their lives. Thus, Solon would have been noble and also most distinguished, as Homer and Hesiod are, not only because of the genuinely poetic qualities of their work, but also because of its educational value. Cf. also the discussion of the moral value of poetry in *Republic* X, especially 607a, where it is decided to accept hymns to the gods and eulogies to good people as the only kinds of poetry allowed into the ideal state. In the *Laws* VII, 817b–d, building up a state is compared to the work of tragedians: "We [the state builders] are poets like yourselves [the tragedians], composing in the same genre, and your competitors as artists and actors in the finest drama." Surely there the quality of the drama is judged according to content rather than to style.

27 In contrast to the memory discussed with the Egyptians, Solon and Critias do not know about the value of the past events, and do nothing to make these events *common* memory. Cf. also Critias' account of his memory in 26b: he vividly remembers this story of his childhood "like the indelible markings of a picture with the colors burnt in," but he is not sure whether he could recall everything from Socrates' speech the day before, which sketched the politically and philosophically relevant structures from his childhood story.

28 Solon seems to have tried to write it down, but felt forced by political troubles to abandon completing it. He treated it, according to the old Critias, as a *parergon*, a by-work, not taking it seriously enough (cf. 21c–d).

29 Timaeus ends his speech at the beginning of the *Critias* by asking the god to grant him knowledge if he was mistaken in anything he said (106a–b). Critias, by contrast, starts his speech by pointing out how much harder his task is, since we all know human affairs so well that we will be able to criticize him much more easily than we could criticize Timaeus (107a ff.). Not only has Critias not learned anything from his story for himself, he also only wants to make sure that he won't be criticized, rather than hoping for enlightenment through the criticism of others, as Timaeus seems to suggest in 54a. And finally, in the *Critias*, Critias' story drifts off into mere narration without any hint of its philosophically important structures, until it breaks off.

human realm based on making use of certain temporal structures. Built on what we called bidirectional temporal structures, the stability of processes—as manifested in actions that are planned and can thus be expected—is established in the human realm due to learning and, further, due to the institutionalization of good laws; one more reason why Plato might have moved on, as is often assumed, from the *Timaeus-Critias* to the *Laws*.[30]

However, while time is the mediator for rationality in the human as well as the natural realm, the temporal structures actually mediating seem to be independent of each other: the succession of before and after on the one hand, bidirectional influences of past, present, and future on the other. The unity of eternity, which is all "at once," the mere "is" (37e6–38a1), seems to be transferred to the world of becoming in two ways: in nature and with the Greeks it is stretched out in a succession of before and after, while for the Egyptians it is developed into "was" and "will be." Nevertheless, the explicit introduction of time in 37c ff. puts an emphasis on the connection of the two temporal structures: the one is bound to the forms of time, the other to the parts of time, but both to the one time.[31] And given that Plato does not assume different kinds of rationalities for different realms, but rather one uniform one, we should not expect more than one time mediating this rationality to empirical processes—one time with different aspects. The intrinsic connection between these two aspects of the one time can also be seen if we look back at the *Timaeus* quotation given at the very beginning (90c–d), where we are told to follow the motions of the universe. Primarily, our understanding should adjust to these motions (cf. 90d),[32] but since our actions are meant to be guided by our understanding, also our actions should adapt to the heavenly ones. For the fully developed rationality of humans will, according to Plato, approximate human actions to courses that are as stable and rational as the courses of the planetary motions are (this stability, though, is based on processes of learning and logic, and not immediately, as with the motions of the planets, on a natural aptitude). Accordingly, the threat of indeterminacy that a Platonist might fear coming in through actions based on bidirectional temporal structures is averted as these human actions should assimilate to those based on unidirectional temporal

---

30 After working out the temporal structures required for good legislation, he could move on to the legislation itself.

31 In the one passage where Plato does indeed seem to talk about times in the plural, 41e, the plural comes in because of the plurality of *organa* that provide different units of time and thus, speaking in an abbreviated manner, different times. Hence, the different "times" talked about in that passage are "times" that themselves are parts of the one unidirectional time.

32 Cf. Gabriela Corone, "The Ethical Function of Astronomy in Plato's *Timaeus*" and David Sedley, "'Becoming like God' in the *Timaeus* and Aristotle," both in: Calvo and Brisson, eds., *Interpreting the* Timaeus-Critias (Sankt Augustin: Academia Verlag, 1997), pp. 327–339, 341–348.

structures. The fully educated will only be left with *one rational* choice, and hence the actions of a fully rational human being will be structured like the motions of a planet are: a certain y will reliably follow a given x. And the circularity of the heavenly motions is mirrored by the resumption of past paradigms in the present and future. However, in order for us humans to adjust our actions correctly to the regular processes of nature, we first have to use the full potential of the bidirectional structure of time. We have to take the detour via learning, as the Egyptians do. The seeming short cut of the Greeks also cuts short the rationality of human processes.*

*I would like to thank the participants of the *Timaeus* conference for feedback on an earlier version of this paper. I am especially grateful to Alan Code for a reply he presented at the conference, to Gábor Betegh, and to Stephen Menn and Verity Harte for detailed comments. Finally, I want to thank Ulrich Bergmann for inspiration and continuing criticism.

17

Narrative Orders in the Timaeus *and* Critias

Kathryn A. Morgan

Introduction

Considerable scholarly effort has been expended on the evaluation of the narratives of Plato's *Timaeus* and *Critias* and on the unfinished trilogy of which they may be a part. What does it mean when Timaeus says that his cosmology is an *eikôs mythos* or *logos*, a likely account? What is the connection of the cosmology with the Atlantis narrative, which, despite its obvious resemblances to philosophical myth, is claimed to be absolutely true? How do the narratives relate to demands made in the *Republic* for ethically reformed poetic production? This essay does not pretend to present solutions to all the problems listed above and to the multitude of further perplexities that arises from them; it will, however, explore a complex of issues centering on the narrative form of the dialogues. My overarching question is: why is narrative necessary? This in turn comprehends further questions: what do we want out of narrative? Can it give us what we want and still remain philosophically respectable? How far do the *Timaeus* and *Critias* go towards meeting our desires? These narrative issues collide with the central physical and metaphysical problems of the *Timaeus*, whose cosmology is a narrative (or is it an analysis?) of what happens when the eternal is mapped onto the physical world, as the Demiurge models the cosmos—the ordered universe—on the eternal world of unchanging being. The narratology of the dialogues thus has philosophical significance, as the movement from paradigm to narrative at the beginning of the *Timaeus* mirrors and generates the account of the creation of the world as an imitation of the world of the Forms. Both the *Timaeus* and *Critias* result, as we shall see, from certain demands placed on narrative. Speakers are asked for certain kinds of accounts, and they spend a fair amount of time justifying their narrative procedures and attempting to direct audience reception. This obtrusive focus on the fit between accounts and pre-existing intellectual standards reinforces the centrality of the issue of paradigm and instantiation.

The analysis that follows is divided into four sections. The first will examine the relationship between the *Timaeus/Critias* and the *Republic*, showing how the narrative protocols of the former correspond to worries about the realizability of the perfect state set out in the latter. A second section considers the relationship between words and the world in light of the famous and controversial passage at *Timaeus* 29, where differing types of accounts are matched up with differing levels of reality. Next comes an evaluation of the arrangement of the narratives in the *Timaeus*, suggesting that (contrary to many readings) the dialogue demonstrates that the ordering of its narratives, its *logoi*, is not always completely under control, and that this lack of control is intimately connected with the perils of narrative concerning the sensible world. Finally, a brief excursus on the Atlantis narrative will illuminate the type of "historical" narrative that fits the requirement of setting a paradigm into motion.

"Still Life": The Republic *and* Timaeus

The *Timaeus* opens by glancing back to a discussion of the ideal state on the previous day that recalls many of the characteristics set forth in the *Republic*: a hierarchically organized society with an educated warrior class at the top and community of property, women, and children within that group (17c1–19a5). It is also clear, however, that the conversation summarized by Socrates cannot be identical with that of the *Republic*. Not only do the two conversations take place at different times of the year, but the summary in the *Timaeus* omits certain crucial aspects of the city of the *Republic*, chiefly the development of the notion of philosopher kings.[1] The *Timaeus*, moreover, presents a Socrates who is somehow dissatisfied with the previous discussion. One immediately suspects, therefore, that the *Timaeus* will present us with a "road not taken" in the *Republic*, and this suspicion is confirmed by the way the *Timaeus* resumes

---

1   For the mismatch in chronology, see Diskin Clay, "The Plan of Plato's *Critias*," in T. Calvo and Luc Brisson, eds., *Interpreting the* Timaeus-Critias (Sankt Augustin: Academia Verlag, 1997), p. 50 with n. 3. Absence of the philosopher kings: Jean-François Pradeau, *Le monde de la politique* (Sankt Augustin: Academia Verlag, 1997), p. 142; John Sallis, *Chorology: On Beginning in Plato's* Timaeus (Indianapolis: Indiana University Press, 1999), p. 23; Christopher Rowe, "Myth, History, and Dialectic in Plato's *Republic* and *Timaeus-Critias*," in R. Buxton, ed., *From Myth to Reason? Studies in the Development of Greek Thought* (Oxford: Oxford University Press, 1999), p. 263 n. 2; Jacob Howland, "Partisanship and the Work of Philosophy in Plato's *Timaeus*," *The Review of Politics* 69 (2007), 10.

and changes metaphors of the *Republic* dealing with the realizability of the ideal state.

Socrates' dissatisfaction centers on the narrative immobility of the previous discussion:

> Please listen now to the consequences concerning the city we described, what I happen to feel about it. This experience was for me something like this, as if someone who had seen beautiful animals somewhere, whether they were constructed by painting or were even really alive but at rest, arrived at the desire *(epi-thymian)* to watch them moving and exercising in struggle one of the motions appropriate for their bodies. I too experienced the same thing towards the city we described. I would hear with pleasure someone narrating a tale of the contests in which the city engages. (19b3–c3)

Socrates wants to see the just city performing some action worthy of itself, at war with some other city and putting the education of its citizens to good use, showing their greatness of spirit in word and deed (19c5–9). He is conscious of his own incapacities in this area but hopes that his interlocutors may be able to help. The experience of the *Republic*-like discussion was emotionally unsatisfying because the ideal state was merely described, but not shown in action; the elaborate education of the guardians needs to be put to some use. This demands a narrative, preferably of the city engaged in a war; it demands a historical account. As yet, we do not know whether the account is to be historical in the full sense, that is, whether it is to narrate something that actually happened (this would correspond to setting in motion animals that were alive but at rest), or quasi-historical, in that it would narrate a story of the city *as if* it were engaged in historical actions (this would correspond to setting in motion painted animals in a kind of cartoon—or even a motion picture).

This reference to painting and the demand for narrative motion take us back to the discussions of the feasibility of the ideal city in the *Republic*. The issue arises at the end of Book V, after Socrates has given a detailed account of the community of women and children, and will indeed lead to the introduction and development of the idea of philosopher kings and, in Book VI, their education. Socrates insists that, in principle, the question of whether the ideal state could be realized is irrelevant. Their task was to seek a paradigm *(paradeigmatos)* of justice, so that they could fix their eyes on it as a model. The original aim of their discussion was not to see whether the city could be realized. A painter would be none the worse who, although he painted a perfectly beautiful man, could not prove it was possible for such a man to exist. Their aim is to create a verbal paradigm *(paradeigma . . . logôi)* (472c4–e4). Socrates does, however, concede that to please Glaucon he will try to show how such a state might come as close as possible to the paradigm they have constructed in speech, although action, *praxis*, cleaves to truth less than speech does (472e6–473b2). This concession is followed immediately by the introduction of philosopher kings (473c11–e5). The art analogy recurs when Socrates imagines how the philosopher kings might create an ideal city. They are political artists using the Forms as their model for the state. First they are characterized as craftsmen (*dêmiourgon*, 500d6) of the virtues who mold themselves and the citizens (like sculptors), and then they are compared to painters (500e2–501c3). They will demand first a clean drawing tablet (that is, they will have impressionable people to work with and will start the city from scratch), then sketch the outline of the constitution, then paint the city using the Forms as models until its citizens are in the likeness of god. Their habits will then be as pleasing to god as it is possible for them to be—the most beautiful picture.[2] Still, we are reminded at the end of Book IX that the ideal city is nowhere on this earth, but its model (*paradeigma*) is laid up in heaven for anyone who wants to look at it and make himself its citizen (592a10–b5).

The Socrates of the *Timaeus* finds the vision of the city as model lacking. It is too much of a still life. We must, moreover, remember that the *Timaeus* summary does not include philosopher kings, the only conceivable means (in the *Republic*) of realizing the ideal city in the world. The summary ends with the commonality of women and children and arrangements for the breeding of superior offspring. In the *Republic,* this topic is followed rapidly by first thoughts about the possibility of realization (466d6–8) and soon afterwards by the fuller discussion summarized above. We conclude, then, that if the conversation between Socrates and Timaeus, Critias, Hermocrates and the unknown fourth on the previous day followed the same lines as the *Republic*, their discussion very probably ended before any debate about whether the state could be brought from paradigm to reality. It then follows that Socrates' fantasy in the *Timaeus* of setting beautiful animals in motion and/or bringing the picture to life occupies a structurally identical position to the debate on realizability in the *Republic*. Rather than following the path of making philosopher kings artists and craftsmen (*dêmiourgoi*) as he does in *Republic*, Plato constructs, through Timaeus, a craftsman god *(Dêmiourgos)* who constructs the physical universe on the model of the eternal paradigm, thus realizing the paradigm to

---

2 Rowe, "Myth," pp. 267–269 connects the painting metaphor of the *Republic* with the status of the city there as provisional and as an example of philosophical myth (cf. p. 272 for the transformation into an "historical" account). For *Timaeus* 19b as an allusion to the *Republic* passages discussed here, see Christopher Gill, "The Genre of the Atlantis Story," *Classical Philology* 72 (1977), 300.

the extent possible.[3] Plato will also address the question of potential historicity through the Atlantis narrative.

As Brague has pointed out, it is interesting that Socrates is unconcerned to make a distinction between a picture of animals and animals that are alive but at rest.[4] I shall argue later that this distinction corresponds to two possible ways of conceiving both the cosmology and the Atlantis narratives: either as certain kinds of historical narratives that are reconstructed as actually having taken place (the way they are conceived by the characters in the dialogue world), or as the animation of basic principles (the way they are conceived by the external audiences of the dialogue). What is important for present purposes is that this formulation, "whether they were constructed by painting or were even really alive but at rest," marks a transition from pictorial to narrative art that recapitulates the transition from the *Republic* to the *Timaeus*. This is a transition from a paradigm that may or may not be effected in our world to a narrative that takes place in it or even constitutes it. The movement is mirrored within the *Timaeus* by the movement from the eternal paradigm to the temporal and created universe. One should note also that this move to narrative is portrayed as the result of a desire: Socrates is like someone who desires to see beautiful animals in motion. The word for "desire" *(epithumia)*, something that operates most insistently in the world of sensible embodiment, suggests the close connection of narrative with the sensible world, a notion to which we shall be returning.[5]

Both the cosmology and the Atlantis narrative, then, answer to Socrates' desire for a narrative account, though in different ways. While Timaeus' account needs some justification, the account of Athens and Atlantis given by Critias corresponds quite closely to what Socrates asks for, in particular his request to see the ideal city at war.[6] There has been an occasional tendency for interpreters to depreciate Critias' narrative contribution in comparison with that of Timaeus. Critias has been called a boor, a cheat, and a liar, a hybristic self-aggrandizer who forces himself into the narrative limelight.[7] The question is whether the summary of the stories of Athens and Atlantis in the *Timaeus*

---

3 On the parallelism between the philosophical rulers of the *Republic* and the Demiurge of the *Timaeus*, see Howland, "Partisanship," pp. 23–24; Thomas M. Robinson, *Cosmos as Art Object: Studies in Plato's* Timaeus *and Other Dialogues* (Binghamton: Global Academic Publishing, 2004), pp. 73–74.

4 Rémi Brague, "The Body of the Speech: A New Hypothesis on the Compositional Structure of Timaeus' Monologue," in D. O'Meara, ed., *Platonic Investigations* (Washington, D. C.: The Catholic University of America Press, 1985), pp. 53–54.

5 Cf. Gill, "Genre," p. 300; Sallis, *Chorology*, p. 27.

6 *Pace* Warman Welliver, *Character, Plot and Thought in Plato's* Timaeus-Critias (Leiden: Brill, 1977), p. 29.

7 Welliver, *Character,* pp. 17–27; Howland, "Partisanship," pp. 6–7.

and the fleshing out they receive in the *Critias* are aggressive perversions of Socrates' request. This seems an unfair interpretation of the information at our disposal. It is certainly true that Critias is not a philosopher in the same sense as Socrates and Timaeus, but downgrading and dismissing his account obscures the important role that his narrative plays in the scheme of the dialogues. At 20b1–6, Socrates says explicitly that he agreed to talk about state formation on the previous day at the urging of his interlocutors (ὑμῶν δεομένων τὰ περὶ τῆς πολιτείας διελθεῖν) because he knew that they would be able to carry on the discourse "in order" *(hexês)* and that they would be able to show the city engaged in a suitable war. "When," he says, "I had finished my assignment I assigned you in return the task which I am speaking of even now" (εἰπὼν δὴ τἀπιταχθέντα ἀντεπέταξα ὑμῖν ἃ καὶ νῦν λέγω, 20b6–7). Socrates' comments have two interesting implications. The first is that his interlocutors had asked for his discourse on state formation (the *politeia*—almost the title of the *Republic*). One might speculate that in the narrative world of the dialogue, Socrates' *politeia* discourse is well enough known that people can ask for it by name. Yet it would not be Socratic practice merely to repeat what he, or indeed anybody else, had said before; the discourse would be recomposed as he and his companions worked through the topic. It is no surprise that when the discussion reached one of its major points of articulation, Socrates decided to come at the material from a different angle. Yesterday, therefore (and this is the second implication), when he had finished talking about the community of women and children, Socrates made the same comments he has just made about wanting to see the city engaged in war and asked for a war narrative. The discussion of feasibility that occurred in the *Republic* and that led to the introduction of philosopher kings was replaced in the *Timaeus* with a different one, the need to see the civic paradigm in narrative motion. Critias has, not, therefore engaged in narrative highjacking, but is doing just what everyone agreed that he and his companions would do.

If we rid ourselves of the notion that Critias' tales corrupt the narrative scheme, we can also look at Timaeus' cosmology with different eyes: it was not necessarily "ordered" yesterday. How, then, was the ordering of speakers arrived at? If we have already concluded that Critias is a liar, what he has to tell us will not be useful. We have no reason to do this, however, especially since his narrative about the ordering of the narratives is told in front of people who had ample reason to know the truth of the matter. On the way home, Hermocrates tells us, Critias summarized the Atlantis story for his friends and he invites Critias to summarize the story (tell, significantly, its *kephalaia*, its headings), so that Socrates may judge whether the story meets his needs (20c6–d3). After the summary, Socrates concurs that it does (26e2–7). The story belongs. What then of Timaeus' cosmology? Here we return to Critias' account: the interlocutors decided between themselves on the correct order.

Timaeus will speak first of the creation of the world and of man. Next comes, in conceptual order, the education, through the system of education Socrates spoke of yesterday, of some of the men Timaeus has created, after which Critias will "receive" these men who have been generated in speech and make them real Athenians in his account of ancient Athens and Atlantis (27a2–b6). The strict chronological order of the accounts (what narratologists would call the time of the *fabula*) would thus be: Timaeus (creation), Socrates (education), Critias (exploits) (Hermocrates will perhaps speak on more contemporary matters). The narrative order—that is, the order in which we actually get the material is anachronic: Socrates (in summary), Critias (in summary), Timaeus, Critias (with breakoff). The discourses of the *Timaeus* and *Critias* consciously supplement the account of Socrates by filling in the chronological gaps before and after and, in the account of Critias, making the transition to history—albeit history of a certain kind.

What is the significance of this ordering of the material? It seems designed to underline the role of contingency in the arrangements for the narratives. Commentators have noted how such contingency is installed right at the opening of the *Timaeus*, where Socrates counts his three interlocutors and asks what has happened to the fourth who was to be present. We are told that illness has caused his absence, and Socrates then demands that his companions "fill in" the part of the absent one (17a1–7).[8] When Critias introduces his Atlantis material, he marvels that he happens to be in possession of the perfect story to satisfy Socrates' requirements, "by some chance and not on purpose" (25e3–5).[9] The "filling in" happens, then, both with regard to supplementing the account of the *Republic* and to making do with an unforeseen lack in the expected dramatis personae. Nor is this the only supplementation that will be required. The reader will in the end be compelled to fill in the history of Athens and Atlantis from the material given in Critias' summary at the beginning of the *Timaeus*, since the account of the *Critias* breaks off before it is complete. At the macro-level of the dialogues, therefore, we are presented with a careful disorder that will also recur in Timaeus' cosmology. Whose disorder is it? That of the narrative god of the dialogues, Plato himself, who has with great sophistication taken pains to show us the generation of a set of narratives whose ordering and internal arrangements are governed by chance and the vagaries of the sensible world.

Given the demand for a narrative of the ideal city at war, we might well think that it is Timaeus' account, not Critias', that was unexpected. Yet a certain

---

8   Welliver, *Character*, p. 34; Clay, "Plan," p. 52; Thomas K. Johansen, *Plato's Natural Philosophy: A Study of the* Timaeus-Critias (Cambridge: Cambridge University Press, 2004), p. 197; Howland, "Partisanship," p. 9.
9   On the transparency of this "coincidence," see Kathryn A. Morgan, "Designer History: Plato's Atlantis Story and Fourth-Century Ideology," *Journal of Hellenic Studies* 118 (1998), 102–103.

teleology operates at the level of Platonic narration, just as it will at the level of demiurgic creation. Timaeus and Critias interpret differently Socrates' desire to see his citizens in motion. For Timaeus, the need is to produce a paradigmatic account of the world being created in time, a likely account that conforms to a set of teleological assumptions (that the universe is the best possible world, its creator good, and so on). If narrative history is a series of causally tied events, the teleological role of the Demiurge is essential as the initial cause that sets the narrative in motion. As Catherine Osborne has pointed out, Timaeus refuses to become bogged down in the way things actually happened, but tries to replicate in his account the creative activity of the Demiurge, wrestling with the necessity of dealing with materials that are sometimes recalcitrant and imposing order.[10] Here we see Plato's own narrative teleology at work, foregrounding the issues involved in realizing an image. Timaeus' account deals with the transition from paradigm to organized motion. It is therefore indispensable as a *foundational* account: the story of the first organized motion that gives the audience of the dialogue (though not necessarily Critias) the conceptual tools to understand the relationship of paradigm to an image moving in time. It is to this relationship that we must now turn.

Words and the World

The execution of this sort of narrative is complicated by the fact that we use words to refer to two different orders of reality. The world is a copy, existing in time, of the eternal model that can be apprehended by reason. Words are in turn related to what they describe. The nature of this connection needs specification:

> We must distinguish in the following way concerning the likeness
> (*eikonos*) and its model (*paradeigmatos*), that accounts are akin to
> the very things that they expound (*exêgêtai*). Accounts of what is
> stable, secure, and manifest to reason will be stable and unchang-
> ing—to the extent that it is possible and fitting for words to be
> irrefutable and unconquerable, they must fall nothing short of
> this—but accounts of what has been made as a copy with respect
> to that [the stable model] and is a likeness are likely (*eikotas*) and
> exist in a proportionate relationship to them [the stable accounts]:

10   Catherine Osborne, "Creative Discourse in the *Timaeus*," in C. Gill and M. M. McCabe, eds., *Form and Argument in Late Plato* (Oxford: Clarendon Press, 1996), pp. 188–189, 191, 204–207; Johansen, *Natural Philosophy*, pp. 190–192. For further reflections on the assimilation of the author of myth to the creative Demiurge, see Luc Brisson, "Le discours comme univers et l'univers comme discours. Platon et ses interprètes néo-platoniciens," in *Le texte et ses représentations*, Études de littérature ancienne 3 (Paris: Presses de l'École Normale Supérieure, 1987), pp. 121–127.

what being is to becoming, this is the relationship between truth
and conviction. (29b3–c3)

Timaeus suggests two possible causes of linguistic imprecision. First,
accounts cannot be completely stable, but only to the extent that it is possible
and fitting. Second, the stability of a narrative will also be governed by the
intelligibility or sensibility of its object. The world of becoming is a copy of
the intelligible realm and any account of it will be "likely." Recent work has
suggested that we should not read this passage as a downgrading or dismissal
of accounts of the sensible world. Timaeus' *eikôs mythos* is not to be glossed in
terms of modern conceptions of probability; rather, it is based on the fact that
accounts of the sensible world are accounts of an image or likeness, an *eikôn*,
and so "like" the "likeness" they express *(eikotas)*.[11] Likeliness thus has connotations of verisimilitude, fitness, and appropriateness; it expresses a standard to
which the account should live up.[12] Emphasis on fitness and verisimilitude, and
on the proportional fit between an image and words expounding that image,
seems proper, yet I think we should be on our guard against too maximalist an
interpretation of the possibilities of accounts of the sensible world. Even if the
cosmology fits the world as a rational and reasonable reconstruction based on
practical reasoning, it still runs up against the restrictions expressed with respect
to accounts of the paradigm at 29b7–c1: "to the extent that it is possible and
fitting for words to be irrefutable and unconquerable, they must fall nothing
short of this" (καθ' ὅσον οἷόν τε καὶ ἀνελέγκτοις προσήκει λόγοις εἶναι καὶ
ἀνικήτοις, τούτου δεῖ μηδὲν ἐλλείπειν). There would be no point in saying "to
the extent that it is possible . . . for words to be irrefutable" if it simply were
the case that absolutely stable accounts of the paradigm were possible. If even
accounts of the paradigm can only be stable to the extent admitted by language,
this will hold to an even greater extent for accounts of the image. Timaeus will
later comment (49c7–50a4) that since the elements are continually presenting
themselves in different forms, it is troubling to apply a demonstrative such as
"this" or "that" to them. Things that change should be described as "such."[13]
The problem with language, then, is partly that it gives the impression of

---

11 Myles Burnyeat, "EIKÔS MYTHOS," *Rhizai* II:2 (2005), 145–148; Johansen, *Natural Philosophy*, pp. 50–56.

12 Robinson, *Cosmos*, pp. 117–118, Burnyeat, "MYTHOS," pp. 146–147, 150. For further thoughts on the criterion of appropriateness in the cosmology (while retaining stress on its provisionality), see Kathryn A. Morgan, *Myth and Philosophy from the Presocratics to Plato* (Cambridge: Cambridge University Press, 2000), pp. 272–273.

13 For discussion of the problematic interpretation of this passage, see Sallis, *Chorology*, pp. 101–103 ("fire and the others elude discourse," p. 101); Johansen, *Natural Philosophy*, p. 120. On problems with language, see Osborne, "Discourse," p. 196.

spurious stability, but it also seems that one might code one's presentation to indicate that the perceptible cosmos is in a state of change.

We can see, then, why Timaeus' cosmology demands *narrative* motion, the description of something changing in time. The sensible world itself is a moving image of eternity, and it is the regular motion of this image according to number that we call "time" (37d5–7).[14] If accounts are analogous to their objects, an account of the sensible world must be a narrative. Both move in time. Socrates' request to set his paradigm in motion was the result of a productive intuition about the functioning of discourse in the sensible world. The model city is staged in that world, and an effective account of it must show the city in change. It takes Timaeus' speech, however, to show why this is the case. The cosmology shows something more fundamental than citizens at war: the philosophical underpinnings that give authority to various kinds of speech. Any account of the created world will inescapably be in motion, since the object of the discourse is the created world rather than the Forms and accounts are analogous to their objects.[15] Such an account will, moreover, inherently lack stability (we shall see that this instability is reflected at the level of narrative form)—not because they are necessarily random or unsatisfactory, but because they do not refer to things that always remain in the same place.

Accounts concerning the created world are *properly* couched as narrative. This realization leads to an old problem in the interpretation of the dialogue, whether the story of creation should be taken literally or metaphorically, and if the former, whether a literal reading was intended only for the sake of teaching.[16] Did Plato think that the world was ungenerated or created? The problem is complex and cannot be resolved here; indeed, if the approach taken in this paper is correct it may be irresolvable. Whether or not creation is a metaphor, it corresponds to what we might call the narrative imperative of the sensible world. The very sequence demanded by description already imports a kind of

---

14 Sallis, *Chorology*, pp. 78–82.

15 Burnyeat, "MYTHOS," 149–152, wants to restrict that application of the principles in 29b3–c3 to special, religiously inflected and philosophically satisfactory accounts of the cosmos (as likeness of its paradigm), but I see no reason for such restriction. Is it not a general principle that words are akin to their referents?

16 Literal (e.g.): Gregory Vlastos, "The Disorderly Motion in the *Timaios*," *Classical Quarterly* 33 (1939), 71–77; Robinson, *Cosmos*, pp. 14–19. Modified literal: Johansen, *Natural Philosophy*, pp. 87–91. Literal for the sake of teaching: Aryeh Finkelberg, "Plato's Method in *Timaeus*," *American Journal of Philology* 117 (1996), 391–409. Metaphorical: Leonardo Tarán, "The Creation Myth in Plato's *Timaeus*," in J. P. Anton and G. L. Kustas, eds., *Essays in Ancient Greek Philosophy* (Albany: State University of New York Press, 1971), pp. 373–392. M. R. Wright, "Myth, Science and Reason in the *Timaeus*," in M. R. Wright, ed., *Reason and Necessity: Essays on Plato's* Timaeus (London: Duckworth, 2001), p. 16, comes at the problem of system and narrative from a different angle: the perceptible world need not have a starting point, but a narrative must.

proto-narrative. When we specify the different parts of the universe and their functions, we are bound to ask of the relationship between them, how one affects the other. These relationships happen in time and orderly causal progression through time makes narrative.[17] N. J. Lowe has argued that as we read a narrative we experience two models of the story: a temporal model based on an "illusion of temporal succession within that universe," and an atemporal one, as we build up a mental model of the story as a whole. Further, "the tension between our twin internal models of the story is the source of the dynamic and affective element in plot. What we, as readers, want is for our temporal and atemporal models of the story to coincide."[18] This perceptive analysis is illuminating for a consideration of the problem of Timaean creation. The distinction between temporal and atemporal notions of a narrative is not identical with that between a created and a non-created universe, but it does suggest that the two different modes of understanding the physical universe (systemic versus chronological) may correspond to two different ways of experiencing the narrative universe. The physical universe demands diachronic narrative and human beings need it, but this does not prevent us from attempting to extrapolate the system. Indeed, the need to visualize the system as a whole may be the necessary counterpart to the desire to see the system take shape in time.

Socrates' longing to see the citizens of his city engaged in some kind of action looks to a fundamental human relationship with narrative, as our experience of "plot" generates emotional affect and satisfaction. His wish for narrative (described in terms of desire, *epithumia*) is a desire for affect. The *Timaeus* and *Critias* thus occupy a special place in the narratology of Plato's dialogues. Most dialogues are reports or dramatic presentations of philosophical conversations in which the action is intellectual. It has been claimed that the Platonic dialogue is "an exemplary case of something it might be useful to term *quasiplotting*: the development of plot*like* structures and reader response in non-narrative texts."[19] Whatever the truth of this contention, it is clear that the cosmology and the Atlantis narrative are exceptional; not only are attempts made to present creation and political activity as stories, but narrative presenta-

---

17   Internal causal structure also generates affective power. See the discussion of Forster in N. J. Lowe, *The Classical Plot and the Invention of Western Narrative* (Cambridge: Cambridge University Press, 2000), p. 14.

18   Lowe, *Plot*, pp. 23–24.

19   Lowe, *Plot*, p. 95, but see also my discussion of the narrative nature of the Platonic dialogue: Kathryn A. Morgan, "Plato," in I. De Jong, R. Nünlist, and A. Bowie, eds., *Narrators, Narratees, and Narratives in Ancient Greek Literature*, Studies in Ancient Greek Narrative, Volume I, Mnemosyne Supplementum 257 (Leiden and Boston: Brill, 2004), pp. 357–376. Note Lowe's observation that in Platonic dialogues, "it is the status of modal worlds themselves that is under discussion."

tion is itself thematized and the two different narratives are arranged within a larger narrative trajectory that connects them.

Narrative Arrangements

If Timaeus' narrative activity mirrors the creative activity of the Demiurge and shares its teleology, we might expect his account to mirror the perfections of its subject matter. Such has sometimes been the conclusion of modern interpreters. One might cite the judgment of Catherine Osborne in her seminal work on creative discourse in the dialogue: "the orderly arrangement of Timaeus' description matches the orderly arrangement of the world itself."[20] In this section, I shall argue that evaluations of this type do not do justice to the recalcitrance of the physical world and the way it is reflected in narrative. Although the best narrative would start at the beginning, go on to the end, and then stop (mirroring the causal chain of the temporal cosmos), this is not the case in the narrative presented to us in the *Timaeus*.[21]

Most interpreters of the cosmology agree that it falls into three main parts, with explicit divisions at 47e3 and 69a5. The first section deals with the workings of reason, the second with the workings of necessity and the receptacle, and the third with the functioning of the human body.[22] The divisions mean that the narrative makes fresh starts, and Timaeus himself comments on this. The introduction of the idea of the wandering cause at 48a5–8 causes him to remark that "we must therefore move backwards again, and begin again from the beginning, taking up another fitting beginning of these same things anew: just as we did in the case of the previous subject matter, so too now concerning it" (48a7–b3). Again, once he has distinguished various types of causes, Timaeus proposes that they, "briefly go back to the beginning again and swiftly travel to the same starting point whence we arrived at our present position" (69a8–9). These are not, however, the only points of discontinuity. At 61c2–d5 Timaeus asks his audience to assume a discussion that has not yet taken place: we are told to presuppose the existence of body and soul so that the account of the affections *(pathēmata)* may follow the account of the elements. At 34b10–35a1, Timaeus' meditations on narrative arrangement come with a crucial explanation. He admits that he has dealt with the creation of

---

20   Osborne, "Discourse," pp. 193–194. Cf. Johansen, *Natural Philosophy*, p. 186, "Just as the four speeches as a whole are carefully planned, so is Timaeus' speech . . . Timaeus' speech has been prepared in advance" (see also pp. 189–191).
21   My argument here is an expansion of my discussion in Morgan, *Myth*, pp. 273–274.
22   Sallis, *Chorology*, p. 8. For a more detailed division, see Johansen, *Natural Philosophy*, pp. 186–187, and for resistance to the idea of a tripartite structure (together with the innovative suggestion that the parts of the speech are intended to match up with parts of the human body), Brague, "Body," p. 61.

the soul and the body in the wrong order. In his account the creation of the soul comes after that of the creation of the body, although the soul is prior to the body. God, he says, would never have allowed the older to be ruled by the younger. Why has this happened? "Somehow," he explains, "because we have a great share of chance and the random, we partly speak in this way also" (ἀλλά πως ἡμεῖς πολὺ μετέχοντες τοῦ προστυχόντος τε καὶ εἰκῇ ταύτῃ πῃ καὶ λέγομεν, 34c2–4).

Here is an explicit acknowledgement that Timaeus' narrative trajectory does not, cannot, match the creative perfection of the Demiurge. The spoiler is the randomness of language, which is in turn dependent on the randomness inherent in the human condition.[23] The account here is indeed akin to the matter it explicates, but the kinship is expressed through disorder. This disorder should be connected with the disorderly motion that characterized the world before the organizing intervention of the Demiurge.[24] Just as the Demiurge works to bring order to the chaotic movement of matter, so Timaeus strives to order his presentation. Even the Demiurge must deal with the "wandering cause" and necessity, although we are assured that his creation is the best that it was possible to be. Can we say the same of Timaeus' narrative? No, because Timaeus, although his creative role is parallel to that of the Demiurge, although he is philosophical and has therefore practiced his whole life to bring his soul into harmony, is yet a human being in a mortal body. Not only this, but he must work with speech that has a great share of chance and the random, proceeding as it does from mortals who are similarly characterized.

Work on the narrative arrangement of the *Timaeus* has generally adopted a more optimistic interpretation. To my knowledge, only John Sallis has focused on the discontinuities of Timaeus' presentation, and although my interpretation of these discontinuities is less Derridean than his, it rests upon the same evidence. How, then does one deal with the obtrusive stress on order found in the speech? Timaeus "seems to be working according to a taxonomy . . . [he] seeks to control his material in order with his plan," and the end of the dialogue uses ring composition to stress completion and closure.[25] It has been suggested that we should compare the fresh starts of Timaeus' narrative to a series of circular

---

23 Wright, "Myth," p. 15, connects the "random" (*eikêi*) in this passage with the "likeliness" of the "likely account" (*eikôs logos*), but see the remarks of Burnyeat "MYTHOS," pp. 145–147.
24 Vlastos, "Motion," pp. 76–77; cf., contra, Tarán, "Creation," pp. 384–388. Contingency of language: Osborne, "Discourse," p. 200. For detailed discussion (along Derridean lines) of the connection of disorderly motion and the "wandering cause" with irregularity of presentation, see Sallis, *Chorology*, pp. 65, 88, 91–97, 132–135.
25 Johansen, *Natural Philosophy*, pp. 187–189. Yet, as Osborne, "Discourse," p. 195, remarks, the end of the speech does not in fact coincide with the end of the dialogue. Plato has, then, carefully avoided perfect closure.

orbits that intersect but trace a different path.[26] On this reading, the motion of the narrative is orderly and circular in a good sense. Certainly, Timaeus strives for regularity and order, but perhaps he protests too much.[27] His revisions and qualifications point to an awareness that the narrative progression is imperfect, even that the subject imposes this imperfection, rather than to the conclusion that his speech is an organic whole in which one part inevitably leads to another.[28]

What, then, do we make of Timaeus' disorderly narrative motion? One solution has been to interpret it as a sign that Plato does not intend the creation myth to be interpreted literally, but metaphorically. The contradictions of chronological order that are said to arise in the narrative presentation must, it is argued, have been noticed by Plato and could have been removed before publication if such removal were possible. Since this is not the case, Plato was not interested in chronological order:

> "The reversal of the 'chronological' order of creation is said to be due to the fact that 'there is in us too much of the casual and the random,' . . . But it is clear that Plato could not have meant this explanation of the reversal suffered by the mythical order in the narrative to be taken literally, for he is himself warning us that the chronological order has been reversed and, consequently, he could have modified the order of creation if he had so wished."[29]

We should, however, hesitate to conflate Timaeus' comments with Plato's voice. Plato presents us with a philosophical narrator who attempts to present in chronological order the creation of the universe, but is prevented from achieving this goal by the restrictions of language and the human condition. Plato could, conceivably, have had Timaeus present things in a different order, but his interest was in showing Timaeus grappling with narrative contingency and conforming to Socrates' request to see a paradigm in narrative motion.

As I have already indicated, Timaeus' imperfect narrative progression is mirrored on a large scale in the anachronic elements of the *Timaeus/Critias* complex. Timaeus' cosmology is narratively, as well as philosophically, teleological. The story of creation is a story of aiming at the greatest good possible, but also at the education of men. His account ends (or almost ends) with material that looks forward to education, how to regulate the motions of our soul. This

---

26   Osborne, "Discourse," pp. 197–198.

27   Note the tension between Johansen's assertions of planning and order with the admission that at 48e, "Timaeus is correcting himself: he was not right in his previous expectations about how the *logos* would go" (Johansen, *Natural Philosophy*, pp. 187–189 vs. p. 195 n. 29).

28   Contra Brague, "Body," pp. 53–83; Johansen, *Natural Philosophy*, pp. 191–195.

29   Tarán, "Creation," pp. 373–375, 383–384; quote at p. 375.

in turn should lead to the narrative of their exploits. Yet we have seen that this is not the case. Timaeus' account should come first but does not, and Socrates' model of education should come second. Socrates' account is summarized right at the start of the dialogue, so that it can be a presupposition for all that follows. The subsequent summary of Critias' account means that, in outline at least, it exists as a subtext during Timaeus' cosmology. Strangely, it then emerges, the two accounts (Socrates' and Critias') that have dominated—at the level of intention—the entire discussion that takes place over the two days, are only ever related in summary, for the *Critias* breaks off precisely at the point where preliminaries and summaries stop and detailed narrative is about to begin.

Atlantis

Critias' Atlantis narrative will illustrate the perils of narrative in a different way. The account perplexingly straddles the borders of myth, history, and philosophy, and the determination of its status has been the focus of intense investigation.[30] In what follows, I shall focus on one central aspect of this narrative, the way it forms a mediating term between paradigm and the chaotic world of history-as-it-happened. The first prerequisite to understanding the narrative is to realize that, just as was the case with Timaeus' cosmology, Critias' story has a different effect upon its internal and its external audiences. First, the internal audience. Critias (and Socrates follows his lead) emphasizes that the tale is historically true. The deed of the ancient Athenians is not merely spoken of, but was actually performed (*Timaeus* 21a4–5). The ideal state that was described "as if in myth" in the *Republic* will now be transferred to the realm of "truth" (26c8–d1). The tale has the great advantage of not being an invented *mythos* but a true *logos* (26e4–5).

What of the external audience? I have argued elsewhere that even if the speakers in the dialogue take Critias' protestations of truth at face value, the reader is under no compulsion to do so.[31] The tale of Atlantis has close connections with the Noble Lie at the end of *Republic*, Book III, and is meant to act as a philosophically informed charter-myth for Athens. The Noble Lie of the *Republic* tells the prospective citizens of Socrates' ideal state that, while they experienced being educated and trained for the new polity, they were really being formed within the earth, their mother and their nurse. Each citizen has a genetic inheritance that places him or her within the new hierarchy. The object of the Noble Lie is to persuade the rulers of the city especially, but failing that,

---

30 See, e.g., Gill, "Genre," pp. 287–304; Rowe, "Myth," pp. 263–264, 271–278; Osborne, "Discourse," pp. 181–189; Johansen, *Natural Philosophy*, pp. 24–47. The analysis offered here is based on Morgan, "History," pp. 101–118.

31 Morgan, "History," pp. 102–104.

the rest of the city (*Republic* 414c1–2), that they should care for the city and each other. Socrates thinks it unlikely that they could induce the first generation to believe it, but hopes that subsequent generations could be persuaded (415d2). Similarly in the *Timaeus* Solon receives from the Egyptians a charter myth/history for Athens and the tale is passed down with the stamp of Solon's authoritative truth on it. This tale persuades Socrates, Timaeus, Critias, and Hermocrates, (the last three of whom are politically important in their cities) to believe that the state described by Socrates on the previous day has *already* been realized. They have entered a compact to receive the narrative as history. The external audience, however, can distance itself and consider the story as narrative, precisely what the interlocutors have agreed not to do. This distancing, this consideration of narrative topoi and arrangements, matches the reaction of the external audience of the cosmology (interpreters of the dialogue), who can argue over the degree to which it is meant to be a narrative at all.

Atlantis represents idealizing history in several senses. The tale is narrated in order to set the ideal city of the *Republic* in motion, but it also has a close relationship to contemporary historicizing genres. Nicole Loraux has pointed out how various elements of the story of Atlantis recur in the Athenian civic genre of the Funeral Oration.[32] The scope of the comparison can be broadened, however. Aspects of the Atlantis myth are closely paralleled in Isocratean epideictic rhetoric, a rhetoric that argued from past civic glories and failures in order to establish the best course of action in the present; the paradigmatic role of the past is here explicitly an issue. In both the Atlantis story and Isocrates we see an Athenian constitution that surpasses all others and deeds of valor that make Athens preeminent in war. Both traditions record that Athens defended the Greeks and Europe against the incursions of hybristic barbarians. In the *Timaeus*, Athens is the leader of Greece, undergoes extremes of danger, and acts as a liberator (25b5–c6), just as, in Isocrates' *Panegyricus*, Athens undergoes danger and preserves the freedom of all. The just administration and leadership of Critias' Athenians (*Critias* 112e2–6) again finds parallels in the *Panegyricus* and *Areopagiticus* of Isocrates.[33]

These links with Isocratean panegyric history do not just reflect a common background in civic panegyric and the Funeral Oration, but take on an added resonance in contemporary political debates. It has long been realized that the story of Atlantis and Athens resonates with the great events in fifth-century history. As Vidal-Naquet pointed out already in 1964, the maritime character of Atlantis is crucial—he makes the myth an allegory of the late fifth century in which Atlantis maps onto the aggressive maritime pride of Athens that led

---

32 Nicole Loraux, *The Invention of Athens*, translation by A. Sheridan (Cambridge: Harvard University Press, 1986), pp. 302–303.
33 Morgan, "History," pp. 104–107.

to defeat at the end of the Peloponnesian War.[34] Yet the maritime model is crucial not just with respect to the fifth-century past. Plato was also playing on topical themes. The period from the 370's to the 350's was characterized by debates over the nature of Athens' maritime alliances. The Second Athenian league was founded in 377, and a central question of the period was whether Athens should embrace (or was embracing) the late fifth-century maritime paradigm. We see in Isocrates, as well as in Plato, the idea that maritime expansion causes constitutional decay.[35] Does Athens want to repeat the mistakes of Atlantis? In this context, the "history" of Atlantis looks to the future rather than the past. Plato's narrative intervenes as an influential paradigm for present decision-making.

The Atlantis narrative is thus paradigmatic history in three senses. It realizes the paradigm that Socrates set up in the *Republic*-like discussion and conforms to contemporary models for paradigmatic history. Finally, it presents models that were deployed and actively debated in early fourth-century Athens. This trajectory from unrealized ideal through the past to the present is based upon a rewriting of the political presuppositions of action. The narrative as we have it, however, despite reminiscences of the practice of Herodotus and Thucydides, is still far from classical historiography as we would recognize it.[36] It refuses to put forward a detailed account of what actually happened in the war between Athens and Atlantis, and remains, with the exception of the descriptive geographical excurses of the two cities, an outline history. It is worth noting that when the *Critias* breaks off, the narrative has just made an obtrusive transition to an epic mode, with a council of the gods about to debate the fate of Atlantis; the continuing story of Atlantis would have had an epic rather than a Thucydidean or Herodotean framework.[37] "History" is not allowed to get as far as a detailed account of how Atlantis attacked and Athens defended. Curiously, once we can dismiss our nagging curiosity about the precise content of this account, we can conclude that the details do not in fact matter as much as we might think. The summaries that Critias has delivered have told us all we need to know.[38] But what has changed since the beginning of the *Timaeus*, where a full-blown narrative of war was desired and promised?

---

34 Pierre Vidal-Naquet, "Athènes et l'Atlantide. Structure et signification d'un mythe platonicien," *Revue des Études Grecques* 77 (1964). Cf. Gill, "Genre," pp. 295–298; Luc Brisson, "De la philosophie politique à l'épopée. Le *Critias* de Platon," *Revue de Métaphysique et de Morale* 75 (1970), p. 436; Clay, "Plan," pp. 53–54; Pradeau, *Monde*, pp. 102–110 (with references to the earlier work of Bartoli).

35 Morgan, "History," pp. 114–118. Cf. Pradeau, *Monde*, pp. 206–229.

36 Herodotean and Thucydidean connections: Johansen, *Natural Philosophy*, pp. 11–15; Pradeau, *Monde*, pp. 156–185.

37 Clay, "Plan," pp. 51–52.

38 Welliver, *Character*, p. 34.

The cosmology has intervened and we have learned more about the relationship of the paradigm to the world of change and history. We have learned not to chase down every detail but be content with verisimilitude, the kind of thing that should be the case (and in the case of Atlantis, many of the details have already been supplied indirectly by resonances with recent and contemporary history). Human beings do indeed need narrative—but perhaps not too much of it. It can be no coincidence that the *Critias* breaks off when, for the first time, the narrator seems to be about to move into direct speech. The *mimesis* of direct speech was revealed to be an ethical problem at *Republic* 393c11–394b1, and modern discussions of Thucydidean method often linger on the puzzles presented by the composition and "historicity" of his speeches. Ventriloquizing the leaders of the past, let alone the gods, is a formidable task. The narrative ceases at a methodological crux.

Conclusion: Discontinuities

The story of Athens and Atlantis ends in a narrative cataclysm as the narrative breaks off in mid-sentence. I join those who believe that this break-off was caused neither by Plato's sickness, nor incompetence, but was intentional.[39] How else to explain the fact that the cataclysm of form corresponds to one of content? Critias' account tells how history has been punctuated by frequent destructions. Floods and earthquakes periodically require most civilizations to start from scratch, and one of these cataclysms followed the war between Athens and Atlantis. It is for this reason that the Athenians do not know the most significant events in the past of their city (*Timaeus* 22b8–23b6, 25c6–d6; *Critias* 109d2–110a3). Critias' ancient Athens is thus cut off from the present by a cycle of natural cataclysms that call into question the possibility (for most people, according to the Egyptian priests at least) of accurate knowledge of the past and thus of learning from the past. This is a world in which Thucydides' hope that people could learn to recognize the processes of history because of their knowledge of a persistent element, the human thing, is vain. It is thus impossible to generalize and abstract from individual details and events of the past. The contingency of the physical world prevents it. The same contingency caused the absence of the mysterious fourth interlocutor. The same contingency (this time taking the form of political *stasis*) prevented Solon from finishing the account that would have made him a poet to rival Homer and Hesiod (*Timaeus* 21c4–d3).[40] Narrative contingency bars us from hearing a full account of the

---

39 Clay, "Plan," pp. 51–52.
40 Clay, "Plan," pp. 51–52, implies that the narrative ends where it does because this is where Solon's epic broke off, but Critias' comments do not indicate that any of the narrative material he received was lacking.

Atlantis war and whatever it was that Hermocrates was going to narrate (teasingly forecasted at *Critias* 108a5–c7).

The arrangement of the speeches in the *Timaeus* and *Critias* ensures that the reader only ever experiences top-down versions of accounts of happenings in the physical world. Timaeus' cosmology is the result of teleological and *a priori* reasoning. Critias' history is narrated as summaries, for which the Greek is *kephalaia* ("headings"). Both present narratives that might be described in various senses as cyclic but erratic. This irregularity expresses the nature of the cosmos and the language that represents it. Yet top-down narrative ensures that the audience does not lose sight of the big picture. In Critias' cyclic universe contingent historical details (what Alcibiades did or suffered) cannot bother us. All we need is the principle. We should not be deceived by Socrates' desire for narrative motion into thinking that we are going to hear a real history of either the universe or Athens. What we get is a complex experiment in narrative orders as the world of the paradigm is emplotted into the world we think we know.*

*I would like to thank David Blank, Andrew Ford, and Andrea Nightingale for helpful comments on earlier versions of this paper. My research assistant Brian Apicella saved me from some lamentable errors.

18

Timaeus *in Tinseltown: Atlantis in Film*

Jon Solomon

Plato's description of Atlantis in *Timaeus* (21e–25d) and *Critias* (108c–120d) has for over two millennia challenged the critical skills of scholars,[1] titillated the irregular rationalizations of mystics,[2] and fueled the frenzy of uncredentialed quacks.[3] Aside from his considerable impact as a philosopher, Plato should be

---

1 The bibliography on Atlantis is very large and diverse, and well beyond the scope of this paper. But for an annotated translation of Plato's texts on Atlantis (from the *Timaeus* and *Critias*), see Diskin Clay and Andrea Purvis, *Four Island Utopias, being Plato's Atlantis, Euhemeros of Messene's Panchaia, Iamboulos' Island of the Sun, Sir Francis Bacon's New Atlantis*, ser. The Focus Classical Library (Newburyport: Focus Publishing/R. Pullins Company, 1999), pp. 36–41 and 53–97. For the allegorical analyses by Proclus and Iamblichus with modern commentary, see now Harold Tarrant, *Proclus: Commentary on Plato's* Timaeus; *Book I: Proclus on the Socratic State and Atlantis* (Cambridge: Cambridge University Press, 2007), pp. 168–304; and Pierre Vidal-Naquet (Janet Lloyd, translator), *The Atlantis Story: A Short History of Plato's Myth* (Exeter: University of Exeter Press, 2007), pp. 47–50. John Michael Greer, *Atlantis: Ancient Legacy, Hidden Prophecy* (Woodbury: Llewellyn Publications, 2007) offers a contemporary summary. Charles R. Pellegrino, *Unearthing Atlantis: An Archaeological Odyssey to the Fabled Lost Civilization* (New York: Avon Books, 1991) examines the Thera-based approach.
2 For the seventeenth-century Olof Rudbeck, who located Atlantis in Sweden, see David King, *Finding Atlantis: A True Story of Genius, Madness, and an Extraordinary Quest for a Lost World* (New York: Random House, 2006). For Edgar Cayce, see Edgar Evans Cayce, ed., *Edgar Cayce on Atlantis* (New York: St. Martin's Press, 1997). For more contemporary examples, see Harry Turtledove's "alternative history," *Opening Atlantis* (New York: ROC, 2007); and Frank Joseph, *The Atlantis Encyclopedia* (Franklin Lakes: The Career Press, 2005).
3 Henry M. Eichner, *Atlantean Chronicles* (Alhambra: Fantasy Publishing Company, 1971) discusses the work of many of his predecessors. Marion Zimmer Bradley, *The Fall of Atlantis* (Riverdale: Baen Publishing Enterprises, 1983) offers just one of many contemporary examples. There are also many websites, e.g., *http://www.lost-civilizations.net/atlantis.html*.

credited as an imaginative artist, for his vivid and detailed description of the island empire of Atlas created one of the longest enduring otherworld legacies in the Western tradition. In the modern era Plato's original Atlantis has been variously reinterpreted in the popular culture, just as it has been geographically diversified. In the cinema this has inspired Atlantean episodes ranging from such exotic locales as the Sahara desert and the Philippine Islands to subterranean locales under the earth and sea. During the Renaissance Atlantis began to be identified as a utopia, but during the industrialized era this utopia frequently became a technologically advanced Atlantean dystopia ruled by seductive empresses and/ or maniacal tyrants. These elements all work very well in the cinema, far better than the Plato's original literary Atlantis, which by design lacked such suggestive dramatic elements—other than one of the greatest catastrophic climaxes in the history of Western literature.

Figure 1: Kircher's 1665 Atlantis Map

We pick up the thread in 1627 with the posthumous publication of Francis Bacon's *New Atlantis*.[4] Incorporating political, social, and cultural elements from

---

4   Francis Bacon, *New Atlantis: A Work Unfinished* (London: J. H. for William Lee, 1627). Bacon seems to have written the treatise in 1624. Christopher Kendrick, "The Imperial Laboratory: Discovering Forms in 'The New Atlantis'," *English Literary History* 70 (2003), 1021–1042; and J. Weinberger, "Science and Rule in Bacon's Utopia: An Introduction to the Reading of the *New Atlantis*," *The American Political Science Review* 70 (1976), 865–885, concentrate on Bacon's political science; while Bronwen Price, ed., *Francis Bacon's New Atlantis: New Interdisciplinary Essays* (Manchester: Manchester University Press, 2003), with J. C. Davis'

Thomas More's *Utopia*, Bacon seems to locate his Atlantis where America now lies, but it is on an island named Bensalem where science and learning were so highly valued.[5] Bacon in turn inspired the ever resourceful, magnificently prolific, and occasionally credible Jesuit polymath Athanasius Kircher to investigate Atlantis in his 1665 study of the subterranean world.[6] His map of Atlantis (**Figure 1**), which is oriented from the perspective of the South Pole, locates the sunken Atlantis between Africa and America.

After America itself developed into the United States, and as these United States began to look outward at the rest of the world in the late nineteenth century, Ignatius Donnelly, after serving as a Republican Minnesota congressman (1863–1868) and state senator (1874–1878) and before running as the People's Party's vice-presidential candidate (1900), wrote *Atlantis: The Antediluvian World*.[7] Derived in part from the theosophist Helena P. Blavatsky and following close upon the heels of Schliemann's excavations at Troy and Mycenae in the 1870's, this very successful 1882 publication was written when the field of anthropology was in its infancy.[8] Donnelly attempted to synthesize our knowledge of Atlantis, ancient Egypt and Babylon, the Biblical flood, and contemporary ethnology into a single comprehensive history of the world.[9]

---

review in *The Modern Language Review* 100 (2005), 1088–1091, offers a variety of discipline specific approaches. For a critical analysis via a "new" form of the New Historicism, see Robert Appelbaum, *Literature and Utopian Politics in Seventeenth-Century England* (Cambridge: Cambridge University Press, 2002).

5   For a survey of Renaissance and early seventeenth-century conceptions of Atlantis, see Vidal-Naquet, *The Atlantis Story*, pp. 55–77. Giuseppe Mazzotta, *Cosmopoiesis: The Renaissance Experiment* (Toronto: University of Toronto Press, 2001), pp. 53–75, offers the most recent examination of Renaissance utopian concepts. Preceding More's publication was Jacopo Sannazaro's *Arcadia* (1502), which popularized another Renaissance image of an ancient, albeit mythological utopia devoid of human society.

6   Athanasius Kircher, *Mundus Subterraneus* (Amsterdam: Joannes Janssonius & Elizeus Weyerstraten, 1665), I, p. 82.

7   Ignatius Donnelly, *Atlantis: The Antediluvian World* (New York: Harper & Brothers, 1882). The following year in *Ragnarok, the Age of Fire and Gravel* (New York: D. Appleton and Company, 1883), Donnelly attempted to demonstrate that the prehistoric world had been struck by a destructive comet. See Martin Ridge, *Ignatius Donnelly: The Portrait of a Politician* (Chicago: University of Chicago Press, 1962), pp. 196–210.

8   H. P. Blavatsky, *Isis Unveiled* (New York: J. W. Bouton, 1877). Another early source will be discussed in n. 40.

9   I have not been able to identify uncited claims that Donnelly reasoned that if Heinrich Schliemann could find the mythical Troy and Mycenae, then he could "find" the mythical Atlantis; cf. Andrew Collins, *Gateway to Atlantis: The Search for the Source of a Lost Civilization* (New York: Carroll & Graf Publishers, 2000), p. 15. That line of reasoning should probably be attributed to Heinrich Schliemann's grandson, Paul, a leader in the subsequent search for Atlantis, or to the theosophist; cf. "Antiquity of Man," *Theosophy* 13 (1925), 308–311 and 401, where Blavatsky expresses the same reasoning, and H. P. Blavatsky, *The Secret Doctrine*, II (Pasadena: Theosophical University Press, 1997), p. 236. For a different association between

In this history he identified Atlantis as the antediluvian womb from which the human race and its civilizations emerged. His Atlantis was the Garden of Eden, Garden of the Hesperides, and the Elysian Fields of ancient myth, its inhabitants were remembered as the Olympian gods of the Greeks, and it produced the original Indo-European and Semitic peoples along with the first bronze and iron technology. Donnelly concludes in his last chapter (p. 479):

> Science has but commenced its work of reconstructing the past and rehabilitating the ancient peoples, and surely there is no study which appeals more strongly to the imagination than that of this drowned nation, the true antediluvians. They were the founders of nearly all our arts and sciences; they were the parents of our fundamental beliefs; they were the first civilizers, the first navigators, the first merchants, the first colonizers of the earth; their civilization was old when Egypt was young, and they had passed away thousands of years before Babylon, Rome, or London were dreamed of. This lost people were our ancestors; the words we use every day were heard, in their primitive form, in their cities, courts, and temples. Every line of race and thought, of blood and belief, leads back to them.

Meanwhile in Europe, exploiting the dawning mid-nineteenth century fascination with science and technology, Jules Verne blended Atlantis into the inchoate science fiction genre.[10] In his 1869 novel *Vingt mille lieues sous les mers (20,000 Leagues Under the Sea)*, Verne had Captain Nemo's submarine stop for just a single day at the ruins of Atlantis. In the first of only ten paragraphs allotted to this brief sojourn in Atlantis, Verne immediately makes his readers aware of the ancient and subsequent controversies about whether Atlantis had been a real kingdom (II.9):

> L'Atlantide, l'ancienne Méropide de Théopompe, l'Atlantide de Platon, ce continent nié par Origène, Porphyre, Jamblique, D'Anville, Malte-Brun, Humboldt, qui mettaient sa disparition au compte des récits légendaires, admis par Possidonius, Pline, Ammien-Marcellin, Tertullien, Engel, Sherer, Tournefort, Buffon, d'Avezac, je l'avais là sous les yeux, portant encore les irrécusables témoignages de sa catastrophe! C'était donc cette région engloutie qui existait en dehors de l'Europe, de l'Asie, de la Libye, au-delà

Troy and Atlantis, see Eberhard Zangger, *The Flood From Heaven: Deciphering the Atlantis Legend* (New York: William Morrow, 1992).

10   On Verne's ability to popularize this fascination and capitalize upon it in the literary representational mode, see Diana Loxley, *Problematic Shores: The Literature of Islands* (New York: St. Martin's Press, 1990), pp. 15–23.

des colonnes d'Hercule, où vivait ce peuple puissant des Atlantes, contre lequel se firent les premières guerres de l'ancienne Grèce![11]

[Atlantis, the ancient Meropis of Theopompus, the Atlantis of Plato, that continent denied by Origen, Porphyry, Iamblichus, D'Anville, Malte-Brun, and Humboldt, who placed the account of its disappearance among the legendary stories admitted by Posidonius, Pliny, Ammianus Marcellinus, Tertullian, Engel, Sherer, Tournefort, Buffon, and D'Avezac, there before my eyes I now had it and all the undeniable evidence of its catastrophe. The sunken region outside of Europe, Asia, and Libya, beyond the pillars of Hercules, was inhabited by those powerful people, the Atlantides, against whom the first wars of ancient Greece were waged. (This is my own translation of the French.)]

Verne often employed this technique, inserting detailed and often extensive lists of historical or scientific facts with the effect of diverting the narrative function of his fictional prose into the temporary guise of non-fiction.[12] Here he describes Atlantis as a ruin and as background provides this summary of scholars and authors who had probed the mythical kingdom, thereby suggestively confirming its reality.[13]

Verne and Donnelly were instrumental in establishing Atlantis as an historical location, putting it back on the map, as it were, precisely during the period in which the "unknown world" was rapidly disappearing. This transformation of Atlantis from a literary and mythological location into an historical one sufficiently prepared the path for their successors to transform Atlantis from merely an historical location into an extant, even vibrant location in which a drama could transpire. Their most important artistic and historical prototype was Pompeii, the

---

11   This paragraph is not always fully translated in English editions of *20,000 Leagues Under the Sea*, including the online Gutenberg edition *[http://www.gutenberg.org/etext/2488]*: "Atlantis! The Atlantis of Plato, that continent denied by Origen and Humbolt, who placed its disappearance amongst the legendary tales. I had it there now before my eyes, bearing upon it the unexceptionable testimony of its catastrophe. The region thus engulfed was beyond Europe, Asia, and Lybia *[sic]*, beyond the columns of Hercules, where those powerful people, the Atlantides, lived, against whom the first wars of ancient Greeks were waged."

12   Timothy A. Unwin, *Jules Verne: Journeys in Writing* (Liverpool: Liverpool University Press, 2005), pp. 184–186, cites as an example Verne's 1884 novel *L'Archipel en feu* [The Archipelago on Fire] (pp. 33–46), where Verne surveys Greece from antiquity to the War of Independence.

13   Verne may have returned to Atlantis in the short story, "Edom," a science fiction work published posthumously as "*L'Éternel Adam*" [The Eternal Adam] in *Hier et Demain* (*Yesterday and Tomorrow*) (Paris: Collection Hetzel, 1910); see William Butcher, *Jules Verne: The Definitive Biography* (New York: Thunder's Mouth Press, 2006), pp. 298–299. For the question of whether Jules or Michel Verne should be credited with authorship, see Herbert R. Lottman, *Jules Verne: An Exploratory Biography* (New York: St. Martin's Press, 1996), pp. 333–334.

catastrophic destruction of which Edward Bulwer-Lytton employed skillfully in his popularly successful 1834 novel, *The Last Days of Pompeii*. Towards the end of the nineteenth century several additional extremely successful popular novels prepared for the promulgation of Atlantean narratives, particularly Lew Wallace's *Ben-Hur* (1880) and Henryk Sienkiewicz' *Quo Vadis?* (1897). The former, set in the Roman province of Judea during the reign of Tiberius, became a huge best seller by 1896 and spawned several different long-running stage representations and a high-profile film (1907).[14] The latter, set in Rome during the reign of Nero, garnered the 1905 Nobel Prize in Literature for its author and was adapted into a Broadway play in 1900 and into one of the first "blockbusters" in cinematic history—Enrico Guazzoni's 1912 epic.[15]

It was during this period that Atlantis was repopulated and then enters the twentieth century as either a thriving utopia or a dystopia doomed to pay for its sins.[16] In either instance it could now be assumed to be either an ancient land, some of whose remnants or descendants may have survived, or a contemporary Neverland which was reachable so long as one had the means of transportation to get there and the good or bad fortune to stumble upon it.[17] It is methodologically important for us to identify the state of this particular element of the Greco-Roman tradition in the latter half of the nineteenth century because with few exceptions the early cinema embraced or rejected particular parts of the tradition on that basis. The archaeological excavations at Troy by Schliemann and Dörpfeld in the latter third of the nineteenth century, for instance, transformed Homer's Troy from a mythological icon to a headline-making historical ruin, and Troy consequently failed to fire the imaginations of artists at the outset of the new century.[18] Fortunately for our purposes, the repopulation of the Atlantean tradition was taking place just as the twentieth century was beginning. The last few decades of the nineteenth century

---

14   Formed in 1888, the Clark & Cox "Ben-Hur Tableaux" toured the United States for nine years. Shortly thereafter the Klaw & Erlanger Broadway production ran for two decades from 1899. The 1907 Kalem film was not nearly so successful: Kalem was sued by Harper and Brothers, along with the Wallace estate, for copyright violation, and ultimately lost its case—Kalem Co. v. Harper Brothers, 222 U.S. 55 (1911)—before the United States Supreme Court.

15   In addition to Ferdinand Zecca's brief film version of 1904.

16   The most notable of dystopic descriptions could be found in David M. Parry, *The Scarlet Empire* (New York: Bobbs-Merrill, 1906), a veritable response to Edward Bellamy's *Looking Backward, 2000–1887* (Boston: Ticknor & Co., 1888); see the introduction by Jerome M. Clubb and Howard W. Allen in the 2001 Southern Illinois University Press edition of the novel (Carbondale, 2001), pp. vii–xxxiv.

17   I use the word "Neverland" specifically because J. M. Barrie's *Peter Pan, or The Boy Who Wouldn't Grow Up* (1904) premiered during the period in question.

18   By comparison, Homer's Ithaca remained relatively unexplored, so Homer's *Odyssey* was still able to inspire such important works as Joyce' *Ulysses* (1918–1922) and Kazantzakis' *The Odyssey: A Modern Sequel* (begun in 1924). For details, see Jon Solomon, "The Vacillations of the Trojan Myth: Popularization & Classicization, Variation & Codification," *International Journal of the Classical Tradition* 14 (2007), 529–530.

had also produced a number of technological inventions that were providing the rapidly growing consumer market with colorful and vivid pre-cinematic images to absorb, purchase, and enjoy. This included the pulp fiction novels that pervaded the popular culture, and between 1886 and 1920 over two dozen novelists and poets crafted book-length sci-fi and pulp fiction narratives set in Atlantis.[19] And so

---

19   William Walton Hoskins, *Atlantis, and Other Poems* (Philadelphia: Sherman & Co., 1881); Mrs. J. Gregory Smith, *Atla: A Story of the Lost Island* (New York: Harper and Bros., 1886); Edward Taylor Fletcher, *The Lost Island* (Ottawa: A. Bureau & Freres, 1889); John Bachelder, *A.D. 2050: Electrical Development at Atlantis* (San Francisco: The Bancroft Co., 1890); Chauncey Thomas, *The Crystal Button: Or, The Adventures of Paul Prognosis in the Forty-Ninth Century* (Boston: Houghton, Mifflin and Co., 1891); Elizabeth G. Birkmaier, *Poseidon's Paradise: the Romance of Atlantis* (San Francisco: The Clemens Publishing Co., 1892); André Laurie [Paschal Grousset], *Atlantis [The Crystal City Under the Sea]* (Boston: Estes and Lauriat, 1896); Augustus Le Plongeon, *Queen Moo and the Egyptian Sphinx* ([author's edition], 1896); Edward N. Beecher, *The Lost Atlantis; or, "The Great Deluge of All"* (Cleveland: The Brooks Co., 1897); Frona Eunice Wait, *Yermah the Dorado* (San Francisco: William Doxey, 1897); H. H. Buckman, *Merope; or The Destruction of Atlantis* (Jacksonville: The DaCosta Printing and Publishing House, 1898); C. C. Dail, *The Stone Giant: A Story of the Mammoth Cave* (New York: F. Tennyson Neely, 1898); Nancy McKay Gordon, *Her Bungalow; an Atlantian Memory* (Chicago: Hermetic Publishing Co., 1898); Ira C. Fuller, *Mysteries of the Formation of the Earth, the Rising and Sinking of Continents and the Introduction of Man and his Destiny Revealed* (Buffalo: Charles Wells Moulton, 1899); Frank Aubrey (Atkins), *A Queen of Atlantis: a Romance of the Caribbean Sea* (Philadelphia: J. B. Lippincott Co., 1900); Roy Horniman, *The Sin of Atlantis* (London: John MacQueen, 1900); Douglas Erskine (John Buchan), *A Bit of Atlantis* (Montreal: A. T. Chapman, 1900); Charles John Cutcliffe (Wright) Hyne, *The Lost Continent* (New York: Harper and Brothers., 1900); D. Bridgman-Metchim, *Atlantis, the Book of Angels* (London: S. Sonnenschein, Ltd., 1900); Edith Nesbit, *The Story of the Amulet* (London: Ernest Benn, Ltd., 1906); Parry, *The Scarlet Empire*; Joseph M. Brown, *Astyanax: an Epic Romance of Ilion, Atlantis & Amaraca* (New York: Broadway Publishing., 1907); William Kingsland, *A Child's Story of Atlantis* (London: Theosophical Publishing Society, 1908); Reginald H. Bolton, "In the Heart of the Silent Sea," (London: *The Boy's Own Annual*, 1909); Melchior McBride, *A Message From the Gods* (London: Rider & Son, 1910); Elliot O'Donnell, *The Sorcery Club* (London: Rider & Son, 1912); Albert Armstrong Manship, *The Ancient of Atlantis, an Epic Poem* (Boston: Sherman, French & Co., 1915); Thomas Charles Bridges, *Martin Crusoe: A Boy's Adventure on Wizard Island* (London: Geo. G. Harrap & Co., 1920); Marion and Franklin Mayoe, *Doomed: a Startling Message to the People of Our Day, Interwoven in an Antediluvian Romance of Two Old Worlds and Two Young Lovers* (New York: Frank Rosewater Publishing, 1920); and Phylos, the Thibetan (Frederick Spencer Oliver), *Dweller on Two Planets or the Dividing Way* (Los Angeles: Poseid Publishing Co., 1920). This list does not include novels in which the name appears in the title but the story does not take place in Atlantis, e.g., Francis Fuller Victor, *Atlantis Risen: Talks of a Tourist About Oregon and Washington* (Philadelphia: J. B. Lippincott Co., 1891); and Gerhart Hauptmann's *Atlantis: A Novel* (New York: B. W. Huebsch, 1912). On the other hand, to the list can be appended entries in both the popular Tarzan and Buck Rogers series: Edgar Rice Burroughs, *Return of Tarzan* (Chicago: A. C. McClurg, 1915); *Tarzan and the Jewels of Opar* (Chicago: A. C. McClurg, 1918); and *Tarzan and the Golden Lion* (Chicago: A. C. McClurg, 1923); as well as Dick Calkin and Phil Nowland, *Buck Rogers in the City Beneath the Sea* (Racine: Whitman Publishing Co., 1924). Eichner, *Atlantean Chronicles*, pp. 135–210, provides plot summaries for most of these

it is no surprise that Pierre Benoit's 1919 best-selling novel *L'Atlantide* was rendered into film already in 1921.[20]

Beneath art deco drawings of an imposing queenly emblem and symmetrically opposed lions, all in a red orange tint, we read the title:

L'Atlantide

> Roman de
> > Pierre Benoit
> > > adapté à l'écran par
> > > > Jacques Feyder . . .
> [Novel by Pierre Benoit, adapted for the screen by Jacques Feyder . . .]

From a black screen an iris opens to reveal a veiled woman draped in a lengthy robe, sitting seductively on an Egyptian-style bed, accompanied by a lioness (**Figure 2**).

Figure 2: Antinéa—Atlantis' *She*-like femme fatale ruler *(L'Alantide)*

---

publications, though not all his bibliographical material is complete or correct. Verne's *L'Éternel Adam* belonged to this period as well.

20 According to Françoise Marchand *[http://www.atlantide-films.net/filmo/feyder.htm]*, the book was released in February 1919, and by the following autumn the film was already in production. This survey does not include the 1913 Danish Atlantis, directed by August Blom, because it was based on the 1912 Gerhart Hauptmann novel which focuses on a Titanic-like, failed crossing of the Atlantic. I have not seen the film, but according to *http://www.cinemaweb. com/silentfilm/13atlant.htm:* "The title reads: 'In his dreams Dr. von Kammacher walks with his friend, Dr. Schmidt, through the sunken town, Atlantis.' The scenes are brief, and are accomplished by a few double exposures of ghostly images walking through a village."

The woman is Antinéa. *L'Atlantide* tells the story of two Frenchmen, Captain Morhange (Jean Angelo) and Lieutenant de Saint-Avit (Georges Melchior), trapped in the Sahara by Antinéa (Stacia Napierkowska), the descendent of Atlantean royalty. Antinéa, they find out, has loved, murdered, embalmed in gold, and then entombed dozens of lovers. This captivating siren holds sway in the desert oasis, which is the last visible vestige of Atlantis:

Figure 3: The archivist's monologue *(L'Atlantide)*

In a sitting room, the wall behind lined with books, the Archivist (Paul Francheschi), a thin, elderly man wearing a robe and a turban, explains to Morhange and de Saint-Avit where it is that they now find themselves. Cursive subtitles transcribe his monologue (**Figure 3**):

ARCHIVIST
"Vous êtes ici au centre de ce qui ut jadis . . . l'Ile 'Atlantide' . . ."

"You are here in the center of what was formerly the Island 'Atlantis'"

Morhange and de Saint-Avit give each others haughty looks of disbelief and disinterest. The archivist continues:

ARCHIVIST
". . . dans la catastrophe qui engloutit l'Atlantide, neuf mille ans avant notre ére, la partie centrale de l'Ile n'a pas été submergee par les flots . . ."

"... in the catastrophe that sank Atlantis, nine thousand years before our era, the central part of the island was not submerged by the floods ..."

Now the two men are mildly interested. He continues further:

"Après l'assèchement de la mer Saharienne seule a subsisté, cette oasis merveilleuse, isolée à jamais du monde vivant, par sa ceinture d'infranchissables montagnes!"

"After the Saharan sea receded, all that remained was this magnificent oasis, isolated forever from the real world, by this ring of impassable mountains!"

The archivist goes to the library wall behind him and retrieves a sizable tome:

ARCHIVIST
"... et ce Platon, unique exemplaire complet du *Critias* qui subsiste au monde, établit de façon indiscutable que cette partie de l'Ile correspond au Hoggar actuel ..."

"... and this Plato, the only complete copy of the Critias *remaining in the world, establishes indisputably that this part of the Island corresponds with the current Hoggar."*

He turns to the specific page and hands it to one of the visitors, who examines the cover, nods approval, and looks at the text.

ARCHIVIST
"C'est dans cette montagne que Neptune enferma sa bien-aimée Clito, aïeule millénaire d'Antinéa!"

"It is in this mountain that Neptune imprisoned his beloved Clito, the one thousand year-old grandmother of Antinéa!"

That Atlantis had been transformed from an ancient island kingdom to a contemporary desert ruin demonstrates the flexible tradition of Atlantean chronology and geography and its susceptibility to contemporary popular trends. Like several of the previous pulp fiction Atlantises, this Atlantis was ruled by a femme fatale, who works her seductive charms on Morhange and de Saint-Avit in an imaginative desert kingdom, and this particular trend developed in the wake of H. Rider Haggard's 1886/1887 serialized novel, *She*.

The director of *L'Atlantide*, the 36-year old Jacques Feyder, insisted on shooting the film in the Algerian desert (predominantly Touggourt) in grueling

Figure 4 and 5: Contrasting color-tinted shots of Atlantis
depicted as a Saharan-style desert *(L'Atlantide)*

heat over a period of eight months, and he employed orange as well as yellow and blue filters to enhance the hues of the Sahara (**Figures 4 and 5**). This and a liberal use of narrative and visual flashbacks, the latter rendered as fetching miniature films-within-a film, enabled his film version of *L'Atlantide* to evoke a visual nostalgia for an alluring but fatal Atlantis (**Figure 6**). The public adored the film.[21] It appealed to the post-war French demographics of independent women and contemporary Dadaists who sympathized with protagonist victims rejecting home and country for an irrational, unrealizable utopia.[22] *L'Atlantide* played in Paris movie halls for an entire year and helped establish Feyder as one of France's most renowned filmmakers.[23] It prepared the way for such other exotic and now well-remembered films as *The Sheik* (1921), with Rudolph Valentino, and *The Thief of Bagdad* (1924), with Douglas Fairbanks. *L'Atlantide* itself was successfully re-released in 1928.

---

21   Martin Danan, "From a 'Prenational' to a 'Postnational' French Cinema," *Film History* 8 (1996), 72–73, points out that *L'Atlantide* not only withstood the influx of American films into France after World War I but even penetrated the American market. For Feyder as part of the generation of French directors who rejected American-style international films and produced culturally specific films in the colonies, see David H. Slavin, "French Cinema's Other First Wave: Political and Racial Economies of 'Cinéma colonial,' 1918 to 1934," *Cinema Journal* 37 (1997), 23–46.

22   Richard Abel. *French Cinema: The First Wave, 1915–1929* (Princeton: Princeton University Press, 1984), pp. 23–26 and 154–156, puts the film into its historical context.

23   *L'Atlantide* was the first successful writing and directing project by Feyder [née Jacques Frederix], and, even though the native Belgian attempted to shoot next Benoit's *Le Roi lépreux* in Indochina, but was unable to raise the required funds, the success of *L'Atlantide* enabled him to continue for the next two decades with another two-dozen projects. His reputation warranted a period in Hollywood (1929–1934), where he directed Greta Garbo in the German version of O'Neill's *Anna Christie* (1931).

Figure 6: Evoking nostalgia while suggesting a film-within-a film *(L'Atlantide)*

Georg Wilhelm Pabst released his filmization of *L'Atlantide* in Germany in 1932 as *Die Herrin von Atlantis,* and in the United States as *The Mistress of Atlantis* and subsequently as *Queen of Atlantis* and *The Lost Atlantis.*[24] Pabst had recently re-established his reputation in the sound era with his musical adaptation of the Gay/Brecht/Weill *Die 3 Groschen-Oper* (*The Threepenny Opera,* 1931), and the demands of sound era films now required Pabst to employ a variety of writers (Alexandre Amoux, Jacques Deval, Ladislaus Vajda, Miles Mander) to create a screenplay with dialogue for German, French, and English versions. They inserted a scene that takes place in a Parisian cabaret, several scenes with the more humane Clementine (Odette Florelle), and two notable scenes featuring Vladimir Sokoloff playing the tipsy Hetman de Jitomir.[25] To enhance the screenplay and the visuals, which were not nearly as costly or elaborate as those in Feyder's version, Pabst had Wolfgang Zeller compose a musical score with middle-eastern evocations for the domestic scenes, and a rousing descriptive passage for the violent sand storm which brings the film to its fittingly Atlantean cataclysmic close. Focusing on the female lead, Pabst, who had developed a national reputation for developing such young female talent as Greta Garbo and Louise Brooks, chose Brigitte Helm. He did so in part because she was already well established after playing the iconic

---

24 For Eric Rentschler, ed., *The Films of G. W. Pabst: An Extraterritorial Cinema* (New Brunswick: Rutgers University Press, 1990) and citations of other works, see Steven Unger and Tom Conley, eds., *Identity Papers: Contested Nationhood in Twentieth-Century France* (Minneapolis: University of Minnesota Press, 1996), p. 130 n. 2.

25 For Pabst's French period, see Lee Atwell, *G. W. Pabst* (Boston: Twayne Publishers, 1977), pp. 105–109.

automaton in Fritz Lang's *Metropolis* (1927), and in part because in the spirit of German nationalism he was expected to rebound from his previous choice of the American Brooks, which had been heavily criticized. Ultimately Pabst's recreation of the imaginary Saharan Atlantis is secondary to the unrequited, desperate love that men receive from the passionless Atlantean mistress, whose sculpted colossal countenance hauntingly looms over several interior segments.[26]

Atlantis and its mysteries as well as the classical tradition in general had relatively little allure for filmmakers during the 1930's and almost the entirety of the 1940's. The Great Depression inspired only four classically themed productions—DeMille's two Paramount films (*The Sign of the Cross* [1932]; *Cleopatra* [1934]), Goldwyn's Eddie Cantor farce, *Roman Scandals* (1933), and RKO's much adapted version of *The Last Days of Pompeii* (1934)—and thereafter the ancient subgenre remained almost entirely dormant until 1949. There was one notable exception, however, although it was a low-budget production aimed at the matinee crowd. Republic Pictures produced its twelve-part serial, *Undersea Kingdom* (1936), less than two months after the initial release of Universal's successful Flash Gordon serial, and their formula was very much the same.[27] Ray "Crash" (cf. Flash) Corrigan starred as himself "Battling Unknown Terrors in a Land of Peril Under the Ocean's Floor," as advertised in contemporary posters, along with his female companion Diana Compton (Lois Wilde), the counterpart to Gordon's Dale Arden (Jean Rogers). That this was Republic's immediate, knee-jerk response to Universal's Flash Gordon serial suggests that by the 1930's it could be assumed by producers of pulp fiction and B-movies and general audiences alike that Atlantis could be considered the equivalent of outer space, in its distance from modern reality.[28]

Characteristically, this Atlantis featured a society run menacingly by the familiar stereotyped cruel and wicked tyrant.[29] The essential mission of Crash Corrigan, a U.S. naval officer, was to thwart the evil connivings of not Ming the Merciless but Unga Khan (Monte Blue).[30] Near the outset of the first episode

---

26 On Pabst's approach to the theme of losing one's identity by falling in love, see Enrico Groppali, *Georg W. Pabst* (Firenze: La nuova Italia, 1983), pp. 74–85.

27 According to Jack Mathis, *Valley of the Cliffhangers* (Northbrook: J. Mathis Advertising, 1975), pp. 10–17, *Undersea Kingdom* had the lowest production budget ($81,924) of any of the sixty-six chapter plays Republic produced. *Undersea Kingdom*, was the second of them to be produced, following *Darkest Africa* (1936).

28 *Undersea Kingdom* locates Atlantis off the southwest coast of Greenland some 10,000 feet beneath the surface of the sea—a considerably more plausible depth than Verne's 20,000 leagues, which can be calculated to approximately 65,000 kilometers (some 40 miles).

29 For a plot synopsis and fifteen stills, see Robert Malcomson's *Those Enduring Matinee Idols*, 1 (1970/1971), pp. 90–93.

30 On the role of the United States military in the Republic serials, see Richard Maurice Hurst, *Republic Studio: Between Poverty Row and the Majors* (Metuchen and London: The Scarecrow Press, 1979), p. 84.

we learn from a briefing by Professor Norton (C. Montague Shaw) that contrary to "popular opinion," i.e., Plato, the cataclysm that destroyed Atlantis did not occur in one day but over a period of years, during which time the Atlanteans constructed a roof of orichalcum to protect themselves from the deluge.[31] Seconds later we learn that Sharad, the High Priest of Atlantis (William Farnum), whose throne room prominently displays a statue of their protective deity Poseidon, is involved in a power struggle with the usurper, whose ultimate goal is to destroy the upper world by disintegrating it—ironically *via* earthquakes—and sending its ruins to the bottom of the sea, which in turn will make Atlantis rise again. B. Reeves Eason, who had served as associate director for MGM's 1925 version of *Ben-Hur*, co-directed the dozen action-filled episodes.[32] Consequently, chariots abound even though the modern arsenal of this Atlantis includes a remote-controlled "Juggernaut" tank, aircraft appropriately termed "Sky Chariots," a "Magnetic Ray," and the "Invisible Wall of Atom Rays." Chariots appear in Sharad's retinue in four of the first five episodes, and the cliffhanger which brings the third episode, "Arena of Death," to an end depends upon a chariot chase that leads into the fourth, "Revenge of the Volkites." (**Figure 7**)

Undersea Kingdom has had a successful afterlife. In 1950 and/or 1966, towards the beginning or end of the 1949–1966 renascence of films set in the ancient world, National Telefilm Associates (NTA) edited the twelve episodes down to 100 minutes and released it as *Sharad of Atlantis* for television syndication.[33] In 2001 the Roan Group packaged the original twelve episodes onto two DVDs.

The renascence of interest in ancient films just referred to began with Cecil B. DeMille's hugely profitable postwar biblical spectacle *Samson and Delilah* in 1949 and then MGM's big-budget, cast-of-thousands, award-winning, spectacular 1951 Roman epic, *Quo Vadis (sic)*.[34] The first Atlantean progeny this movement engendered was Seymour Nebenzal's version of Benoit's novel,

---

31   Cf. Plato, *Critias*, pp. 116–119, where much of the Atlantis Temple of Poseidon was constructed of orichalcum. For a metallurgical analysis of this quasi-legendary alloy of copper and zinc, see Earle R. Caley, *Orichalcum and Related Ancient Alloys: Origin, Composition and Manufacture, with Special Reference to the Coinage of the Roman Empire* (New York: American Numismatic Society, 1964). The idea of building a dome over Atlantis to save her from the deluge dates back at least to the aforementioned 1895 novel by Paschal Grousset released in an English version as *The Crystal City Under the Sea*.

32   Although it is impossible to reconstruct the relative degrees of influence and coincidence, whereas Eason had worked on MGM's *Ben-Hur*, Farnum had initiated the role of Judah Ben-Hur in the original 1899 Broadway production of Klaw & Erlanger's *Ben-Hur*, which also featured an on-stage chariot race.

33   IMDbPro *[http://pro.imdb.com/title/tt0060969/]* offers the 1966 date; Malcomson's *Those Enduring Matinee Idols*, 93, offers the (July 8) 1950 date.

34   The earlier spate of films of which this was a renascence clustered during the silent era. It included such notable films as the Italian *Quo Vadis?* (1912) and *Cabiria* (1914) as well as MGM's first version of *Ben-Hur* (1925).

Figure 7: Atlantis as seen in a popular 1930's Hollywood film serial, *Undersea Kingdom*

Siren of Atlantis, (1949), which was the sole release by Seymour Nebenzal Productions. Nebenzal had co-produced Pabst's 1932 German and American versions of the *L'Atlantide*, and he seems to have been associated with Atlantis Productions, which released six films in 1942 and 1943.[35] This version featured Maria Montez, the Dominican actress who played nothing but femmes fatales throughout the 1940's.[36]

The 1950's were awash in ancient spectacles and science-fiction horror films.[37] One of the many low-budget versions of the latter was *Fire Maidens From Outer Space* (1956), which employed a characteristic mid-1950's scenario following earthly astronauts to a nearby planet inhabited by anthropomorphic, English-speaking, scantily clad females.[38] These "fire maidens" were the descendants of Atlanteans who escaped from the Platonic deluge by building not a dome of orichalcum (as in *Undersea Kingdom*) but a rocket which allowed them to fly to Jupiter's thirteenth moon.[39] These fire maidens are said also to be the last remaining daughters of Aphrodite: subsequent films set in the various locations and forms of new Atlantises will feature different Olympian divinities.

---

35 *http://us.imdb.com/company/co0003169*.
36 The film was directed by Gregg Tallas, a native-born Greek.
37 One minor exception was Ian Hupp's *Bells of Atlantis* (1952), a twelve-minute cinematic poem in which Anais Nin narrates her "House of Incest" while visual evocations connect the pre-conscious state of the poet and primordial Atlantean fluids.
38 Other examples include *Cat Women of the Moon* (1953), *Missile to the Moon* (1958), and *Space Ship Sappy* (1957)
39 In 1956 only eight moons of Jupiter had been discovered; Leda (Jupiter XIII) was discovered in September 1974.

Fire Maidens From Outer Space, despite the poor quality of its production and the derivative nature of its plot, perpetuated the modern fiction and introduced to the Atlantean film tradition the assumption that the ancient Atlanteans had survived because of their superior scientific and technical skills. It also introduced another enduring element into mid-century films set in Atlantis not anticipated by Plato, Proclus, Bacon, or Donnelly, namely, a man-destroying monster.[40] Here the monster is nothing more than an uncredited stuntman in a simple costume and mask, but it is instrumental in the plot in that by the orders of Prasus (Owen Berry), the lone-surviving Atlantean male, the astronauts must kill it before they can return to earth. "Prasus" is otherwise a place name associated with a temple of Zeus on the island of Crete, but in another type of authenticating nomenclature, the lone fire maiden (Susan Shaw) whom the astronauts take to earth is named Hestia. This will become still another narrative motif in Atlantis films—escaping with at least one of the Atlanteans, usually a woman.[41]

Three years later Twentieth-Century Fox' screen adaptation of Jules Verne's *Journey to the Center of the Earth* (1959) ventured down an extinct Icelandic volcano to the center of our planet, where near the end of the film [1'51"] the protagonists literally stumble upon the lost city of Atlantis (**Figure 8**). The protagonists of Verne's original 1864 novel, *Voyage au centre de la Terre*, do not come upon a subterranean Atlantis, but because the protagonists of *Vingt mille lieues sous les mers* do, and because Disney's *20,000 Leagues Under the Sea* (1954) had not taken advantage of this, the penultimate scene of the Fox film takes place inside a cavern which houses the ruins of Atlantis.

Figure 8: Atlantis imagined as a lost sunken city
(Journey to the Center of the Earth)

40   At the dawn of the last century, C. J. Cutcliffe Hyne's *The Lost Continent* followed in 1906 in the ninth chapter of Edith Nesbit's juvenile novel, *The Story of the Amulet*, included prehistoric beasts, e.g. mammoths, in their descriptions of Atlantis.
41   At the end of *Undersea Kingdom* the catastrophe that destroys Atlantis destroys the Volkite, mobile, mechanized army, but Professor Norton salvages one of the robots so that by reconfiguring it he can make sure that "all mankind will be relieved of the drudgery of physical labor."

As Sir Oliver S. Lindenbrook (James Mason) and his colleagues Alec McKuen (Pat Boone), Carla Göteborg (Arlene Dahl), and others descend a long stone staircase, the camera is framed by Minoan-style, red-painted wood columns as it follows the explorers gazing upon serpentine mosaics, seagreen plaster, red-painted dados, and tumbled or broken fluted column drums. They find a long-abandoned, Pompeian-style, open-air tavern, but the Pompeian section bread, which crumbles in Alec's eager hands, is "stale," and the oysters which they find are dry.[42] Sitting near the temple is a large, bowl-shaped altar stone made of "serpentine . . . a massive form of asbestos," which the modern explorers will use to convey themselves, as they do in Verne's original novel, via a volcanic chimney back to the earth's surface. The city consists of simply this sound-stage set, but as the camera takes us and them through its visual features it slowly reveals that lurking beneath their feet is our second cinematic Atlantean monster, in this instance a giant, man-eating reptile (i.e. a lizard shot through a macro lens). Fortunately for the protagonists, the volcano erupts on cue and both kills the reptile and propels them to freedom (**Figures 9, 10, 11**).

Figure 9: The Atlantean monster menacing over Verne's protagonists in *Journey to the Center of the Earth*.

Figure 10: On cue: The erupting volcano's lava causing the monster's demise, while . . . (*Journey to the Center of the Earth*)

---

42   For Pompeian section bread, see the fresco from the House of the Baker in Pompeii, e.g., *http://www.bbc.co.uk/history/ancient/romans/daily_life_gallery_02.shtml*. Similarly, for oysters as a characteristic food of ancient Rome, see the variety and preferences as well as the bibliography collected in Andrew Dalby, *Food in the Ancient World From A to Z* (London: Routledge, 2003), pp. 145–147. The infamous "oyster and snails" sequence in *Spartacus* (1960) is contemporary with this film.

Figure 11: . . . acting as the force which propels the main characters up through the volcanic chimney—and to safety. (*Journey to the Center of the Earth*)

Two years later producer/director George Pal, remembered today for such science-fiction films as *Destination Moon* (1950), *The War of the Worlds* (1953), and *The Time Machine* (1960), set his next science fiction film in Atlantis. Following a tradition that dates back to the pre-Donnelly period, Pal opens *Atlantis, the Lost Continent* (1961) with a historical explanation of the history of Atlantis and its antediluvian importance (**Figure 12**):[43]

> The camera shows us a hand drawn map of Western Asia, Europe, the Atlantic Ocean, and the eastern shores of the Greenland and South America. A black matte moves east to west as small models of Columbus's three ships sail in that same direction.

---

43 Preceding even Donnelly was John B. Newman, *Origin of the Red Men: An Authentic History of the Peopling of America by the Atlantians and Tyrians; the Origin of the Toltecs, the Description and History of Atlantis . . . Legend of Quetzalcoatl . . . the Aztec City of Sumai, etc.* (New York: J. C. Wells, 1852). At the turn of the next century, Alice and Augustus Le Plongeon, Mayan archaeologists, promulgated a connection between the Mayan and Egyptian civilizations: both were established by survivors of the Atlantean cataclysm, Queen Mu fleeing to Egypt where she was known as the goddess Isis; see James W. Mavor, Jr., *Voyage to Atlantis: The Discovery of a Legendary Land* (Rochester: Park Street Press, 1969), p. 39. The similarities between old and new world cultures mentioned at the outset of *Atlantis, The Lost Continent* are more likely derived from one of two popular sources—Lewis Spence, *Atlantis in America* (London: Ernest Benn, Ltd., 1925) [cf. L. Sprague de Camp, *Lost Continents: The Atlantis Theme in History, Science, and Literature* (New York: The Gnome Press, 1954), pp. 103–122], or William Scott-Elliot, *The Story of Atlantis: A Geographical, Historical, and Ethnological Sketch* (London: Theosophical Publishing Society, 1896); as a publication of the Theosophical Society, the latter was re-issued in 1909 and frequently thereafter, including 1954.

NARRATOR[44]

When Columbus discovered America, a series of mysteries arose to confound the scholars of Europe. Here are two continents completely isolated from each other, yet they simultaneously developed similar cultures. For example, the Mayans measured time on the same principle as the Gregorian calendar of Europe. They used the same signs of the zodiac, the same decimal and mathematical system. They valued silver and gold, using it for jewelry and barter. Another mystery was the banana plant—a native of Asia that cannot be grown from seed, yet Columbus found it thriving in the new world. Elephants at that time did not exist in the Americas, yet their likenesses were cleaved on the walls of prehistoric caves in Peru. The pyramids in Mexico and in Egypt were built on identical architectural principles . . . . But the most significant of all: Mayan and Aztec legends shared with Greek, Hebrew, and Assyrian literature an account of a terrible deluge, a deluge many believed had destroyed the link, the mother empire that had spread her civilization to both sides of the Atlantic. The Greek scholar Plato recorded this theory first over 2000 years ago: there was once another continent . . . Atlantis,

[cymbal crash; orchestral chord; scroll with title]

the lost continent.

[title music]

Figure 12: Narrative prelude: The map that appears before the title sequence of George Pal's *Atlantis, the Lost Continent*.

---

44 The versatile Paul Frees served as narrator.

Daniel Mainwaring was the chief writer for the film, but he developed his screenplay from the 1949 film scenario appended to an operatic libretto, *Atalanta, A Story of Atlantis*, written, illustrated, and scored by Sir Gerald P. Hargreaves.[45] In the Foreword (p. 5), Hargreaves specifically cites both Plato's *Critias* and Donnelly and elaborates upon the latter's thesis by proposing that the Trojan War was connected to the vast Atlantean empire that stretched from Mexico to Babylon. He points out that, according to Homer (*Iliad* 7.442–463), Poseidon constructed the walls of Troy and that Poseidon preceded Atlas as the penultimate ruler of Atlantis: when the Greek army defeated Troy, Atlantis then took its revenge on Greece.

As one of the leading exponents of futuristic, science fiction films filled with gadgetry, Pal developed the post-Baconian Atlantean tradition into an island-state that boasted of a thoroughly advanced, pre-gunpowder, pre-petrochemical, pre-electronic, pre-nuclear technology based on crystals.[46] Pal's Atlantis is a Tomorrow-Land island with the now traditional villainous, albeit blonde, crazed tyrant who seeks world domination. Because *Atlantis, the Lost Continent* was produced during the Cold War era, so Zaren (John Dall), who also played the villainous Glabrus in Stanley Kubrick's contemporary *Spartacus*, delivers some paranoiac, hegemonic, war-mongering dialogue designed to turn the typical 1961 American audience member against him (**Figure 13**).[47]

Figure 13: Championing Atlantean world-domination backed by a
weapon of mass destruction (*Atlantis, the Lost Continent*)

45 Sir Gerald P. Hargreaves, *Atalanta, A Story of Atlantis* (London: Hutchinson, 1949), pp. 123–126. It was Cecil B. DeMille who suggested the book to Pal while the latter was still working at Paramount early in the 1950's.

46 This fiction also dates back at least to the aforementioned 1895 novel by Paschal Grousset.

47 On Pal's antitotalitarianism, see Gail Morgan Hickman, *The Films of George Pal* (South Brunswick and New York: A. S. Barnes & Company, 1977), p. 132. For the relationship between the politics of the period and science fictions films in general, see Errol Vieth, *Screening Science: Contexts, Texts, and Science in Fifties Science Fiction Film* (Lanham and London: The Scarecrow Press, 2001), pp. 49–96.

The camera opens the scene by focusing on a table covered with a relief map looking somewhat like Kircher's map.

ZAREN

Here in the middle of our vast ocean is Atlantis, our mighty empire. But no ocean is vast enough to contain our might, our power, our ambitions. In the past, this one great crystal was enough to supply energy for all our needs. But we cannot live in the past. If we are to survive, we must live in the future, and as our monument to the future I have caused to be readied another, a greater crystal in the belly of the crater—a weapon so powerful that with it, governors of Atlantis, we can become masters of the world!

Azor (Edward Platt), the High Priest of Atlantis, objects.

AZOR

You speak of wicked things, Zaren. Do not listen to these words of war.

ZAREN

It's the destiny of Atlantis to rule the world. Do not the gods themselves call us the race of masters? And isn't it also written: conquer or be conquered?

AZOR

Conquered? By whom?

ZAREN

I shall answer you. One country alone may not be an enemy worth fearing but united with other countries would present a strength that would endanger our very existence.

AZOR

No!

ZAREN

Atlantis cannot take that chance. We must attack them one by one. Our only assurance of survival is to attack and attack soon!

George Pal Productions produced the film in conjunction with Metro-Goldwyn-Mayer, though the studio rushed the project in the midst of a strike and gave it a limited budget. This forced Pal to save money by reusing Roman arena segments from MGM's aforementioned 1950 Roman epic, *Quo Vadis*, and this in turn created a sharp visual contrast between the elaborately designed futuristic sets and the spectacular ancient arena sequence. But it also allowed Pal and his technical and artistic crew to spend a greater portion of the budget on the miniature work used to demonstrate the power of Atlantean crystal technology and the climactic, quasi-authentically Platonic destruction of the island capital as it is rocked by violent seismic activity and immediately swallowed by the sea (**Figure 14**). The conclusion of *Atlantis, the Lost Continent* not only follows Plato's scenario but also satisfies the theme which pervades many such mid-twentieth-century science-fiction, quasi-political film fantasies—that the evil empire of Atlantis must be destroyed.

Figure 14: Witnessing the end of Atlantis (*Atlantis, the Lost Continent*)

Even though the island continent and its entire population are condemned and punished, it is primarily the Atlantean ruling class that is malevolent. This sort of punitive injustice is paralleled in the majority of contemporary, high-profile, studio-produced films set in antiquity. In MGM's *Ben-Hur* (1959) the villainous Messala represents the evil power of Rome which condemns, imprisons, and punishes Judah Ben-Hur as well as Jesus. Similarly, in Universal's *Spartacus* (1960) the Roman Senate enables the villainous Crassus to engineer the destruction of Spartacus' rebellion and decimate Spartacus' slave army. And in the aforementioned *Quo Vadis* it is the villainous Nero who oversees the burning of Rome, (scenes from which are reused for the destruction sequences in *Atlantis, the Lost Continent*).[48] The characteristic Hollywood conception of

---

48 For these and additional ancient films, see Maria Wyke, *Projecting the Past: Ancient Rome, Cinema and History* (New York and London: Routledge, 1997).

ancient empires at the time was that their tyrannical regimes paralleled the Nazi empire of the previous war or the contemporary Soviet empire of the Cold War.[49] Atlantis, albeit a mythical ancient empire and at that a futuristic one, represented the same sort of misdirected leadership and militaristic imperialism, and it had its ultimate destruction already pre-ordained by Plato.[50]

In commercialized artistic popular culture it is common for one successful venture to inspire at least one other and often a number of imitations, and that same year in Italy Centroproduzione SpA released another film set in ancient Atlantis, *Il gigante di Metropolis*. Goldstone Film Enterprises subsequently released the film as *The Giant of Metropolis* in the United States in 1963. Exploiting the anachronism well established in the popularized Atlantis myth, this film falls neatly into the "sword-and-sandal" *peplum* genre so popular in Italy, the rest of Europe, and America in the early 1960's while still maintaining a substructure dependent upon futuristic technology.[51] Not to be outdone by Plato's fictionalized historical chronology, the writers of the film moved the kingdom of Atlantis back in time another 11,000 years to 20,000 BC.[52]

> TITLE CRAWL [Rolling Title]: In 20,000 B.C. . . . on the continente [*sic*] of Atlantis, now lost beneath the waters of the ocean, there lived a people who had developed an amazingly advanced civilization and who ruled all other people on earth . . . Obro, a man born in the east dared to probe the mystery of the city of death.
>
> His gigantic strength and courage were pitted against Yotar, the evil King, in a struggle to the finish . . .
>
> . . . When the scientists of Metropolis attempted to penetrate the secret of death, nature rebelled, causing universal destruction . . .
>
> . . . love alone triumphed . . .
>
> . . . and remained the sole source of life . . .

---

49 Historically speaking, Alfred Rosenberg, *Der Mythus des zwanzigsten Jahrhunderts: eine Wertung der seelisch-geistigen Gestaltenkämpfe unserer Zeit* (Munich: Hoheneichen, 1930), had already connected the lost civilization of Atlantis with the origins of the Aryans.

50 Cf. David Seed, *American Science Fiction and the Cold War: Literature and Film* (Edinburgh: Edinburgh University Press, 1999), especially pp. 8–13 and 94–118.

51 For an overview of the *peplum* sub-genre, see Jon Solomon, *The Ancient World in the Cinema* (New Haven: Yale University Press, 2001), pp. 306–323.

52 IMDb *[http://us.imdb.com/title/tt0054924/fullcredits#writers]* assigns writing credits to Sabatino Ciuffini, Ambrogio Molteni, Oreste Palella, Emimmo Salvi, and Gino Stafford as well as director Umberto Scarpelli.

Typically for the period, a consortium of short-lived production companies from different European countries issued a fourth film version of Benoit's novel in 1961.[53] Typically for the period as well, the film was released in several different countries over a number of years, each time and place with a different title. According to IMDb, this version of *L'Atlantide* appeared in 1961 in Italy as *Antinea, l'amante della città sepolta* and West Germany as *Die Herrin von Atlantis*, and then the U.K. and U.S.A. as *Journey Beneath the Desert* in 1964 and 1967.[54] Such co-productions often credited multiple crews as well, but this version seems to have been adapted and directed for the most part by Edgar G. Ulmer, who had amassed nearly fifty film credits dating back to the 1930's.[55] Queen Antinea was played by Haya Harareet, who had recently made a high-profile appearance as Esther in the 1959 MGM *Ben-Hur*. Updating the scenario which brings the outside visitors to Atlantis, Ulmer has the protagonists crash their helicopter near an atomic testing range. They soon find themselves trapped in the city, but this version of Atlantis was not undersea, buried by water, but underground, buried by sand.

Journey Beneath the Desert:

TAMAL

Atlantis did not disappear without leaving a trace. The legend is wrong in one detail. Atlantis did not sink into the sea: it settled in the sand, the very sand of this desert.

ROBERT (James Westmoreland, aka Rad Fulton)

You want me to believe an entire continent would suddenly sink underground?

TAMAL

Thousands of years ago the ocean reached up to these very mountains. There was one of the most violent earthquakes ever known. When it was over, the ocean had fallen back to its present shores, leaving behind it desert rock, this desolation. And slowly over the centuries the sands covered the ruins of Atlantis, buried them for all time. Those who escaped with their lives fled into these caverns, and what's left of that empire has existed here for centuries and will continue so.

---

53 Compagnia Cinematografica Mondiale (CCM), Fidès, and Transmonde Film.
54 *http://www.imdb.com/title/tt0054641/releaseinfo*.
55 Ulmer's "ancient" films included *L'amante di Paride* (1954) and *Hannibal* (1959). IMDb also gives Giuseppe Masini credit as co-director.

Unger develops Benoit's original plot by subordinating Antinea to Tamal (Amadeo Nazzari), the apparent—and, of course, despotic and cruel—ruler of Atlantis, who is as enamored of Antinea as are the visitors. At the film's end an atomic bomb test brings about the ultimate downfall of the Atlanteans. As in *Fire Maidens From Outer Space*, one Atlantean woman befriends and falls in love with an outsider, so she escapes with him.

Film adaptations of the Atlantis tradition peaked in 1961. That year another European consortium issued *Ercole alla conquista di Atlantide*, released in the United States by Woolner Brothers Pictures, Inc., in 1963 as *Hercules and the Captive Women* and in England as *Hercules Conquers Atlantis*.[56] Directed by veteran action and *peplum* director Vittorio Cottafavi, this is one of the dozens of Hercules films that followed Joseph E. Levine's successful 1959 international release of Pietro Francisci's *Hercules (Le fatiche di Ercole)* (1958).

Hercules and the Captive Women illustrates amply the concept of *contaminatio* as applied to contemporary cinema, that is, the commingling of mythological names, events, and motifs to give quasi-historical substance to a recombined mythical narrative.[57] Early on in *Hercules and the Captive Women*, Hercules (Reg Park) consults Teiresias—the Theban prophet best known from Homer's *Odyssey* and Sophocles' *Oedipus Tyrannus*—and hears about "a peril from afar." Hercules and his son Hylus *(sic)* (Luciano Marin) set out towards Atlantis—the ancient Hylas accompanied Hercules on the quest for the golden fleece—with the King of Thebes, Androcles (Ettore Manni)— a literary character best known for his reciprocally beneficial relationship with a lion—and soon encounter the metamorphosing sea god Proteus (Maurizio Coffarelli)—another character best known from Homer's *Odyssey*. Hercules slays Proteus to free Ismene (Laura Altan [Efrikian])—whom we know as the daughter of Oedipus and sister of Antigone, but here is the daughter of Queen Antinea (Fay Spain). Antinea had planned to have Ismene killed in order to satisfy a prophesy and thereby save her kingdom—a mythological motif known best in the story of Andromeda and her mother Cassiopeia. Later in the film we learn that not Poseidon but Uranus is the chief divinity of the Atlanteans, and that Antinea annually sacrifices male children to a rock sacred to him—a motif probably derived from the influential Italian silent film, *Cabiria*. Hercules then foments a rebellion à la Spartacus to rid the island of its tyrannical queen, although a climactic volcanic explosion—one thinks of Pompeii—apparently kills everyone except

---

56   The consortium consisted of SpA Cinematografica and Comtoir Français du Film Production.

57   The term *contaminatio* in its ancient context has been much discussed, e.g., Obafemi Kujore, "A Note on Contaminatio in Terence," *Classical Philology* 69 (1974), 39–42; and Walter R. Chalmers, "Contaminatio," *The Classical Review* 7 (1957), 12–14.

Hercules, Androcles, Hylas, and Hylas' new love Ismene—another Atlantean who escapes to the outside world.

Unlike the Yotar character invented for *The Giant of Metropolis*, these characters all have a pedigree commencing in the ancient Greek mythological or literary corpora. By conflating Hercules, Hylas, Teiresias, Proteus, Ismene, and Androcles as well a several narrative motifs and then associating them with the kingdom of Atlantis, Cottafavi and his team of writers create in *Hercules and the Captive Women* an elaborate matrix that offers a reasonable amount of familiarity and a certain degree of mythological authenticity. Educated members of the audience generally find such contamination to be ludicrous (or camp), but they are not the target demographic. Less discriminating audiences tend to enjoy the action and the novel narrative assembly, and Cottafavi is following a well-established tradition in Italian theater that dates back to Renaissance drama and Baroque opera.[58]

The sword-and-sandal genre was nearing its end when still another co-production, this one Italian/Egyptian, issued the Technicolor, Techniscope *Il conquistadore di Atlantide* (1965), released the same year in the United States as *Conqueror of Atlantis* and in England as *Kingdom of the Sand*.[59] The opening of the film shows us a shipwrecked Heracles *(sic)* (Kirk Morris) being brought ashore in North Africa. Here he meets Princess Virna (Luciana Gilli), whom he will eventually have to rescue from nomadic desert warriors. It is not until the nineteenth minute that we learn that these nomads are "phantoms" from the "Mountains of the Dead Ones," and it is more than half way through the film that we finally venture inside the desert mountains to meet Ramir (Piero Lulli), the crazed Atlantean scientist, who explains that Virna has been chosen to succeed as the twenty-fourth queen of Atlantis (**Figure 15**). The final cataclysm that destroys this reincarnation of the desert Atlantis Heracles himself creates by pulling several giant levers in Ramir's cavernous laboratory, which characteristically for the genre seems to have a doomsday switch with no automatic shut-off valve.[60]

---

58   The story of Giasone *(Jason),* for instance, the Cavalli opera which premiered in Venice in 1649 and became one of the most popular Italian operas of the seventeenth century, follows very much the same methodology with the characters of the various strains of the myths involving Hercules, Jason, Medea, Hypsipile, and Aegeus, while adding an additional character named Orestes. There were no operas set in ancient Atlantis, other than Hargreaves' unperformed work, until Manuel de Falla's *Atlántida,* which was derived from Jacinto Verdaguer's Catalan epic of 1877. But Falla died before completing this "scenic cantata," and excerpts from it were not performed until 1961 or staged until 1962. Interestingly, these were the years which also produced a number of films set in Atlantis.

59   The co-production came from the Roman company P. C. A. Produzione Film and Cairo's Copro Film (The Egyptian General Company for International Film Production).

60   Also released in 1965 was Domenico Paolella's *Operation Atlantis,* aka *Agente 003, Operacion Atlantida,* a James Bond knock-off set again in a radioactive African desert.

Figure 15: Camp meets beefcake in the Atlantis of the
Italian *peplum (Conqueror of Atlantis)*

After the era of sword-and-sandal films ended in the mid-1960's, Atlantis resurfaced during the 1970's in the Philippines. This distant relocation is not as far-fetched nor implausible as it may at first seem, and perhaps at the avant-garde of late-twentieth-century globalization it was visionary to move 1973's *Beyond Atlantis* to the Philippine Archipelago. As we have seen, Atlantis was an imaginary continent that had already been relocated to such divergent eco-systems as those beneath the Atlantic Ocean and the Sahara desert, and we have also seen survivors from the Atlantean deluge flee to a moon of Jupiter. Moreover, from the American and European perspective the Philippines do lie to the far west, as Francis Bacon would have it.[61] But more importantly, director Eddie Romero, one of the most prolific and internationally recognized Filipino filmmakers, had recently made several films aimed at the low end American market, most noticeably *Black Mama, White Mama* (1972), starring Pam Grier and cult-figure Sid Haig. For *Beyond Atlantis* he secured the services of Patrick Wayne, the son of John Wayne. Wayne senior had been recognized as a popular symbol of positive American-Philippine relations ever since the release of *Back to Bataan* (1945). Wayne junior, his unremarkable Hollywood film career in decline, had begun working in television and off-shore productions. *Beyond Atlantis* therefore provided a convenient opportunity for both Romero and Wayne. Nonetheless, it is particularly interesting that out of all the subjects the

---

61 For South Sea locations, see Reinhold Bichler, "Atlantis," *Brill's New Pauly,* I (2006), pp. 373–375.

Western narrative tradition had to offer a film designed to blend the Philippine and American traditions, Romero chose to develop the story of Atlantis.

Rejecting the high-tech, learned Atlanteans of earlier films, and conflating (as in *Fire Maidens From Outer Space*) Hellenic Atlanteans with equally Hellenic Amazons, writers Charles Johnson and Stephanie Rothman required the Atlantean princess Syrene (Leigh Johnson) to mate with an outsider. In Romero's contribution to the film tradition of Atlantis, the eyes of the Atlantean natives have become "pearlized"; that is, the Atlanteans dive so deeply and so frequently into the sea to gather so many pearls that their eyes bulge and shine like pearls. Pearlization apparently happens only to the dark-skinned, lower class Atlanteans, who also provide occasional meals for the deadly piranha lurking in the local pond. The ruling class, light-skinned, aristocratic Atlanteans, like their pearlized counterparts, are quasi-amphibious. They swim underwater for long periods of time without taking a breath, especially Syrene, the blond Atlantean princess. Sparagmos is an element common enough in B-horror films, and this accounts for the piranha, but B-horror films also often provide their audiences with at least one sequence in which an academic provides an expert and authoritative explanation for what seems to be a scientific or historical impossibility. In *L'Atlantide* it was the archivist who did so, in *Undersea Kingdom* it was Professor Norton, and in *Fire Maidens From Outer Space* it was Prossus. In *Beyond Atlantis* Dr. Katherine Vernon (Lenore Stevens) offers a pseudo-historical justification to Vic Mathias (Patrick Wayne) as to how and why bronze-age Minoans might have migrated so far from the Mediterranean:

> Dr. Vernon sits on a beach, Atlantean huts and pine trees behind her. Vic offers her some coffee from the campfire and sits down beside her. She is writing in her notebook.
>
> DR. VERNON
> I saw the exact duplicate of this mask today.
>
> VIC
> At this temple in the jungle?
>
> DR. STEVENS
> Now the one we had at the museum was found on one of the islands of Crete about a half century ago. It's carved in the style of the Minoans. They lived about 2000 BC.
>
> VIC
> Are you making a connection?

DR. STEVENS
I'd like to. They could be descendants. The Minoans supposedly
lived on an island that sank into the sea—Atlantis.

VIC
Are you saying these people migrated here?

DR. STEVENS
It's just a conjecture. Atlantis had a similar climate.

VIC
How do you account for their eyes?

DR. STEVENS
I don't know. Environment possibly. Or a form of genetic mutation brought about by inbreeding.

Of course it is highly implausible that 2,000 years ago Minoans, i.e., Cretan
Atlanteans, made their way to the tropical Philippines, especially for the
improbable reason that it had a similar climate, which it does not.[62] But neither
plausibility nor authenticity applies when conjecturing about the diaspora of
the Atlanteans after the great deluge.

Of greater interest here is the timely introduction of Dr. Stevens' assumption
that the Atlanteans could be related to the ancient Minoans of Crete. After all,
the idea that the historical volcanic explosion of the island of Thera/Santorini
north of Crete was the cataclysmic event to which Plato referred in his *Timaeus*
and *Critias* was unknown to Bacon, Kircher, Donnelly, and the pulp fiction
writers of the early twentieth century. Spyridon Marinatos had first proposed
the idea in 1939, but it was only in 1947–1948 that a Swedish oceanographic
expedition first charted volcanic debris on the Mediterranean floor, and it was
not until the 1960's that subsequent expeditions from Columbia University
and the Woods Hole Oceanographic Institute began to provide scientific data
supporting the idea that the destruction of the Minoan sites on Crete may
have been attributable to the volcanic destruction of Thera.[63] Mary Renault's
novel *The King Must Die* (1958), which describes a violent earthquake on Crete
as the spark that incited the peasant rebellion led by the Athenian Theseus

---

62 It should be noted, however, that Plutarch [*Life of Sertorius* 8] describes two Atlantic
islands specifically in regard to their idyllic climate.
63 Spyridon Marinatos, "The Volcanic Destruction of Minoan Crete," *Antiquity* 13 (1939),
425–439. For the scientific expeditions, see, for instance, "Atlantis Beneath the Vineyard,"
Science News 92 (1967), 125–126.

against the Knossian palace guard, helped promulgate the process among the demographic of lay readers.[64] Meanwhile the Thera/Atlantis hypothesis was growing in acceptance also among a handful of scientists and classicists. In 1960 Angelos Galanopoulos, in "The Origin of the Deluge of Deukalion and the Myth of Atlantis," proposed to the International Union of Geodesy and Geophysics that Atlantis was the island of Stronghyli—the name of the intact predecessor of Thera/Santorini.[65] In 1966 J. Walter Graham, while reviewing Fritz Schachermeyr's *Die minoische Kultur des alten Kreta* (1964), wrote, "The hypothesis that Crete is indeed the prototype of the 'Lost Atlantis', and that the irreparable catastrophe was the result of violent tidal waves and earthquake shocks accompanying the explosion of Thera is an attractive one."[66] Marinatos' scientific excavation of the Theran site of Akrotiri then commenced in 1967, the First International Congress on the Volcano of Thera was held in September 1969, and its proceedings were published in 1971.[67] Dr. Stevens, then, had clearly kept up with the latest developments in her field![68]

The Atlanteans are again portrayed as an evil civilization in 1978's *Warlords of Atlantis* and 1983's Italian-made *Raiders of Atlantis (I predatori di Atlantide)*. The former film was created by specialists in lost civilizations, so to speak. Producer John Dark and Director Kevin Connor had previously realized Edgar Rice Burroughs' Pellucidar, the land inside the hollow surface of the earth, in a 1974 cinematic version of his 1914 novel, *The Land That Time Forgot*; and they realized Burrough's subterranean land of the 1918 Caspak series in *At the Earth's Core* (1976) and *The People That Time Forgot* (1976). The Atlantis of *Warlords of Atlantis* they site out in the Atlantic a little beyond the Bermudas, capitalizing on the Bermuda Triangle panic that gripped the Western world in the mid-1970's, particularly after the publication of Charles Berlitz' *The Bermuda Triangle* in 1974.[69] Berlitz' book

---

64   Mary Renault, *The King Must Die* (New York: Pantheon, 1958), pp. 293–309.

65   Angelos G. Galanopoulos, "The Origin of the Deluge of Deukalion and the Myth of Atlantis," *Athens Archaiologike Hegaireia* 3 (1960), 226–231. Cf. Dorothy B. Vitaliano, "Geomythology: The Impact of Geologic Events on History and Legend with Special Reference to Atlantis," *Journal of the Folklore Institute* 5 (1968), 5–30.

66   J. Walter Graham, review of Fritz Schachermeyr *Die minoische Kultur des alten Kreta, The American Journal of Philology* 87 (1966), p. 363.

67   A. Kalogeropoulou, ed., *Acta of the 1st International Scientific Congress on the Volcano of Thera, held in Greece, 15th–23rd September, 1969* (Athens: Archaeological Services of Greece, General Direction of Antiquities and Restoration, 1971).

68   Prossus in *Fire Maidens From Outer Space* suggests that the architecture the astronauts have identified on Jupiter XIII is not from "the late Minoan period" but "late Atlantis; the two periods of architecture are often mistaken for each other."

69   Charles Berlitz, *The Bermuda Triangle* (Garden City: Doubleday, 1974). Among the numerous books contemporary with Berlitz' book and *Warlords of Atlantis* were Adi-Kent Thomas Jeffrey, *The Bermuda Triangle* (New Hope: New Hope Publishing Co., 1973); Richard Winer,

climbed to the top of The New York Times Best Seller List on February 2, 1975, ultimately sold over twenty million copies, and was awarded the Dag Hammarskjöld International Prize for Non-Fiction in 1976.[70] In 1938 Edgar Cayce had predicted that Atlantis would be discovered near Bimini in the late 1960's, and, *mirabile dictu*, on September 2, 1968 Dr. J. Manson Valentine, Honorary Curator of the Science Museum of Miami, identified the subterranean stone mass off the coast of North Bimini Island in the Bahamas as a remnant of Atlantis.[71]

The action of *Raiders of Atlantis* takes place appropriately off the coast of Miami, where the radiation caused by government attempts at raising a sunken Russian submarine disturbs the nautical equilibrium to such an extent that the domed island of Atlantis rises to the surface, bringing with it a gang of punk-style, motorcycling Atlanteans. Similar to its prototypes, the popular post-apocalyptic *Mad Max* (1979) and *Mad Max 2: The Road Warrior* (1981), *Raiders of Atlantis* is filled with a-historical action. It offers little Atlantean lore other than the characteristic statement from the resident scientist [57"] that long ago a "solar fire, probably a kind of nuclear explosion" had caused the destruction of Atlantis.

Readers of Plato will much appreciate the first exchange about Atlantis that takes place in *Warlords of Atlantis* (1978):

> CHARLES (Peter Gilmore)
> Atlantis!
>
> GREG (Doug McClure)
> Ah, c'mon, Charlie! That's a legend.

The Devil's Triangle (New York: Bantam Books, 1974) and *The Devil's Triangle 2* (New York: Bantam Books, 1975); Martin Ebon, ed., *The Riddle of the Bermuda Triangle* (New York: New American Library, 1975); George Johnson and Don Tanner, *The Bible and the Bermuda Triangle* (Plainfield: Logos International, 1976); William L. Wisner, *Vanished—Without a Trace!* (New York: Berkeley Publishing Co., 1977); and Ian Thome, *Bermuda Triangle* (Mankato: Crestwood House, 1978). In 1975 Lawrence David Kusche's *The Bermuda Triangle Mystery—Solved* (New York: Harper and Row, 1975) succeeded only in continuing the controversy.

70   It was in 1984's very popular *Ghostbusters* [41"] that Winston [Ernie Hudson] was asked during his job interview if he believed "in the theory of Atlantis."

71   For details of this and various explorations in the Atlantic, see Robert F. Marx and Dimitri Rebikoff, "Atlantis at Last?" *Argosy* 369 (December, 1969), 23–27. *Atlantis, the Lost Civilization* (1995), an episode of the "Ancient Mysteries" documentary series produced for the Arts & Entertainment Network, contains diving footage of the Bimini wall, identifying it as a remnant of Atlantis. In comparison, Globe Cinema's 1978's documentary, *The Lost City of Atlantis*, had traced the legend to pre-Colonial America.

CHARLES

No, no, no! Not just the sunken ruins of a city but a living civilization.

ATMIR (Michael Gothard)

That is Troy, the third city. We can rest there.

CHARLES

A third city? What happened to 1 and 2?

ATMIR

They are lost beneath the waters of the outer limits—forever . . .
Eventually the five remaining cities will also disappear.

CHARLES

Seven cities to Atlantis? You know, the Greeks always claimed there were nine.[72]

ATMIR

Plato was not always right!

These Atlanteans differ from the previous cinematic Atlanteans in that they did not escape the deluge by fleeing, as in *Fire Maidens From Outer Space*, to a once unknown moon of Jupiter. Quite the opposite, we next learn from Atsil, Inquisitor for the Council of the Elite (Cyd Charisse), that they are actually Martians who have stopped on earth to refresh themselves in the ocean but soon found our planet to be so primitive that they, a master race, plan to control ours. One of the means by which they plan to do this is by implanting gills in the humans they have captured. Another is to modify the brain of the most intelligent humans, and we eventually [1'01"] see Charles wearing a device on his head which enables him to achieve "the full creative energies of twentieth century science . . . [envisioning] a utopia, a perfect society" powered by neutron technology. This segment is realized by superimposing film and sound recordings of Nazi rallies, which were not only inexpensive to employ but equally clear in their imagery: Atlanteans are evil-minded, militaristic, and power hungry. As in the Burroughs-derived films of Dark and Connor as well as several of the aforementioned Atlantis films, monsters menace this Atlantis as well. (The popular tradition of Atlantis now easily accommodates this.) And once again the Atlanteans have superior firepower, but despite much *Sturm*

---

72 Cf. Plato, *Timaeus*, 119b, where there are ten.

und Drang, all their explosives conveniently miss the favored earthlings, who ultimately escape in a dinghy.[73]

Alien Atlanteans coming to earth to colonize and dominate provide also the narrative essence of *Alien From L.A.* (1988). We are told that the gigantic Atlantean spaceship which transported them to earth sank into the ocean after a cataclysmic earthquake, and that is why the surviving Atlanteans established their earth colony well beneath the earth's surface. The heroine protagonist of the film, Wanda Saknussemm (Kathy Ireland), bears the surname coined by Jules Verne for his 1864 novel *Voyage au centre de la Terre*, and veteran director Albert Pyun used the English title *Journey to the Center of the Earth* for a veritable sequel in 1989. In *Alien From L.A.* Pyun creates a totalitarian Atlantean society with ubiquitous governmental P.A. announcements and informational video screens (à la George Lucas' *THX 1138* [1971]) set amidst a dark and dusty soundstage characteristic of the "future noir" films developed a few years earlier by Ridley Scott in *Alien* (1979) and *Blade Runner* (1982).[74] In *Warlords of Atlantis* the Martian Inquisitor had informed the earthlings that *they* were aliens in Atlantis; here the Atlanteans deny the existence of the surface world entirely and pursue the earthlings as alien spies.

The following year the sequel evolved because Pyun was hired by Menahem Golan and Yoram Globus of Golan-Globus Productions to complete the problematic production of *Journey to the Center of the Earth*, which had fallen into dormancy. Pyun reengineered the script into a near sequel to *Alien From L.A.* and reused some of his former cast, but he moved the entrance portal in this version of his Atlantean totalitarian state from a non-descript archaeological excavation in North Africa to a cave in his native Hawaii. Uniquely, this film ends joyfully as Atlantis joins into global retail capitalism and begins to admit surface people for commerce and tourism.

Once they had been equated with aliens, late-twentieth-century cinematic Atlanteans could begin to appear in various kinds of non-anthropomorphic

---

73   The Bermuda Triangle craze produced as well NBC's network television series *Man From Atlantis*, starring Patrick Duffy. It aired during the 1977/1978 season in seventeen episodes, including #7: "The Hawk of Mu" and #11: "Crystal Water, Sudden Death." The same era inspired Irwin Allen to attempt a return to primetime television with his pilot, *The Return of Captain Nemo*, aired first on CBS March 8, 1978, wherein Captain Nemo [José Ferrer], revived after cryogenic suspension, battles against Tibor [Horst Buchholz], King of Atlantis. The three-hour, three-part pilot was not picked up, though Allen marketed it later that same year as a theatrical release in Europe, e.g., as *Abenteuer in Atlantis* in West Germany and Austria, and *Capitan Nemo, missione Atlantide* in Italy. Preparing the way, Deutsche Film had already produced the dozen, 24-minute, time-traveling episodes of the East German *Unterwegs nach Atlantis*, based on Johanna von Koczian's *Abenteuer in der Vollmondnacht* and *Der geheimnisvolle Graf*, which aired July 28, 1977.

74   For the term, see Paul M. Sammon, *Future Noir: The Making of Blade Runner* (New York: HarperCollins Publishers, 1996).

body forms—the degree of non-anthropomorphism proportionately related to the film's budget. Moving beyond Queen Antinea of the numerous adaptations of Benoit's novel, the alluring women of *Fire Maidens From Outer Space*, the blond Syrene of *Beyond Atlantis*, and the latter's pearlized-eyed Minoan refugees, 1992's *Humanoids From Atlantis* offers up a different kind of body type. There is actually only one humanoid in this film, not several, which may have been one of the many reasons the Movie Police deemed this film worthy of their motto: "Movies so bad . . . there ought to be a law!" But producer, director, editor, actor J. R. Bookwalter specializes in the low-budget horror, zombie, and drug genres, and here he reduces the high-minded, high-tech culture of the received Atlantis tradition to a grunting actor wearing a shabby humanoid suit while attacking two people in a car.

Much more imaginative was the Atlantization of Gamera. Fire-breathing and fanged, this famed, flying Japanese turtle, which was first unveiled in 1965's *Daikaiju Gamera* (released in the United States in 1966 as *Gammera [sic] the Invincible*), takes on an Atlantean pedigree in 1995's *Gamera, Guardian of the Universe*. The original Gamera, like his cinematic exemplar Godzilla, was unleashed from the earth as a result of an atomic explosion. This 1995 installment, the ninth Gamera film, contains the *de rigueur* scientific explanation segment to account for the connection between the suddenly emergent monster and ancient Atlantis:

> FATHER (Akira Onodera)
> Those little trinkets are made of a metal unlike anything I have ever seen . . . . The comma shape may have some relation to symbols used in medieval Japan. Plato mentioned a civilization that used a metal called orichalcum. This could be it.

> DAUGHTER (Ayako Fujitani)
> Hey! Isn't that the metal they used in Atlantis . . . the lost continent? It sank in the ocean eons ago . . . .

> BROTHER
> But we found the atoll in the Pacific.

> FATHER
> If such a continent really existed, then the legend could have spread all around the world. One version was Atlantis, another Mu.

> BROTHER
> You mean that monster was created by men?

FATHER
Well how else would you explain the existence of a turtle that
flies like a flying saucer?

This group of films dating back to 1956's *Fire Maidens From Outer Space*
and culminating with 1995's *Gamera, Guardian of the Universe* was created
by an older generation of filmmakers, foreign production companies, and/or
low-budget specialists. The 1970's brought a newer generation of Hollywood
directors—Coppola, Spielberg, Lucas—who created such widely acclaimed and
financially successful blockbusters as *The Godfather* (1972), *Jaws* (1975), *Star
Wars* (1977), and *Raiders of the Lost Ark* (1981), but had not yet borrowed from
the Atlantis tradition. When Ron Howard, one of their pupils, finally did so in
his popular *Cocoon* (1985), his film reexamined the hostile relationship between
humans and Atlanteans that had served as a basic assumption for most of the
previous films. Based on David Saperstein's 1985 novel of the same name, the
cinematic adaptation was delayed for several years as the original producer
Michael Douglas waited for director Robert Zemeckis to complete *Romancing
the Stone*. But upon screening the rough cut of the latter and thinking it would
be an utter failure at the box office, Douglas fired Zemeckis the next morning.[75]
The project eventually ended up in the hands of producers Richard D. and Lili
Fini Zanuck, and David Brown, and after six major overhauls of the script,
and hiring Ron Howard to direct, the film was finally put into production.[76]

In the release version of *Cocoon*, as in Saperstein's novel, we see again that
Atlanteans travel as easily in outer space as they do underwater. Here a small
group of aliens from the planet Anterea in the constellation Scorpio return to
Earth to recover the fellow Atlanteans they had left behind 10,000 years ago
after the great earthquake and Platonic deluge.[77] The audience discovers their

---

75 Mark Horowitz, "Back With a Future," *American Film* 13 (1988), 32–35. Released in
1987, *Romancing the Stone* turned out to be a very popular film, earning over $100 million
worldwide, and generating a sequel, *The Jewel of the Nile* (1984).

76 Saperstein told Skip Press in *The Complete Idiot's Guide to Screenwriting*[2] (New York: Alpha
Press, 2004), pp. 227–228, that "five writers were hired at various times to adapt his novel. The
fifth one, Tom Benedek, called Saperstein and said he didn't like any of the previous drafts; he
simply planned to adapt the story the way it was laid out. And Benedek got the sole screenplay
credit." See also Aubrey Solomon, *Twentieth Century-Fox: a Corporate and Financial History*
(Metuchen: The Scarecrow Press, 1988), pp. 202–203. Howard, who had been working on his
own (unfunded) project, was not involved in the writing; see Barbara Kramer, *Ron Howard:
Child Star and Hollywood Director* (Springfield: Enslow Publishers, Inc., 1998), pp. 56–57.

77 In the novel (David Saperstein, *Cocoon* [New York: The Berkley Publishing Group, 1985],
pp. 12–16), the Antareans called Atlantis "Antares Quad Three," and their Atlantic island
colony on earth was destroyed by a chunk of Saturn that had broken loose and passed too close
to the earth. I have not been able to determine if the inspiration for this particular apocalyptic
event was the discovery of the Chicxulub crater in the Yucatán in 1978 and publicized in 1981.

alien nature when Jack Bonner (Steve Guttenberg) leers through a peephole to watch Kitty (Tahnee Welch) undress: she thoroughly shocks us when, after taking off her clothes piece by piece and then reaching behind her head, she removes her human skin to air out her dazzlingly bright alien body form (**Figures 16 and 17**).

Figure 16: Unzipping the Atlantean: moving from the human to . . . *(Cocoon)*

Figure 17: . . . reveal the alien *(Cocoon)*

Despite this striking segment early on in the film, *Cocoon's* Atlanteans are portrayed as members of an advanced and pacifist culture of the type so admired by Bacon. We have examined numerous examples of how the mid-twentieth-century popular culture tended to think of the rulers or residents of Atlantis as being either power-crazed or monstrous, neither type being beneficial or salubrious for the human race. But *Cocoon* follows in the tradition of the new wave of alien films that had emerged with Spielberg's mega-hits *Close Encounters of the Third Kind* (1977) and *E.T.: The Extra-Terrestrial* (1982). In both these films the aliens were much more benign, and in *Cocoon* the powerful life force of the Atlanteans invigorates the elderly at a retirement home. Even after some second-act property disagreements and the loss of an Atlantean life, in the third act the generous Atlanteans offer thirty elderly Americans permanent utopia on their planet.[78]

Cocoon helped to establish the relatively benign tone for several of the Atlantean films that surfaced around the turn of the next century. In 2001 Scott Hicks directed William Goldman's film adaptation of Stephen King's 1999 novella, *Hearts in Atlantis*. Typical of King's output in that period, the story is set not in the kingdom of Atlantis but in an American town of the early 1960's where there seems to dwell, particularly in the character of Ted Brautigan (Anthony Hopkins), the benign magic of Atlantis. Brautigan himself aptly describes this aura as he delivers the author's message nearly one hour into the film:

> We're so happy when we're young. It's like being in Atlantis: every-thing is magical. Then we grow up, and our hearts split in two.

The most prominent of this type of Atlantean film was Disney's 2001 ani-mated feature *Atlantis, the Lost Empire*.[79] The Disney Atlantis was a peaceful, sub-Atlantic Water-World decaying under the rule of the aged King Kashekim Nedakh (voice of Leonard Nimoy). His very young-looking but 8,800 year old daughter, Princess Kidagakash (voice of Cree Summer), hopes that the explorers from the surface will help rejuvenate Atlantis, but Commander Lyle Tiberius Rourke (voice of James Garner) hopes to exploit the kingdom for its mineral wealth. (The exploitation of Atlantis for mineral wealth was also a plot device in *Beyond Atlantis*.) As in *Cocoon*, the influence of Spielberg prototypes is evident in the opposition between youthful naïve optimism and cynical establishment greed. This comes to a climax in the quest for the all-powerful "Heart of Atlantis" crystal—à la Paschal Grousset's novel and George Pal's film—which has the power to rejuvenate the kingdom in a final burst of animated splendor.

Atlantis, the Lost Empire makes numerous attempts at what might be considered legendary authenticity. Plato's account is cited frequently, the aerial overviews of Atlantis rigorously contain the walls and canals Plato attributed to the kingdom, and Disney hired Marc Okrand, the creative linguistic specialist who had designed the Klingon language for the Star Trek universe, to develop a plausible Atlantean language, evidenced by the names of the aforementioned

---

78 Demonstrating the equation between space travel and Atlantis at the time was NASA's Space Shuttle "Atlantis," which made its maiden flight on August 8, 1985.

79 The release of the film was accompanied by the publication of Kyle Van Mitchell's "revised and updated edition" of Preston B. Whitmore, *The Mythical World of Atlantis: Theories of the Lost Empire From Plato to Disney* (New York: Disney Editions, 2001).

royals.[80] The film even supplies subtitles to translate the Atlantean passages for us (**Figure 18**). This adds a completely new element of historicity to the Atlantis tradition, but the effect is not dissimilar to that created by Jules Verne. Both Verne's novel and the Disney film attempt at placing Atlantis within an authoritative historical setting, Verne by citing a number of the scholars who had contributed to the study of the authenticity of Atlantis, and the Disney film by creating a plausible Atlantean language. But Disney, like many of its filmic predecessors, in setting almost an entire narrative within the confines of Atlantis—"finding" Atlantis is an integral part of any narrative involving Atlantis—brings Plato's lost continent to life in a vivid manner palatable to contemporary audiences.[81]

Figure 18: Subtitles translating Atlantean for the viewer *(Atlantis, the Lost Empire)*

---

80 For a discussion of the Atlantean language, see Berlitz, *The Mystery of Atlantis*, pp. 157–175. For a general survey of the languages of science fiction creations, see Walter E. Meyers, *Aliens and Linguists: Language Study and Science Fiction* (Athens: University of Georgia Press, 1980), especially pp. 86–103.

81 Not included in this listing of contemporary offerings is Luc Besson's 1991 underwater wildlife documentary named *Atlantis*; or the SyFy channel's 2007 documentary "Quest for Atlantis." Two other Atlantean connections require an accounting, but these films do not take place in Atlantis or directly involve Atlanteans. Dean Silver's *Atlantis Conspiracy* (2000) refers simply to the name of the corporation involved in the film's intrigue. On the other hand, the name of Atlantis is not mentioned in the *Lord of the Rings* trilogy (2001, 2002, 2003), but the land of Númenor from which the line of Aragorn (Viggo Mortensen) derives, was a large island continent boasting of advancements in the science of shipbuilding, which had been destroyed and then risen again with the name "Atalantë in the Eldarin tongue." Tolkien developed this mythology in the 1930's. See J. R. R. Tolkien (Christopher Tolkien, ed.), *The Silmarillion* (Boston: Houghton Mifflin Company, 1977), p. 281; For a discussion, see *http://greenbooks.theonering.net/quickbeam/files/081503.html*. For additional literary adaptations of and parallels to the Atlantis legend in twentieth-century literature, see de Camp, *Lost Continents*, pp. 257–277.

Along the way the new Atlantis phenomenon spilled over into episodes of some of the most successful television series of the period. The mission underlying the second episode of the fourth season of *Star Trek Next Generation*, originally aired on September 22, 1990, was to build a massive underwater environment named Atlantis. The concluding episode of the third season of *Hercules, The Legendary Journeys*, one of the most popular television programs ever syndicated world wide, was named "Atlantis." Aired originally on May 12, 1997, "Atlantis" applied a healthy dose of *contaminatio* to have Cassandra, usually associated with Troy, warn the unmindful King Pantheus (James Beaumont) of Atlantis' impending doom. This Atlantis, like several others, is powered by crystals. *Stargate SG-1*, the longest running (1997–2007) science-fiction series in the history of North American television, had been originally scheduled to conclude its seventh season with the discovery of the "Lost City" of Atlantis under the continent of Antarctica. Determining in 2004 to create a spin-off instead, producers Brad Wright and Robert C. Cooper transferred Atlantis to outer space, specifically the Pegasus Galaxy, and at the end of the pilot the new city emerges triumphantly from the deep much as in the finale of the Disney film; the fifth season of *Stargate Atlantis* concluded in January 2009 (**Figure 19**).[82]

---

82 Another notable television appearance, in addition to NBC's *Man From Atlantis*, was MacGyver's 1994 made-for-television movie, "Lost Treasure of Atlantis."

The commerce of publishing newly developed theories of Atlantis continues apace as well. Alan F. Alford, *The Atlantis Secret: A Complete Decoding of Plato's Lost Continent* (Walsall: Eridu Books, 2001), connects the Atlantis legend to his comprehensive exploded planet theory and describes it as a metaphor for spiritual creation; a paperback edition is being published in 2008. C. E. Albertson, *Tartessus Was Atlantis* ([online]: iUniverse, 2008) is a fantasy novel about an archaeological quest for the city in Andalusia. The back cover of the fourth printing of Shirley Andrews's *In Search of Atlantis* (St. Paul: Llewellyn Publications, 2001) promises to teach us "how the legacy of Atlantis can help bring our own world into a new age of peace and enlightenment." For a more traditional approach, see Luc Brisson, *Plato the Myth Maker* (Chicago: University of Chicago Press, 1998), pp. 25–39.

Figure 19: Mixing science fiction and the Atlantis myth in
contemporary television *(Stargate Atlantis)*

In 2003 Disney released *Atlantis: Milo's Return*, a sequel to *Atlantis, the Lost Empire*. This direct-to-video film represents the complex state of cinematic production in the early years of the twenty-first century. New technologies offer producers and audiences alike a variety of digital media, delivery systems, viewing venues, and commercial synergies which blur the traditional distinctions between various forms and formats of film, video, television, and their by-products—and adding to them considerably. A search for "Atlantis" in YouTube results in approximately 23,000 hits ranging from flights of the spacecraft Atlantis to the "Atlantis" level of the Lara Croft "Tomb Raider" computer game. In Japan the year after *Gamera, Guardian of the Universe* was released, Atlantis made its entry into the rapidly developing anime market in the 26-part television series known in the United States as *The Vision of Escaflowne* (1996), wherein the imperialistic Zaiback Empire seeks access to the legendary destructive power of Atlantis, thereby reviving the evil, threatening Atlantis. In 1998 The Forum Shops at Caesars Palace in Las Vegas opened "Race for Atlantis," billed as "the world's first and only giant-screen Imax 3-D ride," that is, a three-minute motion simulator ride designed to thrill audiences by having them participate in a chariot race (against the diabolical "Ghastlius") through the streets of Atlantis as their seats are being tossed about by huge hydraulic pistons.[83] The following year Terminal Studio issued its computer game, "Atlantis Quest," followed by "Rise of Atlantis." In 2005 BKN International released *Kong: King of Atlantis* as part of its animated "Kong" series, blending cyber forces and musical numbers with a blue animated version of the Merian C. Cooper/Edgar Wallace creature from the 1933 RKO film *King Kong*. This direct-to-DVD

83   *http://everything2.com/index.pl?node=Race%20for%20Atlantis.*

film also portrays the Atlanteans, ruled by Queen Reptilla, as evil again, for a solar eclipse is about to set into motion forces that will allow Atlantis to rise again from the sea to destroy Kong's island "and perhaps the whole world." Majesco Entertainment released the correlative computer game for GameBoy. Cable television recently offered *Atlantis SquarePantis*, the first SpongeBob SquarePants made-for-television movie after an eight-year run on the Nickelodeon network.[84] Airing November 12, 2007, *Atlantis SquarePantis*, featured a light-hearted quest for the world's oldest bubble brought from outer space over one million years ago, when the Atlanteans first colonized earth. Though a critical disappointment, the broadcast drew an audience of some 8.8 million people, and a DVD and computer game version went on sale immediately afterwards.

One could suppose that if he were alive today, Plato would be horrified at what has become of his illustrative descriptions of Atlantis. For him one of the quintessential elements in his account was that the Atlantean civilization no longer existed. But now, populated by cinematic scientists, tyrants, sirens, monsters, and aliens from other planets, and located in or under the sea or desert or in the Philippines, Atlantis has developed since the advent of film into a mysterious, dangerous, or futuristic society that still exists in one form or another. On the other hand, in the spirit of Atlantean fantasy maybe we can envision Plato alive today working closely with an attorney in an attempt to establish his authorship rights and collect his royalties for this unique artistic and successful commercially property. But the world of popular culture often remembers historical figures otherwise heralded for their unique genius, sophisticated output, and unparalleled skills for one of their more unlikely products—Wagner and Mendelssohn for their wedding music, Handel for his "Hallelujah Chorus," Da Vinci for the "Mona Lisa," Dali for melted watches, and Horace for "carpe diem." That Plato's Atlantis lives on in contemporary animation and video games seems to be simply part of that process.[85] Most often Atlantis offered artists and audiences an exotic stage for alluring vamps, scantily clad blonds, menacing creatures, or maniacal scientists. But on occasion twentieth-century popular culture painted Atlantis as a canvas rich in cultural and political allusion. In these portrayals Atlantis could represent the Soviets or Nazis as an alien empire, an

84   For the production history, see Edward Wyatt, "SquarePants Round Trip: SpongeBob's Yearlong Ride to Atlantis, via Korea," *The New York Times* (November 12, 2007), B3.

85   Similarly, Plato's false etymology at *Phaedrus* 244A–B, which laid the foundations for the erroneous tradition that the Delphic Pythia prophesied in a frenzy, still thrives as well. See Hugh Bowden, *Classical Athens and the Delphic Oracle* (Cambridge: Cambridge University Press, 2005), p. 24.

idealistic refuge for humanity, or, as Plato originally conceived it, a mighty empire destroyed by a natural catastrophe in a single day.[86]

---

86 For Plato's mythological invention of Atlantis in a socio-political context, see Kathryn A. Morgan, "Designer History: Plato's Atlantis Story and Fourth-Century Ideology," *Journal of Hellenic Studies* 118 (1998), 101–118; for a historiological reading, see Gerard Naddaf, "The Atlantis Myth: An Introduction to Plato's Later Philosophy of History," *Phoenix* 48 (1994), 189–209. For a discussion of the natural disasters and historical transformations that may have influenced Plato, e.g., the submergence of Helike in a single day in 373 B.C., the imperialistic expansion of Syracuse, and the tsunamis of 426 B.C. that destroyed Atalante in the Opuntian Gulf, see Phyllis Young Forsyth, *Atlantis: the Making of Myth* (Montreal: McGill-Queen's University Press, 1980), pp. 169–181.

19

The Atlantis Effect: The Lost Origins of Architecture

Anthony Vidler

It is a commonplace of the history of utopia that Plato's mythical description of Atlantis, begun in the *Timaeus* and expanded in the unfinished *Critias*, has inspired many imitations and revised versions through to the present. It is also true, but less well-known, that the history of the ideal city since the Renaissance, was founded on this description in many different ways, again through to the present. And since the genre of "utopia," named by Thomas More in 1516, has always been intimately linked to that of ideal city designs, it is no secret that "Atlantis" has hovered behind, and sometimes overtly influenced, many propositions for building the perfect city. Indeed, "Atlantis" became, over centuries of repetition, the name for a perfect and ideal architecture, a veritable paradise filled with the splendors of antiquity, and whose restoration, if not rediscovery was essential for the perfection of the social order. Which is strange, because, as we know, for Plato "Atlantis" was a paradigm of the exact opposite.

For many centuries the myth of the lost Atlantis served as a lure for explorers, geographers, archeologists, and nationalists to search for its supposed site. It was certainly Atlantis that Columbus discovered, at least according to a Spanish priest in 1493; it was equally, according to Bartolomeo de las Casas, the Bishop of Chiapas, originally located in Central America; for Francis Bacon, whose posthumous narrative *The New Atlantis* was published in 1627, Atlantis was more likely to be in South America—specifically Peru; Athanasius Kircher in 1664 identified the Canary Islands as the surviving land masses of the great empire. Then with enormous scholarly care and persistence, the rector of the University of Uppsala, Olof Rudbeck in his *Atlantica* published between 1679 and 1702, proved beyond all doubt that Atlantis had been in Sweden, indeed in Uppsala. He was, not surprisingly, supported by the King of Sweden, and taken seriously by Newton. Others were certain that Atlantis was in Africa, perhaps the Sahara. Ignatius Loyola Donnelly, the utopian founder of a colony in Minnesota, and lieutenant governor of the state, in his *Antedeluvian World* of 1882, that found traces of it in the Atlantic and drew a map of its enormous former extent. Archeologists after 1909 excitedly claimed Crete, proposing the Minoans as survivors of the deluge. Theosophists, reading William Scott-Elliott's *The Story of Atlantis*, also published in 1909, put it back in the Atlantic fully equipped with flying-machines and a colorfully dressed population called the Lemurians. Someone claiming to be the archeologist Heinrich Schliemann's grandson "discovered" the true map of Atlantis in his grandfather's papers and published it in 1912. More recently, the architect H. R. Stahel has provided meticulous drawings showing children (and us) exactly how Atlantis was built and what it looked like in every detail, in his *Atlantis Illustrated* of 1982.[1] And of course every movie-maker knows the city by heart, as in George Pal's "Atlantis, The Lost Continent."

On a more sinister note, Hitler believed that Atlantis was at the origin of German civilization, having read Alfred Rosenberg's *Der Mythus des 20 Jahrhunderts* a work that explained the spread of the Atlantians across the globe to Galilee with the result that Jesus was a direct descendent; following which, Himmler, claiming to be an expert on the subject, identified Atlantis with Germany and occupied France, the capital of which was Heligoland— the sacred *Heiligland*. It was Pierre Vidal-Naquet, whose parents perished in the Holocaust, who pointed out that the French writer Georges Perec, in his autobiography, invented an imaginary land called *W*, that was for all intents and purposes a version of Atlantis, and a metaphor for the death camps. It was also Vidal-Naquet who pointed out the long history of potentially dangerous nationalisms spawned by the idea of Atlantis.[2]

Of course we really know nothing about Atlantis save for the original account of its rise and fall in Plato. For "Atlantis" was nothing more nor less than a story made up by Plato and what we do know comes only from the description developed by the speaker Critias, who, at the beginning of the *Timaeus* gives a long account of the transmission of the story in the dialog of that name.[3] In 1719, the Italian literary scholar Giuseppe Bartoli came to the conclusion agreed upon by most contemporary scholars: that the Atlantis fable was simply that, a convenient fiction invented out of more or less whole cloth

---

1 H. R. Stahel, *Atlantis Illustrated*, with a Foreword by Isaac Asimov (New York: Grosset and Dunlop, 1965).

2 For a comprehensive survey of all these myths, see Pierre Vidal-Naquet, *L'Atlantide. Petite histoire d'un mythe platonicien* (Paris: Les Belles Lettres, 2005).

3 See C. Gill, "The Origin of the Atlantis Myth," *Trivium* 11 (1977), 287–304, and Vidal-Naquet, *L'Atlantide*.

by Plato (with perhaps a little help from Herodotus and Egyptian mythology) as a way of criticizing the Athens of his own day.[4] Thus, in the end, the myth starts with Plato.

Now the centuries of speculation over this myth is what I have called the "Atlantis Effect" in the first half of my title. But what has all this mythical lost continent to do with the subject of my sub-title, "The Lost Origins of Architecture"? Plato's Atlantis story, together with the story of another city, ancient Athens, also told in the prologue to the *Timaeus* and the *Critias,* in fact had an enormous influence on the way in which architecture, as it developed in the Renaissance through to the eighteenth century and well into the present, envisaged its authority. What gave architects the right to build for society? How could architects prove to clients that they were building for the client's good? What was the aesthetic authority by which architects demonstrated their forms to be, as Alexander Nehamas asks, beautiful, true, and, most important for the social role of architecture, just?

This leads me back to the two dialogs, the *Timaeus* and the *Critias.* The *Timaeus* and its unfinished "sequel" the *Critias* are generally thought to follow the *Republic* and perhaps the *Statesman* and to pre-date what historians understand to be the last dialog, the *Laws,* unfinished at Plato's death in 347. The *Timaeus* opens with Socrates asking three of his companions what they remember of the conversation of the day before—one apparently resuming the attributes of the ideal *polis* developed in the *Republic.* Do Critias, Timaeus, and Hermocrates remember yesterday's conversation, he asks, when they had discussed "the kind of political structure cities should have and the kind of men that should make it up so as to be the best possible"? (Zeyl, 17c) Reminded in detail, they concur that they "were all very satisfied with" (Zeyl, 17c) Socrates' description of it, but Socrates himself is far from satisfied. The ideal city he outlined seems in retrospect a still-life, a painting, or at least a picture of animals, "alive but standing still." (Zeyl, 19b) He would now see them "in motion or engaged in some struggle or conflict that seems to show off their distinctive physical qualities." (Zeyl, 19b) Or, in Rivaud's translation, "Well let me tell you now furthermore, regarding this State *(politeia)* which we have described, what kind of feeling I have felt with respect to it. This impression resembles that which one would feel, when, having seen somewhere beautiful living creatures, either figured in painting, or even really alive, but holding themselves at rest, one senses the desire to put them themselves into movement and to carry out in reality some of the exercises that seem to suit their bodies." (19b, Rivaud, 128, my translation) Socrates wants to hear of the struggles of a state and its battles, for a state can only, it seems, act like a state when at war with other states. Thus Critias' offers to recount the story, told by Solon to his great-grandfather, a

---

4 See Vidal-Naquet, *L'Atlantide,* pp. 96–99.

story Solon himself heard from the Egyptians, a story of ancient Athens nine thousand years before, an Athens with laws and a society much like the ideal sketched by Socrates, and whose prowess in war was attested to by the repulsion and defeat of imperial Atlantis. Such a story, retold by Critias, would, it seems satisfy Socrates demands for animation:

> We'll translate the citizens and the city you described to us in mythical fashion yesterday to the realm of fact, and place it before us as though it were ancient Athens itself. And we'll say that the citizens you imagined are the very ones the priest spoke about, our actual ancestors. The congruence will be complete, and our song will be in tune. (Zeyl, 26d)

This, Socrates agrees, will not be a "made-up story," but a "true account." (26e)

It is then that the dialogue shifts to Timaeus, who is designated to speak before Critias, beginning "with the origin of the world" and ending "with the nature of human beings." (27a) Only then, prepared by beginning at the beginning, will the history told by Critias find its place, history thus taking up the discourse of society from the astronomical discourse of the universe. Critias' story is thus deferred, until the second, unfinished dialogue, the *Critias*, and gives way to the cosmology developed by Timaeus. It is now that we begin to see the importance of this dialog for architectural theory.

As Timaeus told it, the universe was created in three stages: the stage before the foundation, where a generalized "place" or *chora* holds the elements of fire, earth, water, and air as they, without form and proportion, move unequally about (this idea would be important, as we shall see, for the idea of architectural "generation" developed by 15th century architects). This was followed by the stage of construction, at the hands of the "demiurge," or craftsman-architect (another important simile—the idea of the creator of the world as an architect could hardly fail to interest Renaissance architects) who then proceeds to shape the elements according to a preconceived ideal in his mind, copying it to form the cosmos itself and doing so with the help of geometry, creating the universe in the shape of a perfect sphere. This "round shape, the form of a sphere, with its center equidistant from its extremes in all directions . . . of all shapes is the most complete and most like itself" with a "smooth, round finish all over on the outside." (Zeyl, 33b) The sphere has held a privileged position in the theory of ideal forms. Endowed with a centrally positioned world-soul, itself the embodiment of reason and harmony, and incorporating, like some perfect armillary, the motions of the seven planetary rings, this world incorporates time within its circularity, marked by the differential motions of the planets.

Such was the world crafted as Plato recounts "by Intellect *(nous)*". (Zeyl, 47e) It was this passage in the *Timaeus* that resonated for Renaissance architects, and later, for the eighteenth century architects of the Enlightenment, from Leon Battista Alberti, to Etienne-Louis Boullée (whose spherical planetarium dedicated to Newton (1784) reflected the scientist's own belief in the geometry of the *Timaeus*) to Claude-Nicolas Ledoux, whose project for a cemetery (1785) emulated the spherical world, and thence to Le Corbusier who adapted the elemental geometrical solids to his abstract theory of "Purist" architecture.

The final stage of creation was that of the human body, with its organs and humors (always a model for the architect seeking an organic and biological analogy for a building that would shelter humanity with the same ecological perfection as the body itself). In a metaphor that, as we shall see, will be repeated by Renaissance architects, Plato compares the model followed by the demiurge to the father; the copy that becomes the tangible reality to the child; and the receptacle within which becoming is realized, to the mother.

All this is, however, preliminary to the detailed description I have mentioned of two mythical cities: that of ancient Athens, and that of Atlantis. It is clear that the description of the formation of the universe, the invention so to speak of the form of the cosmos, is a necessary preliminary to the description of another beginning, this time a historical, rather than a cosmological one, of the society of humankind, the foundation of the *polis*, and its active administration by a statesman *(politicus)* who is at once a craftsman/demiurge and a weaver-architect. The foundation of the *polis*, that is, demands a replication of the cosmic construct—the establishment of territories through geometry, their definition according to classes of inhabitants, and the careful exclusion of non-citizens of the *polis*, into the worldly equivalent of chaos. In sum, the work of architecture.

It was on these conceptual foundations and in the image of his creation myth, that Plato modeled his two archetypal cities—"proto-Athens," and Atlantis: an ideal city—what Athens used to be, and a not-so-ideal city, what Athens had become in Plato's day. Pre-Athens, in Critias' account, was an agricultural state, administered by farmers of talent. Before the *polis*, there was no agora, simply a walled around and extensive acropolis manned by the warriors in barracks, refectories and temples to the north and gardens, gymnasia, and summer refectories to the south. Guarded by Athena and her brother Hephaistos, the city was under the double sign of philosophy and art, guardian and producer, respectively. Outside the walls worked the farmers and craftsmen. A landlocked republic with no ports, harbors, or maritime trade, its virtue and strength resided in its fertile soil, equable climate and unchanging traditions: even the houses were built according to a rule passed down through generations, "to succeeding generations who resembled themselves." (Lee, 112) Only with the cataclysm that destroyed both Athens and Atlantis, was the land washed away, and the great acropolis reduced to its Periclean dimensions.

Atlantis, by contrast was surrounded by water, built on an island, fortified over the ages so as to make it almost impenetrable. In his account Critias cites all the topoi of the genre later to be named by Thomas More "utopos": the site, a fertile plain close to the sea some 600,000 yards long and two thousand broad, surrounded by a moat 200 yards wide. Rivers flowed from the mountain, emptied into the ditch, finally discharging into the sea. Channels and cross-channels a hundred feet wide formed a gridded transportation network. The fortified center, a hill near the middle of the plain, was occupied originally by one of the "original earth-borns," Evenor, together with his wife Leucippe and daughter Cleito, in a city founded and fortified by Poseidon who had taken Cleito for his spouse, with concentric rings of sea and land:

> There were two rings of land and three of sea, like cartwheels, with the island at their center, and equidistant from each other, making the place inaccessible to man (for there were still no ships or sailing in those days). He [Poseidon] furnished the central island with godlike lavishness; he made two springs flow, one of hot and one of cold water, and caused the earth to grow abundant produce of every kind. (Lee, 113)

Over many generations the city grew and prospered, with temples, palaces, harbors, docks and organized farming. A palace was built at the center where the god had lived, a "residence whose size and beauty were astonishing to see." The rings of water were bridged to make a passage to this palace, and canals dug to make the island accessible from the sea:

> They began by digging a canal three hundred feet wide, a hundred feet deep and fifty stades long from the sea to the outermost ring, thus making it accessible from the sea like a harbour; and they made the entrance to it large enough to admit the largest ships. At the bridges they made channels through the rings of land which separated those of water, large enough to admit the passage of a single trireme, and roofed over to make an underground tunnel; for the rims of the rings were of some height above sea-level. The largest of the rings, to which there was access from the sea, was three stades in breadth and the ring of land within it the same. Of the second pair the ring of water was two stades in breadth, and the ring of land again equal to it, while the ring of water running immediately round the central island was a stade across. The diameter of the island on which the palace was situated was five stades. It and the bridges (which were a hundred feet broad) were enclosed by a stone wall all round, with towers and gates

guarding the bridges on either side where they crossed the water.
(Lee, 115)

The buildings were constructed out of stone of many colors, white, black and yellow, and with the outer wall covered in bronze, the inner with tin, and the wall of the acropolis covered with a gleaming substance named "orichalc." At the center of the Palace was a shrine sacred to Poseidon and Cleito, itself surrounded by a golden wall affording no entry. The Temple of Poseidon was huge, a stade in length, three hundred feet wide, and proportionally high, covered in silver, with pediments in gold and a roof of ivory picked out in gold, was, Critias admitted, "somewhat outlandish in appearance."

From this center, the original springs were piped by aqueducts to the outermost ring. The middle ring was used for horse racing, while each ring was furnished with temples, gardens, and exercise areas. Completing the defenses of this impregnable land was a wall, starting at the sea and following a circle at fifty stades distance from the largest ring, a wall "densely built-up all round with houses," (Lee, 117) anticipating Plato's later arguments against free-standing walls not made up of the city fabric itself.

Vidal-Naquet has analyzed the underlying dialectical structure of Plato's two models: their complex relation to "Athens," either as the pure city (proto-Athens) or as the city in disunity (Atlantis); the mirroring of relations between Athena, goddess of the land-based proto-Athens, and Poseidon, god of Atlantis; the intertwined fates of each, as sea-bound Atlantis is swallowed into the earth, and land-bound washed away so as to become surrounded by the sea; and, finally, the political systems of each, the one a fable of stability, the other a moral tale of disharmony and greed.[5]

There were, however, as Jean-François Pradeau has noted, further reasons for Plato's concentration on the Atlantis description in *Critias*.[6] Not only was it the case that without Atlantis "there would be no war, no story," but more importantly for our investigation of the spatial nature of architectural utopia, the distinction between the two cities, Athens and Atlantis, rested on a temporal divide incorporated into the spatial order. Thus Athens, the perfect model, was static, occupied in working its own, bounded territory; Atlantis by contrast, was constantly extending its boundaries, improving its ever-expanding lands. This resulted in what Pradeau calls a "morphological incoherence," one that would mark geographical utopia ever since; Louis Marin has identified similar spatial

---

5 Vidal-Naquet, "Athens and Atlantis: Structure and Meaning of a Platonic Myth," *The Black Hunter: Forms of Thought and Forms of Society in the Greek World*, translated by Andrew Szegedy-Mascak, with a Foreword by Bernard Knox (Baltimore: The Johns Hopkins University Press,1986), pp. 263–284.

6 Jean-François Pradeau, *Platon et la cité* (Paris: Presses Universitaires de France, 1997).

dislocations in Thomas More's version. In the *Critias* however, the incoherence is temporal, but obscured by the apparent "timelessness" of the description. Thus the circular harmonies traced by Poseidon are cut through by the rectilinear canals of his descendants; the citizens of Atlantis are "distributed among different towns and villages separated by encircling walls, gates, or canals"; in Athens they were "brought together in the same place." (Pradeau, 93) In Pradeau's, and Plato's, terms these geometrical figures are representative of political and social morality—the rectangular susceptible to corruption, the circular enclosed and thereby resistant to decay. Pradeau concludes: "The unity of Athens (which is a city) and the imbalanced Atlantis (an immense colonial empire) are precisely opposed with respect to the limits drawn by their respective frontiers. This is the indication, supported by the detail attention paid to geographical frontiers, of what a limit determines and defines what it circumscribes." (Pradeau, 93)

Perhaps we can infer from this that the circular form of Ancient Athens, as against the rectangular gridded form of the extensions of Atlantis, were allegories of Plato's own resistance to the modern, and "democratic" Hippodamian plans of Greek colonial foundations, or, closer to home, the gridded plan of the Piraeus, said by Aristotle to be "divided up" by Hippodamos. If we follow the trail of Socrates' conversation, beginning with the *Republic*, we note that the discussion of the just city started precisely in the modern port of the Piraeus, on the day of an equally modern festival, both emblems for Plato of the decayed state of Athenian democracy. Ancient Athens then would be, in its refusal of maritime adventures, and its bounded, circular form, reflecting that of the original cosmos, the image which the *Republic* was seeking. It would be definitively affirmed in the plan of Magnesia, the circular city of the *Laws*, the dialog that completed Plato's experiment in philosophical urban planning.

From the mid-fifteenth century, and the discovery of the Latin manuscripts of the *Republic*, the *Timaeus*, the *Critias*, and the *Laws*, architectural theorists have seized on the variety, and exploited the ambiguity, of the "origins" explored by Plato, and the ideal forms of figures and cities, joined to the ideal forms of social life, legal and political institutions that gave life to Plato's imaginary *polies*. I give only two of the most outstanding early examples. First, that of Leon Battista Alberti, who is normally credited with introducing Roman thought into architectural theory in order to outdo Vitruvius himself, whom he considered an inferior writer. While the *De re aedificatoria* was explicitly concerned with Roman virtue, in its elegance of language and its emphasis on decorum, drawing on the Cicero of *De officiis*, and there is little mention of Greek sources beyond lip service to the *Republic*, Alberti's satirical novel, *Momus* is another story. Recounting the antics of Momus, the "god of fault-finding and the personification of embittered mockery," the story may be read as a satirical treatment of the circle of Florentine humanists and the statesmen who were their patrons. Some have interpreted the story as an attack on the grandiose ambitions of the papacy for the reconstruction of Rome, perhaps in response to Alberti's personal relations with Nicolas V. In either case, *Momus* was a non-too subtle warning of the dangers of architectural hubris and at the same time an affirmation of the role played by architecture in the public life of a patron.[7]

Read carefully in the light of the *Critias* however, *Momus*, in fact, was Alberti's attempt to complete what was left unfinished in the *Critias*—an almost literal continuation of the last lines following the account of the catastrophe of Atlantis and proto-Athens, and the degeneration of human society: "And the god of gods, Zeus, who reigns by law, and whose eye can see such things, when he perceived the wretched state of this admirable stock decided to punish them and reduce them to order by discipline. He accordingly summoned all the gods to his own most glorious abode, which stands at the center of the universe and looks over the whole realm of change, and when they had assembled addressed them as follows: . . . ." (Lee, 121)

But perhaps the most startling influence was evinced in the extraordinary, and underestimated treatise of the Florentine architect Antonio Averlino, who adopted the name "Filarete," from the Greek word *philaretos*, or "lover of beauty," a treatise that has the distinction of having delineated the very first ideal city of the modern period, both in plan and in the detail of its various quarters and buildings.[8] Working from his knowledge of the Platonic dialogs, the *Timaeus*, the *Critias*, and the *Laws*, Filarete wrote his *Libro architettonico* sometime between 1460 and 1464, dedicating it first to Francesco Sforza, Duke of Milan, and then in a hasty politically motivated revision to Piero de' Medici in Florence.[9] Like the *Sforziad*, the eulogy of his intellectual mentor by the humanist Francesco Filelfo, Filarete's discussion of his ideal city, named "Sforzinda" in honor of his patron, was never printed, remaining in manuscript with only a few copies of its first and second state in libraries in Italy and Spain, and was not to be properly recognized until the end of the

---

7   See Manfredo Tafuri, "'Cives esse non licere': The Rome of Nicholas V and Leon Battista Alberti: Elements towards a Historical Revision," *The Harvard Architectural Review* 6 (1989), 60–75. Tafuri opines that the character of Jupiter in *Momus* could be either Eugene IV or Nicholas V.

8   Antonio de Piero Averlino, Filarete, *Libro architettonico* (c. 1460–January 31st 1464). Filarete was born and educated in Florence. In Rome between 1433–1445 he fabricated the still existing bronze doors for the central portals of St Peter's; in Venice around 1450 he worked in mosaic and fresco, and between 1451 and 1465 he was in Milan in the service of Francesco Sforza, working on the Castello Sforzesco, the Cathedral, the Ospedale Maggiore (1457–1465), and the Cathedral of Bergamo (1457).

9   See Luisa Giordano, "On Filarete's *Libro architettonico*," in Vaughan Hart with Peter Hicks, *Paper Palaces: The Rise of the Renaissance Architectural Treatise* (New Hvane and London: Yale University Press, 1998), pp. 51–65 for the best recent summary of the scholarship and interpretation of the treatise.

19th century, although as we shall see, portions of it were known to a certain current of utopianism in late 18th century France.

The *Libro* is written in the form of a Platonic dialog between the architect Filarete and his clients, Francesco Sforza, his wife Maria Visconti, and their son, Galazzeo, following every step in the designing and construction of the new city. He opens: "I shall first describe a city, as I think it can be made good and beautiful. I shall describe its circumference, all the buildings within. I shall show you the proportion, form, and dimensions of these according to their quality." (*Libro architettonico*, II, 10)

Filarete was fully conscious of the radical nature of his revival of antiquity. In his narrative he portrayed Alberti's Mantuan patron, Lodovico Gonzaga, visiting the city of Sforzinda, in discussion with Francesco Sforza over the benefits of ancient as opposed to "modern" (Gothic) practice: responding to Filarete's projects Gonzaga states: "I seem to see again the noble buildings that were once in Rome and those that we read were in Egypt. It seems to me that I have been reborn on seeing *[mipare rinascere a vedere]* these noble buildings." (*Libro* XIII, 100r; Spencer I, p. 175) More than an ideal city, *Sforzinda* was also a framework for re-imagining Milan itself, a matrix for seeing the program of construction begun by Sforza—the cathedral, the castle, and the hospital—as a part of a larger *rinovatio*, and a way of transposing the mythic onto the real, in Garin's terms "translating a metaphysical myth in urbanistic terms."[10]

Filarete's conception of the architect's role in society was clear: the architect was a mortal version of the demiurge-constructor, the divine architect, whose business it was to create a *polis* for humanity according to the divine model. Accordingly Filarete's city was based on an ideal cosmology of forms set in a verdant landscape where nature will provide abundant water, fertile soil, and fair breezes. This model was then inhabited by the roster of social groups common to the *Republic* and the *Laws*: princes, soldiers, craftsmen, merchants, with all the institutions needed to house them properly. I don't have time to go through them all, but they are described and drawn in detail. In this way Filarete develops, not only what could be called the first truly philosophical treatise on architecture but also the first complete modern ideal city—a model for many of the ideal cities of the future, from Ledoux in the 18th century to Ebeneezer Howard in the nineteenth century, to Le Corbusier in the twentieth.

John Onians has convincingly demonstrated Filarete's deep reliance on the *Timaeus* and the *Critias* in the development of his ideal plans. Filarete states

---

10   Eugenio Garin, *Umanisti artisti scienziati. Studi sul Rinascimento italiano* (Rome: Editore Riuniti, 1989), p. 198. Garin also makes the important point that Filarete, the admirer of Alberti, stressed the Platonism of his utopia, as against the more empirical Aristoteleanism of the Florentine.

that the plans of his city are based on a so-called "Golden Book" translated by on Iscofrance Notilento, and anagram of Francesco da Tolentino, or Filelfo, a well-known Greek scholar at the Sforza court and close friend of Filarete from the early 1440's. Filelfo, we know, was in contact with the library of Pavia, which held Latin translations of the Platonic dialogues, including the *Laws*, the *Timaeus*, and, most importantly, the *Critias*. But other internal evidence supports the thesis that Filarete is working from Plato: The use of Plato's creation myth as a narrative of architectural creation; the delineation of two cities, the one on land, the other by the sea; the second "sea" city, Plousiapolis, designed according to the guidelines provided by a mysterious and newly discovered "Golden Book"; the castles, the mazes, the moats and canals of both Plato and Filarete; even the color of the stones used to build Atlantis and Sforzinda. All attest to the excitement of the texts, or summaries of texts, supplied to the architect by his friend the Milanese humanist, Filelfo.

The parallel even extends to the role of the *chôra* in creating an ordered universe, or, for Filarete, a rational architecture. For Filarete, every architectural "body" embodies the proportions and functions of its human builder: "the building is constructed as a similitude to the human figure," and, like the body, "buildings need members and passages, that is, entrances and exits," located in the right place. (I.5v-r. Spencer p. 12) Every building needs to be born, its creator, the architect, acts as its mother, conceiving and modeling it in order to demonstrate its virtues to its father, the client; whence the architect acts as the wet nurse for the building until it is fully grown. Like humans too, buildings can become sick—for excess and corruption, as in society, can ruin a building—and require the architect to cure them. (II.7v. Spencer, p. 15)

In all this Filarete, under the influence of the scholar Francesco Filelfo who had, like Filarete, moved from Florence to Milan, is evidently and polemically countering the Romanist Alberti, with new Greek knowledge. Like Filelfo's own *Sforziad*, modeled on the *Iliad* in 24 books, so Filatete's *libro*, modeled on the *Timaeus, Critias* and *Laws* was composed in 24 books, is filled with Greek inscriptions, and rejects the Roman orders. That Filarete's architecture is not entirely "Greek" is, as Onians points out, the result of his reliance on Plato, and Plato's description of the opulent Atlantis. Filarete was reported to have died on the way to visit Constantinople, following Filelfo, to see the works he had dreamed of through Plato.

There followed the long line of utopian ideal cities stretching from Thomas More, through to Claude-Nicolas Ledoux in the late eighteenth century, and thence to Ebeneezer Howard's "Garden Cities of Tomorrow" in 1898 and Patrick Geddes's "Biopolis" in the early 20th century. All were in some way influenced by and responded to Plato's *Republic* and *Laws*, but all, in their physical plans, were deeply indebted to the geometries and monumental programs of Atlantis. In this way Atlantis crept unseen into the urban plans of twentieth century modernism—the ideal cities of Le Corbusier, Bruno Taut, and even the geometries of geographers like Walter Kristaller in Germany or planners like Ludwig Hilbersheimer in the U.S. after the Second World War.

The question of the influence of the *Timaeus* as a whole on architecture is more complicated and has been well covered with respect to the Renaissance, and its affection for numerical ratios, harmonies, and geometrical origins. Its influence on the modern period is less understood: Le Corbusier's liking for primary geometrical solids, and Paul Valéry's re-framing of the Socratic discussion of beauty with Phaedrus as the architectural subject of *Eupalinos ou l'architecte* (1921) are well-known. But more recently, Jacques Derrida has awakened interest in the role of the *chôra* in the act of creation—a role welcomed by feminist architectural theorists—and specifically in the questioning of architectural origins per se.

In a 1986 interview Derrida asked the question (one for which his interrogation of the meaning and role of chôra in the *Timaeus* would become a potent vehicle for its exploration) of how to think "architecture" before, so to speak, architecture itself came into being as an already formed and disciplined institution:

> Let us consider architectural thinking. By that I don't mean to conceive architecture as a technique separate from thought, already representable in space, and constituted as an object of thinking [distinct from constructing], but rather to raise the question of architecture as a *possibility* of thought, a potential which cannot be reduced merely to the status of a representation of thought.[11]

Not then to think *about* architecture (which would assume that we already knew what we were talking about) but rather how architecture itself might be thought, in and as its essential character. Derrida was, as he said, looking for "an undiscovered way of thinking," one that related to a moment of architecture before the fatal separation of so-called "theory" and so-called "practice," that separation that immediately reduced architecture to a technique subordinate to thought. For Derrida, this pre-technical, pre-professional, moment was one that was motivated by simple "desire," a desire for and toward architecture, but an architecture that did not yet know itself *as* architecture. Derrida is, so to speak, looking for a way to imagine a pre-existent state, a "before" when architecture was not severed in two, separated between form and function, idea and material, intelligible and sensible, art and *techne*. Against all the philosophic uses of architecture as a metaphor for rational or well-built thought, from Aristotle

---

11 Derrida, "Architecture Where the Desire May Live," interview with Eva Meyer, *Domus* 67 (1986), 17.

to Kant and Heidegger, such a quest for beginnings, demanded for Derrida a moment of pioneering, a gesture of "clearing of a path"—a "path that does not have to be discovered but to be created" and that makes possible both arrival and departure at the same time.[12]

I cite this passage only to indicate how, even today, architectural thinking is still tied to a Vitruvian theoretical schema that assumes an "architecture" already pre-formed and applies it to distinct and instrumental ends—those celebrated ends of *firmitas*, *commoditas*, and *venustas*, [strength, utility, beauty] or, as Henry Wotton, a British 17th century writer so aptly translated them, "firmness, commodity, and delight." Thus, today, architecture (as if we knew what it was) is still divided among the partisans of one or another of these ends—we get the high-tech partisans of strength, the social instrumentalists of use, and the post-modern avatars of "beauty." So in returning architecture to a reading of the *Timaeus* I am simply attempting to return architecture to a condition of thinking its "origins" in such a way that we might fashion an alternative to the disciplinary structure we have inherited from the Roman Vitruvius; that would be a "Greek" and philosophical origin. In this sense, even as Jean-François Pradeau, in his introduction to his translation of the *Critias* expresses a desire to rid Atlantis of its mad mystical followers, and give it once more "the dignity of a Platonic dialog," I would wish to do this for architecture.

And this leads me to my second reason for returning to Plato; not for any nostalgia for the anti-democratic order he espoused, nor for his strictures on representation in the arts, nor even to found a new ideal city; but for the example he provides us of two cities: both mythical, but both paradigms, so to speak, of urban behavior. What is important about pre-Athens is that it articulates the values of a self-sufficient, non-expansive, non-consumerist, non-imperialistic society that despite all this operates in balance with its natural environment. Atlantis on the other hand, city of luxury and expansion, was the epitome of a city over-stretching its boundaries and degenerating in its power: "to the perceptive eye, the depth of their degeneration was clear enough, but to those whose judgment of true happiness is defective they seemed, in their pursuit of unbridled ambition and power, to be at the height of their fame and fortune." Such words ring as true today as then.

Perhaps from these "rational fictions" as Pradeau calls them, we can draw our own paradigms, now framed even more seriously by our disastrous experiences of war and attempted conquest, both of nations, and of the environment. It is here that I will conclude: in looking at pre-Athens, in working through Plato's attempt to address cause and effect, form and necessity in the cosmos and the material world, even in reading Filarete's careful and respectful treatment of nature in the founding of his city, we can perhaps counter the

---

12 Derrida, "Architecture," 17.

neo-liberal, expansionist myths of today's global developers, who, like the late luxury-sated kings of Atlantis ravage the entire earth, unwittingly devouring the source of their own wealth, and in the rush to build at all costs, reduce the social *polis* to ruins.

20

Plato's Timaeus *and the Aesthetics of "Animate Form"*

Ann Bergren

Spurred by the span of the conference for which it was written, "Life, the Universe, Everything—and More: Plato's *Timaeus* Today," this essay is a time-traveler, shuttling back and forth to forge lines of transit between contemporary architecture, the model of architectural beauty in the *Timaeus*, and another, earlier tradition of "Homeric beauty."

We begin with the latest movement of 20th-century architecture, the "animate form" designed with the aid of animation software. Visually striking, with irregular, often biomorphic curvatures, for all of their formal innovation, the works of "animate form" still provoke the age-old aesthetic question—"which one is beautiful?"

Pursuing this question, we turn to the foundation of the Western conception of architectural beauty, the account of cosmic construction in the *Timaeus*. There Plato's creator god is a mighty *dêmiourgos* "craftsman" who builds the world as a material copy of an ideal, immutable, and beautiful Form in *chôra* "place, space." As this medium of *chôra* is wholly passive and character-free, contributing nothing to compromise the likeness, the *kosmos* can perfectly imitate its Formal model. Before the creation of the *kosmos*, however, the pre-cosmic *chôra* was in no way passive, but rather shaking and being shaken by the unequal weights of the primeval "footprints" of the four elements, earth, wind,

It is a pleasure to thank Lorenzo Garcia, Alex Press, Bruce Rosenstock, Mario Telò, and Anthony Vidler, who have given critical reading and illuminating suggestions at various stages of my project, and the "Athena-inspired" *dêmiourgos* "craftsman" of our conference, Richard Mohr.

water, and fire, in perpetual *anômalia* "unevenness." It is the achievement of Plato's cosmic architect to replace this reciprocal dynamic with equilibrium—the condition that emulates the unchanging stability of the Forms—and thereby to endow his *kosmos* with *schêma* "pattern" and every possible relation of mutual measurability, the features that render it *kallista arista te* "most beautiful and good" (53b5–6). Can this model of the creation and the criteria of beauty decide which work of "animate form" is beautiful?

Bringing Plato's text back to "animate form," we find that it is not the beautiful *kosmos*, but rather the characteristics of the pre-cosmic *chôra* that pre-figure its fundamental features. Does this mean that the *Timaeus* offers nothing to help us determine beauty in "animate form"? No, for the pre-cosmic *chôra* of the *Timaeus* points back to an alternative tradition of Classical beauty, the pre-Platonic tradition of "Homeric beauty."

The attributes of the pre-cosmic *chôra* of the *Timaeus* resonate with a conception of craft that precedes the Platonic. In the material works of art and craft that are termed "beautiful" in the Homeric epics, we find features that anticipate the essential aesthetic attributes of "animate form" articulated by its pioneer, Greg Lynn. What links these earliest and latest layers of Western architectural culture, what makes them comparable despite their distance, is their shared difference from Platonic ontology. Each lies on the other side of the model of beauty in the *Timaeus*.

Finally, we speculate upon the influence of the transcendent beauty ascribed to artifacts in Homer upon Plato's choice of a *dêmiourgos* "craftsman" as the creator of the *kosmos*, an influence that would make the goddess Athena the ultimate precedent with whom the divine craftsman of the *Timaeus* aims to compete.

Embryological House, Greg Lynn, 1999: "Which one is beautiful?"

The decade of the 1990's saw the development of architecture designed by means of calculus-based animation software. It was pioneered by Greg Lynn under the title of "animate form."[1] His research during this decade culminated in a project entitled *Embryological House*. (**Figure 1**)

After presenting this series of houses at an ANY (Architecture New York) Conference in New York in 2000, Lynn recalls being asked the founding question of Classical aesthetics, "Which one is beautiful?"[2] In this formulation, with its aim at a legitimate singularity from a field of contenders, the question presupposes the model of beauty in the *Timaeus*, the paradigm for Classical

---

1   See Greg Lynn, *Animate Form* (New York: Princeton Architectural Press, 1999).
2   Tape-recorded interview with Lynn, 13 March 2007.

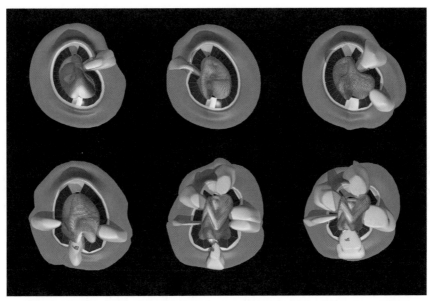

Figure 1: *Embryological House,* Greg Lynn, 1999. (Courtesy of Greg Lynn Form)

architectural excellence in antiquity and the Renaissance.[3] Can this model determine the beautiful one among works of "animate form"?

The model of beauty in the *Timaeus: kosmos* "order" vs. pre-cosmic *chôra* "place, space"

In Plato's dialogue, the title character, Timaeus, describes the creation of the world, designated by the Greek word *kosmos* "order."[4] Its creation becomes the Classical model of the nature and criteria of architectural beauty. For unlike

---

3 See, for example, Rudolf Wittkower, "Proportion in Art and Architecture," in Rudolf Wittkower, *Architectural Principles in the Age of Humanism* (New York and London: St. Martin's Press, 1988), pp. 144–155.

4 Because it denotes formal order, considered in Greek thought to be a feature of beauty, a more complete translation of *kosmos* might be "order that makes for beauty, beautiful order." For an example of how the mere condition of *kosmos* creates beauty out of even the most conventionally unbeautiful objects, see Xenophon, *Oeconomicus* 8.19: "How beautiful *(kalon)* is the sight of all sorts of shoes, provided they are in sequence, beautiful *(kalon)* is the sight of all sorts of clothes, when they are separated, beautiful *(kalon)* are bedcovers, beautiful *(kalon)* are bronze kettles, beautiful *(kalon)* is tableware, and beautiful *(kalon)* is also what of all things would be most laughable, not to the serious but to the comic man—namely, the fact that I say even cooking pots appear with good rhythm *(euruthmon phainesthai)* provided they are distinctly arranged *(eukrinôs keimenas)*."

those cosmologies in which the world is the product of some mode of natural growth, from a seed, or an egg, or divine copulation, for example, here the *kosmos* is a work of construction. Its creator god is a *dêmiourgos* "craftsman."[5] And his building is "most beautiful and good" *(kallista arista te)*.

Timaeus tells the story of this creation in three phases, employing the *hysteron-proteron* "later before earlier" order characteristic of Homeric epic. In the first phase, Timaeus explains how the *dêmiourgos* "builds" *(tektainô)* and "constructs" *(synistêmi)*[6] the *kosmos* as an *eikôn* "likeness, copy"[7] using a Form as *paradeigma* "model"[8] in *chôra* "place, space" (48e2–52d1).[9] He then moves back in time to describe the characteristics of pre-cosmic *chôra*—how *chôra* was before the building of the *kosmos* (52d1–53a7). And then he returns in time to complete his account of the cosmic construction, stressing the features that form its surpassing beauty (53b1–69a5).

---

5   The *dêmiourgos* "craftsman" is an apt choice for the creator of the *kosmos* insofar as this role comprises the whole world of construction and production, both concrete (for example, shoes, *Gorgias* 447d1–3, *Theatetus* 146d1; beds, *Republic* 597d9–11; images of animals and houses, *Republic* 401b1–7; women's *kosmos* "ornament," *Republic* 373b8–c1; musical instruments, *Republic* 399c10–d1; Silenus-statues, *Symposium* 215b2; brass-ware, clay pots, cooked meat, *Euthydemus* 301c3–6; Pheidias' Parthenon sculptures, *Hippias Major* 290a5–9; refined gold, *Statesman* 303d10–e5) and figurative (for example, justice, *Protagoras* 327c7; moderation, justice, and virtue, *Republic* 500d4–8; crimes, *Republic* 552d3–6; freedom, *Republic* 395c1; love between gods and men, *Symposium* 188d1; painted images in the soul, *Philebus* 39b3–7; names, *Cratylus* 431e1; noble deeds, *Laws* 829d2; beautiful *eikones* "likenesses" in speech, *Laws* 898b3). The particular craft of architecture is indicated in the *Timaeus* by the use with the *dêmiourgos* of verbs of building: *tektainô* (compare *tektôn* "builder" and *architektôn* "architect") and construction: *sun* "together, with" + *histêmi* "make stand, set up." The *Timaeus* is not the only dialogue in which a *dêmiourgos* figures as architect of the *kosmos*: see also *Republic* 530a4–7, *Statesman* 270a5, 273b1–2, and *Republic* 507c6–8 for the *dêmiourgos* as fabricator of the "lavish power of seeing and being seen."
6   For the verbs *tektainô* "build" and *suntektainô* "build together" of the Demiurge and the gods as his deputies, see 28c6, 33b1, 36e1, 68e5, 70e3, 91a2, and 45b3. For the verb, *sunistêmi*, see 29e1, 30b5, 30c3, and 32c7. For the two verbs together, see 30b4–5 and 36d8–e1.
7   See 29b1–2, 37d5,7, 52c2, and 92c7 (for the *kosmos* as *eikôn tou noêtou* "likeness of the intelligible").
8   See 28a6–b1: "Whenever the *dêmiourgos*, by looking always toward what is the same and using something of this sort as model *(paradeigmati)*, produces the visible form *(idean)* and power of his work, by necessity everything he accomplishes in this way must be beautiful *(kalon)*." See also, 31a4 for the *kosmos* as "crafted" *(dedêmiourgêmenon)* in accordance with its model *(paradeigma)*, 37c8–d1 for how the *dêmiourgos* "took thought to make it [the *kosmos*] even more like *(homoion)* its model *(paradigmati)*, 38b6–c3 for time as *homoiotatos* "most like" its *paradeigma tês diaiônias* "model of eternal nature." For the Forms as *paradeigmata* in which things participate by resemblance and imitation, see *Parmenides* 132d1–4.
9   For the need for the third ontological kind, the "receptacle" and "as it were, nurse" of all *genesis* "coming-into-being," see 48e1–49a6.

In the first phase of his story, Timaeus defines the three ontological kinds, the Form as "model," the *kosmos* as "likeness, copy," and *chôra* "place, space." The Form is an ideal model of a real object, as in the familiar example from the *Republic*, the Form of a bed, the idea or ideal of which a material bed is a particular instance.[10] The Form is "intelligible" *(noêton)*, perceivable not with the senses, but only by thinking *(noêsis)*.[11] Not being material, it never changes: it never undergoes *genêsis* "coming-into-being, becoming" and thus does not pass away. A Form is eternal and thus immortal, like a god.[12] That Form which contains all others is the *paradeigma* "model" used by the *dêmiourgos* in constructing the *kosmos*.[13]

The *kosmos* is an *eikôn* "likeness, copy" of this transcendent Form of all Forms. Being material, it is perceivable with the senses. And because it is material, it changes, coming into being and passing away.[14] So that the *kosmos* can be a true copy of its model, the *chôra* "place, space" in which it is built must be

---

10 See *Republic*, 595c7–597e4. On the discrepancy between this account in the *Republic*, where *theos* "god" creates the Form, and the *Timaeus*, where the divine *dêmiourgos* uses the Form as *paradeigma* "model," see Alexander Nehamas, "Plato on Imitation and Poetry in *Republic* 10," in J. Moravcsik and P. Temko, eds., *Plato on Beauty, Wisdom, and the Arts* (Totowa: Roman and Allanheld, 1982), pp. 73–74 n. 32d.

11 See 48e5–6: ἓν μὲν ὡς παραδείγματος εἶδος ὑποτεθέν, νοητὸν καὶ ἀεὶ κατὰ ταὐτὰ ὄν "one [ontological kind] posited as the Form of the model, intelligible and always being the same" and 52a1–4: ὁμολογητέον ἓν μὲν εἶναι τὸ κατὰ ταὐτὰ εἶδος ἔχον, ἀγέννητον καὶ ἀνώλεθρον . . . ἀόρατον δὲ καὶ ἄλλως ἀναίσθητον, τοῦτο ὃ δὴ νόησις εἴληχεν ἐπισκοπεῖν "it must be agreed that there is one, the unchanging Form, ungenerated and indestructible . . . not-visible and also otherwise not-perceptible by the senses, it is this which in fact thinking has obtained as its portion to look upon."

12 For the *paradeigma* of the *kosmos* as eternal, see 37d1.

13 See 30c3–31a1: "In likeness to which of the living things did the constructor *(ho sunistas)* construct *(sunestêsen)* it [the *kosmos*]? Not to any of those things that belong by nature to the category of the part, let us deign to claim. For nothing that is like to that which lacks completeness *(atelei)* could ever become beautiful *(kalon)*. Rather let us lay it down that it is most like to this of all things: that of which all other living things are, one by one and according to their families, parts. For indeed that holds contained in itself all intelligible *(noêta)* living things, just as this *kosmos* contains us and as many other creatures as have been constructed as visible."

14 See 48e6–7: μίμημα δὲ παραδείγματος δεύτερον, γένεσιν ἔχον καὶ ὁρατόν "and the second [ontological kind], the copy of the model, possessing coming-into-being and visible" and 52a4–7: τὸ δὲ ὁμώνυμον ὅμοιόν τε ἐκείνῳ δεύτερον, αἰσθητόν, γεννητόν, πεφορημένον ἀεί, γιγνόμενόν τε ἔν τινι τόπῳ καὶ πάλιν ἐκεῖθεν ἀπολλύμενον, δόξῃ μετ᾽ αἰσθήσεως περιληπτόν· "The second [ontological kind] is of the same name and like to that one, perceptible by the senses, generated, always having been moved, both coming-into-being in a certain place and again passing away from there, graspable by opinion with the aid of perception."

absolutely passive, a *tabula rasa,* contributing nothing of itself to the copying.[15] To explain this requirement, Timaeus makes use of analogies, one from gold sculpture and another from perfume, in which the absence of contaminating elements in the medium ensures the fidelity of the copy to its model.[16] Such passivity was not, however, the condition of *chôra* before the building of the *kosmos.*

After summing up the relation among the three cosmic kinds (51e6–52d3), Timaeus turns in a sort of "flash back" to the earlier *(proteron)* state of *chôra,* before the construction of the *kosmos* by the *dêmiourgos.* Rather than character-free inertia, this pre-cosmic *chôra* manifests a condition of reciprocal dynamics, in which unequal forces produce perpetual and simultaneous shaking and being shaken (52d4–53a7):

> Before heaven came into being, the nurse of becoming [that is, *chôra*], being made wet and fiery, and receiving the shapes *(morphas)* of both earth and air, and undergoing *(paschusan)* as many other conditions *(pathê)* as go with these, showed appearances of every sort *(pantodapên)* to see. And because of being filled with forces *(dynameôn)* that were neither the same *(homoiôn)* nor of equal weight *(isorropôn)*, in no part of herself was she equally balanced *(isorropôn)*. But swaying everywhere unevenly *(anômalôs,* from *an* "not" + *omalos* "even, level")*, she herself was shaken *(seiesthai)* by those unequal forces, and by being moved *(kinoumenên)*, she shook *(seiein)* those forces back in turn *(au palin)*. By being moved *(kinoumena)*, they were continually separated and carried in different directions—just as when things are shaken *(seiomena)* and winnowed by baskets and tools for the cleaning of corn, the thick and heavy corn goes in one direction, and the thin and light husks in another. At that time *(tote)*, in the same way, the four kinds *(genê,* that is, pre-cosmic water, fire, earth, and air) were shaken *(seiomena)* by her who received them, which was herself being moved *(kinoumenês)* like a tool producing a shaking *(seismon)*, so as to separate the most unlike *(anomoiotata)* kinds farthest from one another and to thrust the most alike *(homoiotata)* close together. Indeed, in this earlier time *(pro toutou)*, all these four kinds were incalculable *(alogôs)* and unmeasurable *(ametrôs)*.

---

15   See 50d4–e1: "and it is also necessary to understand that if an impress is going to be variegated *(poikilou)* to see with respect to all variegations *(pasas poikilias)*, this in which what is impressed is placed must be well prepared, not otherwise than being without the shape *(amorphon)* of all those forms, as many as it is going to receive from elsewhere."

16   For the example of gold sculpture, see 50a5–b8, and for that of perfume, 50e4–8.

After this description of the pre-cosmic *chôra,* Timaeus resumes his account of how the *dêmiourgos* built the *kosmos,* now articulating the attributes that make it a "beautiful order" (53b1–b6):

> But when he [the *dêmiourgos* "craftsman"] took it in hand to make a *kosmos* of the universe *(kosmeisthai to pan),* fire first and water and earth and air had some traces *(ichnê* "footprints") of themselves, but were in all ways indeed to be sure disposed as it is likely that anything is, when the god is absent from it. To these, being then *(tote)* by nature in this condition, he gave *schêma* "pattern" for the first time *(prôton dieschêmatisato)* by measurable solid forms *(eidesi te kai arithmoîs* "by both forms and numbers," that is, the "Platonic" geometrical solids). And that the god constructed *(sunistanai)* them, to the degree that it is possible, as most beautiful and good *(kallista arista te)* out of what is not thus, beyond all else let this be asserted by us always.

And in conclusion he recapitulates (69b2–c3):

> For just as was said at the beginning, because these things [the pre-cosmic elements] were lacking order *(ataktôs),* in each—in relation both to itself and to the others—the god created symmetrical relations *(summetrias,* from *sum* "with" + *metria* "measurability") in all the ways it was possible for them to be proportional *(analoga)* and measured together *(summetra).* For before *(tote)* they had no share of these qualities, except insofar as it happened by chance, and there was nothing at all worthy of the names we now use—like fire and water and the rest. But all these he first put in beautiful order *(dieskosmêsen)* and then from them constructed *(sunestêsato)* this universe, one living thing having all living things in itself both mortal and immortal.

Putting together the first and third phases of Timaeus' story, we have a composite of the characteristics that make the *kosmos* a model of architectural beauty. From the first, we know that the *kosmos* is a true copy of its Formal model, because its medium *chôra* "place, space" is wholly passive, contributing nothing of itself to the copying. From the third, we know that the material solid forms that give to the *kosmos* its *schêma* "pattern" are *kallista arista te* "most beautiful and good" and that they possess every possible relation of mutual measurability. For example, a Platonic solid like the pyramid is always and everywhere a true copy of its Formal model, and by virtue of this uniformity, every such solid can be symmetrical—"measured with"—another, and the measurements of one solid can be proportional to those of another.

These features of the beautiful *kosmos* stand in sharp contrast to those of the pre-cosmic *chôra*. As opposed to the uniformity of the elementary cosmic solids, the four elements—water, fire, earth, and air—in their pre-cosmic state are formally heterogeneous, with their own "shapes" *(morphas)*, and visually variegated, "of every sort *(pantodapên)* to see." In relation to its cosmic condition, each element is already a "trace"—a footprint before the foot, an index before its origin, as it were—a mimetic abstraction of its condition yet to come. And because these elementary forces are of unequal weight, pre-cosmic *chôra* is in a state of continual *anômalia* "unevenness" producing a perpetual "loop" of "shaking" and "being shaken" at the same time. Over against this on-going *anômalia* of the pre-cosmic *chôra*, is the condition of the *kosmos* in which unevenness is episodic: sometimes there is equilibrium and sometimes the disequilibrium necessary for movement.[17] Indeed, in the *kosmos,* opposite conditions like "evenness" and "unevenness" exclude each other, but in the pre-cosmic *chôra,* the opposite conditions of "shaking" and "being shaken"—the opposite conditions of "active" and "passive"—are simultaneous. And unlike the presence of all possible calculable symmetries and proportional relations in the *kosmos*, pre-cosmic *chôra* is "incalculable" *(alogôs)*, "unmeasurable" *(ametrôs)*, and proportional or symmetrical only "insofar as it happened by chance."

The beautiful *kosmos* "order" vs. pre-cosmic *chôra:* which prefigures "animate form"?

We may now return to the question with which we began: can the model of the *kosmos* in the *Timaeus*, the foundation of Western architectural beauty, determine aesthetic merit in the latest architectural innovation of the 20th-century? The answer would seem to be, no. For in the works of "animate form" we find not a counterpart of the beautiful *kosmos,* but a far-flung kinship between the earliest layer of Timaeus' cosmology and architecture's latest manifestation. The *Timaeus* is the ultimate antecedent for "animate form," but not in the figure of the *kosmos*. Rather, by virtue of its mathematical base, animation software can generate forms prefigured in the features of the pre-cosmic *chôra*. Pre-cosmic *chôra* was "incalculable and unmeasurable" because classical mathematics could not calculate and measure continual *anômalia* "unevenness." But because it is calculus-based, animation software can calculate, measure, and construct continuously irregular curved surfaces, continual architectural "anomaly."

---

17 See 57e2–58a2.

As pre-cosmic *chôra* is simultaneously active and passive, so the surfaces of "animate form" can turn back on themselves, thus erasing the distinction between active and passive movement—as, for example, in the configuration termed "bleb," a "pocket of space formed when a surface intersects with itself, making a captured space."[18] A "bleb" is created by connecting curves that turn back so as to overlap themselves. (**Figure 2**) For example, such self-intersecting curves are lined up vertically. (**Figure 2a**) Then, the input operation called "lofting" connects the curves and forms a surface. (**Figure 2b and 2c**) Then the surface can be trimmed to form an enclosure. (**Figure 2d**) The "bleb" technique is used by Greg Lynn in

Figure 2: The Formation of a "Bleb." (Model by Ann Bergren)

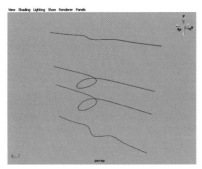

2a. Self-intersecting curves lined up.

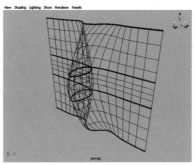

2b. Loft the curves to form the surface, wireframe view.

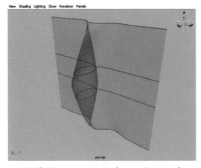

2c. Loft the curves to form the surface, shaded view.

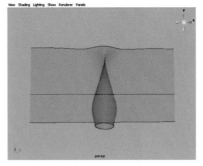

2d. Surface trimmed to form an enclosure.

---

18   For this definition, see Greg Lynn, "Learn, Bleb" at *www.platostimaeustoday.com.*

Imaginary Forces New York, an office renovation of 2000. (**Figure 3**) First, a series of bleb-formed surfaces is created. (**Figure 3a**) Then the surfaces are trimmed to form enclosures. (**Figure 3b**) These trimmed enclosures become the new rooms in the existing building. (**Figure 3c**)

As pre-cosmic *chôra* is animated by a "loop" of dynamic forces, so by the application of the "blend shape" tool, forms transform, one into another. Lynn uses this operation to design a large, interior lantern for the *Bloom House,*

Figure 3: *Imaginary Forces New York,* Greg Lynn, 2000. (Courtesy of Greg Lynn FORM)

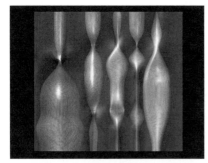

3a. A series of bleb-formed surfaces.

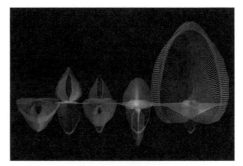

3b. Bleb-formed surfaces trimmed to form enclosures.

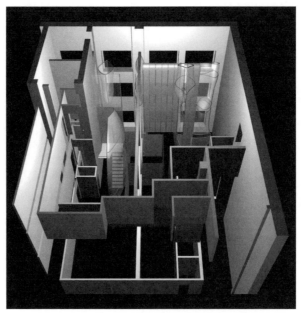

3c. Trimmed enclosures become new rooms in the existing building.

2008. (**Figure 4**) First, a surface is formed by lofting curves that will form the ribs where the panels of the lantern are connected. Then the "blend shape" tool undulates that surface into the form that maximizes the opportunities of the room's spatial parameters. To see the animation, go to Figure 5 at *www.platostimaeustoday.com*. (**Figure 5**)

And as the four elements in pre-cosmic *chôra* are *ichnê* "footprints" of their concrete, cosmic condition, so in their stylized biomorphology, many works of "animate form" display a penchant for abstract *mimêsis*.[19] The six houses that make up Greg Lynn's *Embryological House,* for example, are proleptic "traces"

Figure 4: Lantern of the *Bloom House,* Greg Lynn, 2008. (Courtesy of Greg Lynn FORM)

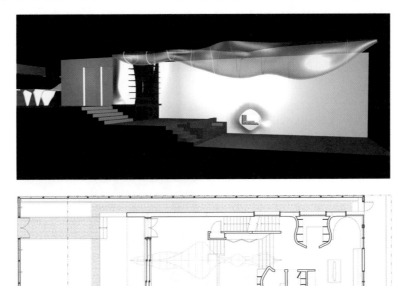

Rendering and reflected plan of the *Bloom House* lantern.

---

19 I use the term "abstract" here in a sense akin to that developed by John Rajchman in his analysis of Giles Deleuze's "anti-Platonist" concept of "abstraction" in philosophy and art, in "Abstraction" in John Rajchman, *Constructions* (Cambridge: MIT Press, 1998), pp. 55–76. Against the "view of abstraction as a process of extracting pure or essential Forms, emptying a space of its concrete contents," Deleuze posits "an abstraction that consists in an impure mixing and mixing up, prior to Forms, a reassemblage that moves toward an outside rather than a purification that turns up essential Ideas or in toward the constitutive 'forms' of a medium." Against a process of negation or subtraction—abstract as "what is *not* figurative, not narrative"—this abstraction is a "great, prodigious, conceptual 'And . . .'."

of literal embryos. (**Figure 6**) Having emerged from vectoral forces applied to primitive spheres, they begin life as a group of what Lynn calls "gastrulated rooms," a non-Platonic abstraction of the process by which an embryo folds on itself to form a *gastêr,* the Greek word for "stomach."[20] (**Figure 6a**) From this initial host of gastrulated forms, Lynn chooses six that display wide variation and invents a structural system for them. The selected volumes are then developed through interaction of their forces with the forces of a ground plane: in another instance of the simultaneity of active and passive forces in pre-cosmic *chôra*, here the ground deforms the volume, as the volume deforms the ground, thus nesting the house in a folded plinth. (**Figure 6b**) Further mutual deformation between volume and ground creates interstitial zones for transitional elements, such as the pod-shaped gardens or the patio, which is rendered in glass, so that the house appears to be floating above the ground.[21] (**Figure 6c**) The composite is shown in a plan view of the six houses together with an exploded axonometric compilation of their components: the roof, the house volume, the structure, the glass transition, and the ground. (**Figure 6d**)

Figure 6: Phases of the Design of *Embryological House,* Greg Lynn, 1999. (Courtesy of Greg Lynn FORM)

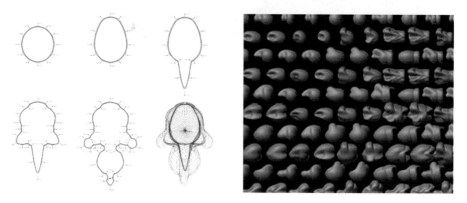

6a. Vectoral forces transform primitive spheres into a host of "gastrulated rooms."

---

20 Lynn's "gastrulated rooms" are not an example of simple abstraction from natural models. For these forms were neither generated by looking toward a *gastêr* "stomach" in the mind's eye beforehand, like the *dêmiourgos* "craftsman" looking toward the Formal model, nor motivated by a desire to abstract one of its qualities, its curved surfaces, for example. They were altogether formed before they were "gastrulated." They emerge from a conceptual "and" that "mixes" *gastêr* and "room" with no clouding or reduction of the material specificity of either. We will find a similar mimetic abstraction in the artifacts of "Homeric beauty," see below, pp. 362–368.

21 The garden is formed as a bleb: the equator of the gastrulated shape of the house is copied and offset repeatedly until it turns around on itself.

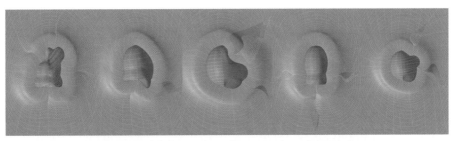

6b. The ground deforms the volume, as the volume deforms
the ground, nesting the house in a folded plinth.

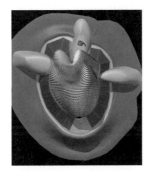

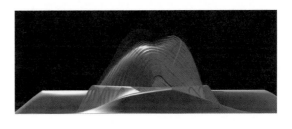

6c. Plan view (left) and front elevation (right) show pod-shaped gardens and a
glass-paneled patio formed by mutual deformation between volume and ground.

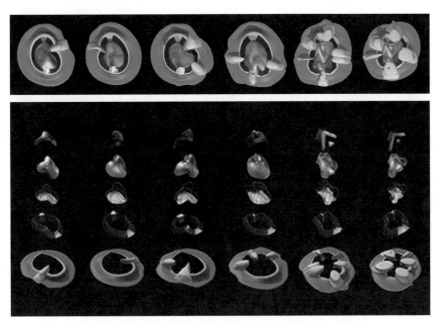

6d. A plan view (above) of the six houses with an exploded
axonometric compilation of their components (below).

An animation recaps this design process. To view the animation go to Figure 6e at *www.platostimaeustoday.com*. (**Figure 6e**)

But which one of these six houses is beautiful? Even if they are formally cognate with the pre-cosmic *chôra*, can the model of architectural beauty embodied in the *kosmos* not determine their aesthetic status? Let us recall its criteria: to be beautiful like the *kosmos*, a material object must be a perfect copy of its Formal model. As such, it will display the features that render the *kosmos* "most beautiful and good" *(kallista arista te)*: the *schêma* "pattern" of its elements, the Platonic solids, all proportional *(analoga)* and mutually measurable *(summetra)*. Gauged against this model, it would seem that no work of "animate form" could be beautiful. For insofar as it exemplifies the perpetual "loop" of dynamic transformation that we saw in the pre-cosmic *chôra*, no such work can have an ideal, unchanging, immortal Form as a model. Applying this model of beauty, the answer to our question must be "no one of these houses is beautiful."

But are we assessing the category of the "Form" too narrowly? Could we perhaps say that in the case of "animate form," an input operation in the animation software, the "blend shape" tool, for example, functions like a Form, a Formal model, in relation to its series of outputs? If that is the case, then the Platonic model of beauty in the *Timaeus* would be confounded, even as it is confirmed. For every phase, every moment—every frame—of any animation is an equally perfect instance of its input operation. It would thus not be possible for any of them to be a less than perfect "copy" of their "model," a less than perfect instantiation of the animating script. In the Platonic model, if an object claims to be beautiful, this claim can be verified as true, because it can be falsified. It can be shown to be false by showing that the claimant is an imperfect copy of its Form. But in the case of a work of "animate form," no such claim to beauty can be falsified, so none can be shown to be true. If an animating operation is a kind of Form, then the answer to our question would have to be "every one and no one of these houses is beautiful."

But, finally, is there yet another way in which the Platonic category of the "Form" might be interpreted with regard to architectural beauty? What if the true model of an architectural project, the ideal against which the real object is to be measured, is the architect's preconceived concept of a project, the drawing and model he or she makes of it in the mind's eye? In this conception of aesthetic merit, the architect's intention is like a Platonic Form, in that a work of architecture is "beautiful" to the degree that it represents the architect's subjective vision. But here, too, the theory would fail to discern beauty in "animate form." For while the design process may be motivated by a method of fabrication, as in the *Bloom House* lantern, or influenced by a figural analogue, as in *Embryological House,* in the case of architecture designed with animation-based software, no fully pre-conceived, subjective vision of the final form *inside* the mind's eye of the architect is possible before the design process begins. It would seem, then, that in "animate form," the Platonic *kosmos* has met a limit in its capacity to model and to adjudicate architectural beauty.

This limit does not, however, mean that the *Timaeus* is irrelevant to the aesthetics of "animate form." For the pre-cosmic *chôra* not only points forward in time by prefiguring this new architecture. It also reaches back, before the advent of Platonic philosophy, by echoing features of another tradition of Classical beauty, features that themselves predict the attributes defined by Greg Lynn as constituting beauty in "animate form."

In this other aesthetic tradition, the word "beautiful" is used of material works of art and craft that fall under the category of *mêtis,* "transformative intelligence," the mental and the material process common to every artisanal *technê* "craft."[22] The working and the work of *mêtis* share with the pre-cosmic *chôra* the attributes of variegation, perpetual shape-shifting, simultaneity of opposites such as active and passive, and an allo-Platonic mode of *mimêsis.* As the pre-cosmic *chôra* "showed appearances of every sort *(pantodapên)* to see," so a work of *mêtis* is *pantoios* "multiple, manifold, of every sort or kind," *poikilos* "variegated, differentiated," and *aiolos* "glittering, mobile, animated."[23] As the pre-cosmic *chôra* is constituted of the different *morphas* "shapes" of the pre-cosmic elements, themselves of different weights, so *mêtis* is forever polymorphic and polyvalent.[24] As the different weights of the pre-cosmic elements produce a simultaneity of shaking and being shaken, so creatures endowed with *mêtis* possess qualities ordinarily opposite, like the cuttle-fishes with their eyes on one side and their mouth on the other, with their "heads haloed by their waving feet," and by their swimming sideways, every direction is at once both front and back.[25] And as the pre-cosmic elements display an enigmatic resemblance across the boundaries of present and future, and effect and cause, being proleptic *ichnê* "footprints" of their exemplars yet to come, so the arts of *mêtis* produce "diagonal imitations" across ontological divides, as when the living fox plays the dead one, thus reversing without erasing the line between animate and inanimate.[26] By virtue of a shared semantic field, the concept of

---

22   For the definitive work on *mêtis,* see Marcel Detienne and Jean-Pierre Vernant, *Cunning Intelligence in Greek Culture and Society* (Chicago: University of Chicago Press, 1991). For the role of *mêtis* in early Greek architectural thought, see Ann Bergren, "Architecture Gender Philosophy," in Ann Bergren, *Weaving Truth: Essays on Language and the Female in Greek Thought* (Cambridge: Harvard University Press for the Center for Hellenic Studies, 2008), pp. 260–265. The absence of *mêtis* from Platonic thought, except in the figure of the goddess Metis, the mother of Eros' father Resource, at *Symposium* 203b3, may be motivated by the fact that there could be no Form of such continual shape-shifting.

23   See Detienne and Vernant, above note, p. 27.

24   Detienne and Vernant, p. 27.

25   Detienne and Vernant, p. 38.

26   The idea of "diagonal imitation" across natural *genera* derives from the "diagonal science" of Roger Caillois described in Claudine Frank, ed., *The Edge of Surrealism: A Roger Caillois*

mêtis leads to the fullest expression of this other Classical beauty, the objects termed *kalos* "beautiful" in the Homeric epics.

The "Homeric beauty" of "animate form"

Together with the analysis contained in his book, *Animate Form,* Greg Lynn has published several essays that articulate the aesthetics of "animate form." This 21st-century aesthetics echoes the model of beauty in the foundation of Greek thought, Homeric epic. For in the *Iliad* and the *Odyssey,* more than of either gods or humans or the phenomena of nature, the words for "beautiful," *kalos* and its compounds, are used of material works of art and craft.[27] By this preponderance of usage, the verbal medium pays tribute to the visual, material artifact. The epics also name the attributes that make an object beautiful. Three in particular belong to the semantic field of *mêtis* and also forecast aesthetic virtues of "animate form" described by Lynn: *daidalos* "elaborately crafted, detailed (in an architectural sense)" and *poludaidalos* "with much elaborate craft, with much detail"; *poikilos* "variegated, differentiated, multiplicitous" and *pampoikilos* "all-variegated"; and *aiolos* "glittering, mobile, animated" and *panaiolos* "all-glittering." In addition to these key features, many artifacts in epic qualify as beautiful (as do objects in the *Timaeus*) by virtue of a mode of imitation, but the model of *mimêsis* in Homeric epic differs in fundamental respects from the Platonic relation between material copy and Formal model and looks forward instead to the tropes of "animate form." After charting these analogies between the features of beautiful artifacts in epic and aspects of Lynn's aesthetics, we will observe some examples of this "Homeric beauty" in works of "animate form" by the architect and engineer, Elena Manferdini.

daidalos and "intricacy"

When artifacts termed "beautiful" in Homeric epic are described by the poet, it is not symmetry or structure or proportion—prime elements of the model of beauty in the *Timaeus*— that are singled out for notice, but rather attributes of technical execution.[28] One of these is denoted by the adjective *daidalos.*[29] Since the etymology of this word is uncertain, its meaning must be deduced from the traits of the objects it describes.[30] In Homer *daidalos* does not designate any

---

Reader (Durham and London: Duke University Press, 2003).

27   60% in the *Iliad* and 48.25% in the *Odyssey.*

28   See Hanna Philipp, *Tektonon Daidala: Der bildende Künstler und sein Werk im vorplatonischen Schrifttum* (Berlin: Bruno Hessling, 1968), pp. 4–5.

29   For a magisterial study of *daidalos* in Greek literature and art, see Sarah P. Morris, *Daidalos and the Origins of Greek Art* (Princeton: Princeton University Press, 1992).

30   See Morris, p. 3.

single method of fabrication, but is used of the entire range of artifacts. Some employ the various modes of intertwining or interlocking of discrete elements taught by the goddess Athena—weaving, embroidery, furniture, shipbuilding, and the *choros* "dancing floor" at Cnossus built by the legendary master architect Daedalus, himself named for this quality of his art.[31] Some are works of fusion taught by the metallurgic god Hephaestus—armor, jewelry, and cups in bronze, tin, gold, or silver, and the divine smith's own self-moving tripods with gold wheels on their legs. And some combine these techniques, as when metal strips or nails are inlaid in fine cabinetry. What is common to all these *daidala* is the elaborate, complex, and always precious craftsmanship.[32] In architectural terms what *daidala* share, the attribute that contributes to making them beautiful, is that they are permeated and constituted by "detail." In the Homeric description of beautiful artifacts, there is no sign of the later hierarchical discrimination of structure over detail, whole over part.

As such the word *daidalos* looks forward to Greg Lynn's concept of "intricacy" as an intrinsic feature of "beauty." In his catalogue essay for the exhibition he curated entitled "Intricacy," Lynn describes the features by which "these works make a claim toward elegance, rigor, expertise, and, dare say, beauty."[33] In Lynn's conception, "intricacy is the fusion of disparate elements into continuity, the becoming whole of components that retain their status as pieces in a larger composition. Unlike simple hierarchy, subdivision, compartmentalization or modularity, intricacy involves a variation of the parts that is not reducible to the structure of the whole."[34] Accordingly, intricate objects share with *daidala* a ubiquity of detail:[35]

> Detail need not be the reduction of concentration of architectural design into a discrete moment. In an intricate network, there are no details per se. Detail is everywhere, ubiquitously distributed and continuously variegated in collaboration with formal and spatial effects. Instead of punctuating volumetric minimalism with discrete details, intricacy implies complexity all over without recourse to compositional contrast.

Like *daidala*, these intricate works employ Athena's art, the "compositional practices of weaving, folding, and joining," for "intricacy occurs where

---

31 For other *redende Namen* of craftsmen in Homer, *Tektôn* "Builder" and *Harmonidês* "Joiner," see Morris, p. 3.

32 See Morris, p. 30.

33 Greg Lynn, *Intricacy: A Project by Greg Lynn FORM* (Philadelphia: University of Pennsylvania, 2003), p. 1.

34 Lynn, *Intricacy*, p. 1.

35 Lynn, *Intricacy*, p. 1.

macro- and micro-scales of components are interwoven and intertwined.[36] And in their continuous variegation, the details of intricate objects recall the closeness in sense between *daidalos* and the attribute of beautiful artifacts in Homer designated by the adjective *poikilos.*

poikilos and "variation"

Greg Lynn continues his delineation of the concept of "intricacy" in the essay "Calculated Variations."[37] There he stresses the capacity of calculus-based design tools to create "variation" within "a high degree of continuity" and explains that "this combination of variability and continuity yields a quality I call 'intricacy'."[38] The surfaces thus created are "meshes made from networks of curves," the curve functioning, "even if straight" both to unite and divide differing entities. This linkage between "intricacy" and "variation within continuity" aptly parallels the relation between *daidalos* and *poikilos* in epic.

The meaning of *poikilos* seems so close to that of *daidalos* that the two are sometimes taken for synonyms. And the collocation in *Odyssey* 1.130–132, where Telemachus seats Athena-Mentes, would seem to support that conclusion:

> He led and seated her in an arm-chair, after spreading a fine cloth on it, an armchair beautiful *(kalon)* and intricate *(daidalon)*. And for her feet there was a stool underneath. And nearby he himself placed a variegated *(poikilon)* chair.

The variegation of the chair here may be in colors of paint or in materials, wood inlaid with ivory, for example. Such a chair could also be termed *daidalos,* as is the armchair. And *poikilos* is used of a range of artifacts similar to that of *daidalos*—woven or embroidered fabric, wooden furniture,[39] armor,[40]

---

36 Lynn, *Intricacy*, p. 1.
37 Greg Lynn, "Calculated Variations," in Bernard Tschumi and Irene Cheng, eds., *State of Architecture at the Beginning of the 21st Century* (New York: Monacelli Press, 2003), pp. 72–73.
38 Lynn, "Calculated Variations," p. 72.
39 *Odyssey* 1.132.
40 See the collocations with *teuchea* "armor" at *Iliad* 3.327, 4.432, 6.504, 10.504, 12.396, 13.181 and 14.420, with *entea* "armor" at *Iliad* 10.75, with *sakos* "shield" at *Iliad* 10.149, and *thôrax* "breastplate" at *Iliad* 16.134. Note also the use at *Iliad* 18.590 of the verb *poikillô* of metalwork in Hephaestus' creation of the *choros* "dancing floor" on Achilles' shield.

chariots,[41] a chariot-board.[42] The specific nuance of *poikilos* seems to be one of comprehensive quantity, of multiplicity within a singularity, of differentiated, serial elements in the same entity—the many interwoven threads, perhaps of different colors, functioning, like curves in a work of "animate form," simultaneously to "unite and divide" the *peplos* "gown," or the several twists in the *poikilos desmos* "complex knot" that Odysseus learned from Circe (*Odyssey* 8.448), or the various spots on the skin of a leopard or a fawn (*Iliad* 10.30, *Odyssey* 19.228), or the *throna* "flowers" of variegated color or form that Andromache weaves into a double, purple web, while Hector is defending Troy (*Iliad* 22.441), or *thektêria panta* "all the enchantments" figured in Aphrodite's irresistible girdle (*Iliad* 14.214, 220). Hence the intensive form of the adjective *poikilos* is not formed with *polu* "much," as in *poludaidalos* "with much elaborate craft," but with *pan* "all"—*pampoikilos* "all variegated."

aiolos and "animation"

In the world of Homeric epic, beautiful objects, although stable, are not static. The appreciation of pervasive detail in *daidalos* and continuous variegation in *poikilos* give rise to an aesthetics of mobility and signs of life. This feature of beautiful artifacts is highlighted in the adjective *aiolos* "glittering, mobile, animated." Like *daidalos* and *poikilos*, it has an intensive form, *panaiolos* "all-glittering." Etymologically cognate with Sanskrit *âyu* "force of life" and Greek *aiôn* "life,"[43] the word denotes liveliness and rapid movement, often that of light as it flashes from metal. For also like *daidalos* and *poikilos*, *aiolos* is used of armor, the artifact most frequently called "beautiful" in the *Iliad*.[44] But it also describes various animals in motion, "wriggling worms" (*Iliad* 22.509), a "writhing snake" (*Iliad* 12.208), "flickering wasps" (*Iliad* 12.127), a "darting gad-fly" (*Odyssey* 22.300), and the "swift-glancing feet" of Achilles' horse Xanthus (*Iliad* 19.404).[45] In each case, the movement is vital, the proof that

---

41 *Iliad* 5.239, 10.393, 13.181, 537 and 14.431, *Odyssey* 3.492 and 15.145, 190. Both *teuchea* "armor" (*Iliad* 6.504, 13.18, 14.420) and *armata* "chariots" (*Iliad* 4.226, 10.322) are qualified as *poikila chalkôi* "variegated with bronze." For the possibility that the reference is to bronze rivets, see Richard Janko, *The Iliad: A Commentary* Volume IV: Books 13–16 (Cambridge: Cambridge University Press, 1994), p. 334.

42 *Iliad* 10.501.

43 See Emile Benveniste, "Expression Indo-européenne de l' 'éternité'," *Bulletin de la société de linguistique de Paris* 38 (1937), pp. 103–112.

44 The form *aiolos* is used of a seven-layered bull hide *sakos* "shield" with an eighth layer of bronze on the top at *Iliad* 7.222, of another *sakos* "shield" at *Iliad* 16.107, and of *teuchea pamphanoônta* " all-gleaming armor" at *Iliad* 5.295, and the intensive form *panaiolos* is applied at *Iliad* 4.186 and 11.236 to a warrior's *zôstêr* body-girdle of leather and metal plates.

45 Note also the use of the verbal form *aiollêi* of a man "turning back and forth" as he cooks a haggis (*Odyssey* 20.27).

the animal is alive. Thus *aiolos* as a feature of "Homeric beauty" looks forward to the heart of "animate form," animation itself.

Closely related, like "variation," to the concept of "intricacy" is Lynn's concept of "animation." Lynn uses the word in a wide sense, one that recalls the semantic range of its kernel in Latin *anima* "the air breathed by an animal, life breath, principle and sign of vitality, consciousness, soul." Thus *Animate Form* opens: "animation implies the evolution of a form and its shaping forces; it suggests animalism, animism, growth, actuation, vitality and virtuality."[46] And in the essay *Intricacy* this vision of animation is extended even to include the machine. Under the heading "Vital Mechanisms" he writes:[47]

> Intricacy of movement is one of the characteristics of a regime of machines that began to express a new kind of mechanical complexity in the 16th century and continues to do so today. The robot is, and has been, the ultimate expression of a machine capable of detailed organic movements . . . . All the work in this exhibition is in one way or another robotic.

This praise for mechanical vitality echoes the aim of *mimêsis* in the beautiful artifacts of epic.

mimêsis and "animate form"

The metallurgic god Hephaestus, pre-eminent maker of "Homeric beauty" in the shield of Achilles, is aided in his artifaction by a troop of "vital mechanisms," his golden female robotic assistants. As the lame Hephaestus departs from his forge to greet Achilles' mother Thetis, these golden maidens are described (*Iliad* 18.416–420):[48]

> He went out
> limping; and to aid their lord there moved swiftly handmaidens
> made of gold, like to living young women.
> In these is intelligence *(nous)* in their minds, and in them speech
> and strength, and from the immortal gods they know handiwork
> *(erga)*.

---

46 Lynn, *Animate Form,* p. 9.
47 Lynn, *Intricacy,* p. 3.
48 On these golden maidens, see Morris, p. 226. See also the golden dogs "immortal and ageless all their days" made by Hephaestus to guard the palace of Alcinous (*Odyssey* 7.91–94).

These animated sculptures are apt agents of Hephaestus' art. For the aim of *mimêsis* in works of "Homeric beauty" is literally "animate form." Imitation in epic artifacts is a cross-genus resemblance that maintains even as it defies generic specificity. For Homeric epic accords to plastic artifacts its own mimetic power: as the poem imitates motion and sound while remaining silent and inert, so it describes the creatures in artifacts as animated—in motion and making sounds—"even though of gold." This broach on Odysseus' cloak is exemplary (*Odyssey* 19.225–231):[49]

> Noble Odysseus was wearing a fleecy purple cloak
> double-folded, but the broach upon it was fashioned of gold
> with double clasps, and on the front it was intricately wrought
> (*daidalon*):
> in his front paws a dog was holding a dappled (*poikilon*) fawn,
> twisting and turning (*aspaironta*) as the dog is gripping (*laôn*) it.
> And at this all the people were continuously amazed:[50]
> how, although they were of gold (*hoi chruseoi eontes*), the dog was
> gripping (*lae*) the fawn, strangling it,
> but the fawn by struggling with its feet is striving to flee.

Similarly, on the shield Hephaestus makes for Achilles, ascriptions of motion and sound are combined with repeated assertion of the work's metallic medium.[51] In contrast to the Platonic model in which the *kosmos* imitates perduring, unchanging, static Forms, *mimêsis* in Homeric artifacts is rather like the contemporary technology of "motion capture."[52] Nestor's marvelous cup similarly captures motion (*Iliad* 11.632–635):

> and beside them, an exceedingly beautiful (*perikalles*) cup, that
> the old man brought from home,
> studded with golden nails. Its ear-handles were
> four in number and about each of them two doves,
> made of gold, were feeding, and below there were two supports.

---

49 See Morris, p. 227.
50 Note the frequentative *thaumazeskon*.
51 See the advancing army of the besieged city, led by Ares and Athena, "both of gold and wearing gold clothes" (*Iliad* 18.517), the field that "grew black and looked like ploughed land, even though being gold: indeed that was the marvel (*thauma*) that had been wrought (*tetukto*)" (548–549), the vineyard with its "trench of dark-blue lapis" and "fence of tin" (564–565), and the lowing cattle of gold and tin with their golden herdsmen walking beside them (574–577). On this feature of the shield, see Philipp, pp. 7–8 and Morris, p. 227.
52 See *http://en.wikipedia.org/wiki/Motion_capture*.

Like the "abstract *mimêsis*" of Lynn's "gastrulated forms," these "gold doves feeding" maintain, even as they transcend, the difference between animal and mineral.

This vision of an artificial, metallic artifact animated with sound and motion looks forward to the powers attributed in the time of Socrates to the works of the foundational artisan Daedalus. But before looking at them and their possible influence upon the choice of a *dêmiourgos* "craftsman" as Plato's divine creator, let us see how the aesthetic correlations we have been tracing between "Homeric beauty" and "animate form" appear in the architecture of Elena Manferdini.

"Homeric beauty" in the "animate form" of Elena Manferdini

In addition to works by Greg Lynn himself, a variety of projects by architect-engineer, Elena Manferdini, display the features of "Homeric beauty" in "animate form." Manferdini uses animation software to make constructions in fabric that can also be realized in full-scale building. In order to work with fabric, she starts with surfaces that are "developable," always able to return to flat without stretching or tearing. In comparison with surfaces of complex curvature, developable surfaces admit of a wider range of fabrication methods. This technological economy facilitates the hallmark of Manferdini's designs, an immense series of intricate apertures, both repeating and gradually differing, an aesthetic of serial progression and differentiation evocative of minimalist music. Once gravity and air currents work upon these openings, what started as two-dimensional fabric becomes a three-dimensional architecture with its planes in perpetual motion. And once fabric turns into building, we find full-scale analogues of "gold doves feeding."

Manferdini's method is applied to fabric in *Clad Cuts*, 2005. (**Figure 7**) An animation using the "blend shape" tool generates a series of curves. To view the animation go to Figure 7a at *www.platostimaeustoday.com*. (**Figure 7a**) From this series, a curve is chosen to create the contours of openings that will be laser cut in the fabric and sealed. The goal is maximum curvature within the material tolerances of the fabrication process: if the configuration is too complex, the fabric will not hold together. But even with a single curve, variation in the openings emerges from five gradations of the area excised. (**Figure 7b**) Applying the algorithm to the laser cutter makes possible thousands of cuts, more than could be drawn or cut by hand, producing a virtually endless *anô-malia* "unevenness" of undulating opacity and aperture. (**Figure 7c**)

When such fabric is worn by a moving body, its planes become literally animated, in constant *chôra*-like movement. In the dress entitled, *Cherry Blossom*, Manferdini exploits the mimetic potential of this mobility, crafting an intricate spray, never static, of abstract "cherry blossoms." (**Figure 8**) First worn

Figure 7: *Clad Cuts,* Elena Manferdini, 2005 (Courtesy of Atelier Manferdini)

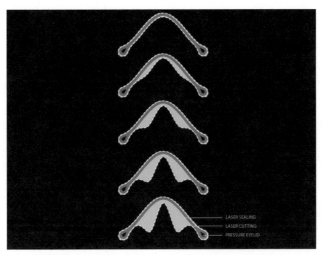

7b. Contours to be laser cut and sealed in the fabric.

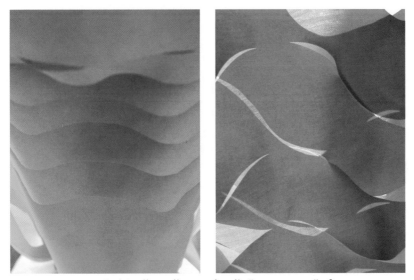

7c. A virtually endless *anômalia* "unevenness" of
undulating opacity and aperture.

in a fashion show to open the Beijing Biennale of 2007, the dress pre-figures
the outdoor pavilion Manferdini built for the same event. (**Figure 8a and 8b**)
Once rendered in a full-scale architectural structure, the design remains fluid,
as the wind sways the strips of twirling plastic.

Ceaseless motion and architectural allegory likewise mark Manferdini's
design of the dress and installation entitled *Merletti*inter*Lace: suspended canopy*

Figure 8: *Cherry Blossom*, Elena Manferdini, 2007 (Courtesy of Atelier Manferdini)

 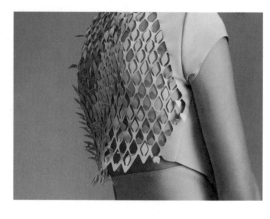

8a. An intricate spray, never static, of abstract "cherry blossoms."

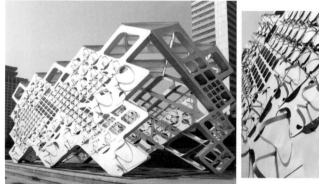 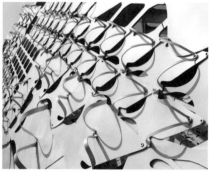

8b. An outdoor pavilion of abstract "cherry blossoms" with
twisting plastic strips that sway in the wind.

of 2008.[53] (**Figure 9**) This project is an abstraction of the Italian term, *merlétto,*
which designates both the lace made by women in Venice during the Renaissance
and the crenellation of perimeter walls.[54] (**Figure 9a**) This conceptual "mixing"

---

53   For a description of this installation, see *http://www.sciarc.edu/exhibition.php?id=1081.*
54   Translated from the *Dizionario Garzanti della Lingua Italiana*: (1) *merletto:* "Lace: decorative
border/motif of small points and generally patterned with open holes, obtained using different
braided threads; light and transparent fabric, constructed by different threads woven to form
an intricate and decorated surface. The word comes from "*merlo,*" because of its pointy border
that recalls the crenellation in military architecture." (2) *merlo:* "Merlons: the raised portions

Figure 9: *Merletti*inter*Lace: suspended canopy,* Elena
Manferdini, 2006 (Courtesy of Atelier Manferdini)

9a. *Merletti* "lace" in architecture and fabric.

9b. Cut-outs forming multiple, hanging filigrees.

of fabric and building is composed of twenty-six catenary cables suspended across an approximately 50' x 25' gallery. Strung along each cable are panels, their cut-outs forming multiple, hanging filigrees. (**Figure 9b**) As if inhaling and exhaling, the number of panels across a cable gradually increases and decreases three times—from 10 to 13 to 10, from 11 to 15 to 10, and from 9 to

---

of the wall-crown that frames the top of the perimeter walls of castles, towers, palaces, with the scope of defense or decoration."

9c. Model wearing the dress-version of the project wanders through the panels.

13 to 9. Also subtlety varying along the expanse are the patterns of the panels themselves, four in all, with increasing degrees of opening, through which a model wearing the dress-version of the project can wander. (**Figure 9c**)

And finally, in the 100-meter high *Fabric Tower* for Guiyang-Huaxi, China, Manferdini has designed a gigantic robot of "Homeric beauty." (**Figure 10**) Like *Merletti*inter*Lace,* the tower is an abstraction of a female's fabrication— here, the headdresses worn by the Miao women native to that area of China. (**Figure 10a**) Turned from the scale of a headdress, to the scale of a tower, the filigree becomes—like "golden doves feeding"—a "steel and glass gown flowing." In grand sweeps of colossal draping, pleats cascade from the crown, swelling and swerving, as if blown by winds from mountains nearby. (**Figure 10b**) And like the bottom of a curtain longer than its window, the folds curve at the base to lie in a lattice upon the grass, turning into landscape. (**Figure 10c**) An animation traces this design process. To view the animation go to Figure 10d at *www.platostimaeustoday.com.* (**Figure 10d**)

Why the *dêmiourgos* "craftsman"?

When composing Timaeus' cosmology, what was Plato's motive in making his creator god a "craftsman?"[55] Why did he think that a god who wanted to create

---

[55] In "Nature as Craftsman in Greek Thought," in Friedrich Solmsen, *Kleine Schriften* (Hildesheim: Georg Olms, 1968), pp. 339–344, Friedrich Solmsen derives Plato's choice from what he says about craftsmanship in other dialogues, in particular, *Gorgias* 503e with

Figure 10: *Fabric Tower,* Guiyang-Huaxi, China, Elena
Manferdini, 2008. (Courtesy of Atelier Manferdini)

10a. Filigree headdresses worn by Miao women, the inspiration for
the design of *Fabric Tower.* (Courtesy of Weizhong [Frank] Chen)

10b. Pleats of steel and glass swell and swerve.

10c. Folds turn into a lattice, forming a landscape.

beauty needed to emulate a human *dêmiourgos*? Perhaps the Homeric model of crafted beauty exerted some competitive influence. The sort of "animate form" we have seen in Homeric artifacts is ascribed in the fifth century to works by the legendary Daedalus.[56] As with epic objects that move and make sounds "while still being gold," the animated statues of Daedalus do not loose their material specificity. In fragment 188 (Kassel-Austin) of the comic poet Plato, for example, a statue of Hermes identifies itself thus: "I myself am Hermes, having a voice from Daedalus, made of wood, but walking on my own (*automatos*) I have come." Indeed, whether of wood or bronze or gold, "the statues made by Daedalus" are so "animated" that they must be "bound in order not to run away."[57] With this power of craftsmanship, sustaining material difference while exceeding its limits, and "mixing" within inert matter the sound and

---

its stress upon the crafted work as *tetagmenon kai kekosmêmenon* "arranged and ordered," *Republic* 506b6–10, and *Laws* 903c5–d1. In "Teleology and Craftsmanship," in *Plato's Natural Philosophy: A Study of the* Timaeus-Critias (Cambridge: Cambridge University Press, 2004), pp. 69–91 Thomas K. Johanson stresses that because its *dêmiourgos* "craftsman" looks toward an external, ordered, and unchanging model, the *kosmos* is necessarily beautiful and concludes that "Timaeus focuses upon the particular case of causation where the cause is a craftsman because this is the kind of cause that can *necessitate* the beauty of the outcome."

56 Morris, pp. 215–237 describes the "discourse on voice and animation in the inanimate" surrounding Daedalus as architect and sculptor in fifth-century drama and philosophy.

57 Aristophanes, *Daidalos,* fr. 194 (Kassel-Austin). On these comic fragments together with Cratinus, *Thracians,* fr. 75 (Kassel-Austin), see Morris, p. 220.

movement of life, the figure of Daedalus plays for Plato's Socrates a role of paternal precedent and opponent in constructive skill.

In the *Meno,* Socrates likens *doxai alêtheis* "true opinions," if left "unbound" to the soul by *logismos* "causal reasoning" via the process of *anamnêsis* "recollection," to Daedalus' statues: "unless they are bound, they run away as fugitive slaves," but "if one of them is bound, it is of great worth. For they are altogether beautiful works *(panu kala ta erga)."* When thus "bound," these opinions turn into abiding *epistêmê* "knowledge." "And this is why knowledge is more honored than right opinion: knowledge transcends right opinion by virtue of its bond *(desmos)"* (*Meno* 97d–98a). Socrates' philosophical craftsmanship rids Daedalic opinions of their mobility, leaving them stationary, "altogether beautiful works."

In "binding" Daedalic mobility, Socrates deposes a father. For in the *Euthyphro,* after Euthyphro complains that "whatever statement we put forth moves around and will not stay where we put it," Socrates says "your statements are like works of our ancestor *(progonos)* Daedalus" (11b7–c1).[58] The two banter about which of them is playing the "philosophical Daedalus" here by making the statements move around. "It is not I," insists Euthypro, "who makes these statements move around and not stay put, but you are the Daedalus—for they would have stayed, so far as I'm concerned" (11c7–d2). Socrates' response is first to supersede his ancestor, claiming that he is "more amazing in skill" *(deinoteros tên technên)* than Daedalus "inasmuch as he made only his own works move, but I, it seems, make others' move in addition to my own." Having thus supplanted Daedalus' mastery of movement, he disavows it, insisting "the most exquisite thing about my skill is that I am wise *(sophos)* against my will *(akôn),* for I would rather my words stay put and sit still without motion *(akinêtôs hidrusthai)* than possess the wisdom *(sophiai)* of Daedalus and the wealth of Tantalus besides" (11d3–e1). What Socrates wants, in other words, is the unchanging fixity of a Form, rather than Daedalus' "animate form."[59]

If Plato, like Socrates, wanted to supplant his Daedalic ancestor, if he wanted to replace a vision of god-created beauty whose ideal is "animate form," if he wanted to arrest errant *mêtis,* then his ultimate model in making his creator god a *dêmiourgos,* the figure this craftsman is designed to rival and replace, may be Metis' daughter, the goddess Athena herself. For in the ultimate tribute by Homeric epic to material craft, when Athena creates living beauty—as does the *dêmiourgos* in creating the living *kosmos*—the living beauty of Odysseus,

58 For the tradition of Socrates' father's occupation as a stone-sculptor and the possibility that he, too, had done stonework, see Diogenes Laertius, *Vitae philosophorum,* book 2, sections 18.1, 19.4–5, 20.11–12 Long. Socrates claims descent from Daedalus also at Plato, *Alcibiades* I 121a3–4. See Morris, p. 235.

59 For another contrast between the objectives of Socratic philosophical method and the works of Daedalus, see *Republic* 529c4–530c3, where the truths of astronomy must be learned through problems rather than diagrams drawn by Daedalus.

in an honorific reversal of apparent cause and effect, she is likened to a metal-lurgical craftsman, one, indeed, she and Hephaestus have taught, who makes of curling hair an abstract flower (*Odyssey* 23.156–162):[60]

> Over his head Athena poured *(cheuen)* beauty *(kallos)* in abundance,
> making him greater to look upon and broader, and down from his head
> she cascaded curling locks, like to a hyacinth flower.
> And as when a man pours gold around silver *(chruson pericheuetai argurôi)*,
> a skillful one *(idris)*, whom Hephaestus and Pallas Athena have taught
> every sort of craft *(technên pantoiên)*, and full of grace *(charienta)*
> are the works he produces, even so the goddess poured grace around *(pericheue charin)* both his head and his shoulders.

In the *dêmiourgos* of the *Timaeus*, Plato has made his own "Athena," one who takes over her emulation of a mortal craftsman and would also supersede her, binding her animated works within the *desmos* of a Form.

---

60   For the same image of Athena's beautification of Odysseus, see *Odyssey* 6.229–237. For additional instances of Athena's beautification likened to metallurgic art in her "pouring down" *(katacheuo)* of "grace" *(charis)*, see *Odyssey* 2.12, 8.18–19, 17.63. For the same verb used of her "pouring down mist" to hide Odysseus, see *Odyssey* 7.40–42, and 140. And for the same verb used of pouring gold around the horns of a heifer sacrificed to Athena, see *Odyssey* 3.384, 425–426, and *Iliad* 10.294.

21

Time and Change in an Eternal Universe

Sean M. Carroll

The origin and nature of the wider universe around us have fascinated every human culture. In the era of modern science, we understand a great deal more about the laws of physics and the evolution of the universe than ever before. Nevertheless, there remains a great deal that we *don't* know, including the answers to some of the questions raised by Plato's *Timaeus* and other ancient speculations on the origin of the universe. It's instructive to look back on what we've learned and compare our progress to the cosmological scenarios put forward by our predecessors.[1]

Of course we now know a great deal about the universe that Plato could never have guessed at. We know some of the basic laws of nature, including quantum mechanics, and general relativity. We have observed the large-scale structure of the universe, resolving our own galaxy into billions of stars and finding billions of other galaxies scattered throughout space. We know that the universe is expanding, and that about 14 billion years ago it emerged from a hot, dense phase we know as the Big Bang. We can observe the left over radiation from that era, as well as the light elements that were synthesized in the first few minutes.

But there are bigger questions left unanswered. In this discussion I want to concentrate on two of them:

1. Did the universe have a beginning, or is it eternal?
2. Was the universe created by an external agent, or is it self-sufficient?

---

1 This short paper is an informal summary of my talk at the *Plato's* Timaeus *Today* conference, and as such it does not include references to the literature. Readers interested in more may see my recent book, *From Eternity to Here: The Quest for the Ultimate Theory of Time* (Boston: Dutton Adult, 2010).

I hope to make the case that, while we don't yet know the answers to these questions, we have made a certain amount of progress in the last two thousand years, and there's good reason to hope we may eventually come to a conclusion.

The Big Bang

Let's recall some basic facts about the standard Big Bang model of contemporary cosmology. We should distinguish between the Big Bang *model,* which is the basic framework of a universe expanding from an initially hot and dense state, from the Big Bang *singularity,* the hypothetical moment of infinite density at the beginning of that story. The "model" is extremely well supported by a wide variety of data, and no serious cosmologist doubts its basic truthfulness. The Big Bang singularity, on the other hand, is simply a placeholder for our ignorance—our current knowledge doesn't stretch back that far.

The Big Bang model is based on general relativity, Einstein's conception of gravity as a manifestation of the curvature of spacetime. Although we make a big deal in relativity about "spacetime" being the relevant theoretical construct, rather than "space" and "time" separately, in the specific case of cosmology the universe actually does provide us with a fairly unambiguous division of spacetime into space and time. That is, we live in a universe that is homogeneous and isotropic on large scales—as far as we can tell, it looks the same throughout space. But it's changing dramatically through time, as space expands and galaxies move further apart.

The expansion of space can be a confusing concept. The universe is not, as far as we know, expanding *into* anything; there is an intrinsic geometry to space, and the amount of space between any two far-apart galaxies is growing with time. There is no need to imagine anything outside the universe, nor is there a central point from which all matter is moving away. Space is expanding uniformly, so that the apparent recession velocity of galaxies is larger for those that are farther away. As space expands, not everything expands along with it; in particular, bound objects (such as galaxies, atoms, or human beings) remain the same size. Fortunately for observational cosmologists, waves of light are not bound objects; their wavelengths get stretched as the space through which they travel expands, a phenomenon known as the cosmological red shift. This causes the universe to cool as well as grow increasingly dilute with time.

We don't know empirically what happened at the earliest moments in the universe's history, but we do know that the early universe was opaque—it was sufficiently hot that light couldn't travel very far before bumping into free electrons. That means there is only a finite piece of universe that is directly amenable to observations. The speed of light is finite—one light-year per year—and slightly less than 14 billion years ago the universe was opaque. So it is easy to imagine objects that are outside our "horizon"—they are so far away that light from them has not had time to travel to us within the history of the observable universe. (For technical reasons the current distance to the horizon is about 40 billion light years, rather than 14 billion light years as one might expect.)

The finiteness of our observable universe comes with a profound consequence. Even though the universe we see looks extremely uniform on large scales, there is no guarantee that this uniformity stretches forever. The universe on unobservably large scales might very well be a continuation of the conditions we observe nearby, or it might feature any number of regions with dramatically different conditions, even different low-energy laws of physics. We don't have any evidence one way or another, so at this point it pays to keep an open mind.

The Fate of the Universe

So that's a bit about the past of our universe; what about the future? The ultimate fate of our universe has been a longstanding puzzle, but one that came a bit into focus in 1998. That year, two groups of astronomers discovered an astonishing fact: the universe is not only expanding, it's also *accelerating*. The rate of expansion—what astronomers call the "Hubble parameter"—is not actually increasing, it seems to be asymptoting to a constant. But a constant expansion rate is equivalent to an accelerating universe, through the miracles of non-Euclidean geometry. If the expansion rate is constant, that means it takes a fixed amount of time for the universe to double in size. So if we observe one particular galaxy for the amount of time (billions of years) it would take to move twice as far away as its current distance, in the same amount of time after that it will move four times as far away, and the same time later it will be eight times as far away, and so on. (**Figure 1**)

Cosmologists are not sure what is causing the acceleration of the universe (which has subsequently been verified by completely independent observations), but there is a leading candidate: vacuum energy, or what Einstein called the cosmological constant. This is simply the idea that empty space itself carries a fixed amount of energy in every cubic centimeter; an energy that doesn't change with time or vary from point to point in space. If vacuum energy is indeed responsible for the acceleration of the universe, it comes with a deep consequence: the expansion of space will never end. The universe will continue to grow increasingly dilute and cold, for all of eternity.

It's worth pausing to reflect on the story we are telling. We live in a vast universe, containing over a hundred billion galaxies with a hundred billion stars each, spread over billions of light years. It is expanding from a moment 14 billion years ago of unimaginable temperature and density. But it will expand into the future *forever*, growing emptier with each passing moment. It might seem like 14 billion years is a long time, but compared to the future history of the universe it's literally nothing at all.

Figure 1: The Hubble Deep Field, showing the distribution of distant galaxies. (Courtesy of NASA, ESA, S. Beckwith [STScI], and the HUDF Team)

The Arrow of Time

There is an apparent imbalance between the past and future of the universe. The past was hotter and denser, beginning 14 billion years ago; the future will be colder and emptier, stretching forever. But there is a more profound difference between past and future, as codified in the Second Law of Thermodynamics: the statement that the entropy of the universe (or of any closed system) will only increase, not decrease, as time passes.

Entropy is usually glossed informally as a measure of the "disorder" of a system. A stack of papers piled neatly on a desk has a low entropy; the same stack, scattered haphazardly across the desktop, has a high entropy. This notion was formalized in the late 19th century by Austrian physicist Ludwig Boltzmann. (**Figure 2**) He noticed that there might be many ways to rearrange the atomic constituents of a physical system while leaving its macroscopic appearance unaltered. Furthermore, there would be more ways to perform such rearrangements if the system were in a messy high-entropy configuration than if it were in an orderly low-entropy one. This helps us understand why entropy tends to increase with time: there are simply more ways to be high-entropy than to be low-entropy.

Figure 2: Ludwig Boltzmann's tombstone in Vienna, showing his formula for entropy. (Courtesy of Martin Röll)

This somewhat arid understanding of the arrow of time in terms of macroscopically indistinguishable arrangements of atoms tends to understate the tremendous power of the idea. The tendency of entropy to increase underlies nearly all of the various ways in which we perceive the past to be different from the future. Ice cubes melt, but warm glasses of water never form ice cubes; we can turn eggs into omelets, but not omelets into eggs; we remember the past, but not the future; we feel we can make choices that will influence the future, but not the past; we believe that effects precede causes; we are born, grow old, and die, never the reverse order. All of these widely disparate phenomena can ultimately be traced to increasing entropy.

But a mystery lurks beneath. Boltzmann's logic helps explain why the entropy of the universe will be larger tomorrow than it is today. But it says absolutely nothing about why the entropy was smaller *yesterday*. The fundamental laws of physics are perfectly symmetric under time reversal; following Boltzmann's demonstration, we could argue that the entropy was higher yesterday with equal conviction as we argued that it will be higher tomorrow.

This puzzle has been the subject of numerous arguments over the years, but the basic solution is fairly unambiguous: in addition to Boltzmann's definition of entropy and the reversible microscopic laws of physics, we need a new piece of input. This extra ingredient takes the form of a boundary condition, sometimes dubbed the "Past Hypothesis"—the observable universe began in an extremely low-entropy state. In other words, the reason why the entropy of the universe was lower yesterday was because it was even lower the day before that. And this logic stretches all the way back to the origin of the universe.

In other words, the arrow of time is ultimately a question for cosmology. Our observable universe began at the Big Bang, and at that time the entropy was extremely low. (This is another confusing and subtle topic, but the basic lessons are clear.) The entropy has been going up ever since, in accordance with the Second Law. But *why* was the entropy low at early times? Modern cosmologists pride themselves on their understanding of the early universe; we should be able to explain this low-entropy condition, not simply posit it.

Beyond the Big Bang

There are basically two options for dealing with this situation. The first is to imagine that there really is some new part of the fundamental laws of physics; not a dynamical rule, that relates configurations of the universe from one moment to the next, but a boundary condition that fixes the state of the universe at some time. It may be the "no-boundary proposal" of James Hartle and Stephen Hawking, or some other prescription. Ultimately this possibility comes down to an assertion that the early universe simply is that way, and there is no explanation for its low entropy in terms of some dynamical laws.

The other possibility is that the Big Bang isn't truly a boundary at all—that there was a universe even before the Bang, and that this larger picture helps explain our apparently unnatural early conditions. This option may come as a surprise to anyone who is used to hearing the Big Bang described as the singular boundary of the universe, before which space and time simply didn't exist. The truth is that such a description might be accurate—or it might not be. Our current understanding of the laws of physics simply isn't adequate to let us decide. General relativity predicts unambiguously that spacetime becomes singular at the Bang; however, that doesn't imply any actual singularity, only that general relativity itself breaks down. Without a better understanding of how quantum mechanics is reconciled with gravitation, we have no way of knowing whether the Big Bang was truly a beginning, or merely a phase through which the universe passed. Indeed, cosmologists are considering an increasing number of scenarios that feature a universe before the Big Bang, out of which ours arose.

If that's true, we can still hold out hope for an explanation of the arrow of time that relies solely upon the dynamical laws of physics, without recourse to any additional input in the form of a finely tuned boundary condition. We can imagine that the mysteriously low entropy of our observable universe is in fact a natural consequence of the way we emerged from the pre-Big-Bang spacetime.

Can we go beyond imagining it, to developing a more specific model? Not while remaining on solid ground, but we can certainly speculate.

Consider again the far future of our universe, where matter has dissipated away, leaving nothing but empty space. But that empty space still has vacuum energy. As a consequence, there is a nonzero temperature to empty space, just as Hawking showed that there is a temperature around black holes. Empty space isn't completely empty, but is filled with incredibly cold thermal radiation (with a temperature of about 10–30 Kelvin).

Because of this temperature, there are thermal fluctuations—particles that appear out of empty space and occasionally (very rarely) collect into random configurations. Indeed, if we wait long enough, even incredibly rare configurations will appear—and we are imagining that we have infinitely long to wait. Among those rare configurations, we can imagine that spacetime itself fluctuates enough to create a *baby universe* (**Figure 3**). This is a tiny patch of space with a very high energy density, and just the right conditions to pinch off from its parent spacetime and go its own way. To an observer inside that baby universe, it would appear to start in a very dense low-entropy state, and expand and cool over the course of billions of years. It would, in other words, resemble our very own observable universe.

So the scenario might be as follows: there is an eternal background universe that never started in a Big Bang, but simply remained as empty space (with a small vacuum energy) for all time. Over the course of eternity, this universe gave birth to occasional baby universes, which expanded and cooled according to the traditional Big Bang story. One of those baby universes is our own. The

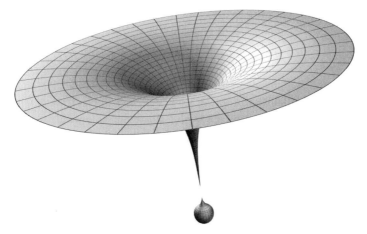

Figure 3: Creation of a baby universe. (Model by Derryl Rice / Parmenides Publishing)
To view the animation, go to Figure 3 at *www.platostimaeustoday.com*.

Figure 4: A sketch of a multiverse that is time-symmetric
on large scales. (Courtesy of Jason Torchinsky)

overall picture is eternal; it has no beginning or end. And it is symmetric in time; baby universes can be created toward the very distant past, as well as the distant future. In this picture (**Figure 4**), the entropy of the larger multiverse has no maximum value; it appears to be increasing in our local neighborhood because we are a byproduct of the tendency of entropy to always increase overall.

Lessons

This story is obviously highly hypothetical—it's grounded in sensible ideas in modern physics, but is very far from being accepted as a promising scenario. For our present purposes, it helps us relate back to the cosmological picture of the *Timaeus,* and reexamine the two questions we originally asked.

First, did the universe have a beginning, or is it eternal? At the moment, we simply don't know—both options are very much on the table. The growth of entropy in our observable universe relies on a low-entropy condition near the Big Bang, but that condition may or may not represent a true beginning for the entire universe. No amount of *a priori* philosophizing will be able to answer this question; both alternatives are coherent, and ultimately we will have to make considerable progress in both theory and experiment before we can be making a choice between them.

Second, does the universe require some sort of cause (such as Plato's demiurge), or can it be self-sustaining? There are many reasonable-sounding arguments in favor of the need for something outside the universe; however, over the last five hundred years science has gradually eroded these arguments one by one. It was once thought necessary to invoke a Prime Mover to explain the motions of earthly and celestial bodies, in a framework where objects were thought to naturally come to rest; but the concepts of conservation of energy and momentum have rendered that point moot. Similarly, it was thought necessary to invoke a designer to explain the marvelous complexity of living organisms; but Darwin's theory of evolution showed how random mutation and natural selection could achieve the same purpose without any external guidance.

When we appreciate the vastness of space and the intricate order of the cosmos, we may nevertheless be tempted to believe that some sort of external agent is required to make it all come into existence in the first place. The lesson of our discussion here is that such a conclusion is far from warranted. The complexity of the universe, which Plato suggested was imposed on primordial chaos by the demiurge, is a natural outgrowth of undirected evolution, once we grant the low-entropy conditions of the early universe. And those conditions may well have a dynamical explanation in terms of a larger multiverse.

As for the existence of the multiverse itself, it's hard to say whether further explanation is required. It is certainly possible that the multiverse "just is." Modern physics conceptualizes the world, not in terms of causes and effects, but in terms of configurations that obey inviolable patterns that we call the "laws of nature." These patterns may simply hold true for all eternity in an everlasting cosmos. Only a great deal of further investigation will allow us to draw any firm conclusions.

Index Locorum

General Index

acceleration of universe, 375

account/story. *See* narrative.

Adam, belly button controversy and, 11–12

Aesop, 222–224

aetiological myth, 222–224

affect, narrative and, 277

agôn ("struggle"), 241, 244

aiolos ("glittering, mobile, animated"), 357–358, 361–362

air. *See* primary bodies.

akolouthia ("following-upon-ness"), 51

Alberti, Leon Battista, 333, 336–339

Alcinous

  On the Demiurge 86–87, 99

    Father of all things 87

    First god 86

    Identical with the Idea of the Good 89

    Identical with the Paradigm 89

    Maker of the universe 87

alliteration, 235, 236

anachronism, 244, 247

anachrony, 273, 280

ananke ("necessity"), 31, 34, 50, 65, 74, 119, 130, 148–149, 174, 194, 197

Demiurge and, 44, 48–49, 126

  Presocratic causes and, 148–149

Anaxagoras, 180–183

  conception of God, 41

  origin of the universe and, 107–108

animate form

  beauty and, 343–345, 350–358, 362–368, 370–371

  Homeric beauty and, 358, 362–368, 370

  mimêsis and, 362–364

  Timaean cosmology and, 350–357

animation, 356–357, 361–362

  Atlantis narrative and, 331–332

anômalia ("unevenness"), 344, 364–365

Antedeluvian World, 330

anthropic principle, 35

Antinea, l'amante della città sepolta, 310

apeiron ("indefinite, indeterminate"), 71–72, 74–75, 130

Apuleius

  on the Demiurge, 86–88, 99

    Father and Maker of all things, 87

    Father of the world-soul, 88

    highest god, 86–87

    Maker of the world-body, 88

PRE-SOCRATICS

By Being, It Is: The Thesis of Parmenides by Néstor-Luis Cordero

To Think Like God: Pythagoras and Parmenides. The Origins of Philosophy
Scholarly and fully annotated edition by Arnold Hermann

The Illustrated To Think Like God: Pythagoras and Parmenides. The Origins of Philosophy by Arnold Hermann with over 200 full color illustrations.

The Legacy of Parmenides: Eleatic Monism and Later Presocratic Thought by Patricia Curd

Parmenides and the History of Dialectic: Three Essays by Scott Austin

The Route of Parmenides: Revised and Expanded Edition, With a New Introduction, Three Supplemental Essays, and an Essay by Gregory Vlastos by Alexander P. D. Mourelatos

The Fragments of Parmenides: A Critical Text with Introduction and Translation, the Ancient Testimonia *and a Commentary* by A. H. Coxon. Revised and Expanded Edition edited with new Translations by Richard McKirahan and a new Preface by Malcolm Schofield

PLATO

God and Forms in Plato by Richard D. Mohr

Image and Paradigm in Plato's Sophist by David Ambuel

Interpreting Plato's Dialogues by J. Angelo Corlett

One Book, the Whole Universe: Plato's Timaeus *Today* edited by Richard D. Mohr and Barbara M. Sattler

The Philosopher in Plato's Statesman by Mitchell Miller

Platonic Patterns: A Collection of Studies by Holger Thesleff

Plato's Late Ontology: A Riddle Resolved by Kenneth M. Sayre

Plato's Parmenides: *Text and Translation* by Arnold Hermann. Translation in collaboration with Sylvana Chrysakopoulou with a Foreword by Douglas Hedley

Plato's Universe by Gregory Vlastos

ARISTOTLE

One and Many in Aristotle's Metaphysics—*Volume I: Books Alpha-Delta* by Edward C. Halper

One and Many in Aristotle's Metaphysics—*Volume 2: The Central Books* by Edward C. Halper

HELLENISTIC PHILOSOPHY

A Life Worthy of the Gods: The Materialist Psychology of Epicurus by David Konstan

ETHICS

Sentience and Sensibility: *A Conversation about Moral Philosophy*
by Matthew R. Silliman

AUDIOBOOKS

The Iliad (unabridged) by Stanley Lombardo
The Odyssey (unabridged) by Stanley Lombardo
The Essential Homer by Stanley Lombardo
The Essential Iliad by Stanley Lombardo

FORTHCOMING

'Parmenides, Venerable and Awesome': *Proceedings of the International Symposium* edited by Néstor-Luis Cordero
Platonic Realism and Quantum Theory: *Metaphysics and Mysticism in Modern Physics* by John Spencer
Plotinus The Platonist: *A Comparative Account of Plato and Plotinus. Their Mysticism, Epistemology, Metaphysics, and Ethics* by David J. Yount
Presocratics and Plato: *A Festschrift in Honor of Charles Kahn* edited by Arnold Hermann, Vassilis Karasmanis and Richard Patterson
Reading Aristotle Physics 7,3: *"What is Alteration and What is Not." Proceedings of the International ESAP-HYELE Conference* edited by Stefano Maso, Carlo Natali, and Gerhard Seel

ANNOUNCING

A New Series of Commentaries on
THE ENNEADS OF PLOTINUS:
Translations with Introductions and Philosophical Commentaries on Individual Treatises
Series edited by John M. Dillon and Andrew Smith